THE STORY OF THE THEATRE

By GLENN HUGHES

THE STORY OF THE THEATRE. A short history of theatrical art from its beginnings to the present day.

NEW PLAYS FOR MUMMERS. A book of ten burlesques.

RED CARNATIONS. Comedy in one act. Appears only in *One-Act Plays for Stage and Study*, Second Series.

BOTTLED IN BOND. Comedy in one act.

PIERROT'S MOTHER. Comedy in one act.

LADY FINGERS. Comedy in one act.

HARLEQUINADE IN GREEN AND ORANGE. Comedy in one act.

THE EVE IN EVELYN. Comedy in one act. Appears only in *Fifty More Contemporary One-Act Plays*.

SHOWING UP MABEL. Comedy in one act.

HAPPINESS FOR SIX. Comedy in three acts.

NONE TOO GOOD FOR DODO. Comedy in one act.

THE REAL GLORIA. Comedy in one act.

KOMACHI. Romantic drama in three acts.

ART AND MRS. PALMER. Comedy in one act. Appears only in *One-Act Plays for Stage and Study*, Fifth Series.

———

SOULS AND OTHER POEMS

BROKEN LIGHTS: A BOOK OF VERSE.

———

Translated or Edited:

THREE MODERN JAPANESE PLAYS. (*With Y. T. Iwasaki.*)

THREE WOMEN POETS OF MODERN JAPAN. (*With Y. T. Iwasaki.*)

FIFTEEN POETS OF MODERN JAPAN. (*With Y. T. Iwasaki.*)

BALZAC IN SLIPPERS. (*With Babette Hughes.*)

UNIVERSITY OF WASHINGTON PLAYS. (*First, Second and Third Series.*)

UNIVERSITY OF WASHINGTON POEMS. (*First, Second and Third Series.*)

UNIVERSITY OF WASHINGTON CHAPBOOKS.

From Nicoll's *Development of the Theatre.*

THE STORY OF THE THEATRE

A SHORT HISTORY OF THEATRICAL ART FROM ITS BEGINNINGS TO THE PRESENT DAY

BY

GLENN HUGHES

PROFESSOR OF ENGLISH AND DIRECTOR OF THE DIVISION
OF DRAMA, UNIVERSITY OF WASHINGTON

SAMUEL FRENCH

NEW YORK   LOS ANGELES

SAMUEL FRENCH Ltd.   LONDON

1935

MANUFACTURED IN THE UNITED STATES OF AMERICA
BY THE VAIL-BALLOU PRESS, INC., BINGHAMTON, N. Y.

To My Friends
RICHARD ALDINGTON
E. T. BELL
BARRETT H. CLARK
Scholars and Gentlemen All

PREFACE

This book is intended primarily for students of the theatre, secondarily for the general reader. So far as the writer knows it represents the first attempt in English to summarize in one volume the main events of theatrical history from the earliest times to the present. It does not reveal much that is new, but it selects and organizes the old in a useful way. Its compactness gives, it is hoped, a sense of the continuity of theatrical development—something which fifty or a hundred volumes in scattered fields can scarcely give.

In an outline of this sort the problem of selection is a terrifying one, and is inevitably a matter of personal judgment. The author anticipates much criticism on that score. "Ten pages to so-and-so, and not a line to such-and-such!" No doubt there will be justice in some of the complaints, but it is manifestly impossible to satisfy everyone.

No space has been given to the theatrical arts of certain ancient civilizations: Assyrian, Egyptian, and the like, for the simple reason that not enough is known on the subject. Religious dances and festivals, puppets, and other elementary dramatic forms constituted, we may assume, the only theatre which they possessed. A more serious omission, and one that is regretted, is that of the development of the theatre in colonies, provinces, and republics culturally dependent upon Europe. Canada, Australia, Mexico, and the countries of South America and Africa have been completely ignored. The only defense is that in most of them the theatre is little more than an extension of the European theatre. Where a language goes, its drama goes also.

vii

The reader will soon discover that little emphasis has been placed upon dramatic literature. To give anywhere near an adequate survey of this colossal subject would require at least a separate volume. He will discover, also that slight attention has been paid to social, political and economic conditions. Important as these matters are in the interpretation of such an institution as the theatre, they are of secondary significance to the student for whom this book is written—that is, the student of the *arts* of the theatre.

The aim of the writer has been threefold: brevity, clarity, and accuracy. The first of these has surely been realized; the other two are open to question. In a volume which contains so many names and dates it is difficult to avoid errors—especially so because of the extraordinary number of conflicting statements which occur in theatrical histories and biographies. To check back to original sources of information in every case of doubt would entail the labor of more than one lifetime.

It may appear unscholarly and even ungrateful to have omitted the customary footnote references to authorities, but to have included them would have changed the whole nature of the book. It was not conceived in the spirit of true scholarship, for no true scholar would dream of chronicling in a few hundred pages the dramatic events of more than two thousand years. One footnote would have required ten thousand more, and these would have left no room for narrative.

The works on which I have based my narrative will be found listed at the back of this book. Some of them are extremely scholarly; others are tinged with romantic imagination. From some I have taken nothing; from others a great deal. In gratitude I wish to acknowledge that I have leaned heavily on works pre-eminent in their field, for instance: Chambers' *Mediaeval Stage,* Zucker's *Chinese Theatre,* Kincaid's *Kabuki,* Hornblow's *History of the Theatre in*

America, Hawkins' *Annals of the French Stage,* Sand's *History of the Harlequinade,* Haigh's *Attic Theatre,* Rennert's *Spanish Stage,* Mantzius' *History of Theatrical Art,* and the brilliant treatises of Prof. Allardyce Nicoll. My purpose is not to save the student the necessity of reading such excellent accounts, but rather to stimulate him to do so.

Finally, I wish to acknowledge my indebtedness to my colleagues, Burton W. James and John Conway, for bibliographical suggestions; to my wife, Babette Hughes, and my friend, George Savage, for patient assistance in proofreading.

—G. H.

University of Washington, Seattle.
January 15, 1928.

NOTE

The author is grateful to the publishers and editors of various books and magazines for permission to use illustrations.

The publishers listed below have kindly allowed their material to be reprinted:

Harcourt, Brace & Company, Theatre Arts Monthly, The Orient Magazine, The University of Chicago Press, The John Day Company, Samuel French, and The Ward Leonard Electric Company.

CONTENTS

ILLUSTRATIONS

PRIMITIVE THEATRICALS

CHAPTER I

PRIMITIVE THEATRICALS

IT is utterly impossible to say how long the human race has indulged in some form of action which may be called drama. As far back as records go, men are discovered executing rites which must be classed as theatrical, though of course their purpose is religious rather than aesthetic. It has been said repeatedly that the basis of all art is religion, and the statement is certainly irrefutable in the case of dramatic art.

Primitive man, wherever his home, whatever his era, employs dancing and music (the foundation of drama) in the worship of his deities. He is almost certain to include poetry in his ceremonials, and if he develops properly, he will add prose dialogue, though by that time he is well on the way towards civilization. He does not have to learn these things from any one else; they are instinctive with him. Thus we have in every corner of the earth, races of men cut off from each other, and yet arriving at fundamentally the same practices. Forms differ, but the spirit is invariably the same. Still, it must be admitted that the dramatic instinct is present in varying degrees among different peoples, even when those peoples are on the same plane of civilization. It is obvious, for example, that while the Hebrews, Egyptians, and Turks never advanced beyond a rudimentary sort of theatrical expression, the Greeks, the Hindus, the Chinese, and the Japanese achieved early in their history, elaborate and extraordinarily effective theatrical systems. This is not the place for a discussion of

3

possible reasons for such divergence. Anthropologists may explain the matter satisfactorily, or they may not; but racial temperament, climate, religion—these would all have to be taken into account. One thing is indisputable: namely, that the non-theatrical races mentioned above are only cases of arrested development. They were not wholly devoid of dramatic instinct—they merely failed to develop it beyond a certain point. The Jews held religious feasts which involved symbolic action; the Egyptians performed religious dances, and quite certainly had puppet-plays; the Turks at least had shadow-puppets.

Fom one point of view man is an actor even before he acquires standardized language, for gesture precedes speech as a means of communication. Low-grade savages express nearly everything in pantomime, or sign language. And for a considerable time after words are used, gestures must accompany them or they are not perfectly clear. There are tribes in existence today whose members are not intelligible to each other in the dark, so inadequate is their spoken language.

But communication is only one motive in primitive man's use of pantomime. Another, more significant to us, is his belief in sympathetic magic. Surrounded by the mysteries of nature, and lacking any scientific explanation of them, he evolves the naïve theory that imitation is a potent act. It is a perfectly logical theory—for a savage. If you make a sound like rain falling, real rain will fall as a result of your act. If you disguise yourself in a buffalo skin and do a buffalo-dance, you will be successful in the next buffalo-hunt. If you make a clay image of your enemy and then smash it, or burn it, or mutilate it, your enemy will suffer and perhaps even die. Nothing is simpler or easier to understand than this belief. The point in it for us is, however, that it leads inevitably to the art of imitation, or acting. It is religious at heart, because magic is a divine process, and to invoke magic is to appeal to the gods. But it is a very practical kind of religious observance: it aims at immediate results.

It may be asked at this point why it is that imitative action invariably resolves itself into a rhythmical pattern, following a regular musical beat. The answer is that man is rhythmical by nature—especially on the emotional side. The more intense his emotion, the stronger his sense of rhythm. He does not have to be taught to beat a drum with regular cadence, or to dance to the beating of the drum; he knows how. The beating of his own pulse, the rhythm of his breath—these have given him from birth a sense of rhythm. Only in civilized man is the sense of rhythm deficient. Only civilized man writes prose—the savage is limited to verse.

In primitive drama there is always the mask. Why? There are several reasons. First, because the performer wishes to look like the animal or object or person whom he is imitating. The mask is magic. The wearer becomes for the time being like the original of the mask. If it is the mask of a god, the wearer absorbs something of the divine essence; if it is an animal mask, the qualities of the animal are imparted to the dancer, or, in some cases, the animals are made more plentiful by the magic of the dance. Then, there is the business of war. It is desirable to strike terror to the hearts of the enemy. A hideous mask will accomplish it, even though it is worn long before the battle, during the war-dance. The enemy, miles away, dancing around his own camp-fire, will feel the baleful influence of this mask. Such is magic. Again, there is the initiation ceremony—an extremely important part of primitive life. Nearly all savage tribes, whether of Australia, North America, Africa, Polynesia, or elsewhere, conduct elaborate initiation rites. Boys of the age of puberty are the neophytes. Sometimes the ritual is extended over a number of days, during which time the boys are subjected to rigid discipline by the men of the tribe. Women are always excluded from the ceremony, and it is carried on in strict secrecy. The chief purpose of the event is to impress the boys with the responsibilities of manhood; another is to acquaint them with the myths and history of the tribe; still another is to implant within them a fear of the tribal gods. To accomplish these ends, some of the men have to impersonate supernatural beings; others find it necessary to act out tribal legends; but in any case, masks must be resorted to. We can see, therefore, that the mask is indispensable to primitive drama. When it is not working magic on the wearer, it is at least instilling righteous fear in the hearts of the younger generation. As drama develops, the mask obviously takes on other significances than these, but they must be reserved for later discussion.

The idea of penance and sacrifice is naturally behind many forms of primitive drama. The savage usually feels that gods must be appeased by human suffering, and the greater the suffering, the greater the favors of the gods will be. This belief leads to the sacrifice of human beings and animals, and to self-inflicted torture. The early Greeks offered the lives of virgins to their bloodthirsty deity; later they substituted sheep and other animals for the human victims, and finally conducted sacrificial rites without taking life at all, the whole ceremony being symbolic action. Such an evolution illustrates very well the growth of drama.

Another fundamental drama is contained in the love-dance. Most tribes offer specimens of it. The occasion may be either the betrothal, the wedding, or both. Usually it is performed by the bride and groom, with the rest as spectators, but among some peoples it is a general dance. It may follow the theme of flirtation, pursuit, resistance and capture (a motive common in modern exhibition dancing), or it may symbolize the many aspects of married life. It is not

From *Theatre Arts Magazine.*

Plate 1 : Green Corn Dance. American Indians in Mexico.
Drawing by William P. Henderson.

apt to be delicate, for sexual matters are treated frankly by those who live close to nature. Seductive dances by women play an important part in the ceremony, and it is this phase which has been most imitated and admired by civilized communities.

It has already been stated that one of the first dance-dramas to develop in primitive society is the hunting-dance, as most savage tribes depend mainly on the flesh of animals for food. But eventually agriculture takes its place beside hunting as a practical pursuit, and logically, as a dance theme too. Magic is applied to the vegetable kingdom—chiefly to the process of sowing seeds, and to rain-making. The early Greeks are said to have believed the seed-sower could influence the height of the grain by leaping in the air as he sowed. The higher he leaped, the higher the stalks would grow. It is easy to see that from this belief a sower's dance would evolve, first as a practical magic, later as an aesthetic form admired for its own sake. The high leaping in modern ballet-dancing may perhaps be traced to some such original motive. As for rain-making—it is almost a universal drama. From the moment man puts his faith in vegetation he feels that his life is in the hands of the rain-god, and the least sign of drouth will send him into the throes of supplication. Tribal priests invent the ritual, which commonly includes imitations of falling rain, thunder, and lightning, and the tribe keeps at its devotions until actual rain falls or until the supplicants are exhausted.

In addition to these dramas of love, hatred, food-getting, initiation, and sacrifice, a primitive people may perform historical pantomime in which the element of magic is present in only the slightest degree. The lives of heroic ancestors and mythical heroes furnish the stories, and the action is in the nature of a spectacle. But even though we class these separately we must realize that they are closely bound up with the other forms of drama, and that their motives are not primarily aesthetic. Their prime function is to promote loyalty and courage in warriors—a motive which attaches them firmly to the war-dance.

Fortunately it is not necessary for the student of primitive drama to base his conclusions on ancient history. There are still plenty of savage tribes in existence, and although civilization has in certain instances curbed their traditional theatricalism, there are a sufficient number of ceremonials practised today to furnish an investigator with all the illustrations he needs. In the Congo, black men whirl to the incantations of the voodoo; in Australia, bush-men terrify each other with masks and unearthly music; in Polynesian islands, oily-skinned natives beat the tom-tom and dance their magic rituals of love, hate, and war; in Alaska and British Columbia the Indians and Eskimos perform their mysteries in awful masks beneath the towering totem-poles; in Arizona and New Mexico the Zunis and the Navajos enact the solemn rites of the Sun-God. Torture has been eliminated from some of the rites—forbidden by white men in authority, but the dramatic spectacle is as seriously conducted as it was a thousand years ago.

There is no line of demarcation between primitive and civilized drama. Whatever distinctions are made must be purely arbitrary. In beauty of physical movement, richness of costuming, effectiveness of music, impressiveness of masks, primitive drama is often superior to the drama of culture; in literary expression, subtlety of thought, mechanical equipment, and organization, the latter is obviously superior. Perhaps a better means of distinction is the element of comedy. Savage drama is invariably tragic—its seriousness is overpowering; civilized drama introduces the comic spirit.

Whatever our conclusions in this matter, we must be aware of the strong influence savage art has exercised on the modern theatre. Barbaric rhythms of the Congo have invaded not only vaudeville and cabaret entertainments, but have reached even the semi-sacred precincts of the opera and the symphony concert. Dance-patterns from Tahiti, Mexico, and Burma have found their place in our theatre. Stage-decoration and costume are reflecting the colors and designs of primitives; the mask and the puppet have been returned to popular favor, and their virtues have been sounded from high places. The theatre of nineteenth century Europe, so smug in its civilized pseudo-realism, has been challenged by the vigorous and imaginative art of the savage. How far it will go in accepting inspiration from such a source is conjectural, but that it has already taken new life from the contact is incontestable.

SELECTED REFERENCES

For a general study of primitive magic and religion, consult Frazer's *The Golden Bough*. The standard work on primitive drama is Havemeyer's *The Drama of Savage Peoples*. A fairly good account is also contained in Mantzius' *History of Theatrical Art*, Vol. I. Excellent in the same field is Ridgeway's *Dramas and Dramatic Dances of the Non-European Races*. For illustrations and illuminating descriptions of the use of masks in primitive theatricals see Macgowan and Rosse's *Masks and Demons*.

THE THEATRE IN ASIA

CHAPTER II

THE INDIAN THEATRE

THE Orient has for long been the despair of exact historians, for the Oriental mind seems definitely opposed to the scientific accumulation and ordering of fact. In all ancient matters of the East, mythology blends inextricably with history, speculation fills in the absence of record, and spiritual values take precedence over physical realities. All this is remarkably true of India, where time is mystically ignored.

No one has a very clear idea of the origin of Indian theatricals, but it is fairly certain that until the modern era there were no playhouses erected as such. There were, in ancient times, however, at least three distinct types of theatrical entertainment, all of them more or less connected with religious worship. The first of these, and obviously the oldest, is the open-air festival. Scarcely any race is without this form of drama, and the Indians (or the Hindus, let us say) have cultivated it persistently for three or four thousand years. It is safer not to venture dates, but we may without hesitation affirm that long before the Greeks sang and danced about the altar of Dionysus, the Hindus paid spectacular homage to Rama and other deified kings. And these early religious rites grew into drama (well-formed and with literary appeal) even as did the savage dithyrambs in Attica. Dancing and song flourished in ancient India ; the symbolic dance still calls India its home. The open-air festival was filled with dancing, music, and poetry. At times it became pageantry. And even today the Hindus celebrate in this manner the sacred lives of Rama and Krishna. The Festival of Rama lasts sometimes during the entire month of October; the Festival of Krishna occupies at least a week.

The second type of theatrical in India is the secular or semi-religious drama, written by cultivated poets, to be played in the halls of palaces before princes and invited guests. Such a performance corresponds closely to the dramas of the Renaissance in Europe, and is the natural outcome of a period which produces a highly educated upper class and at the same time a number of wealthy rulers with leisure and good taste. As the early drama in a country is always religious in theme, it is inevitable that for a considerable time after theatrical art has separated itself from the actual place and occasion of worship, the drama will continue to reflect its origin, and will retain many of its sacred features even though its motivation is secular. Besides, as poetic drama tends to depict the lives of renowned heroes, it turns naturally to kings, and as kings so frequently become gods in legend, it is easy to understand why plays continue to be built around the same material that inspired the ritualistic song, dance, and pageant. This principle holds true in India no less than in Greece or Japan.

It is useless to estimate the antiquity of court plays in India. It seems probable that they existed before the Christian era, but if so, the dramas themselves have disappeared. The finest Hindu drama extant is the "Shakuntala," written by Kalidasa, probably in the sixth or seventh century A. D. Scholars cannot find conclusive evidence on this point, but all of them agree that the play belongs to the Christian era, and that it could scarcely have been written later than the eleventh century A. D. The Hindus themselves, although very fond of the "Shakuntala," seem to care little when it was written. Their point of view is that so long as it is a beautiful play it doesn't matter how old it is. (An admirably idealistic attitude, but how irritating to the Occidental believer in card-catalogues!) At any rate, this classic drama was translated into English for the first time in 1789, and ever since has brought profound delight to successive generations of Western dramatic students.

Another Hindu drama of about the same period is "The Toy Cart," by an unknown poet. This, too, has been translated into English, and like the "Shakuntala," has been performed successfully in our modern theatre. About a dozen other old plays exist, but these two are the best examples of the type, and they illustrate clearly to what a high degree of excellence dramatic literature attained in the courts of the Hindu princes. They are written in mixed prose and verse, are based on extremely diverting stories, and offer splendid opportunities for subtle acting. They are in the nature of comedy rather than tragedy, though they do not exclude pathos. They contain suspense, but avoid violence. In every line they breathe restraint and delicacy born of long sophistication. They do not attempt, as Greek dramas do, to lay bare the depths of the human soul as it strives with fate. They mirror a more submissive spirit—one that is too wise to war with destiny. Love plays an important part in them, and so does nature—in fact, a lyric atmosphere is dominant in them.

The manner in which these plays were presented is a subject for speculation. It is likely, though, that they were performed on temporary raised stages in banquet or reception halls, that the prince and his attendants occupied a dais in the center of the hall, facing the stage, and that a considerable audience was invited to fill the remaining space in the hall. It is doubtful if a front curtain was used, but it is almost sure that draperies were hung at the rear of the stage, serving as a background for the action. These may have been painted to represent the scene of the action, or they may merely have been neutrally decorative. The plays themselves suggest the latter as the more likely hypothesis, for the action moves from place to place rather rapidly, and so, had the curtains represented specific localities, a number of quick changes would have been necessary, and such changes involve a system of stage mechanics which can hardly have been known at that time, and which is not indicated at all in native treatises on the Indian theatre. The plays themselves were written in a highly conventional manner, and it is reasonable to suppose that they were not produced in a spirit of realism. Besides, it is well known that the Indian actors were extraordinarily clever at pantomime, and when pantomime is cultivated, scenery is almost certain to be simple.

A most significant point is that there appears never to have been any fundamental objection to the presence of women on the Indian stage. As a matter of fact Hindus pride themselves on their idealization of women, and on the intellectual and artistic achievements of that sex during the long centuries of India's history. The fact that actresses were permitted in the days of Kalidasa may account somewhat for the extraordinary delicacy and refined humor to be discovered in "Shakuntala." It may account in part, also, for the lack of a definite tradition of masks in the Hindu theatre. It is pleasant, anyway, to think of the delightful heroine created by Kalidasa being portrayed by a flower-like maiden rather than by a masked effeminate male. The practice of female impersonation, so common in other Oriental countries, was not unknown in India, but there it became a most chivalrous custom, for the only feminine characters delineated by men were the old and ugly ones.

Play-writing and play-acting were taken very seriously in mediaeval India, and elaborate rules were laid down for the guidance of dramatists and actors. Theorizing has always been a favorite practice with the Hindus, and in the field of theatrical art their analytical thought was given full scope. The plays themselves were classified in every conceivable manner, and appropriate forms were assigned to each type. The number of acts, the style of language, the kinds of characters—these were carefully sorted out and arranged according to formula. There were two main language divisions—Sanskrit and Prakrit. The former, dignified, archaic, and learned, served only a literary purpose, and was put into the mouths of principal male characters (gods and heroes), the latter, the conversational language of the time, was used by all female characters, whether mortal or divine, and by minor male characters. Prakrit, furthermore, included seven or eight distinct dialects, and these were employed in a conventional manner to distinguish specific types of character, the dialect suggesting the social status, profession, and geographical origin of each type. (A somewhat parallel system is found in the *Commedia dell' Arte* of sixteenth-century Italy, with its clown types from Venice, Naples, and other cities, all retaining characteristic localisms of speech. Had certain characters of the Italian comedy spoken pure Latin, the parallel would be complete.)

The theorists of the Hindu theatre attempted also to discover and classify the many moods or impressions created by dramatic presentation. Beginning with such broad categories as Exotic, Comical, Pathetic, Tragic, Heroic, Awful, Hateful, and Miraculous, they went on to subdivisions of these *ad infinitum*. Exhausting this subject, they assembled, grouped, and classified the rôles of the actor. The result was forty-eight types of hero, three hundred and eighty-four female types, and many varieties of villain, comedian, confidant, *et cetera*. All this labor seems, at least to the Western mind, curiously futile, but to the Hindus it apparently was a satisfactory exercise. Its interest to the modern student lies in the proof it offers of the seriousness with which the theatre was taken by Indian scholars.

Those who performed in the court plays were undoubt-

edly of high caste. None but the educated could have inter
preted the subtleties of such plays, not to mention the prope
use of Sanskrit. It is reasonable, therefore, to suppose tha
court actors were as fully respected as the poets, and tha
they lived comfortably under the patronage of the princes

The third traditional sort of Hindu theatrical, of which
we know practically nothing except that it has long existed,
is the traveling show, composed of singers, dancers, jugglers, magicians, and puppeteers. Such entertainers have
always been of low caste, and though popular with the
masses, have ever been despised by the cultured. Possessed
of no theatre, and at best only a make-shift platform stage,
they wander from village to village, exhibiting their tricks
and earning a scanty livelihood. They leave no literary record, and their names vanish into air. The best of their
songs, their dances and tricks pass on to the new generation,
but that is their sole immortality. That these ephemeral
forms of entertainment have for untold centuries flourished
in India is beyond question. If one follows the history of
the puppet, one is led back, inevitably, to the shores of the
Ganges; if it is legerdemain that intrigues the scholar, the
road is the same. Even today the traveler in India is mysti-
fied by age-old feats of disappearance and transformation,
while our own Western charlatans pay homage to the birth-
place of their art by dressing in Hindu garb.

The professional playhouse did not make its appearance
in India until the nineteenth century, when European influence became so dominant. During the last half-century
theatres not unlike those of modern Europe have been built
in the large cities, particularly in Bombay, and professional
companies have been organized to perform native and
foreign drama. Shakespeare is a great favorite on the Indian stage, and now a new school of Indian playwrights is
rising to supply a native modern drama. A company of
Indian actors has recently been seen in London, and it is

to be expected that other tours into Europe will follow. A modern revival of dramatic music and poetry has been instituted by Rabindranath Tagore and other gifted Indian writers, and it seems that shortly there will come into being a considerable body of excellent Hindu drama. It will not be free from Western influence, but it will in all probability retain much of the classic beauty of old India. It will be intrigued by the realistic effects of the Western theatre, and may at times succumb to them, but, considering the depth of Hindu character, and the strength of Oriental mysticism, it can scarcely fail to retain a large measure of poetic symbolism and spiritual atmosphere. The new theatres of India are mixtures of old and new; the scenery, the conventions, and the mental attitudes of actors and audience, are confused and inharmonious. Eventually these matters will have to be straightened out. Two types of theatres should survive: one reflecting the best of native tradition, the other imitating competently the spirit and method of modern Occidentalism. In this period of transition it is not possible to predict which theatre will emerge the stronger.

SELECTED REFERENCES

There are few good accounts of the Hindu theatre. One is to be found in Mantzius' *History of Theatrical Art,* Vol. I., another in Horrwitz' *The Indian Theatre.* A discussion of ancient Hindu puppet-plays is contained in Pischel's *The Home of the Puppet-Play.* Worth reading, also, are the introductions to the various editions of Kalidasa's *Shakuntala.*

CHAPTER III

THE JAVANESE THEATRE

THE history of theatricals on the island of Java is not complex, and does not differ tremendously from that of several other minor civilizations in the Far East, but it is clearer in outline than the others, and has appealed more to the modern Western mind. If we except the major civilizations of India, China, and Japan, we find Java exerting the strongest Oriental influence on our present-day arts, and most of this influence comes directly from the Javanese theatre, for in Java none of the arts exists independently of the theatre.

The Malayan race (to which the Javanese belong) is given to ancestor worship, and in this practice may be discovered the origin of the Javanese theatre. In their desire to evoke the spirits of their sacred forebears, the Javanese created shadow-puppets carved from the hides of animals, and painted with conventional designs. These flat puppets, called *vayang purva,* are characterized by sharp, exaggerated profiles, long thin arms and legs, and curved, pointed fingers. They are controlled by means of wooden sticks attached to the arms, and are held above the head of the operator, who sits on a mat between a lamp and a screen. The attention of the audience is not drawn to the puppet itself, but to the moving shadows cast by it on the screen. Originally the *vayang* were manipulated by the head of each household, and the spectators were members of a particular family, but eventually this duty passed into the hands of priests, and, as the art became secularized, into the hands of *dalang,* or professional manipulators.

It is not possible to say how ancient the *vayang purva* are. They have been traced back as far as the seventh century, but are thought to be a great deal older than that. Like other Oriental phenomena, they recede into the recordless mists of time. What can be said is that, in the customary manner of religious ritual, the art of *vayang purva* outgrew its original use, and came to interpret all sorts of Malayo-Polynesian myths, later, under the influence of Hindu religion and philosophy, blending these with Oriental legend and history. The Mahabharata and the Ramayana, epic tales of India, provided drama for the Javanese theatre no less than for the festivals and court plays of Hindustan.

Not only did the repertoire of the shadow-puppets widen, but a complete evolution of the puppets themselves set in. The first step in this evolution was the creation of *vayang klitik,* or puppets carved from soft wood in double-sided relief (i. e., not entirely rounded) which were much more human in appearance than the hide-shadows, and which were not used to cast shadows, but were themselves observed by the audience. This step toward physical reality coincided chronologically with the secularization of the plays, and may be considered an indication of the departure from ancestor worship.

Next came *vayang golek,* wooden puppets carved in the round, capable of being shown from all sides. These puppets are unique and generally recognizable from the fact that they are naked from the waist up, but dressed in real clothes from the waist down. They are manipulated by means of a rod passed through the center of the body, and by sticks fastened to the hands. In design they retain many resemblances to their predecessors, but they exhibit a marked tendency toward normal human appearance.

The fourth stage in this interesting theatrical development is a significant one. It offers us, under the title of

vayang topeng, not puppets at all, but living actors costumed
and masked in imitation of puppets. The masks are made of
skin or wood, and are held to the face by a strap on the
inside, which the actor grips in his teeth. The actor does
not speak, for all the lines of the play are recited (as in the
case of puppets) by the *dalang.* The movements of the actor
are close imitations of puppet-movements, and are extremely conventionalized. They are not natural, but are
stylized dance patterns. The performance is always accompanied by music (an orchestra of native instruments furnishes this), and the dialogue is a mixture of song and
chant. The masked figures do not all represent human beings, but frequently portray animals. Bears, tigers, horses,
crocodiles are common subjects. This innovation, the appearance of the living actor, is supposed to have occurred
somewhere around the year 1000 A. D.

From the mask it is only a little way to the paint make-up.
As conventional drama approaches reality it tends to drop
the paraphernalia of savage ritual and of gross exaggeration. So we find in *vayang kedok* the living actor of the
Javanese theatre without his mask, but still painting his
features into a moderately close resemblance to the mask.
His movements, too, though changing slightly from the
marionette manner, retain the rhythmic angularity of the
past. Acting is still a dance.

Finally, but not until the nineteenth century, and from
contact with European civilization, the *vayang orang* appears. In this ultimate form of dramatic evolution, the
actor reduces his make-up to the minimum, he sings and
speaks his own share of the dialogue, he imitates the movements of normal human life. Yet this modern fashion has
not supplanted in Java the older theatrical traditions. Fortunately for the historian, all the evolutionary types have
been preserved, and have even retained their popularity.

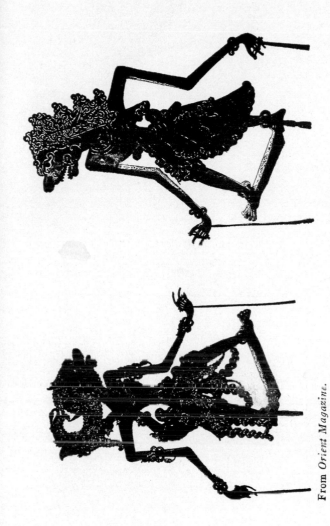

From *Orient Magazine*.

Plate 2 : Javanese Shadow Puppets.

Vayang purva, oldest of all, has still its following, and may outlive its rivals. Certainly it is this first form of Javanese theatrical that has made the deepest impression on the Western world. In the revival of puppetry which has taken place in Europe and America in the twentieth century, the Javanese shadow has found an honored place. His exotic profile and fascinating gestures have enthralled artists and public alike.

As was stated at the beginning of this chapter, the theatre is the origin of all the arts in Java. Carving and painting are limited to the creation of puppets; literature is almost exclusively the drama of the *vayang;* dancing is the heart and soul of their theatrical expression; music is composed and rendered in terms of dramatic accompaniment; the *pendoppo* (a pillared hall with a roof, but open to the air on two or three sides) is a type of building designed for *vayang* exhibitions, and is the only strictly native contribution to architecture. Even the batiks, so familiar nowadays to all Westerners, find their principal motifs in theatrical figures and symbols. Indeed it is unlikely that any other civilization is so completely expressed in terms of theatrical art as is the Javanese.

This theatre, off the beaten path, and without great pretensions, may well be considered by students of the theatre as a striking example of the evolution from religious ritual to secular art, from a world of superstition to a world of reality—the evolution which in nearly all parts of the world is the story of the theatre.

SELECTED REFERENCES

Considerable space is given to Javanese puppets in Joseph's *A Book of Marionettes.* There are some excellent comments and illustrations to be found in various numbers of *The Marionette,* a magazine published during 1918 under the editorship of Edward

Gordon Craig. Several articles on the same subject have appeared from time to time in *The Mask* and in *Theatre Arts Monthly*. A brief but very interesting description of Javanese shadow-plays is given in Anderson's *The Heroes of the Puppet Stage*.

CHAPTER IV

THE CHINESE THEATRE

INDIA may acclaim herself the mother-country of dramatic art, but her claim may be disputed by China, who, as we know, attained a very high degree of civilization before the dawn of the Christian era. It cannot be stated at what date the Chinese developed a theatrical art, but it is believed by authorities that as early as 2000 B. C. they had dramatic religious festivals, court fools, jugglers, acrobats, sword dancers, and other forerunners of legitimate drama. In ancient times there were, presumably, no playhouses, but the temples and palaces served the purpose. The Chinese have always manifested a lively interest in spectacle, and have always been fond of music. They invented fireworks, and used them in an elaborate way long before they were known to the Western world. Yet, early as Chinese theatricals must have flourished, drama seems not to have appeared until a comparatively late period. The oldest specimens of Chinese dramatic literature go back no farther than the sixth century A. D., and these specimens are decidedly rudimentary in structure. In fact it was not until the Yuan Dynasty (1280–1368), the time of the Mongol emperors, that any considerable number of well-developed plays were composed.

The Chinese themselves point to the eighth century as the beginning of professional theatricals. In that century the Emperor Ming-Huang employed a number of actors at his court, and established the tradition of organized players. He called his comedians "Students of the Pear Garden," indicating, perhaps, that they performed in one of the royal gardens, and this poetic name is still applied to actors. It is said that Ming-Huang had as many as three hundred actors in his company, and that he himself directed them. Be that as it may, it is pretty certain that through the patronage of the court, the Chinese drama was established as something more than a religious celebration, and was given a basis of definite artistic principles.

In spite of royal favor, however, the drama was not accepted as a major art by the ancient Chinese sages. Poetry, philosophy, and painting were rated highest, and to these professions the finest minds turned. The chief objection to drama held by the scholars was that it must by its very nature be written in the vernacular, whereas poetry and philosophy, intended for the learned few, could be written in the learned language. The Chinese had at that time, and have always had, a classical language quite distinct from that of their conversation, and it was obviously impractical for such a public art as the drama to employ a medium so restricted in its appeal. The reason drama took a turn for the better during the Yuan Dynasty was that the Mongol rulers threw the old court scholars out of their honored positions and let them shift for themselves. Left thus to their own resources, the pundits compromised with necessity by stooping to the composition of plays and novels—in other words, to popular forms of literature.

Taking plots which had been evolved by their humbler predecessors, the fourteenth century playwrights improved them in dialogue and structure. Typical plays of the period are in several acts, from four to twenty, and are usually arranged in groups of four acts each, these tetralogies forming independent units of production. They include many monologues, and these passages contain the strong emotional appeals, dialogue concerning itself chiefly with exposition. The characters announce themselves as they come upon the stage, in the manner of all early drama, and a different character dominates each act in a given tetralogy, thus allowing four star performers to show to advantage.

With the close of the Yuan Dynasty a great change took place. The Mongols were driven from power, and a period of great prosperity and expansion was begun. The Ming Dynasty (1368–1644) was a golden age in China. It corresponds remarkably with the Elizabethan era in England, both in matter of time and the nature of its accomplishments. Dramatic art spread throughout the country, and innumerable plays were written, of which six hundred are known. Plays were not only more numerous than before, but were longer. Some of them reached the disconcerting length of forty-eight acts. But they were still capable of being divided into rather independent sections, and the total number of acts was always divisible by four. They should be thought of as cycles rather than as single plays. They corrected the previous tendency toward the star system, and allowed for a more equitable distribution of parts.

The Manchu Dynasty (1644–1912) saw the further development of the theatre, and brought into vogue the noisy military drama. Sword-fighting became an integral part of stage action, and historical warriors became the popular heroes. In the older drama the hero was usually a student, who by his brilliant scholarship and his consequent ability to pass the government examinations, succeeded in elevating himself from the rôle of humble schoolboy to that of high and mighty mandarin. This theme, as a matter of fact, did not disappear, for it is still popular on the Chinese stage, but under the warlike influence of the Manchus its supremacy was seriously challenged.

Chinese plays, or operas, as they should be called, for they are acted to music, with most of the dialogue sung, are both perplexing and amusing to the Occidental. Students frequently inquire why it is that there are no English translations of Chinese plays. The answer is that, aside from the apparent difficulties of translating them, they are scarcely worth the effort. They are almost without exception sentimental, melodramatic, moralistic and verbose. Like the average libretto of an Italian opera, a Chinese play is written as an excuse for singing and dancing, and lays no special claim to literary distinction. Always considered a democratic art, the theatre in China has taken the intellectual level of the mass as its guide, and has, with few exceptions, avoided subtleties and profundities. Its twin purpose has been to entertain and to instruct. That alone is sufficient explanation of the Sunday-School-story quality which permeates it. In Chinese drama the hero is always triumphant, the villain is always punished. It is said by competent authorities that in the whole repertoire of the Chinese theatre there is not a true specimen of tragedy.

If, however, an examination of Chinese drama does not enrich our store of literature, the theatre art which has grown up about it does assuredly repay our study. The theatre building itself is interesting. Architecturally simple, it is quite uniformly reproduced in all parts of the country. The chief difference between various playhouses is that of size. The building is rectangular, nearly square, and seats as a rule seven or eight hundred persons. Often it is unroofed, except above the stage and galleries, but may have a flat roof with sky-lights in center. The principal entrance to the theatre is through a large ornamental doorway facing on the street, and at the opposite end of the auditorium is the stage, a platform about twenty-five feet square and five or six feet high, projecting into the audience. Over the stage is a roof supported at the corners by two high columns which are brightly painted and covered with gilt inscriptions. A carved and painted balustrade runs around the stage, forming a barrier between the actors and the audience, and a similar ornamental railing surrounds the stage-roof. The entire stage is a traditional representation of the front of a temple—testifying unmistakably to the origin of the drama.

The back wall of the stage is covered with richly embroidered hangings, and contains two doorways, symmetrically placed at right and left, which are also covered with draperies. Small bits of mirror are sewn on these hangings. The floor of the stage is covered with a gorgeous rug, and a few pieces of furniture, chairs, a table, *et cetera,* stand in view of the audience. There is no front curtain.

The main floor of the auditorium is divided into boxes which contain benches, tables, and chairs. Each box holds five or more persons. The gallery runs around three sides of the auditorium. The first tiers of seats in the side-galleries are divided into boxes, and are considered the best locations. Women who attend the theatre generally occupy these seats. The galleries are reached by staircases situated on either side at the rear of the auditorium.

Performances begin late in the afternoon or early in the evening, and continue until past midnight. A six- or seven-hour performance seems unbearably long to a Westerner, but the Chinese are patient. One must remember, too, that these are operas rather than plays, that the audience has heard them over and over, and pays attention only when it pleases. Discriminating patrons come late to the theatre, for the best actors often do not appear until nine or ten o'clock, and during dull or trivial scenes the audience can drink tea, smoke, and relax. The atmosphere of such a theatre is far less strained than that of a Western legitimate playhouse, where dignity and silence must be maintained in spite of a cramped body. There is really something of the cabaret spirit in the true Oriental theatre. The playhouse itself is surrounded by tea-houses and restaurants, and it is possible to relieve the boredom of the opera with a minimum of exertion. These privileges are augmented by another which has almost disappeared from Western theatres—that is, the right of the spectator to express himself freely in regard to the actor or the play at the very moment his emotion is aroused. Shouts of approval or censure punctuate the typical Chinese performance, and add greatly to the spirit of the occasion. Although a modern sense of decorum has prohibited this natural display of feeling in our own theatre, there are persons who believe that artistic standards have been lowered by the banishment of the hiss. Be that as it may, the Chinese actor must look to the temper of his audience.

Perhaps the most striking feature of the Chinese theatre is the conventions of its stage. Properties, costumes, gestures, all are simply but definitely symbolic, and follow a tradition as familiar as it is ancient. Whatever annoyance or ennui the foreigner may suffer at a Chinese opera, he is almost certain to be vastly amused and considerably puzzled by these non-realistic and frequently naïve customs. He may be convinced that there is something extremely subtle and mysterious about the whole business, for Occidentals are given to exaggerating the cryptic qualities of Orientals. As a matter of fact the Chinese stage conventions are childishly simple, once they are put up for examination. This does not mean that they are inferior to the conventions of the Western stage, nor that they are lacking in artistic quality, but merely that they are easily understood. They have served an intelligent race of people for many centuries, and in doing so they have proved their worth beyond any argument. In reality it is possible to show a superiority of the Chinese theatrical system over our own, if one grants that the stage is to be judged according to purely aesthetic principles. The first requirement of any work of art is that it leave something to the imagination, and this the realistic stage does not do.

The Chinese theatre, springing from ritual, has never lost the ritualistic point of view—that is, the desire to pre-

From *Theatre Arts Monthly.*

Plate 3: Conventional make-up for the part of General Kiang Wei.

From *Theatre Arts Monthly.*

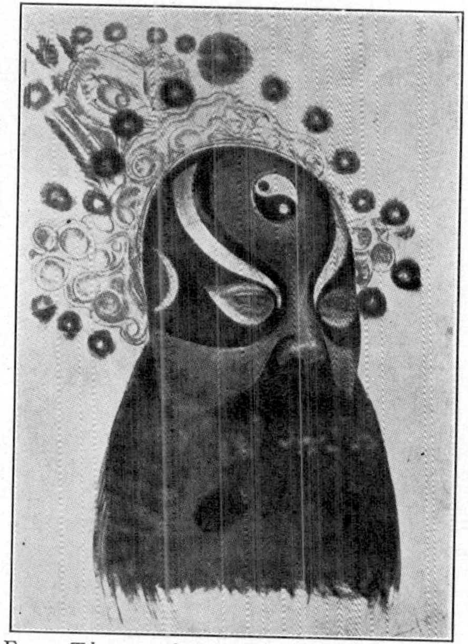

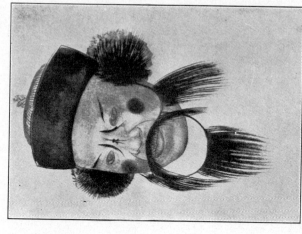

Plate 4: Comic Mandarin.

sent rather than to represent. It does not compete with reality; it reduces life to an art formula. Thus the Chinese actor lifts his foot eight inches from the floor to indicate that he is crossing an imaginary door-sill, or throws his leg in a certain manner to show that he is descending from a horse. He commits suicide, not by leaping from an artificial rock into the wings, but by doing a graceful acrobatic fall from a table, all in full sight of the audience. A sword duel on the Chinese stage is filled with action and color, but no blows are struck: whirls, passes, and slashes weave a thrilling but harmless pattern in the air.

Economy of means is also extended to the matter of supernumeraries. No mobs litter the stage even in battle scenes; instead, a warrior-general carries banners indicating the number of his followers. One banner does service for a thousand foot-soldiers, two banners for twice that number, and so on. With the army reduced thus to the figure of one bespangled general, it is simple to provide the armed wall of a besieged city. A screen, painted to suggest a battlement, is set forth upon the stage, and is held in place by the property-man and his assistant (both visible to the audience) while the symbolically numerous warrior executes a Terpsichorean attack on the fortress. There is no real impact of warrior and wall, but the spirit is present.

A decorated screen is really the chief pictorial device of the Chinese stage. It is used to suggest everything from a palace wall to a single tree, yet it never, either in size or realistic detail, passes out of the realm of symbolism, nor is there any attempt on the part of the stage-hands to lessen the consciousness of the audience that the screen is only a screen. In the same way, an oar signifies a boat, or even a fleet, and a series of small banners decorated with conventionalized waves and fish creates a river.

The costumes and facial make-ups of the actors are in keeping with this strict stylization. Yellow costumes are worn by emperors, a red veil by a bride; a yellow cloth covers the face of a sick person, a red cloth the face of one dead. Gods and spirits carry horse-hair switches, and enter upon the stage at the sound of a gong. A red face is given the god of war or a famous warrior, a black face means a rough but honest man, a white face means cunning and treachery coupled with dignity, gold on the face is the sign of a god, and green the sign of a devil. Only good characters, it may be added, wear mustaches.

Characters tend to follow fixed types, as they invariably do in a non-realistic theatre. In Chinese drama we find most frequently the young military hero (with a headdress of pheasant feathers), the young scholar hero (carrying a fan), the admirable old man with a long beard (a general, or perhaps an emperor), the middle-aged warrior (acrobat, sword-fighter, and boxer), the honest simple girl, the girl of doubtful reputation (a comedy part requiring skilled performance) and of course a clown, who, like all clowns, does a great deal of improvisation.

Masks are worn occasionally on the Chinese stage, but they are the exception rather than the rule. When they are used it is generally in the depiction of comic or supernatural characters. The paint make-up, however, is applied so thick that it often has the effect of a mask. In warrior rôles, particularly, the actor's countenance is apt to be completely concealed by the excessive amount of paint put over it in bizarre designs.

Preparation for a life of acting in China is rather an ordeal. Young boys from the poorer classes are apprenticed to directors of theatrical companies for a period of six or seven years, and during that time the student must learn acrobatics, swordsmanship, singing, reciting, and dancing. He must commit to memory a large number of plays, and in doing so must learn not only the dialogue and music, but every detail of stage-business. Chinese acting is regulated by tradition, and this tradition overlooks not even the flicker of an eye-lash. But when the years of training are over, the student is given parts to play, and proceeds, by six or seven years of professional acting, to pay off his indebtedness to the director. At the end of that time he is free to manage his own career. His social position will always be rather low, but he may, if he becomes popular, make a good deal of money.

Women have had little to do with the development of Chinese theatre art. A good deal of the time they have not been allowed on the professional stage. There were actresses during the time of the Mongols (1280–1368), but when the Emperor K'ien-long succumbed to their charms and made one of them his mistress, they were banned, and did not reappear on the stage until the beginning of the twentieth century. Since the founding of the Republic (1912) the feminine movement has advanced rapidly, with the result that there are now eleven theatres in Peking where women are allowed to perform, but only in all-female casts. Mixed companies exist in Shanghai and other progressive cities, but are frowned upon by adherents to the older civilization. Chinese actors through centuries of practice have developed the art of female impersonation to an extraordinary degree, and have actually set the standard of feminine beauty and deportment. Mei Lan-fang, called the greatest actor on the Chinese stage today, is a female impersonator, and is so popular that he receives a small fortune for a single performance. His favorite rôle is that of the demi-mondaine.

To the foreigner the most astonishing thing about a Chinese production is the music. Loud and penetrating, it accompanies the play almost continuously, and to the unaccustomed ear becomes intolerably monotonous. It emanates from an orchestra of eight or ten pieces, the musicians sitting in plain view of the audience, at the back of the stage between the two doors. The two-stringed violin is the most important instrument, for it carries the melody for the singer. Important, too, is the *pankou* (a sharp-toned drum), which beats the tempo. Then there are cymbals, clarinet, castanets, flute, guitar, and *pang-dze* (a hollow piece of wood beaten with a stick). The squawking and clanging of Western jazz, even in its worst phases, cannot compare with the racket of a Chinese orchestra. It was not ever thus. In ancient times Chinese music was soft and refined, overflowing with tender melody. It was tuned to the quiet subtlety of the philosophic mind, and many a Celestial scholar has testified to its soothing influence. But not many centuries ago, six or seven perhaps, the Mongols brought their savage music from the North, and made it the fashion in China. Only in this century is there a reaction against its raucous vulgarity. Mei Lan-fang is one of the leaders in the movement to restore to the theatre a pre-Mongolian type of music, in which harsh instruments are subdued, and the gentle voice of the flute predominates.

Members of the orchestra, like the property-man, are in a figurative sense only, invisible. That is, they are dressed in black, and black is the symbol of invisibility on the Chinese stage. They tend strictly to business, maintaining in lax moments a passivity truly remarkable. They exhibit no interest in the play that is being acted under their noses, nor in the audience that is gazing full upon them. The musicians sit stoically through so many hours that after a time they blend with the draperies of the background, and are, if not invisible, at least unnoticed. The property-man comes and goes according to the demands of the play, moving a table to the center of the stage, placing a pillow on the floor to support the head of a dying man, holding a screen while it plays the part of a temple, setting out two chairs for a love scene—sitting calmly at one side when there is nothing to do. His combination of efficiency and nonchalance never fails to captivate the foreign spectator, though it is taken for granted by the Chinese.

Another singular custom is that relating to entrance and exit. The actor always enters from the doorway at stage right, and leaves by the one at stage left. Where he is supposed to be coming from, or where he is going, has nothing to do with the case. The action thus moves in a continual circle, and can scarcely become confused. Directly behind the stage is a green-room, where all characters wait their entrance cues, and where minor characters dress and make up. Stars have private dressing-rooms.

Prices of admission to Chinese theatres vary greatly, as they do in all countries. Theatres of the newer type, built and managed in semi-Occidental fashion, are of course the more costly. In the old-fashioned Chinese theatre no fee is charged at the door, and no collection is taken until the performance is more than half through. Those who enjoy the play and sit through it, thus pay for their pleasure; those who are bored and leave early, pay nothing.

All the principal cities in China today have permanent theatres, and the villages are supplied with theatricals by traveling companies. Peking is the theatrical capital, and sets the style in plays. It also furnishes the dialect in which most of the plays are performed. There are said to be at present at least thirty theatres operating in Peking, these not including the various restaurants and other public places where special shows are staged. In most cases the company works on a percentage basis, receiving seventy percent. of the income, the theatre-owners taking the remaining thirty percent. In recent years these metropolitan playhouses have been put on a thoroughly commercial basis, and from the standpoint of business organization are comparable (naturally, being imitations) with our own.

It is presumed that during the process of Westernization which is now well under way in the Orient, the Chinese theatre will lose many of its traditional characteristics, and will (like the Indian and Japanese theatres) attempt a compromise between new and old. As a matter of fact there are already in China groups of amateurs who are producing European plays in an imitation of the European manner. The professional theatre may or may not be swept off its feet by the foreign fashion. Whatever may take place in the large cosmopolitan cities, it seems extremely unlikely that the less penetrable parts of the country will succumb very soon to anything so alien as a realistic theatre. Still, there is the motion picture to act as vanguard, and where it goes, anything Western may follow.

SELECTED REFERENCES

The best treatise on this subject is Zucker's *The Chinese Theatre*. Excellent illustrations but rather slight reading matter may be found in Chu Chia-Chien and A. Jacovleff's book bearing the same title. Another rather slight essay in this field is Buss' *Studies in the Chinese Drama*. Mantzius, in the first volume of his *History of Theatrical Art*, goes into the subject in some detail, but his account is not entirely accurate. A number of travel books contain brief notes regarding the theatre in China, and the files of *Theatre Arts Monthly* will yield valuable information.

CHAPTER V

THE JAPANESE THEATRE

THE development of a literary drama and a conscious art of the theatre did not occur so early in Japan as one might imagine. In fact Japanese drama is of approximately the same age as English drama. Until the latter part of the fourteenth century there was, it seems, no attempt in Japan to gather up the loose threads of dramatic expression and weave them into an elaborate and significant pattern. There were plenty of loose threads in existence, even as there were in mediaeval Europe. Religious dances (with masks), accompanied by chants and instrumental music, were regularly given before the temples; ballad-singers, acrobats, magicians, and puppet-manipulators were known throughout the country; poetry and painting flourished among the upper classes. It remained only for someone to look upon the scene with a co-ordinating eye.

ORIGIN AND DEVELOPMENT OF THE NŌ

Somewhere around the year 1375 the Shogun Yoshimitsu was impressed by the dramatic dancing of a priest named Kwanami, and at the conclusion of the Shinto ceremony of which the dance had been a part, invited him to take up his residence at the Shogun's palace in Kyoto, then the capital city of Japan. Kwanami, installed at the court, enjoying the patronage of the Shogun, proceeded then to develop the art of dramatic representation. Just what steps he took, and in what order, we can scarcely know, but it is clear enough

37

that he and his fellow-priests arranged what may be considered the first real dramas of Japan. For their themes they drew largely upon the religious literature with which they were familiar, and in all their work they retained the sacred atmosphere. Their performances at court were as austere as though they had been given under the eaves of the temple, but their appeal was more than religious; it was remarkably aesthetic. The words chanted by the chorus, and those sung and recited by the dancers, were filled with poetic subtlety, whereas the gestures, postures, and rhythmical movements of the dancers were based upon a symbolic system which only the erudite could hope to appreciate.

This classical performance was called *Nō* (a word meaning the same as our word "drama"; i. e., "something done," or "accomplishment"), and when today we speak of *"Nō plays"* or *"Nō dances,"* we mean only the plays or the dances devised in mediaeval times by Kwanami or his disciples for the edification of the feudal aristocracy. Other names are used to designate more modern and more popular types of theatrical art.

Capable as Kwanami must have been, his rôle was that of a pioneer. He laid the foundations for one of the most absorbing and most nearly perfect theatre arts in the world's history, but it was his son, called Seami (1363–1444), who brought the *Nō* to completion. Devoting his whole life to the task, Seami carried the art of *Nō* as far as it was possible to go, leaving behind him a large number of excellently composed plays, a group of disciples trained to the ultimate point of efficiency, and a treatise on the art of acting, which for profound insight, exquisite taste, and practical suggestion can hold its own with any treatise on the same subject, ancient or modern, Oriental or Western.

Theatre buildings did not come into existence immediately after the foundation of *Nō*. It was not until the seventeenth century, when popular drama was in the ascendant, that public playhouses appeared. The *Nō* stage was erected in a royal hall, in a garden, or before a temple, and the audience was a small, aristocratic one. The stage was a square projecting platform, surmounted by a canopy resembling the roof of a temple, and connected with a green-room (where the actors dressed and waited their entrance) by a rather long, narrow bridge (*hashigakari*). The audience sat on three sides of the stage, as in the theatre of Shakespeare's London. The musicians sat along the back of the stage, the chorus along the left-hand side from the view-point of the actor. The front of the bridge was decorated with three small pine trees (real ones) set at regular intervals, and at the back of the stage proper was a curtain on which was painted a single large pine tree. The pine, to the Japanese, is the symbol of immortality.

The chorus consisted of from eight to twelve men dressed soberly in civilian clothes, whose business it was to sing an interpretation of the actor's movements, sometimes expressing his inward thoughts, again describing objectively his action. There were two main actors, or dancers, as perhaps we should call them, and as many subordinates as the particular play required. Seldom, however, does a *Nō* play require more than three or four actors. Only men took part in the performance, female rôles being played with great skill by actors in masks. Demons, ghosts, and old men were also represented by masks, whereas young men and children were usually portrayed unmasked. These *Nō* masks, many of which are still in existence, are carved from wood, and are considered the finest theatrical masks in the world. They are of great variety, and often a single mask contains in its features a dozen different moods and expressions which can be released at will by an accomplished dancer.

The costumes of the *Nō* actors contributed much, also, to the effectiveness of the performance. Elaborate ceremonial robes of rich brocade, bizarre head-dresses, cloaks, swords

—in short, all the paraphernalia of mediaeval Japanese civilization, made the wardrobe of the *Nō* a magnificent assemblage of color and design. It was seldom, indeed, that the actors themselves could afford to own the costumes. As the *Nō* became a regular event among the nobility, and companies of players moved from one palace to another with their plays, the lords and princes made private collections of costumes, keeping them in readiness for the visit of the players, and priding themselves individually on the excellence of their collections.

Properties, like the stage itself, were non-realistic. As in the Chinese theatre, detail was barely suggested, the rest being supplied by the imagination of the audience. Such necessary properties as boats, carriages, wells, *et cetera,* were represented by simple wooden frames, only vaguely suggestive of the actuality. A fan became, in the actor's hand, any small object: a knife, a brush, or what not. Weapons (being essentially part of the costume) were the sole realistic equipment of the actor.

Three or four musicians made up the orchestra: two or three drummers and a flute-player. The drums, large and small, accompanied most of the action, the flute entering only at special times. This, on paper, does not seem particularly complicated, but those who have heard *Nō* performances have testified invariably that the rhythms created by the drums (even when there were only two, a large and a small) were so extraordinary as to baffle analysis. The rhythm of one drum is woven inextricably into the rhythm of the other, and together they form a pattern against which the actor dances. The rhythm of his own movements, sharply accented by loud stampings of his feet on the floor of the stage, is related to the duple rhythm of the drums, yet it is in opposition to it rather than in accord with it.

The *Nō* plays are short. None of them is of more than one-act length. Some of them are so slight as to consist of little more than a poetic atmosphere out of which rises a dance; others contain considerable plot, but in a highly condensed form. Years pass and great distances are covered in the interval between two short speeches. Many of the plays have to do with the supernatural, and it is a common thing for them to show a character in life, and a moment or two later his death (acted in a most poetic and stylized manner), followed by an appearance of his ghost. Revenge themes are frequent—especially those which display ghosts or demons as avengers. Buddhism dominates nearly all *Nō* plays, not only in fundamental thought, but in detail as well. The average *Nō* text is filled with Buddhistic allusions, and is obviously by and for the adherents to that faith, expounding its principles and emotionalizing its ritual.

The brevity of the *Nō* plays allowed several of them to be presented at a single occasion. But whatever number of plays were included in a production group, they were carefully chosen and arranged according to a well understood formula. The entire program was conceived in three movements, introductory, development, and climax, each play fitting naturally into one of these categories. Introductory pieces were naturally gentle of movement, and permeated with the spirit of salutation and good wishes. Development pieces, on the other hand, were more arresting, while climax pieces reached the zenith of emotional power.

Realism was faithfully excluded from the *Nō*, and so was comedy. Indeed, during the early period of Japanese drama, realism and comedy appear to have been considered synonymous. The *Nō* was not always deep tragedy, but it moved ever in the domain of the serious. Yet its audience was not deprived of the comic spirit, for almost as soon as the *Nō* found solid footing, its producers adopted a kind of homely farce called *kyogen* as an interlude to the *Nō*. The *kyogen* treats generally of rustic or lower class life, and calls for perfectly natural acting. It is faithful to reality, and is screamingly funny as well as astoundingly ingenious. Actually it is identical with the mediaeval farce of France and England, which, it will be remembered, flourished alongside the miracle plays, and served to relieve their religious tedium, even as the *kyogen* relieved the strain of the *Nō*. But whereas in Europe, and particularly in England, the farce mingled with and sometimes destroyed the dignity of the miracle play, the *kyogen* was never permitted to encroach on the *Nō*. The two types were performed alternately before the same audience, but they were kept strictly apart.

The *Nō* may be classed not only as an aristocratic art, but specifically as a possession of the feudal lords who ruled Japan from mediaeval times until 1868, when they were overthrown and the Mikado restored to power. Companies of *Nō* actors were really clans or families, each with its characteristic traditions and secrets of technique. All the members of a company took the family name of its head, and zealously guarded its possessions. There were never more than five of these companies in existence at a given time. At the fall of the Shogunate the art of *Nō* came near to extinction, for the actors feared the new régime, and with the exception of one company, disbanded. Umewaka Minoru, the head of a company, braved the possible persecution of the Mikado and continued his activity. In 1869–70 he built himself a new theatre and kept alive the tradition of *Nō*. Suffering no evil consequences, he became an inspiration to the other leaders, and within a short time all five families were re-established. Today the *Nō* is still alive, though it is somewhat of an anomaly in the twentieth century, and depends upon the patronage of the ultra-conservative Japanese, whose ranks are rapidly thinning. If it survives long, it will very likely do so on aesthetic rather than on religious grounds, for its theology is archaic. That its purely aesthetic appeal is great may be concluded from a study of its history as well as from direct observation of its modern productions. The literature of the *Nō* is unsurpassed for lyric beauty; its technique of acting and its beauty of physical equipment are, in their way, perfect. It is probably not rash to assert that the *Nō* is the most significant specimen of ritualistic theatre art in the word today.

THE RISE OF THE DOLL-PLAY

It was more than two centuries after the founding of *Nō* that a popular drama was established. Like its aristocratic prototype it rose from the religious dance, but instead of exploiting the sacred legends of Buddhism, and considering itself a vehicle of enlightenment, it turned to secular ballads and realistic comedy, with entertainment as its principal motive. It had two distinct branches: the Doll-play, and *Kabuki*. It seems impossible to say which of the two was first to be organized into what may be called a theatre, but it is thought that they developed side by side, one influencing the other, and both attaining popularity at the beginning of the seventeenth century.

Dancing dolls had long been known in Japan. Carried by minstrels from village to village, they had been used all through the mediaeval period to supplement songs and tricks. Then there were blind men who sat near the temples and sang long dramatic ballads, but who of course lacked any means of interpreting their songs by action. Eventually these performers were drawn together, by mutual interest, and, according to one authority, by the introduction into Japan of the *samisen,* a stringed instrument imported from the Loo Choo Islands, though probably of Chinese origin. The *samisen,* which ever since has been the musical mainstay of the popular theatre, proved an exciting substitute for the rather sombre drum and flute of earlier theatricals, and lent itself admirably to the accompaniment of long narratives. The result was that around the year 1600 the Doll-theatre made its appearance, and ballad-dramas, called *Joruri* (after the leading character in the first famous one) acted by puppets to the strains of the *samisen*, while the story itself was chanted.

Japanese theatrical dolls are relatively large. Some of them are nearly life size, and are constructed in a complex way, allowing the finest effects of expression and gesture. They are not controlled by strings from above, nor by rods from beneath, but by the hands of the puppeteer, who, unlike his European counterpart, stays in sight of the audience all the time the doll is in action. He dresses in a simple, dark garment, so as to attract as little attention as possible, and by skillful manipulation, keeps the attention of the audience focused on the doll rather than on himself. In the case of the more elaborate specimens, two or even three puppeteers attend a single doll.

During the seventeenth century the Doll-theatre expanded and progressed most remarkably, attaining a large following in every city of importance. It attracted a host of playwrights, and soon had an extensive repertoire of plays. Early ballad-dramas gave way to complicated and enormously lengthy military plays, while all the thrilling events of history and mythology were exploited by the energetic dramatists. The two outstanding playwrights of Japan, Chikamatsu Monzaemon and Takeda Izumo were the product of the Doll-theatre.

Not only did the puppets inspire dramatic literature; they were responsible for the invention of stage machinery and realistic settings. Japanese craftsmen, world-famous for their skill, were attracted to the Doll-theatre by the opportunity it offered for novel and ingenious effects. The art of conjuring had always been more or less associated with puppetry in Japan, and now that so many dramas of the mysterious and the sensational were being performed, me-

:hanical cleverness was eminently desirable. One result of Doll-theatre craftsmanship was the revolving stage (its first appearance in the world), a device which was later taken over by the *Kabuki* theatre, and finally by European and American producers. Scenes painted in perspective also appeared: landscapes, houses, temples, bridges, all represented with faithfulness to reality, and in sharp contrast to the classic, unadorned setting of the *Nō*.

The Doll-theatre reached the height of its development in the middle of the eighteenth century. From that time to the present it has declined, though its lowest ebb was suffered in the early part of the nineteenth century. Recently it has revived, and in Osaka, its modern home, enjoys rather remarkable popularity. There are traveling Doll-theatres nowadays, but outside of Osaka, scarcely any permanently established ones. They have suffered, not only from competition with the theatre of living actors, but perhaps even more from their silent enemies, the motion pictures. In one sense it is a defeat of puppets by puppets.

THE STORY OF *KABUKI*

We have now to consider the other, and more important branch of popular Japanese theatre art—that is, the *Kabuki*. Surprisingly enough, credit for the origin of *Kabuki* is given to a woman, for it is said that this type of performance sprang directly from the activity of O-Kuni, a religious dancer attached to the Shinto Shrine of Izumo. Moved by heaven knows what ambition, O-Kuni betook herself in the year 1596 to the city of Kyoto, which at that time was not only the very rich and gay capital of the kingdom, but was larger than any city in Europe, having a half million inhabitants. There, in the dry bed of the Kamo River, she had a platform erected whereon she exhibited her dances, wearing the garments of a priest. Presumably there was art in her performance, for she drew good crowds, and more than that, captured the affections of a handsome young samurai Sansaburo by name, whom she presently married. Sansaburo was a cultivated man, familiar with the arts of music, poetry, and dancing. He was even familiar with the *Nō* drama, and the *kyogen* which accompanied it. With uncommon good sense, he directed the activities of his talented wife, steering away from the religious toward the secular and the comic. He composed popular songs for her, taught her bits of *kyogen*, and danced with her. O-Kuni now dropped her priest's garb and donned the robes of a male warrior, an alteration which greatly increased her vogue with the public. She and her husband called their entertainment *Kabuki*, a word already in existence, but heretofore not applied to a specific type of drama. They performed before royalty and before the common people, not only in Kyoto but also in Yedo (Tokyo), the military center of Japan at that time. Sansaburo eventually was killed in a quarrel with another man, and O-Kuni retired to lead a quiet life near the shrine where she had first danced in Shinto ritual.

O-Kuni had created a sensation, and her success inflamed the minds of countless women who fancied themselves as entertainers. The opening years of the seventeenth century saw many companies of female singers and dancers touring the country. They carried men with them to serve as musicians, and the women actors took the parts of male warriors after the fashion of O-Kuni. Within a short time, however, the male musicians began to take part in the acting and dancing, assuming feminine rôles. This interchange of the sexes delighted the public, though it caused some consternation among the protectors of morals. To make matters worse, the *geisha* (professional women entertainers, often of questionable character) now were attracted to *Kabuki*, and once they got a foot-hold on the stage, the reputation of the popular theatre sank. It was also about this time that the *samisen* came into use in Japan, and the stimulating quality of its music augmented the already too frivolous atmosphere of *Kabuki*. The consequence was that in 1608 a government proclamation limited *Kabuki* performances to the outskirts of cities, and in 1629 a more drastic order forbade all women to appear as participants in public entertainments. Not only were women driven from the *Kabuki* stage; they were expelled from the Doll-theatres where many of them had been engaged as singers, and some even as manipulators. There were from time to time violations of the edict against women performers, but they were offenses of minor significance. It was, on the whole, an efficient law—so efficient that it changed the entire course of the popular theatre. Not until the beginning of the present century did Japanese women again take their place on the stage, and even now they have not won back the prestige which they perforce relinquished in 1629.

Before the banning of women, however, *Kabuki* had been taken up by groups of young men; the first all-male company had been organized in Kyoto in 1617, another in Osaka in 1624, and a third in Yedo the same year. The abolition of women's companies left these young men's groups without competition. Thereafter *Kabuki* developed in a perfectly logical manner, older men gradually taking supremacy over the boy actors, rôles becoming classified and conventionalized, clans (families) becoming crystallized around particular traditions and possessions, wooden theatres with galleries being erected, plays and music being accumulated. By the end of the seventeenth century it was a thoroughly organized and well-rooted theatre art.

The *Kabuki* stage was at first nothing more than a platform set in an open space, in a dry river-bed or on a lawn. The name for theatre in Japanese is *shibai,* which means literally, to sit on the grass. The *Nō* stage naturally influenced that of the *Kabuki,* especially in the matter of the *hashiga kari,* or bridge, connecting the stage with the green-room But this bridge was soon abolished by the craftsmen of *Kabuki,* and in its place were built two long runways, called *hanamichi* (flower-paths), from the corners of the stage through the audience, the one at the audience's left being the wider and more important one. The *hanamichi,* recently adopted by European and American producers of spectac ular plays, is perhaps the outstanding physical characteristi of the *Kabuki* theatre, and has influenced the style of acting the arrangement of plays, and in fact the whole spirit of the Japanese popular theatre. It establishes an unusually inti mate relationship betwen actor and audience, and permits extraordinary effects of pageantry. It is used for the sensa tional entrance and exit of warriors, for religious proces sions, for long journeys, and sometimes for trick appear ances and disappearances, its floor being equipped with trap-doors just as is the floor of the stage proper.

From the Doll-theatre *Kabuki* borrowed the revolving stage, a mechanical device which allows the setting of two or three scenes in advance, and which, in a theatre bent on realistic representation, is a tremendous saver of time. From the same source it borrowed its ideas of scenery— landscapes in perspective, movable house-sets, temple fronts, and other inventions of the realistic craftsman. Over the stage in the earliest theatres was the reproduction of a temple-roof, but gradually that has shrunk to a mere decorative suggestion of the original. The auditorium of the typical *Kabuki* theatre has not altered much in the last two centuries. The lower floor is cut into a large number of square enclosures designed to hold four persons each. Mats and cushions take the place of chairs or benches, the spec tators resting on their knees throughout the performance. A gallery surrounds the auditorium on three sides. The walls are rather flimsy, and allow the air to blow through

From Mantzius' *History of Theatrical Art.*

Plate 5: Interior of Japanese Theatre, Kabuki type.

the theatre freely—adding to the comfort of the audience in summer, but decidedly increasing its discomfort in winter. The theatre is roofed, but in an airy manner. The earliest theatres, of course, were not roofed, but those built since about 1700 have been. An interesting architectural feature of the old theatres is the *yagura,* or drumtower. This is a square platform built out over the main entrance, from which a large drum was beat to announce the impending performance.

In older times *Kabuki* began at daybreak and lasted at least until sunset. Travelers from afar came the evening before and put up at the adjoining teahouse. Those who came from a moderate distance left their homes in the darkness of early morning. Women sat up all night arranging their hair (an exceedingly important part of a Japanese woman's toilet), not daring to lie down for fear of destroying the perfection of their elaborate coiffure. The theatre was lighted by candles, tall candle-sticks serving for footlights, and at times lighted candles attached to the end of long, pliable poles were held out from the wings by property-men, illuminating the faces of the actors.

Kabuki has many powerful traditions, but perhaps the most powerful of all is its tradition of acting. There are, broadly speaking, two schools of acting, one that inclines toward the natural, another that aims at the grotesque, the sensational, the picturesquely unreal. The former style is said to have been created by Sakata Tojuro (1645–1709); the latter by Ichikawa Danjuro (1660–1704). Tojuro was in his day the greatest actor of Kyoto, the city of ancient culture, and the technique which he expounded was a reflection of the refined and graceful life which surrounded him. Danjuro, on the other hand, performed in Yedo (Tokyo), which during the seventeenth century was the military center of Japan, and overflowed with rough-and-ready warriors. The spirit of *aragoto* ("rough-style") as

Danjuro's acting was called, was the spirit of the city. Its exaggerated heroics were imitated somewhat from the military plays of the Doll-theatre.

Tojuro left no direct descendant to carry on his name, but his style has lived steadily in the *Kabuki* theatre. Danjuro, on the other hand, left his name and art to a son who did him justice, and who in his turn bequeathed the legacy to Danjuro the Third. The last of the line, Danjuro the Ninth, who is said to have been the greatest actor ever produced in Japan, died in 1903, after a life filled with honors. In 1887 he played an invitation performance before the Emperor—the first time in two hundred and fifty years that Imperial favor had been bestowed upon popular theatre art.

Some times the great actors of *Kabuki* have won their fame in masculine rôles; again they have triumphed as *onnagata,* or female impersonators. Even today, with women resuming their place in the theatre, *onnagata* are great favorites, and are in no immediate danger of being supplanted. It is even said that women to succeed on the modern Japanese stage must not act natural, but must rather imitate the cultivated femininity of the *onnagata.* One of the most famous *onnagata* of the past, Yoshizawa Ayame (died 1729), left some interesting comments on his perverse profession, one of them being to the effect that a good *onnagata* must lead as gentle a life offstage as on: eating daintily, and blushing when his wife's name is mentioned.

With all their fame, however, *Kabuki* actors have always occupied a social plane beneath that of the upper classes. Many of them have been men of excellent education, connoisseurs of poetry, painting, and other arts, yet even these have, because of the stigma attached to their profession, been considered unfit for association with persons of rank. At some periods actors have been restricted to specified districts of the city, but this practice no longer obtains. Gradually honor and respect are being fastened to the names of *Kabuki* actors, and the old prejudice against them (dating back to the sixteenth century, when they were little more than beggars performing on the outskirts of the city) is vanishing. It is true that their morals have often stood in the way of their social progress, but these, it seems, are improving in the light of modern standards and public opinion.

But if the actors have not been accorded the highest social privileges, they have at least basked in the warmth of over-whelming admiration. For three centuries they have been the idols of the mass, and relatively speaking they have been well paid. A star of the *Kabuki* stage can make a fortune. The playwrights, on the contrary, have invariably received less adulation and less pay. Many of the most accomplished playwrights have earned only a bare living. In the old days there was an extraordinary amount of collaboration in writing for the theatre. Each theatre had its chief playwright, a secondary one, and several minor ones. In a long play the work was divided: the minor playwrights (rather poor at the business) did the opening scenes, which were supposed to be dull anyway; the secondary playwright did the next scenes, which were intended to capture the interest of the audience and prepare for the climax; the chief playwright wrote the climax. Besides doing unimportant passages of the plays, the minor playwrights composed the programs, the announcements which were posted in front of the theatre, and in their spare moments copied individual parts for the actors.

The first *Kabuki* playwright of importance was Fukui Yagozaemon. Until he turned his hand to the theatre, *Kabuki* plays had all been short, like the *Nō* plays. They had really been one-acters. But in 1664 Yagozaemon, writing for an Osaka theatre, composed "The Beggar's Revenge," a play in three acts. From that time on the plays grew longer and longer, some of them reaching the length of twenty acts. But as was said previously, the two most famous playwrights of Japan are Chikamatsu Monzaemon (1660–1724), and Takeda Izumo (1688–1756). The former of these is often referred to as the Japanese Shakespeare or the Japanese Sophocles, but these appellations must be taken as symbols of unbounded admiration rather than as definite challenges to a comparison of Chikamatsu with the European giants. He was, however, an exceedingly able dramatist, and a fertile one. In thirty years he composed no fewer than one hundred and thirty pieces, some for the *Kabuki* stage, but mostly for the Doll-theatre. Takeda Izumo, considerably younger, was Chikamatsu's most brilliant pupil and collaborator. They wrote numerous plays together, and in 1713 opened a Doll-theatre of their own. Their masterpieces, written for puppets, were in time all taken over by the *Kabuki,* where they still hold the boards.

The best known of all *Kabuki* plays is the "Chushingura" or the "Vendetta of the 47 Ronin." The story is sometimes called in English, "The Faithful." This play was worked out in rough draft by Chikamatsu shortly before his death, but was written by Takeda Izumo and two others. Another classic, perhaps second in popularity, is the "Suguwara" tragedy, one act of which has been translated into English under the title of "The Pine Tree" ("Matsu"). This play was also the work of Takeda Izumo and his friends, and stands out unmistakeably as a masterpiece. Even in English translation it is very powerful.

Let us see now what features of *Kabuki* we have neglected to mention. Properties, make-up, and certain conventions have been overlooked. As for properties, they are a mixture of realistic and suggestive, with the emphasis on the former. In some plays, where the influence of the *Nō* is felt (and that is not infrequent), the actor relies on classic symbolism, and lets the fan or whatever the prescribed article may be, do duty for any number of objects. But generally the *Kabuki* actor is liberally supplied with realistic properties: swords, candle-sticks, helmets, pictures, *et cetera,* and these are not merely made to look real to the audience; they are authentic, and are usually excellent specimens of the craftsman's art.

The settings, too, alternate between decorative simplicity and ornate realism. It is as though the spirit of the *Nō* and the spirit of the Doll-theatre struggled for mastery of the *Kabuki*. But some sort of pictorial effectiveness is always achieved, and usually it is of a rather elaborate type. Not only are ponds, bridges, orchards, castles, and seashores the favorite settings on the *Kabuki* stage, but the favorite effects are snowstorms, earthquakes, and fires! It is doubtful if the Western theatre has much to offer the *Kabuki* in the way of novelty.

The make-up of the *Kabuki* actor is a complicated affair. In its most extreme form it becomes virtually a mask. Ghosts and demons are, logically, the characters on whom the most extravagant designs are lavished, but warriors and villains come in for their share of conventional decoration. The various clans of *Kabuki* actors have their own traditions of make-up, and do not always agree in detail, but certain principles generally hold true. Samurai, for example, are represented as having very white faces, with broad black eyebrows, and touches of red on the eyes and at the corners of the mouth. Villains, on the contrary, have red faces, and country people, brown. There are fine distinctions also, for a defeated warrior who is still defiant may carry different markings from a warrior who is defeated and submissive. The Japanese block-print has immortalized and made familiar to the whole world not only the typical make-ups of *Kabuki,* but its postures as well.

There are two personalities of this theatre that must be mentioned, for they are vital to its existence. One is the property-man, the other is the horse with the human legs. The former dresses entirely in black (sometimes covering even his face) and performs the hundred miscellaneous tasks that belong to every stage production. Part of the time he is in sight of the audience, part of the time concealed. It does not matter, for he is dressed in black, and that is a sign that he is not to be noticed. Besides handling properties, this indispensable man must act as prompter, and see that actors get on and off the stage properly. His life in the theatre is a model of devotion. As for the horse, it is a grand animal indeed! Its body is of velvet, its trappings most gorgeous. Two men provide its locomotion. Their legs neatly clothed to harmonize with the horse's body, the rest of their selves lost to view, these actors create a remarkably good illusion, rearing magnificently in battle, drooping with pathos beneath the hand of the disconsolate warrior-master, trotting happily home from victory, or cavorting ludicrously in the midst of a comic situation. The *Kabuki* horse represents a very interesting compromise between the purely imaginary steed of the Chinese stage and the flesh-and-blood animal occasionally seen in the realistic theatre of the West. Perhaps it is a true symbol of *Kabuki*—an art which hovers between the real and the unreal.

Incidental music is of the utmost importance in *Kabuki*. It gives the tempo to every scene, establishes the emotional pitch, and creates the needed mood or atmosphere. So large is its share in the production that one might without exaggeration designate *Kabuki* as opera. Flute, samisen, and drums are the principal instruments used. At times the orchestra is noisy, again it is subdued. Its effects are often barbaric to the Occidental ear, but frequently it achieves a beauty of melody or a rhythmic pattern that has a distinctly universal appeal.

Every *Kabuki* actor is a dancer. Necessarily so, for the

essence of *Kabuki* acting is stylization. Its entire background is the dance—the ritual of O-Kuni and her followers, the classic dances of the *Nō*, the multiform movements of the acting dolls. And when he is not engaged in the actual performance of a dance, the *Kabuki* actor is busy posturing. His pantomime is always studied, always pictorial, always pointed with dramatic significance. At his best he is the master-pantomimist of the world—in tragedy, at any rate. It is nothing for him to hold an audience breathless for ten or fifteen minutes without his saying a word—and without moving from one spot. Infinite variety, infinite care, and no effort without meaning, expresses, perhaps, his point of view.

And this fascinating theatre art has developed almost exclusive of foreign influence. The Chinese are the only outside people who have given anything vital to *Kabuki*. After the overthrow of the Ming Dynasty in 1644, many Chinese refugees found their way to Japan, and exercised considerable influence on the various arts. Their presence was felt especially at Kyoto, which for a time adopted many Chinese fashions, and as *Kabuki* was in a formative state during the latter part of the seventeenth century, it could scarcely escape the touch of foreign taste. Costumes and make-up were the branches which borrowed most from the Chinese. There were, of course, Europeans of several nationalities in Japan during the late sixteenth and early seventeenth centuries. The Portuguese arrived in 1543, and were followed by the Spanish, the English, and the Dutch. Christianity was introduced, and so were many products of Western civilization. But soon a reaction set in, all foreigners were expelled from the country, Western books were banned, Christianity stamped out, and Japanese themselves forbidden on pain of death to travel abroad. So far as authorities can discover, the sole effect of this early contact with Europe on the *Kabuki* was the introduction in certain plays of non-

Oriental properties, such as guns and telescopes. It would be difficult to find another theatre art so expressive of national ideals and taste, for *Kabuki* is the mind and heart of Japan.

TODAY AND TOMORROW

Recent events have of course worked changes in Japan. The Great War brought undreamt-of prosperity, and along with it a restoration of faith in native institutions. *Kabuki* flourished as never before. But in 1923 nearly all the theatres of Tokyo were destroyed by the earthquake. Only two survived, but they were, fortunately, the most important ones. The Imperial Theatre, built in 1911, and the finest theatre in the Orient, was not damaged so badly but that it could be repaired within a short time. The Kabuki-za, which had been burned in 1921, and was being re-built at the time of the earthquake, escaped disastrous injury, and was completed in time for its public opening in January, 1925. It, like the Imperial Theatre, is entirely modern in its appointments, though it has retained the characteristic features of Japanese architecture, whereas the Imperial is thoroughly Western. The Kabuki-za seats four thousand persons, and the Imperial approximately the same.

There is one more type of drama to be found in Japan —the modern realistic drama, which has little or nothing in common with the *Nō*, the Doll-plays, or the *Kabuki,* and is a frank imitation of the drama of Europe and America. No theatre has as yet been dedicated exclusively to this type, but ever since the beginning of the twentieth century there have been sporadic productions of plays by Ibsen, Strindberg, Tolstoy, Synge, Shaw, and other Western dramatists, supplemented by native plays written after Occidental models. At the Imperial Theatre the program has often included a short realistic modern play by a Japanese author, and in the universities there have been formed student dramatic societies whose purpose is to study and produce new plays that are expressive of the new civilization. This movement appears to be gaining force year by year, and there are those who predict that eventually *Kabuki* will travel the path of the *Nō,* and will become, instead of the popular theatre art of Japan, merely a curious heritage from an antique age. Whether or not this will happen depends mainly on whether Japan continues to Westernize herself. If the process continues for another half-century at its present rate, *Kabuki* will then be a distinct anomaly. On the other hand, *Kabuki* itself may change with the changing times. It contains enough realism on which to build, and could, without a tremendous struggle, relinquish its too-archaic features. Another possibility is that the art will branch, becoming in one direction a theatre of realism, in the other, conventional opera. Such an evolution occurred in Europe some centuries ago.

Finally, there is the motion picture. The Japanese are excellent photographers, and they are first-rate pantomimists. Why should they not achieve wonders in this latest form of theatrical expression? As a matter of fact they have already produced some very fine films, but they are on classical subjects, and have little appeal to non-Japanese. Their modern pictures have been entirely too imitative of American types. In this field, as in many others, the Japanese are suffering from infatuation with Westernism. They have been bowled over by the thrill of a new and exciting civilization, and until they have recovered their equilibrium, their talents will be wasted in vain efforts to do the Western thing that only Westerners can do. Some day, however, Japan should contribute richly to the art of the motion picture. Her ingrained love of pictorial art combined with her acknowledged mechanical ingenuity should make such a contribution inevitable.

SELECTED REFERENCES

There are three good books relating to the classical stage of Japan: Fenollosa and Pound's *'Noh' or Accomplishment*, Waley's *Nō Plays of Japan,* and Stopes' *Plays of Old Japan: The Nō.* Of the popular stage there is but one complete account: Kincaid's *Kabuki.* Interesting chapters on the doll-play are contained in Joseph's *A Book of Marionettes,* in Anderson's *The Heroes of the Puppet Stage,* and in Miyamori's *Tales from Old Japanese Dramas.* Notes on various types of theatre in Japan may be found in Edward's *Japanese Plays and Playfellows,* as well as in the several histories of Japan and the numerous travel books dealing with that country.

THE THEATRE IN EUROPE

CHAPTER VI

THE GREEK THEATRE

ORIGIN OF THE DRAMA

THE origin of Greek drama was in the ceremonial worship of Dionysus (Bacchus), god of wine and fertility. The early Greeks were in the habit of holding numerous festivals in honor of this deity, the most important and pretentious of which took place in spring, when both earth and the spirit of man testified to the re-birth of life. The combination of song and dance employed in the observance was known as a dithyramb. In the beginning the dithyramb was very likely an improvisation inspired by a liberal use of wine and an ardent religious frenzy; eventually, however, it took on premeditated form, and was composed by a skilled poet. The first example of such a composition dates back to the middle of the seventh century B. C.

During the course of the sixth century B. C. the dithyrambs became fairly well standardized, and were interpreted by a chorus of fifty men dressed as satyrs, followers of Dionysus. The name *tragoidia* ("goat-songs") then was applied to the dithyrambs, either because of the costume of the chorus or because a goat was sometimes offered as a prize for the best poetic composition. There was no real attempt at first, however, at impersonation. The members of the chorus did not think of themselves as actual satyrs; they wore their costumes merely as appropriate symbols of the religion which they practised. Nor did the early leaders of the chorus think of themselves as other than leaders. The performance corresponded to a sacred oratorio.

The mimetic instinct, however, was not long in appearing. Thespis supposedly took the first dramatic step. About the middle of the sixth century B. C., while acting as leader of a chorus, he dressed himself to represent the god Dionysus, and caused the other performers to act the part of the god's followers. From that time forth, impersonation played an increasingly important part in the Greek religious ceremonials. There were some who objected to the idea, among them being Solon of Athens (639–559 B. C.), who declared that impersonation was a dangerous practice, and that if it were allowed to develop it might transform great numbers of the population into deceivers who would delight in taking advantage of others beneath their disguises.

Objections and warnings were of no avail. Aeschylus (525–456 B. C.), the first poet to give tragedy (*tragoidia*) real literary significance, added the second actor (the leader having been the first), and thus devised the first dialogue independent of the chorus. Sophocles (495–406 B. C.) added a third, and the drama was well established. The chorus was not abandoned, but its importance decreased steadily thereafter.

The term tragedy, however, was not applied to all the dramas which developed from the early religious exercises. It was used to designate particularly those which portrayed the more serious aspects of the religion, which had been the chief themes of the choral odes or dithyrambs. The primitive revel, also religious in motive, but frivolous and vulgar in spirit, permeated with hilarious obscenity, developed into comedy (*"comus"* meaning "revel"), and followed a course quite distinct from that of tragedy. A third type of drama, the satyr-play, also took form, but its characteristics and history are too vague to allow elaboration.

By some scholars it is considered only a stage in the development of tragedy, by others it is thought to have had a separate existence parallel with tragedy and comedy. Only one complete specimen of the type has survived, the "Cyclops" of Euripides. We have today of the tragedies, seven by Aeschylus, the same number by Sophocles, and eighteen by Euripides. Of the comedies, we have eleven by Aristophanes.

EVOLUTION OF THE THEATRE

The religious festivals of which the plays were a part became during the fifth century B. C. extremely impressive. They were under the management of the state, and were conducted with great care. The chief festivals of the year, the only two at which plays were performed, were The Lenaea, in January, and The City Dionysia, about the first of April. The latter was the more splendid of the two, and was the greatest event of the year in Athens. It lasted approximately a week, and included, besides two or three days of drama, numerous oratorical and choral contests. Foreign rulers and ambassadors were invited to the festival, the city was decorated, and the entire population joined in the celebration. Prisoners were even released from jail that they might witness the festivities. The holiday was a sacred one, however, and crimes committed during the period were punished with extraordinary severity. Any disturbance was considered a capital crime. Performances began soon after daybreak and continued throughout the day. Spectators often took food and drink with them to the theatre, and refreshed themselves during intermissions.

Early in the development of the drama, while it was still in the dithyramb stage, it had been put by the state on a competitive basis, and this fact undoubtedly contrib-

uted to the excellence of the plays and to the popular interest in them. The sixth century prize of a goat or a basket
of fruit was supplanted in the fifth century by awards of
large sums of money and increased public honor. The winning playwright was crowned before the audience with a
laurel wreath, was banqueted by the state, and revered
by the people. Such an honor must naturally be bestowed
judiciously, and to that end, the rulers of Athens devised
an elaborate scheme of judging.

First of all, a long list of names was chosen from members of the ten tribes of Attica. The names from the ten
tribes were put into ten separate jars, and one name was
withdrawn from each jar. The ten judges thus named by
lot were escorted to the theatre, and when all the plays had
been witnessed, each judge wrote down the name of the
playwright whom he considered the winner. These ten decisions were put into a jar, and only five of them withdrawn.
The winner was declared on the basis of this drawing, only
one place being given. The decision of each judge was then
made public. Prejudice and graft were in this manner reduced to a minimum of influence. It is said, however, that
decisions were often affected by the action of the audience,
the judges of that period being no less susceptible to public opinion than the judges of today, and citizens of Athens
were bound to have favorites among their playwrights.
Aeschylus is reported to have scored thirteen victories, and
Sophocles twenty.

It is obvious that only a small number of playwrights
could have their work exhibited at the festivals. Who the
contestants were to be was determined well in advance by
an archon or magistrate, who examined all manuscripts submitted to him, and chose the most worthy. Customarily
three tragic poets and either three or five comic poets were
allowed to compete at a single festival. Comedy was given
the preference at The Lenaea, tragedy at The City

Dionysia. Each poet was expected to submit four plays, which might or might not be related in theme. This fact explains the existence of trilogies and tetralogies in Greek drama.

As the festivals became better organized, prizes were also awarded to the producer (*choregus*) of the winning plays, and also to the principal actor. The producer's position must be explained. Although the plays were performed under the supervision of the state, public funds were not employed to any great extent for the purpose. The state provided and paid the salaries of the three principal actors in each production. It assigned three actors to each poet arbitrarily. All other expenses incurred during production had to be met by the producer, that is, by some wealthy citizen who, to show his civic and religious patriotism, agreed to finance the work of a certain poet. He it was who engaged the chorus, gave them board and lodging during the rehearsal period, costumed them, and paid their salaries. Music, properties, and all incidentals were supplied by him. Furthermore, it was necessary for him to engage the services of a professional instructor for the chorus. The poet often assisted in training the chorus, but not always. At any rate it can be seen that the success of a group of plays might depend considerably upon the magnanimity of the producer, and lucky was the poet who succeeded in enlisting the aid of a liberal *choregus*. It is said that considerable rivalry developed between producers, and that a sum equivalent to several thousand dollars was often spent on a single production. Such rivalry must have delighted the poets.

The climate of Greece encouraged open-air performances, and its theatres from first to last were uncovered. Had its temples been, like modern churches, places of assemblage, the drama might have been housed therein; but the Greek temple was a shrine only—the abode of a deity,

where people came individually to pour libations and mur
mur prayers. It was natural, however, that the sacrec
dramas should be played in the vicinity of the temple, and
such was generally the case.

Before the dithyramb had attained the complexity oi
drama, it had been performed in an open place, about a
sacrificial altar, the audience forming a circle around the
chorus. Just how the physical theatre evolved from this
practice is a controversial matter, but one theory is as
follows:

When the leader (*choryphaeus*) began to impersonate—
that is, to dress and act in the manner of Dionysus or other
deities, instinct prompted him to improve his position by
leaping onto the sacrificial table near the altar, thus creating the first elevated stage. As he developed his art and
scope, he found it necessary to erect, just outside the ring
of audience, a temporary tent or shelter, where he might
make his costume changes. His next step was to move the
table nearer his dressing-room. Finally, he forced a gap in
the audience and put his stage directly in front of the shelter, which became automatically a background for his action—an accidental setting. The Greek word for this shelter
or hut was *"skene,"* from which our word "scene" is derived.

This arrangement forced the audience into a horseshoe
formation, and divided their interest between the acting of
the leader at one end and the movements of the chorus
about the altar in center, a development which adapted itself admirably to the use of natural amphitheatres. Athens
offered well-situated hillsides for the purpose, and these
were promptly utilized. Wooden benches were supplied at
first, but later were replaced by stone seats. The rude dress-
ing-tent grew into a dignified stage-building.

The above account of the evolution of the Greek stage
must not be considered indisputable, however. It is only an

hypothesis, and is given no credence by some scholars. It is advanced by those who believe the Greek stage to have been at all times an elevated one, and is denied by those who believe that the Greek actors always performed on a level with the chorus. True or not, it has a certain picturesque quality which justifies its repetition in this summary.

Whatever we may believe regarding the embryo of the Greek theatre, we know pretty well what it was at maturity. Ruins, many of them excavated in modern times, tell an accurate story of its final construction. Of course there were many Greek theatres built, and they differ in size and contour, but fundamentally they are alike. The auditorium is built on a concave hillside. At its base is a circular *orchestra,* or dancing place. This is either paved with flat stones or left natural. In the center of the *orchestra* stands a *thymele,* or altar. Back of the *orchestra,* in some cases encroaching slightly upon it, is the stage-building, a wide but shallow structure of one or two stories. In its face are three doors, the center one larger than the others. At either end are wings projecting toward the audience. These are called *parascenia.* In each of them is a door at right angles with the doors in the face of the building. A row of columns along the face of the building supports a platform or *logium.* The row of columns is called the *proscenium.* In the rear of the stage-building are dressing-rooms and property-rooms. The stage-building is not connected structurally with the auditorium. The gaps between the ends of the stage-building and the corners of the auditorium are called *parodi,* or side-entrances. They are used by both audience and chorus. In some cases they are provided with ornamental gateways.

THE PROBLEM OF THE STAGE

The most irritating problem in connection with a study of the Greek theatre may now be stated. Did the actors, that is, the three actors who assumed the leading rôles, perform on the ground, behind the chorus, with the lower story of the stage-building as a background, or did they perform on the *logium,* atop the *proscenium,* some twelve feet above the heads of the chorus? Violent war has been waged over this point, and is still being waged, though the violence has decreased. Most modern scholars seem to favor the first of the two theories, and recent investigations support their view. If the actors performed on the ground, then, one may ask, who used the *logium?* The answer is that the gods did. It is an unquestioned fact that in the performance of Greek plays, divine characters appeared on a higher level than mortals. Sometimes they descended to the mortal plane, but they first had to appear as from the heavens. Those who contend that mortal characters used the twelve-foot *logium* are forced into assuming a second story surmounted by a platform to be used by the immortals. There is nothing impossible in such an arrangement, and it was accepted as decidedly probable until very recently. There are good arguments on both sides of the question, and that is why concrete evidence is so necessary to its solution.

THE THEATRE AT ATHENS

The oldest known Greek theatre, and the most important, is the Theatre of Dionysus at Athens. It was discovered in 1765, but excavations were not completed until 1895. It was built on a hillside near the temple which housed the image of Dionysus. The auditorium was irregular, following the contour of the hill. The seats were made largely

From Flickinger's *The Greek Theatre and its Drama.*

Plate 6: Theatre of Dionysus at Athens.

of limestone, and were set on the bare ground. There were seventy-eight tiers of seats in the center section. The front row was very elaborate, being formed of sixty-seven throne chairs, each chair twenty-five inches wide, twenty-three inches deep, and fifteen inches high. The center chair was larger and more elaborate than the others, and was surmounted by a canopy. It was reserved for the high priest of Dionysus. The auditorium held approximately 17,000 persons, and was cut by fourteen aisles arranged like the spokes of a wheel. The last row was three hundred feet distant from the stage, and a hundred feet above the level of the orchestra. It is thought that the stone seats were not constructed until 330 B. C. During the great period of Aeschylus and Sophocles the seats had been of wood.

The *orchestra* of this theatre was eighty-eight feet in diameter, and was unpaved until the second century B. C., when it was laid with marble slabs by the Roman remodelers. The stage-building was one hundred and fifty-two feet long, twenty-one feet deep, with wings projecting seventeen feet forward. It was built of wood, and was very likely reconstructed more than once. A stone *proscenium* supporting a wooden *logium* supplanted the early stage when the Romans made their alterations.

SCENES AND MACHINES

Scenery and stage machinery were not unknown to the Greeks, though their use of them was limited by a shallow stage, lack of artificial lighting, the absence of any theatrical tradition, and finally by their own love of simplicity. For the most part the plays were performed before permanent, conventional settings. Tragedies were supposed to take place before either a temple or a palace. For this purpose the formal background of columns and paneled walls served well. The large central door in the scene was assumed to be the chief entrance to the temple or palace. Comedies were generally laid in a public square or on a street, and the formal exterior of the scene was not inharmonious with their purpose. Special temporary structures were used, however, to supplement both comedies and the satyr-plays. Balconies, house-windows and shop-fronts assisted the former; trees, caverns and mountains the latter. In the later period of the Greek theatre scenery (like the plays) became decidedly realistic, but during the fifth and fourth centuries B. C. only suggestions of special locations were offered.

Changes of scene during the course of a play were very infrequent, and only one appliance for effecting such changes is recorded. That appliance was a large triangular prism, called a *periaktos*. On each of its sides was painted a different scene, and it could be turned easily, presenting one side at a time to the audience. Two *periaktoi* were used at the same time, one at each side of the stage. It is likely that some kind of backdrop was used in conjunction with them, though how the backdrop was supported is purely a matter of conjecture.

Another interesting and valuable adjunct of the Greek stage was the *ekkyklema*. This was a small wooden platform rolling upon wheels, and limited to such dimensions as would permit its entrance through the main central doorway. It was used chiefly in the presentation of tableaux depicting scenes which had occurred offstage. Murder (frequent in Greek drama, and not permitted to take place within sight of the audience) was suggested first by the screams of the victim, then by a figure or group of figures posed on the *ekkyklema* and wheeled onto the stage. In certain situations characters could descend from this portable platform and join in the action of the other characters on the stage. The necessity of some such device will be apparent to those who realize that the Greek stage allowed no inner stage similar to the one employed in the Elizabethan theatre. No curtains could be withdrawn to show a bedroom. When vital action occurred within doors, the audience could not be let into the scene, therefore the scene (or its aftermath) had to be brought to the audience. Modern theatre-goers will realize that the *ekkyklema* has survived the centuries, for it appears in some of our most up-to-the-minute productions—mechanically perfected, of course, and its mechanics made less obvious by skillful lighting and manipulation. In "Johannes Kreisler," produced in New York in 1922, the *ekkyklema* may be said to have been the principal actor.

The third important device used regularly on the Greek stage was the *mechane* (machine). This was a crane with a pulley and lines supporting a basket or box capable of holding two or three persons. The machine was located at the left side of the stage, at the top of the back-scene. By means of it a god or hero could be lowered from heaven to earth or lifted from earth to heaven. Its operation in broad daylight, with ropes that probably creaked, and stage-hands who probably grunted as they heaved, not to mention the gods who probably clung fearfully to the edges of the basket as they hung in mid-air—all this may strike the modern student as ludicrous. As a matter of fact it struck some of the Greeks as ludicrous; they frequently burlesqued the serious plays. But the majority of people in any age are tolerant of theatrical absurdities. Our own theatre has its weak points, and no one objects but the critics. Then it must be remembered that the Greek plays were religious and patriotic ceremonials, and in religious and patriotic matters the public is notoriously indulgent. Our twentieth century historical pageants and church rituals offer many specimens of theatre-craft fully as ludicrous as the *mechane*. According to Aristotle the Greek playwrights were too fond of the *mechane*. A difficult situation could always be saved by the sudden appearance of a god. And today, when our comedies are brought to a happy conclusion by the discovery of a rich uncle's will, stern critics murmur reprovingly, *"Deus ex machina"*—the god from the machine.

Other mechanical contrivances of the early Greek stage are recorded, but they are of minor importance, and are vaguely described. One of these produced the sound of thunder, another imitated lightning, and still another facilitated the appearance of ghosts. The latter was perhaps nothing more than a trap-door. There is also mentioned a revolving apparatus (*stropheion*) which was used to represent heroes in heaven, and deaths at sea or on the battlefield. This machine would seem to have something in common with the *ekkyklema*. It is unlikely that the Greeks used drop-scenes. There is no real evidence of any curtain being lowered or raised on the stage to conceal or discover action or settings until the theatre came into Roman hands.

COSTUMES AND MASKS

If the background and physical equipment of the Greek stage were slight, the costumes were sufficiently elaborate to make up the deficiency. They were tremendously varied in style and color, and their effectiveness was increased by the masks which all Greek actors wore. The costume of a tragic actor included a tunic reaching to the ground, and over this a richly colored mantle. Sleeves were long, and the girdle high. The shoes (*cothurni*) had thick wooden soles which lifted the actor six inches or more off the ground. The mask covered the entire head, front and back, and was surmounted by an *onkos,* a cone-shaped prolongation of the forehead, which gave height and dignity to the figure. The actor's body was padded to be in proportion with his increased height. The effect desired was that of a god or hero.

The masks worn were made of various materials, linen,

cork and wood. They were painted and modeled both, with grossly exaggerated features—not only because of the extreme passions which dominated the plays, but also because of the distance from which they were to be seen. Delicate lines and subtle expressions cannot carry to an audience of 17,000. It was imperative too that the voice of the actor be not muffled by the mask, and so we find in the typical Greek mask a wide-open mouth of rather terrifying size. Sometimes a small megaphone was built on the inside of the mask, and this helped to project the voice clearly into the huge auditorium. The white of the eye was painted on the mask, but a place for the pupil was left open so that the actor might see.

Convention dictated the style of costume and mask used to represent well-known individuals or types. In a theatre where printed programs were unheard of, it was found advisable to follow popular tradition in picturing characters in order that the audience might recognize them without difficulty. Emblems carried in the hand of the actor also served this purpose. Hermes carried his wand, Apollo his bow, Hercules his club. Messengers bringing good tidings wore crowns of olive or laurel. Persons in misfortune wore black, grey or yellow.

The costumes of the comic actors differed strikingly from those worn by the tragedians. They included a very short tunic, flesh-colored or striped tights, and light-weight shoes. The actor's body was padded before and behind, making it grotesque and ludicrous. Masks were worn, and these often were realistic portraits of contemporary celebrities. Many comedy-types—stock characters, as we would call them— existed: the red-haired roguish slave, the irascible old father with one eye-brow turned up and the other normal, the courtesan with gold ornaments in her hair, the hero with curly hair and sunburnt complexion, the rustic with leather tunic, wallet and staff.

Actors in the satyr-plays wore tunics almost as long as those worn in tragedy, and masks much like the masks of tragedy. They did not wear the *cothurnus,* however. The chief character in the satyr-plays was Silenus, the drunken old follower of Dionysus. His costume was sometimes made of skins.

Chorus costumes in all three branches of the drama differed from those worn by the principal actors. In tragedy the chorus usually represented a group of old men, women, or maidens, and therefore wore the ordinary Greek tunic and mantle, but with special white shoes. The entire chorus wore masks of uniform style. In certain productions, however, the tragic chorus departed from its rather normal human appearance, and assumed the features and actions of fantastic beings. It is said that in the performance of Aeschylus's "Eumenides," the chorus caused a sensation by rushing into the *orchestra* garbed as Furies, with black dresses, distorted features and snaky locks. The effect was so unexpected in tragedy that the spectators were electrified and almost thrown into a panic.

The costumes of the comic chorus varied amazingly, for the comic poets were whimsical and romantic and required the chorus to impersonate every conceivable kind of person, creature and abstraction. At various times they are known to have portrayed groups of athletes, sorcerers, poets, Furies, Amazons, towns, clouds, birds, wasps, frogs, fishes, bees, and seasons. Most of their costumes were fantastic and novel, and generally were designed to allow plenty of free movement, for the dances required of them often verged on the athletic.

The satyric chorus dressed almost invariably as satyrs. In the middle of the fifth century B. C. the satyr was usually conceived as half man and half goat, but half a century later the horse element was introduced, and thenceforth a combination of man, goat and horse prevailed. Shaggy skins around the loins and horns/on the head suggested the goat; horse-tails and sometimes horse-heads suggested the horse. In addition to these emblems, a phallus was worn as a symbol of Dionysus.

ACTORS, CHORUS, AND AUDIENCE

Greek actors needed to be versatile, for three kinds of vocal expression were required of them, besides very exact pantomime. The plays which they interpreted were composed of song, chant, and speech, with definite rules for the rendition of each passage. It is as though they were a combination of grand opera, Shakespearian tragedy, and modern realistic drama. The lyric passages were sung by the actors as solos, duets or trios, or by actors and chorus alternating. These songs, as well as the passages delivered by chanting or recitative, were accompanied by one or more musical instruments, a flute or a harp or both. The flute was preferred because it blended better with the human voice. The laws of harmony were unknown to the Greeks, consequently all singing was done in unison. The music was written in "modes," corresponding somewhat to the "keys" of today, one mode being dignified and majestic, another pathetic, and still another bright and enthusiastic. Seldom were there passages of instrumental music only, for the music existed for the sake of the poetry, and was strictly subordinated to it.

The Greek actor prided himself particularly on his voice, and bent every effort to improve it. He spent years developing its range and resonance, and for its sake was even abstemious in eating and drinking. At times, it is feared, he was so carried away by his pride in vocal power that he overstepped the bounds of good taste and appealed to the less discriminating auditors with imitations of roaring animals, the sound of the sea, and other impressive phenomena. But in spite of these lapses from aesthetic propriety, the Greek actor must have been an artistic interpreter. His diction and phrasing were held up to the most severe criticism, and in tragedy especially, considerable restraint was practised. The tragic actor's pantomime was studied and statuesque, filled with significance, and free from the spontaneous or accidental. In the delineation of gods and other idealized characters, perfect poise is the inevitable aim of acting.

The chorus performed, too, with precision; in fact, with military regularity. They seem never to have imitated the confused movement of a crowd, or as we would say, a mob, but invariably used a rectangular formation, with ranks and files. The typical tragic chorus had five ranks of three men each, and thus three files of five men each; the comic chorus six ranks of four men each, and thus four files of six men each. The chorus entered either by rank or by file, though the latter was preferred as it prevented crowding at the entrance and also gave the audience a better spectacle. Nearly always the left *parodus* was used for the first entry of the chorus, and the best members were placed in the file nearest the audience, the worst being relegated to the middle file, where they were fairly inconspicuous. The *coryphaeus,* or leader, held the middle position in the left-hand file, with assistants at either side of him in the same file. When the *orchestra* was reached, the formation was changed from files to ranks, but the movements of the chorus during the performance are not definitely known. The dance of the tragic chorus, called *emmeleia,* was undoubtedly slow and dignified; the comic dance, called *kordax,* was wild and lascivious; the satyric dance, *sikinnis,* was violent and grotesque. The chief purpose of the choral dance, however, was certainly to illustrate and emphasize the words of the play, and this illustrative action was not confined to the songs of the chorus itself, for the songs and speeches of the principal actors were accompanied by choral dumb show.

All participants in the Greek plays were men. In fact it is thought by some scholars that women were not even allowed in the audience. This view is not generally accepted, but it is probable that special sections of the theatre (not the best sections, either) were set aside for women. It may be, too, that women attended only the more decent of the plays, and that the comedies were given for "men only." One authority states that courtesans were seated separately from other women.

No citizen of Athens was expected to miss the festival. If one pleaded poverty as an excuse, he was told to apply to an official of the state, who would give him money to buy a ticket of admission. The fee, as a matter of fact, amounted to only a few cents, so there cannot have been many honest claims to this gratuity. The fees collected at the festival went into the upkeep of the theatre, which was the property of the state. There was no attempt, evidently, to realize a profit from the sale of tickets.

SUMMARY

It can be readily seen that the theatre held an important place in Greek life. Its motives were religious, patriotic, educational, and aesthetic. Devoted in its early days to mythology, it came soon to embrace recorded history, and finally to interpret and evaluate contemporary life. Its tragedies plumbed the very depths of human emotion; its comedies subjected life to the most penetrating rays of human intelligence. Rising from orgiastic ritual during the sixth century B. C., it developed in the course of a hundred years into a magnificent combination of poetry, acting, and pageantry. After the fifth century B. C. tragedy declined, but comedy persisted and flourished until the end of the fourth century B. C., when culture moved from Athens to Alexandria, and Greek civilization gave way to Roman. Probably the first well-organized theatre in the world, the Greek remains one of the most inspiring.

SELECTED REFERENCES

For inclusiveness and clarity the two best books in this field are Flickinger's *The Greek Theater and Its Drama,* and Haigh's *The Attic Theatre.* The best brief summary is to be found in Nicoll's *The Development of the Theatre.* Interesting material is also included in Tucker's *Life in Ancient Athens,* Le Grand's *The New Greek Comedy,* and Murray's *Euripides and His Age.* There are innumerable treatises on the Greek theatre and drama, many of them highly technical.

CHAPTER VII

THE ROMAN THEATRE

THE torch of theatrical art passed from Greek hands to Roman, and it was in Roman hands that the flame was all but extinguished. The Romans by nature were not a dramatic people. At least they were not dramatically creative. Their instinctive form of amusement was athletics. And so, when tragedy and comedy were introduced into Roman life by Greeks during the third century B. C., they did not inspire any great enthusiasm in the mass of the people. The classics of the Greek stage were performed in Rome, but they were altered in production, made less literary and more spectacular. Certain Roman poets were moved to imitate Attic tragedy, but their plays were largely ignored. Seneca, the tragic dramatist of the first century, followed Greek models, and composed plays which were revived, read, and performed in Europe during the Renaissance, influencing tremendously the Italian, French and English playwrights of that later period, but it is considered doubtful whether his plays were performed at all during his own lifetime.

What Rome wanted was spectacle, and lacking that, farce. Its citizens were as devoted to magnitude as are the motion-picture crowds of today. They did not want to think; they did not want to be serious in the theatre. The gasp of wonder or the shriek of ribald laughter—these were the measures of success. Such standards were perhaps inevitable in a city overflowing with slaves and foreigners, where diversity of language would militate against literary drama, if taste did not.

The festivals of ancient Rome were called *ludi,* and took place at regular intervals throughout the year—more frequently than in Athens. The largest of the festivals occurred in April, July, September, and November, but minor ones were frequent. Besides the regular holiday performances, there were also innumerable special celebrations given in honor of such events as dedications of public buildings, anniversaries of the death of great men, *et cetera.* In all *ludi,* some kind of theatricals were given, and as in the case of the Athenian festival, the cost of production was met by a wealthy citizen. The *editor,* for such was the title given to the benefactor, frequently went so far as to furnish noonday lunch to the spectators. The performances began in the early morning and lasted throughout the day.

The state had relatively little to do with Roman theatricals. In the early days of its development, official Rome even considered the theatre a nuisance. But the power of the theatre in controlling public opinion could not be overlooked for long by wise senators. In the year 194 B. C. the senate officially attended its first theatrical performance. It occupied seats in the *orchestra.* From that time on to the death of the theatre, the state took an interest in theatrical art. Sometimes it supported it and sometimes it attacked it, but it could never again ignore it.

When the Romans came into world-power, they found many Greek theatres standing—some of them built of stone. These they remodeled to suit their own productions. They cut down the *orchestra* to a semicircle, and filled it with spectators. They introduced a low stage (about five feet high), and transferred to it all the action of the play. They built higher and more elaborate scenes. They closed the *parodi* (entrances between the stage-building and auditorium), for their choruses performed on the stage, not in the *orchestra.*

The Romans did build stone theatres of their own, in

certain provincial cities and in Rome, but for the most part they depended on remodeling those left by the Greeks. In Rome itself only three stone theatres were built, and these not until the first century B. C. The first was erected in 55 B. C. under the direction of Pompey; the other two arose in 13 B. C., one under the direction of Balbus, the other of Marcellus. They were built on level ground, and thus architecturally were much greater achievements than the theatres built by the Greeks. Their seating capacities are variously estimated at between eleven and forty thousand persons. The latter figure may be considered an exaggeration, but there is no doubt that these theatres were tremendous—fully as large as the hillside amphitheatre at Athens. The stage-building, an integral part of the theatre structure, was of the same height as the walls of the auditorium. Boxes (raised platforms holding seats) were introduced in the corners of the auditorium near the stage, and were occupied by the *editor* and his friends. Entrance to the auditorium might be had from stairways at the rear, or through vaulted passages under the seats near the stage. Most significant of all, a front curtain was introduced on the stage, but instead of being lowered from above, it was raised from a space between two low walls along the front of the stage. It was elaborately embroidered, and worked on a roller. At the beginning of a play it was let down into its groove, and at the end of the play was pulled up to shut off the scene.

The Roman theatre did not advance to any extent the art of moveable scenery. Its directors were content generally with the permanent background, which, as has been stated, was high and ornate. The typical scene was composed of three stories, formed of three rows of heavy columns atop each other, each row of columns supporting an entablature. Between the columns were niches filled with statues, busts, and ornamental objects. It is recorded that in one theatre, the first story was of marble, the second of glass, the third of gilded wood. (A background capable o obliterating anything less than a glaring spectacle!) Three doors were cut in the back wall, the center one being the largest. Other doors opened onto the stage from the side walls. In comedies, house-fronts were sometimes set before this background, and *periaktoi* (the revolving prisms of the Greek stage) were also employed, but the art of scene painting was not developed to a marked degree.

The magnificent theatres of Rome are dust, but two theatres at Pompeii have left good remains. The smaller seated only fifteen hundred persons, the larger, five thousand. It is thought that they were roofed with wood. They were also distinctive in each having a small balcony along the rear of the auditorium, and under this a *crypta,* or vaulted lobby, from which doors led to the various aisles.

It is considered extremely unlikely that the large theatres of Rome were permanently roofed. It may be, however, that huge awnings were stretched over the auditorium during performances.

Definite information is lacking concerning the mammoth temporary theatres which were erected in Rome on special occasions. They would seem, however, to have been most extraordinary. Their primary purpose was to exhibit the wealth of plutocrats, and if we are to believe the legends concerning them, this purpose was amply fulfilled. It is said, for example, that a theatre constructed by one Aemilius Scaurus seated eighty thousand spectators, had three hundred and sixty pillars in its scenic background, and three thousand statues between those pillars. Its interior is said to have been sumptuously furnished with purple carpets and pictures. This palatial edifice, according to the story, was set on fire by the owner's slaves, and burned to the ground, the loss being approximately four million dollars.

Equally remarkable, and certainly more unique, was the theatre reported to have been built by Scribonius Curio during the first century B.C., the occasion being his father's funeral. Curio had two auditoria constructed with their backs to each other. Plays were then performed for each audience, and at the conclusion of the plays, the auditoria, audiences and all, were swung about, forming a huge closed stadium, in the center of which athletic spectacles were given. This highly ingenious and romantic conception lacks the authority of trustworthy historians, but it is not classed as an absolute myth. The Romans were first-rate engineers, and Curio had, we may believe, plenty of money to indulge his fancy.

The properties, costumes, and traditions of acting in the Roman theatre were borrowed directly and with slight alteration from the Greeks. The Greek mask, on the other hand, was slow in being adopted by this new generation of actors. Grease paint and wigs sufficed the Romans until 115 B. C., but in that year the mask came back into favor, and was used continuously so long as legitimate drama was performed. The typical Roman mask was made of terra cotta.

The number of principal actors was increased during Roman times. The Greeks had held to the rule of three actors, allowing them to double in parts (made easy by a change of mask) when necessary, but the Romans used as many as six principals in their productions. In serious plays no women participated (the Greek tradition again), but in light farces and pantomimes they were not only allowed, but were featured. All actors were looked down upon by Roman society. Most of them were slaves or foreigners, and as such had no civil rights anyway, but if a Roman of good standing entered the profession, he immediately lost whatever civil rights he had possessed. Actors were frequently persecuted and beaten for trivial offenses. One comedian was publicly executed by Caligula (an emperor of the first century) because of slanderous remarks uttered

by him in the course of a satirical farce. Great popularity
was acquired by the best actors, however, and with popularity a good deal of respect on the part of the public. The
most famous Roman comedian, Q. Roscius Gallus, of the
first century B. C., became a veritable idol of his time, and
made a huge fortune on the stage. The name Roscius is
still applied to actors of marked ability.

It has already been stated that the Romans were intolerant of literature in the theatre, and especially intolerant
were they of the heavy tragic style so admired by the
Greeks. In producing the classic tragedies, they improved
them according to their own standards by introducing a
soloist who occupied one side of the stage with the flute-
player, and who sang the lyric passages (formerly the part
of the Greek chorus) while in the center of the stage an
actor danced an interpretation of the songs. When this
method was first employed, the actors were still accustomed
to reciting the dialogue passages of the play, but eventually
the dialogue was judged less interesting than the dancing,
and was dropped from the text. Later, the soloist was
supplanted by a full choir, the flute-player by a group of
musicians, and the actor (the tragedian) became merely a
dancer (*pantomimus*). The interpretative dance then proceeded to degenerate from something intellectual to something purely sensuous. The noble Greek themes became
a camouflage for Roman obscenity. And it was this sort of
theatrical art which was most admired by the upper classes.
It reached the height of favor during the excessive days
of the Empire under Nero (first century A. D.), and was
to be seen not only in the theatres, but at every public and
private banquet. Nero himself grew so enamoured of pantomime that he indulged in it as a performer. More and
more women dancers were employed, and fewer and fewer
clothes were worn by them. The climax was reached when
it became customary for women to dance on the tables at

banquets, attired in nothing at all. (An ironical destiny for Greek tragedy!)

Sharing in the popularity of the sensuous pantomime was the mime (*mimus*) or farce. These were short pieces made up of monologue, dialogue, song and dance. They correspond to modern vaudeville skits, and were very likely on approximately the same moral and intellectual plane. Men and women both took part, and the favorite theme was domestic infidelity. Political and social satire were practiced, and often with telling results, for there are evidences of more than one Roman official who feared the lampoons of the comedians. The monologist was a familiar figure in the mimes, and so was the jokester accompanied by a stupid fellow to act as his foil.

The Romans were the originators of the circus. Their insatiate love of action on a huge scale, coupled with their predilection for cruelty, led to the presentation of the most thrilling spectacles. Gladiatorial combats, wild animal fights, races, and gymnastics vied with each other for popular approval in the thronged arenas.

But such revels were not to continue long without bitter opposition. They were attacked from two sides, on the one hand by Romans whose sense of dignity and propriety had not been lost, and on the other by the newly established Christian church. For the first time in history, religion and drama were at war with each other—engaged in a conflict that has never entirely ceased. Even pagans of the late Roman Empire attacked the theatre on the ground that it profaned the sacred elements of their faith. Actors converted to Christianity were forced to renounce their profession, and vigorous sermons were preached against all forms of theatrical art. But the populace was hard to wean away from its amusements. So strong was the hold of the theatre on the affections of the common people that the church did not dare forbid its members to attend performances. As late as the year 399, during Holy Week the circus and theatre were crowded, and the disgust of churchmen was unbounded.

Strangely enough, what civilized Christians could not accomplish, barbarians could. Tyranny proved more effective than righteous indignation, for it was during the reign of northern barbarians that the theatre as an institution was destroyed. The Goths (who ruled Rome during the fifth and early sixth centuries) despised theatrical exhibitions, and would gladly have tabooed them all. Some concessions, however, were made, and a few *spectacula* were allowed the people. The death blow was struck in the year 568, when the Lombards came into power. They were ruthless Germans who hated everything that reflected the gaiety of the south, and they immediately suppressed whatever theatricals had resisted the attacks of the past. Roman theatres everywhere were emptied and left to decay. In Italy, in France, in Greece, in Spain, their ruins still survive— monuments to a grand and frivolous chapter in the history of the theatre.

Human instincts, however, are never crushed completely. If the Roman theatre was dead, the *mimus* and the *pantomimus* were not. Dancers, jugglers, tight-rope walkers, singers, buffoons—these persisted. Driven from the arena and banquet-hall, they took to the road and market-place. Singly or in pairs, they set out to make a living by amusing others, and through the long centuries that led to a rebirth of the theatre, they were the sole custodians of the oldest art. The clown is the only immortal in the world of the theatre.

SELECTED REFERENCES

For a brief account of the nature of Roman theatricals, the student should read Chapter II in Nicoll's *The Development of the Theatre*. Valuable also is the essay entitled "The Roman Theatre,"

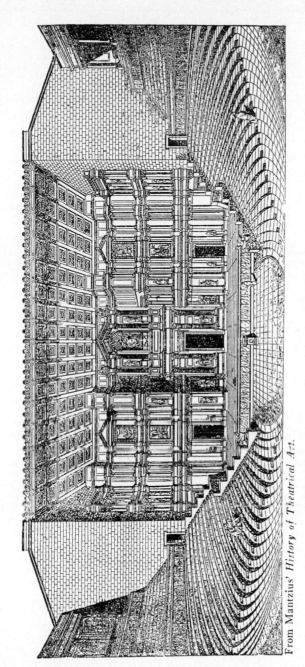

Plate 7: Roman Theatre at Orange, Southern France (reconstruction).

by Charles Knapp, which appeared in *Art and Archaeology*, Vol. I. A book of general information is Johnston's *Private Life of the Romans*. The decay of the Roman theatre is described excellently in the early pages of Chambers' *The Mediaeval Stage*. For Roman architecture see Wilkins' translation of *The Civil Architecture of Vitruvius*, or the digest of that work contained in Campbell's *Scenes and Machines on the English Stage During the Renaissance*.

CHAPTER VIII

MEDIAEVAL THEATRICALS

MINSTRELSY

THE darkest period in European theatrical history extends from the sixth to the eleventh century. During that time no organized theatre existed, and only the slightest records of individual performers are to be found. But from the Dark Ages emerged a composite type of entertainer—a combination of Roman mime and German scôp. The mime was a low comedian, a juggler, a buffoon; the scôp was a singer, and a respected one. From this blending came the minstrel.

From the eleventh to the fourteenth century the minstrel flourished in all European countries, but particularly in Southern France, where both climate and public temperament favored him. He lived in a number of ways, now as a wanderer from village to village, performing in the market-place, again as a hired entertainer in the household of a feudal lord. One day he played for the coppers of the poor, another day for the patronage of a prince. Occasionally he was lucky enough to be retained for several years in a single castle. He was often reviled, particularly by the clergy, but he was more often welcomed and fed. Frequently, no doubt, he deserved a bit of discipline, for he was inclined toward drink and gambling, and was quick to take advantage of the gullible.

In the course of the eleventh century a distinction was made between two kinds of minstrel—the composer and the interpreter. The composer of songs came to be called a *trobaire,* or *trouvère* (troubadour), and the interpreter, who sang, recited, and played some instrument, a *jonglar,* or *jongleur.* In still a separate class was put the vulgar comedian, or *bufo* (buffoon). As time went on the *trouvère* became a less romantic figure, and took on a clerical rather than a theatrical quality. During his transformation from entertainer to professional literary man, printing was invented, and the process was brought to a sudden culmination. The real minstrel vanished.

Minstrelsy had not been limited, however, to the composition and rendition of songs. A list of the minstrel's accomplishments includes the full repertory of the Roman circus and vaudeville tricks. Tumblers, knife-throwers, rope-walkers, prestidigitators, and contortionists—all were represented in the minstrel ranks. But in the whole business of minstrelsy there was scarcely a trace of acting. No characterization seems to have been attempted, in spite of the fact that recitations and songs were the minstrel's specialty. Gestures were used, but little action, and nothing that could be called drama was performed by these picturesque entertainers. In a later period, when their own day had passed, they were at times engaged to take part in festivals and plays, but they never originated a drama of their own.

FOLK-PLAYS AND FESTIVALS

Meanwhile the dramatic impulses of the common people were not without a channel of expression, for the folk-festival persisted in every European country, a heritage, in most cases, from Rome and Greece. It developed independently of minstrelsy, and because of its pagan origin and symbolism, was frowned upon by the church. It was generally connected with the seasons and matters of fertilization, and retained many of the features of early Dionysiac ceremonials.

The most important of the folk-festivals during medi-aeval times was the one held on May Day. Processions were formed, a king and queen chosen for the day, a May-pole was set up and danced around, animals were sacri-ficed and eaten, and all sorts of games were played. Al-though the games early became secular in character, it is considered almost certain that they developed from pagan cult. Football, for example, is thought by scholars to have originated in the animal-sacrifice, the head of the animal being considered capable of bringing good luck to its pos-sessor, and therefore a suitable object of contention be-tween two groups of men. Another feature of May Day was the sword-dance. It was this dance, in fact, which gave rise to the earliest form of English folk-drama.

The sword-dance was a direct inheritance from ancient times. Whatever its primary significance may have been—some say military, others sacrificial—it goes back at least as far as the Romans. Even the barbarians who sacked Rome had their own types of sword-dance. The minstrels kept it alive during the Dark Ages, and during the medi-aeval period it flourished everywhere. Its structure varies, but its symbolism is usually the same in every country: it celebrates the death of winter and the birth of spring. Sometimes a double intent is apparent, for winter is identi-fied with evil, and spring with good. But the movement remains unaltered: the conflict between two forces, the climactic triumph of one, and a general joyous dance to celebrate the victory. (The very rudiments of dramatic plot, as anyone can see).

In some forms of the sword-dance, winter is represented as an old man dressed in white. His adversary's dress is green. Another arrangement is to have a man in green caught and killed in mimicry, then to have a doctor appear and bring him back to life; a form which represents the death and resurrection of the year very logically. In both

France and Russia a ritual on this theme took a more gentle turn and represented a leaf-clad man being awakened by the kiss of a maiden. In this is found the origin of the Sleeping Beauty legend. There are still other examples—one in which the death of winter is portrayed by the burial of an old woman in effigy, but such a type is not of the same dramatic importance as that which is based upon a conflict between men.

It was the violent sham battle which bore such remarkable fruit in England. Having lost long before any special religious meaning, the sword-dance, or morris-dance (two forms so closely allied as to be almost inseparable), became the most popular amusement in England during the fourteenth and fifteenth centuries. As it was elaborated it drew into its structure a whole mass of ballad-material and topics of contemporary appeal. National heroes were characterized by the dancers, and rustic clown-types were added for the sake of comedy. Among the most popular figures were Robin Hood, Maid Marian, and St. George, together with Tommy and Bessy (male and female clowns), A Skipper, Captain Slasher, Turkish Knight (the villain, born of the Crusades), Beelzebub, and most amusing of all, the Noble Doctor, a character well-nigh indispensable to such a bellicose plot.

First, the dance, then music and song, and finally dialogue. This is the order in which all drama grows. When the English sword-dance reached its full stature it became the Mummers' Play, one of the most rollicking and delightful types in dramatic literature. It flowered into drama during the fifteenth century, and spread throughout the British Isles. Always a rural product, it never became professionalized. Its actors were farmers and small-villagers; its stage was an end of the great hall in the nearest manor-house; its audience the lord of the manor, his family, friends, and servants. Some of the Mummers wore masks, and the clowns often blacked their faces. The costumes were home-made, designed and sewed by the women during the holiday preparations. The dancers' costumes commonly had bells on them. At the end of the performance, one of the actors took up a collection among the audience, and thereupon the entire troupe retired to the kitchen, where their efforts met a suitable reward in the form of mince pie and beer. And as the Mummers' Play grew in favor, its perform-ances became more frequent. It appeared not only on May Day, but at Easter, at harvest celebrations, and even more conspicuously, at Christmas. In fact the Christmas Eve productions came to be the most important of all. Father Christmas was added to the cast of characters, and carols were included in the musical program. Thus a pagan rit-ual may, in the course of a few centuries, become a secular amusement, then in turn, an adjunct of a Christian holiday.

The modern Christmas celebration is indeed an astonish-ing mixture of pagan and Christian elements. In pre-Chris-tian days, the Germano-Keltic tribes of Central Europe had held mid-winter festivals, celebrating more than any-thing else the return of warriors from distant forays. Cat-tle were killed, and great feasts were held around the hearth. This celebration took place generally in November, and it was called Yule. With the introduction of Roman customs, other winter holidays were inaugurated: the Feast of the Sun, on November 24th; the Feast of Saturn, on December 17th; and Kalends, or the festival of the new year, on January 1st. But with the spread of Christianity, Christmas appeared as a rival holiday. During the fourth century Christmas had been fixed as December 25th (an arbitrary date, as there is no record of Christ's birthday), and it was the desire of the Christian church that this be made the greatest of winter holidays. From the seventh century on, every effort was made to establish Christmas in popular favor, and to that end, many of the customs of pagan festivals were transferred to the Christian festival. Holly and other evergreens had long been symbols of the fertilization spirit; the sacrifice of boars was a pagan rite; the renewal of fire on the hearth by means of the Yule-log was an ancient folk-custom; good-wishes and prophecies for the coming year had been a part of the New Year's celebration; all these and other ceremonials were gradually absorbed by Christmas. In a similar manner, Easter competed with May Day—the resurrection of Christ with the resurrection of Dionysus. Neither won a complete victory, for both have survived, but the Christian holidays won in the sense that their religious significance is understood, and the pagan holidays are empty of meaning. When school-children of our time dance about the Maypole, they are not consciously worshipping Dionysus. Were their parents and teachers fully aware of the symbolism involved in this naïve ceremony, May Day games might suffer a relapse.

CHRISTIAN FESTIVALS

In addition to the folk-festivals, pagan in origin, secular or Christian by evolution, there were during the Middle Ages in Europe a number of standardized revels which sprang directly from the church. Some of these received the sanction of high churchmen, others did not. An example of the latter sort was the Feast of Fools, which was conducted by the priests and inferior clergy, and gained a strong hold in Europe, especially in France. It was known as early as the twelfth century, reached the height of its popularity in the fourteenth century, and after that time gradually disappeared. It was denounced regularly by Pope and Cardinals, but persisted in the face of their opposition. Its strength lay in the fact that it allowed the minor clergy to escape once a year from the tedious solemnity of their ritualistic religion, to blow off steam in a wild orgy of burlesque, ridicule, and general tomfoolery. It was the safety valve of Catholicism. During its celebration the clergy feasted and drank to their hearts' content, sang festal songs, performed crude farces based on the mass and on various Biblical themes, indulged in masking and dancing, elected the village idiot or some other local object of ridicule as King of the Fools (sometimes designating him Pope, or Bishop), and carried on most scandalously for several days and nights. Laymen joined the revel, and turned the whole countryside into a mad carnival. The church itself was frequently over-run by the merry-makers, though orders were issued against such profanation. It has never been made clear just why this was called the Feast of Fools, though the title seems apt enough. As an institution it was rather typical of mediaeval life, for it was curiously paradoxical in its mixture of reverence and sacrilege, solemnity and gaiety. Its spirit was not unlike that of the cathedral architecture of the period, in which saints and grotesque vulgarities were intimately mingled.

Simultaneously with the Feast of Fools occurred another celebration called the Boy Bishop. This festival was conducted by the choir-boys of the churches, and although it was not so riotous as the Feast of Fools, its purpose was partially burlesque. It began with the election of one of the boys to the office of Mock-Bishop, and included in its program processions, maskings, and the performance of miracle plays. The Boy Bishop was dressed in full ecclesiastical regalia, and was treated with utmost respect; his temporary position, unlike that of the King of Fools, was an honor. The event was common in Germany, France, and England, and did not die out until the latter part of the sixteenth century. The choir-boys' organizations took an exceedingly important part in theatrical and educational development during the Middle Ages and the Renaissance.

It was from them that the great European universities arose, and it was they who, with their well-trained dramatic societies, performed not only the best specimens of mediaeval drama, but the plays of Shakespeare and his contemporaries.

RELIGIOUS DRAMA

More significant, perhaps, than these great festivals, were the sacred plays given within the church with all the pomp and earnestness that a powerful ritualistic religion could command. The liturgical plays (so-called because of their derivation from the liturgy or Mass) may be traced back almost to the very founding of the Church of Rome. From the fourth century onward the service tended steadily to increase in dramatic effectiveness, and as early as the eleventh century certain forms of the Mass were composed entirely of dramatic dialogue. The chants used in the early Roman Church had been antiphonal in structure (that is, they were based on statement and response, or question and response, two divisions of the choir responding to each other, or else to a soloist) and it was this characteristic that led the Mass directly toward drama. Mimetic action, appropriate costuming, and certain stage properties eventually combined to form the sacred play.

The principal theme of the liturgical drama was that of the life of Christ: the Nativity, the Crucifixion, and the Resurrection. Christmas and Easter were, then, naturally, the occasions for the most important performances. At such times the altar was used for the crib or the sepulchre, and in some instances was transformed for the purpose. The Disciples and the two Marys were nearly always portrayed, and occasionally Christ himself. The Wise Men, Lazarus, and Herod were also familiar rôles. The performers were priests, nuns, and choir-boys. The plays were entirely in

Latin, and were fully evolved by the middle of the thirteenth century. From that point on they underwent changes which robbed them of their purely liturgical character.

SECULARIZATION OF THE DRAMA

The process which set in during the latter half of the thirteenth century was the secularization of the plays. Gradually they passed from the hands of the clergy into the hands of the laity, and became more entertaining, but less devout. One cause of this transition was the increasing size of the productions, which had become so spectacular as to necessitate moving them outdoors, into the cathedral yard. For a stage the steps of the cathedral were sometimes utilized, but frequently special stages were constructed in the yard. These stages were either round or rectangular, but were of considerable dimensions, and were divided into a number of stationary scenes ranged side by side. The multiple scene was unique, and has proved extremely interesting to modern students of theatre craft. A stage of this type erected at Freiburg in 1504 was one hundred and ten feet long.

When the plays were established as outdoor events, the weather became a factor, with the consequence that the Easter production absorbed the others. And this, in turn, meant that one day would not suffice for all the plays that were to be given. A cycle of plays covering a period of several days was the final result. This practice extended to all European countries where Roman Catholicism had a hold, but it was strongest in France and England.

But as the plays were participated in more freely by non-churchmen, they changed materially in text. Latin gave way to vernacular, and a greater variety of Biblical episodes made their appearance in the action. Whatever stories appealed to the villagers, they dramatized. In fact they

From Nicoll's *Development of the Theatre.*

Plate 8: Stage for a Valenciennes mystery play, 16th century.

often went so far as to insert non-Biblical matter for the sake of comedy. This type of drama, founded on Biblical history, but not confining itself to the Mass, was known as the Miracle Play. In France, and occasionally in England, the term Mystery Play was employed, but its derivation proves that the terms are practically synonymous.

The last step in the evolution of the Miracle Play was its change from a stationary performance to a movable one. Even in the early period of its development, before it had left the confines of the cathedral, it had included as a kind of prologue, a sacred procession through the streets. Later this procession was elaborated until it took the place of the stationary performance. Particularly was this true in England, where, during the fourteenth century, at least four towns devised great processional cycles of Miracle Plays. The towns were Chester, York, Wakefield, and Coventry. The plays were under municipal control, and the various episodes were provided by organizations of merchants and craftsmen. These groups, called guilds, were not unlike our modern craft and trade unions. Practical judgment was exercised in assigning the plays, with the result that the play of Noah and the Ark was given to the shipwrights; the Last Supper, to the bakers; the Wise Men and their gifts, to the goldsmiths; the Harrowing of Hell, to the cooks. Each guild had to finance and perform its own scene. Costumes, properties, and scenery were kept carefully from year to year, and were repaired, repainted, or replaced when necessary. Each scene was placed on a float, or decorated wagon, of at least two levels, the lower curtained off to form a dressing-room, the upper containing a platform for the action and whatever scenery was required. Thrones, houses, mangers, tombs, and hell-mouth were among the representations. The floats were drawn through the streets in preconceived order, stopping at specified corners long enough to exhibit the play. The stage was visible from all sides. The number of stopping places varied from three to sixteen, the number of days consumed by the processional performance, from one to three. Many villages of course had lesser cycles involving slighter time and effort. But the guild plays died out during the sixteenth century, giving way to secular drama. Before their decay, they had themselves become so secular as to justify the charge often brought against them—that they were more profane than sacred. The church had started something which it could not control. The normal human desire for amusement had triumphed over religious feeling, and the theatre as an independent institution was emerging.

The secular drama developed along several lines. On one hand was the morality play—ethical rather than religious, and with characters representing abstractions. The conflict between virtue and vice was the theme of the morality, and "Everyman" is the best English example of the type. These plays were acted sometimes in the churches, and at other times on stationary scaffolds erected for the purpose. They were more French than English in origin, and owed much to the *Danse Macabre,* a kind of dance of death, which was so frequently performed in France in mediaeval times. The first traces of the morality play occur toward the end of the fourteenth century. The type was at its best in the century following.

On the other hand there was the history-play. Non-religious historical matter began to appear in the miracle plays during the fifteenth century, and proved such a popular theme that it eclipsed all others. In the sixteenth century, when professional playwrights arose, the history-play was a favorite type, and attracted the greatest authors. Marlowe and Shakespeare have left immortal specimens.

And with the rise of secular drama came professional players. The miracle play, whether in the hands of clergy or laity, had been an amateur performance. The early moralities were of the same nature. But as the plays passed from the sphere of religious observance to that of pure entertainment, it was only natural that there should come into existence organizations of players whose purpose it would be to earn their living by play-production. And it was natural, too, that these organizations should travel from village to village, for their repertory was limited, and their potential audiences small. The first troupes of English actors made their appearance during the latter part of the fifteenth century, and by 1520 were well established in their profession. The normal troupe was composed of four or five men and a boy—the latter being assigned to feminine rôles. As there were no theatres in existence, these companies had to perform wherever they could find accommodations. Sometimes they got the use of a municipal hall; again they obtained engagements in the banquet halls of nobility; frequently they inveigled the authorities into allowing them the use of a church; as a last resort they played outdoors in the village square. Most of the pieces in their repertory were short—averaging about a thousand lines, and requiring from thirty to forty-five minutes for performance. This type of short play (a transitional type, from religious to secular) was commonly called an interlude, perhaps because it was commonly presented as a between-piece at a banquet or public affair.

But these pioneer troupes had many troubles. Recruited from vagabonds, down-at-the-heel minstrels, and adventurers, they were in constant danger of persecution. They were so persistently subjected to attack by civil officers and others, that they were forced to obtain patronage of the nobles. Like the minstrels of an earlier time, they appealed to the aristocracy for protection, and in that way secured themselves and their profession. A troupe, having succeeded in pleasing a nobleman, would ask the privilege of wearing his livery and calling themselves his players. If he agreed, they were reasonably free from petty persecution, for in the eyes of the law they were under his care, and he was answerable for their conduct. Thus we find that throughout the sixteenth century, all troupes of professional actors were attached to persons of high degree, whose personal vanity or kindly interest made possible the advance of theatrical art.

In addition to those already mentioned, three theatrical phenomena belong to the general period of the Middle Ages. One is the court spectacle. The masque or pageant appears early in court history. In France and Italy it attained greater significance than in England, but in every country, during the fourteenth and fifteenth centuries, it had its place in the life of the nobility. No state occasion was complete without some kind of costumed spectacle. In the ball-room or on the grounds surrounding the castle, kings and queens, lords and ladies engaged in magnificent displays of history or mythology. In this manner was vanity served and tedium relieved.

In the schools and colleges there was also theatrical activity. Farces were written and performed by the students, and early in the sixteenth century the colleges were finding inspiration in the newly discovered plays of Latin poets—Seneca, Plautus, and Terence. Out of this study grew a strong curiosity as to the nature of the Roman stage. Theatrical research was begun, and presently traveling students were to return from Italy with exciting news of the theatrical revival.

Finally, there were the puppet-plays. Invented who knows when, the puppet-play had existed in Athens, in Rome, and now it was becoming a vogue in all the countries of Europe. Very likely it had never died at all. Records are scarce, but it may well be that during the dark centuries following the decay of the Roman Empire, the puppet, like his brother,

From Cheney's *Stage Decoration.*

Plate 9: A Wagon Stage used in a Coventry Miracle
Play.

the minstrel, kept himself from annihilation. Certainly he was very much alive in Mediaeval Italy, and during the later mediaeval period, he worked his way into France, Germany and England. When he crossed the Channel is problematical, but he was performing miracle plays for delighted Englishmen early in the sixteenth century. "Motions," as the puppet-plays were called in Shakespeare's day, specialized in scenes depicting the Creation, the Flood, and other Biblical episodes of a sensational nature. Managed by professional showmen, often Italians, they offered serious competition to troupes of flesh-and-blood actors, and not until the nineteenth century did they fall on evil days and become the playthings of children.

SUMMARY

At the close of the mediaeval period in Europe (specific dates cannot be given, of course, for the Renaissance took place gradually, and at different times in the various countries) there is, then, great confusion in theatrical matters. Minstrelsy is not entirely dead, though it is waning; folk-drama (ballads, dances and games) still survive, though their hey-day has passed; miracle and morality plays are performed at irregular intervals, but the church has lost its hold on drama; great religious festivals have declined; court masques and pageants are becoming more popular; students in schools and colleges are beginning to study Latin tragedy and comedy, and to imitate these in compositions of their own; small professional companies of players are performing interludes in villages and at court; history and biography are supplying new dramatic themes; puppet-plays (both religious and secular) are popular; the amateur is giving way to the professional; the need of theatre buildings is being felt. In short, a dozen forms of dramatic expression are converging, and that convergence results in the organized theatres of the Renaissance—the direct origins of the theatre of today.

SELECTED REFERENCES

The finest work in this field is Chambers' *The Mediaeval Stage*. For a brief summary see the chapter on the Mediaeval Theatre in Nicoll's *The Development of the Theatre*. For minstrelsy see Jusserand's *English Wayfaring Life in the Middle Ages*. Other specialized references of value are Stuart's *Stage Decoration in France in the Middle Ages*, Pollard's *English Miracle Plays, Moralities, and Interludes*, Spencer's *Corpus Christi Pageants in England*, and Withington's *English Pageantry*. There are innumerable histories of the drama which contain chapters on this subject.

CHAPTER IX

THE RENAISSANCE IN ITALY

THE CLASSICAL REVIVAL

THE rebirth of the theatre took place in Italy. With the revival of learning came the discovery of Latin and Greek plays, and in addition to these, the manuscript of "De Architectura," a comprehensive work by Vitruvius, a Roman of the first century B. C., in which were described in detail all types of classical architecture, including the theatrical, together with a careful exposition of the laws of scientific scene-painting, the use of stage-machines, and the entire process of mounting plays. While many of the assumptions of Vitruvius regarding the Greek theatre are not credited today, his word was taken as gospel by the eager Italian students who discovered him early in the fifteenth century.

Now, all during the fifteenth century there were being formed academies for classical research. These were headed generally by wealthy aristocrats whose interest in the arts and sciences of antiquity amounted to a passion. Each academy specialized in a particular field of study, and more than one of them fixed upon the theatre as the subject of their labors. The first fruitful effort of this nature was put forth by the Roman Academy, headed by Julius Pomponius Laetus (1425–1498), and it was upon the conclusions of Laetus that the most significant revivals of classical drama were based. The Roman Academy met an obstacle in 1468, when Pope Paul II suppressed it on the ground that it was fostering pagan religion, but the set-back was brief, for a few years later, under Pope Sixtus IV, it was allowed to resume activity. The new Pope was in fact of great assistance to its development, for he appointed two of his young nephews cardinals, and both of these, Cardinal Riario especially, were enthusiastic supporters of the Academy, and were willing to expend huge sums of money (supplied them by the Pope) on play-productions. From 1473 onward frequent performances of Latin plays were given in palace rooms on temporary stages, and the art of staging was given a tremendous impetus. Contemporary poets were also stimulated to dramatic composition, and their plays (close imitations of the Latin models) were sometimes honored with presentation.

Meanwhile a similar series of revivals was being held in Ferrara under the patronage of Duke Ercole d'Este, whose court was the center of another dramatic academy. This group is credited with a production as early as 1471, and in 1491 it is said to have mounted a play with full scenic investiture, the designer being Niccolo del Cogo. Of considerable importance, too, is the fact that to this court was attached the leading dramatic poet of the time, Ludovico Ariosto. So impressed were the Duke and his followers by the genius of Ariosto that they constructed a special theatre for the production of his plays, and this structure may well have been the first modern theatre building in Europe, but exact information regarding it is missing, for it was burned down in 1533, two years before the death of Ariosto.

By the year 1500 there were dramatic academies in nearly all the important cities of Italy—in Venice, Mantua, Milan, Naples, Florence, and Vicenza. And in all these centers, the drama was studied not as mere literature, but as living material for the stage. The best artists of the Renaissance were engaged to paint the scenes, and scrupulous attention was paid to mechanical equipment. Nearly all stagecraft of the period, however, owed its being to Vitruvius, whose treatise was digested word by word with fanatical reverence, and followed in the veriest detail. For the members of these academies were scholars, and to them the laws of antiquity were infallible. From top to toe they were academicians. What, then, did they learn from Vitruvius? First, that there must be three kinds of stage-settings, each adapted to a particular type of drama: tragedy, comedy, and the satyr-play. This classification is recognizable to the student as that of the Greek theatre, and also of its imitative successor, the Roman theatre. The setting for tragedy, according to Vitruvius, must be composed of stately houses, fit for the great, and noble public buildings and monuments; that for comedy, of common houses, an inn, a church, and a brothel; the satyrical scene must be a rural landscape, with country houses, trees, herbs, flowers, *et cetera,* the foliage and flowers to be made of fine silk. All settings must be devised according to the scientific laws of perspective (which the author sets forth) and the buildings are to be constructed of canvas stretched on wooden frames, with doors and windows cut out. The horizon is to be fixed somewhere on the back-drop (which may also be painted in perspective) and the buildings are to be graduated in height according to their position on the stage, so that they recede naturally toward the horizon. All ornamental mouldings and details on the buildings must be painted according to the same laws of perspective, in order that the illusion of reality may be complete.

The painters of the Renaissance were so thoroughly engrossed in this newly-revived geometrical design that anything which did not conform absolutely to its principles was looked on with abhorrence. The naïveté of mediaeval painting was scorned, and its beautiful, if technically incorrect, principles of space and relationship were buried

beneath the Vitruvian avalanche of scientific draughtsman-
ship. It is the student of the modern theatre who is privileged to witness a revolt against ornate geometry and a
return to the decorative simplicity of the days before Neo-
Vitruvianism obtained its hold on art. "De Architectura"
transformed Europe. Published first (in Latin) in 1486,
it was presently translated into the vulgar tongue
(Italian), and in 1547 was issued in French. It appeared in
Spain in 1602, and in England in 1692. By the end of the
seventeenth century it had gone through thirty different
editions. How sweeping its influence was, and how tena-
cious its hold on the theatre, can be realized best by a visit
to almost any provincial (and many a metropolitan)
theatre in Europe or America, where one may observe traditional scenes, back-drops, street-drops, wings, borders,
tormentors, and grand draperies, done in almost pure
Renaissance (Vitruvian) style. The tragedy scene (with
its noble buildings and monuments) serves now the acrobat of the two-a-day; the comedy scene, with its converging
streets, its shops, its church, its hotel, provides atmosphere
for the low comedian and the ballad-singer; the satyrical
scene, with its back-drop of distant lake, hills and forest,
and its woodwings and foliage borders, suffices for the
imitator of bird-calls, or for the burlesque golfer. Even in
so-called legitimate houses (the home of standard drama)
the permanent equipment follows the same tradition. What
theatre does not have in its scene-room, the three indis-
pensables: the grand drawing-room set, called "fancy interior," the humble cottage kitchen, and the "woodland
set"? The grand drawing-room is even built with a large
double entrance in the center of the back-wall, making it
worthy of the common appellation, "center door fancy"!
What is this doorway but the palace entrance of the theatre
of Sophocles? Traditions in the theatre do not die quickly.

The stage-machinery of the early Italian stage was, like

its scenery, derived principally from antiquity. Thunder-machines, lightning-makers, and other paraphernalia necessary to mythological drama were duly revived. But there were innovations, and we owe to Sebastiano Serlio, an architect of the sixteenth century, a description of them. Serlio, who was one of the most ardent disciples of Vitruvius, published an "Architettura" of his own. His work, which is in seven books, was published in separate parts during the years 1537–1547, and in it we find a discussion of every phase of Renaissance theatre architecture and equipment. According to Serlio, the Italians made use of invisible wires, revolving globes, colored lights, and moving mechanical figures. The latter were cut out of pasteboard, represented animals, men, and various objects, all capable of being drawn across the scene without their method of operation being discerned. The colored light effects (of which the audience is said to have been inordinately fond) were obtained by placing bottles of wine and other colored liquids behind window-openings, and placing lamps behind the bottles. Sometimes, to strengthen the effect, a bright basin was held behind the lamp to act as reflector. Such devices were indeed ingenious, and demonstrate how remarkably the Italian producers anticipated the mechanics of the modern theatre.

But in spite of the deep interest taken in classic drama by the learned aristocracy, the movement was by no means a popular one, and this fact explains why so few permanent theatres were erected during the Renaissance. The audiences for the plays were exclusive, and could be accommodated nicely in the large rooms of private palaces. One theatre of the time did survive, however, and may be considered an expression of the architectural ideals of the Italian Renaissance. It is the Olympic Theatre, also called the Theatre of Palladio, at Vicenza. It was built for the Olympic Academy of that city from plans drawn by Andrea

Palladio, a geometrician, who died before the theatre wa
completed. Palladio's son carried on the architect's work
and the structure was finished in 1584. It was gracefull
designed, with a semi-elliptical auditorium that allowed :
good view of the stage to all members of the audience
and seated about three thousand persons. The lowe
floor of the auditorium was arranged as a series of curvec
steps, encircled at the rear by a colonnade, the intervals be
tween the columns forming boxes. Stairs led from the rea
of the auditorium to the gallery. A semi-circular playin
space opened directly before the front row of seats, anc
beyond this forestage was the stage proper, which wa
set with the typical Renaissance scene—rows of house
forming three streets which ran toward the audience and
debouched on the forestage—the latter serving in the
action as a public square.

THE COMEDY OF MASKS

Thus much for the classical revival, and the theatre of
the aristocracy. Let us now consider another dramatic
movement of a strikingly different character which took
place in Italy during the same period: that is, the rise of
the *Commedia dell' Arte*.

It was not only the rich and the learned who felt the stir-
ring of theatrical instinct. The common people were to
have their own theatre, and a marvelous one too. Just
when and exactly why the *Commedia dell' Arte* came into
being cannot be stated, but it is certain that at the beginning of the sixteenth century it achieved popular success, and
established a theatrical tradition which has extended even
to the present day. Its nucleus was a company of comedians,
each representing a stock character with a distinctive mask,
a particular dialect, and clear-cut mannerisms. The origin
of the characters is difficult to trace, but some of them were

From Cheney's *Stage Decoration.*

Plate 10: Interior of the Olympic Theatre at Vicenza.

urely derived from the Roman clown types, which had
een preserved through long centuries by minstrels; others
vere in all probability imitations of favorite marionettes
 for the little wooden actors had never disappeared from
he public eye) ; still others were original—created by the
enius of natural comedians.

The first company of this sort of which there is a record
vas organized in 1528 by Angelo Beolco (an actor who
erformed under the name of Ruzzante). The success of
is venture seems to have been instantaneous, for similar
ompanies were formed almost immediately, and by the
nd of the century the movement had not only swept Italy,
ut had invaded France, Spain, and England. From the
tandpoint of popular success it eclipsed all other contem-
orary theatrical movements, and may possibly be con-
idered the greatest success in the entire history of the
heatre.

The *Commedia dell' Arte* was a theatre without a
drama, if by drama we mean a set literary form. The actors
vere furnished with a scenario of action, which was posted
n the wings, and the dialogue was invented by them as
he play ran its course. This did not mean that an actor
always invented his lines at the moment—he usually had
a wealth of stock jokes and repartee up his sleeve—but it
did mean that he was at liberty to improvise as much as
he pleased, and to build up the dialogue in his own way so
ong as it was appropriate to the action. Such freedom al-
owed each comedian to extend himself to his full capacity,
and at the same time it necessitated an extraordinary *esprit
de corps*. Actors playing in the same company over a long
period of time naturally developed a harmonious co-
operative style of performance which proved most delightful. Dialogue was liberally employed, but pantomime was
given special emphasis. Entire scenes were frequently
played without words, and the *Commedia dell' Arte* be-

came noted for its brilliant pantomimists. Dancing an
acrobatics, too, were featured, and musical specialties wer
nearly always included in a performance.

THE CHARACTERS OF THE ITALIAN COMEDY

Chief among the characters of this human comedy wa
Alecchino (Harlequin), the real immortal in the Eurc
pean theatre. In the early companies he was played a
a stupid fellow, the butt of jokes, and the tool of othe
characters. In the seventeenth century, however, he undei
went a change at the hands of Domenico Biancolelli (on
of the great performers of the rôle), who made him
brilliant wit, a jester whose sudden repartee was devastat
ing to his fellow-characters. Thereafter Harlequin was ;
rôle to be played by only the supreme artists of the *Com
media dell' Arte*. Biancolelli was followed by his son Fran
cesco, and by Evariste Gherardi, both of them successful i
upholding the Harlequin tradition. The eighteenth cen
tury contributed at least two renowned Harlequins: An
tonio Tomaso Visentini (called Tomassino or Thomassin)
and Carlo Bertinazzi (called Carlin), the latter an ad
mired friend of David Garrick. Changes in temperamen
and costume are inevitable when a character lives for cen
turies, and Harlequin is no exception to the rule. Still, h
and the other masks of the Italian comedy have retainec
enough of their original quality to be always recognizable
Stupid or witty, Harlequin is ever the fascinating, athleti
creature with diamond-checked, tight-fitting costume. H
cannot be confused with his companions.

To the modern theatre-goer Harlequin has only one equa
in popularity—Pierrot, or to give him his original Italiar
name, Pedrolino. We learn that in the early Italian com
panies, Pedrolino was a rather sly and malicious character
fond of using Harlequin as his tool; but when the latter

became a wit and a clever rascal, Pedrolino had, perforce, to become the stupid one. In French hands, however, Pierrot grew complex, and nowadays it is possible to see a dozen variations of the rôle. In fact the modern tendency has been to make Pierrot the symbol of all phases of romantic youth—sophistication, eagerness, boredom, tenderness, poetic idealism, and worldly disillusionment. His enduring characteristics are his youth, his loveableness, his white face and loose white costume. His neck-ruff has appeared and disappeared at the pleasure of countless actors, and his head-piece has been now a flapping white felt hat, again a black skull-cap, but these changes have been minor ones; they have not transformed him beyond instant recognition.

Another famous mask in this theatrical group is Pulcinella, who made his appearence about the year 1600, and who still survives in pantomimes, puppet-shows, and harlequinades. He is an amiable rogue, a great practical joker, and a favorite everywhere. He is particularly admired by the Neapolitans, and perhaps owes his origin to their locality. In France he acquired a hunched back, and is known there as Polichinelle. Some writers advance the belief that the English puppet, Punch, is a descendant of Pulcinella, but the theory is disputed by other authorities, who claim an antiquity for Punch that would preclude the possibility of such ancestry.

Then, there are Mezzetino, an idiotic clown; Brighella, an unscrupulous bandit and father of intrigues; Scapino, akin to Brighella, adopted and immortalized by Molière; Pantalone, the greybeard, the conventional father; Burattino, a cross between Arlecchino and Pedrolino; Scaramuccia (Scaramouche), noted for his songs and mimicry; Flavio and Leandro, young lovers; Isabella, the heroine; Colombina, the pretty maid-servant; Zanni, the jesting valet; the Doctor, and the Captain. These are the princi-

pals of the *Commedia dell' Arte;* less notable names woul
make a long list. Pierrette (the feminine counterpart o
Pierrot) is not one of the original characters; she cam
into being no earlier than the eighteenth century, whe
the *Commedia dell' Arte* was on the decline.

The two most famous directors and organizers of thes
troupes were Flaminio Scala and Francesco Andreini. Bot
these men achieved great success with companies durin
the latter half of the sixteenth century, dividing their tim
between the several countries of Europe, but finding th
greatest favor in France, where they enjoyed the patron
age of kings and cardinals. At times Scala and Andrein
were the heads of rival troupes; again they combined forces
The tie that united them was Isabella, a young woman en
gaged by Scala in 1578 to play in his company, and who i
the same year (she being sixteen years of age) was marrie
to Andreini. Isabella (whose name was perpetuated by th
character she created) became the most celebrated actres
of her time. Tasso, the Italian poet, wrote sonnets to her
Henry IV entertained her in Paris; and in Rome, by orde
of a cardinal, her portrait was hung between those o
Tasso and Petrarch. When she died in 1604, Scala retire
and disbanded his troupe, so great was the blow to hi
profession.

THE ITALIANS IN PARIS

The separate history of each of these companies o
comedians is too difficult to unravel, and is not really im
portant. But their success, singly and combined, in Pari
is worth mention, for it was there that they brought their
art to its finest flower, and it was there that they shed their
influence upon one of the great dramatists of all time,
Molière.

The first record of the Italian comedy in Paris is in

1571. The troupe went under the name of *I Comici Confidenti* (The Confident Comedians). They were followed almost immediately by a rival company, *I Comici Gelosi* (The Zealous Comedians). In 1574 the two troupes combined under the name *I Comici Uniti* (The United Comedians), but separated again in 1576. Scala was certainly the head of one company. Again in 1577 we find the Italians playing at the Hôtel de Bourbon. In July of that year their performances were prohibited, but were resumed once more in September by order of the King. During the season 1584–85 a troupe established itself at the Hôtel de Cluny, but was soon driven out. In 1600, Henry IV engaged Scala and his actors to play at the Théâtre Rue Mauconseil, and paid their salaries himself.

After the death of Isabella Andreini in 1604, her son Giovanni organized *I Comici Fedeli* (The Faithful Comedians) and held his company together for many years, playing in France and Italy. In 1613 this troupe was called to Paris by Marie de Medici, and performed at court and in the Hôtel de Bourgogne until 1618.

During the entire course of the seventeenth century the Italians were in and out of Paris, always popular with the public, but unpopular with French actors. In 1653 a company settled down at the Petit Bourbon Theatre, and gave regular public performances. They played only in the afternoon, however, for the streets of Paris were dark and full of thieves after nightfall. In 1660 this company was moved to the theatre of the Palais-Royal, which it shared with Molière's French company, the two troupes playing on alternate days. The Italians played with continuous success until 1697, when a misunderstanding caused their sudden expulsion from Paris. The fatal incident arose from an announcement by the Italians that their next bill would be a piece called "La Fausse Prude" (The False Prude). Now it so happened that shortly before, a novel of this title had been suppressed because it attacked the character of Mme. de Maintenon, the mistress of Louis XIV. The play which the Italians purposed giving had nothing to do with the banned novel or with Mme. de Maintenon, but no explanations were invited, and the company was ejected before the play could be performed and its innocence demonstrated.

This was the last official engagement of a *Commedia dell' Arte* company in Paris. Occasionally, during the next twenty years, an Italian troupe would set up its stage at a public fair, and it was always well patronized by the public, but French actors were gradually getting the upper hand, and they made life extremely unpleasant for the foreign entertainers. They had injunctions issued against them; they even attacked them with physical violence. In 1709 a temporary Italian theatre was mobbed and its equipment burned by irate Frenchmen. But if the French routed the Italian actors and burned their stages, they were wise enough to retain their art. Public preference for *Commedia dell' Arte* was unmistakable, and French actors prospered by imitations of their beaten rivals. One by one the famous masks were taken over and incorporated in the repertory of the French stage; characters, costumes, scenarios and all were seized upon and slightly modified. Even the name of the art was kept, for as late as 1780 there flourished in Paris the Théâtre des Italiens, though there was no longer in its company a single Italian actor. The entire range of French comedy from the sixteenth century to the present day has reflected the brilliance and charm of the *Commedia dell' Arte,* and it must be admitted that if the French did not originate the style, they at least have kept it alive, and have from time to time ennobled it with great actors and great dramatists.

The typical company of Italian comedians included twelve or fifteen players, three or four of whom were

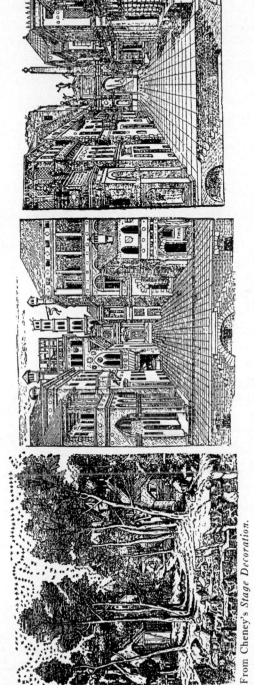

From Cheney's *Stage Decoration.*

Plates 11–12–13: Scenes for Pastoral, Comedy, and Tragedy, from Serilo.

women. There seems seldom to have been any objection to women appearing on the Italian stage during the Renaissance, though criticisms were made against obscenities which the comedians frequently indulged in. Comedy has always leaned toward the risqué, and it is not to be wondered at that in the sixteenth century it should practice much the same sort of sensationalism as it practiced in the days of Aristophanes, and is practicing today. Whether performing on trestles erected in the public square of a village, or on the private stages of the royal palaces in Paris, the Italian comedians were human enough and clever enough to appeal to various tastes, and they must have had their share of sensual spectators. Prudery was not common in sixteenth century Europe.

THE SURVIVAL OF THE COMEDY OF MASKS

Although the characters of the *Commedia dell' Arte* are universally referred to as masks, it is a fact that not all the characters wore masks. The women did not, nor did the young male lovers. The rest, with the possible exception of Pedrolino, whose face may merely have been whitened, wore half-masks—that is, masks which covered only the upper portion of the face, leaving the mouth unhampered. The nose of the mask was exaggerated and made to express individuality. Such masks were extremely practical; they disguised the actor, yet they did not interfere with his speech. In the modern theatre heavy make-up has been substituted for the mask, but the aesthetic principle remains the same. A comedian is most successful when he standardizes his appearance. The three modern parallels to the *Commedia dell' Arte* are the comic strip in the newspaper, the motion-picture comedy, and the burlesque show. In each of these institutions the twentieth century theatre finds its favorite masks. Mutt and Jeff and Krazy

Kat are as inalterable in appearance as were Pulcinella
and Pantalone; Charlie Chaplin (the supreme modern
mask) is never minus the cane, the derby, the comedy
mustache, the flapping shoes; the Jewish and Irish low
comedy types are almost identical in every burlesque house.
Situation, incident, dialogue—these change, but the masks
do not. They are the easy, familiar symbols of humanity;
the better we know them the more pleasure we have in seeing them again. Only in the drama of photographic realism
(the drama of external differentiation) are masks avoided,
and even there they may be found by the discerning, for
what are the typical make-ups of negroes, Chinese, minis-
ters, cowboys, financiers, detectives, *et cetera,* but masks?
They really do not differ from each other so much as they
pretend to. *Commedia dell' Arte* is not, therefore, an
archaic form of theatre art; it is as vital as it ever was. If
Harlequin has tumbled from his throne, Chaplin has
climbed into it. Harlequin played to thousands; Chaplin
plays to millions. In every corner of the earth are men and
women and children who laugh and applaud the Chaplin
mask. One cannot doubt for an instant that were time to flow
backward, and Ruzzante or Scala to see a Chaplin film, the
sixteenth century would pay homage to twentieth century
pantomime. Chaplin, born earlier, would have vied with
Scaramouche for the favor of Louis XIV. Scala's dozen
comedians, alive today, would sweep Broadway like fire, and
could they be coaxed to Hollywood, they would make an
art of the motion picture.

THE RISE OF OPERA

But we must turn to a consideration of still another
form of theatrical expression which had its origin in Renaissance Italy: namely, opera. We have seen that the
revival of interest in literature led to the resurrection of

Latin and Greek plays, and to their performance in the halls of the aristocracy. We have seen, too, that the releasing of the human instincts of the common people of Italy resulted in a most remarkable theatre of conventionalized comedy. It remains now to be observed that music was the last of the ancient arts to be taken up by the academies of classical research, and that consequently, opera, which is music adapted to theatrical action, was the latest of the three theatrical types to make its appearance.

It is difficult to say who originated opera, and any opinion on the subject depends considerably on the definition of the word. The Greek plays were accompanied by music, and more passages were sung than were recited. Much of the same thing is true of Chinese, Japanese, and other early types of drama. But laying that point aside, we can assert that during the Middle Ages in Europe, opera was unknown. Music had developed during that period, and church music had arrived at the use of counterpoint, but it had not followed a theatrical course. Finally one of the academies bent its energies to the restoration of classical dramatic music, but this did not occur until the end of the sixteenth century, a hundred years after classical and modern drama had been put before the public. Led by Giovanni Bardi, Jacopo Peri, and Jacopo Corsi, the academy declared war on mediaeval music, with its composite harmonies, and demanded a return to the simple music of the Greeks. They required of music that it be entirely plastic, that it take its form from the poetry which it accompanied, and that it follow the natural emotional rise and fall of the voice, the accents of the verse, et cetera. To this method they gave the name stile rapresentativo (corresponding roughly to our term "recitative.")

The first plan of the academy was to produce Greek drama with its proper musical setting, but for reasons unrecorded, this aim was abandoned in favor of the production of original opera. Their first performance was of "Dafne," the music by Peri, the book by Rinuccini, both members of the academy. The opera was staged in the palace of Jacopo Corsi in 1595. It was successful enough to justify several repetitions before private audiences. Five years later the first public performance of an opera was given at the Pitti Palace in honor of the wedding of Henry IV and Marie de Medici. The opera was entitled "Eurydice."

From 1600 on the new art flourished. Beginning with themes drawn from classical mythology and appealing to the cultured classes, it shifted gradually to historical romantic themes and popular appeal. The first public opera house was opened in Venice in 1637 with the name Teatro di San Cassiano (a name derived from a nearby church). Nor did the musical style follow the principles laid down by academicians. Singers and composers both deviated at will from the path of Greek simplicity which the founders of opera had so carefully marked out. Trills and flourishes were found irresistible, and music groped its way toward modern forms, refusing to play an utterly plastic rôle.

Another development took place in opera before it was a half-century old. Comedy and farce made their appearance beside the serious mythological or historical themes. The lighter type came into such vogue that by 1650 it was considered a distinct form, and was classified as *opera buffa*. The older form, or *opera seria,* then suffered a decline. Its action diminished until it became only oratorio, that is, opera in which costumes and scenery are used, but in which the singing is of a concert nature, the actors sitting or standing still during most of the performance. *Opera seria* (i. e., grand opera) did not revive until well along in the eighteenth century.

Like the other forms of theatricalism, opera spread from Italy to other European countries. In 1627 the first

From Cheney's *Stage Decoration*.

Plate 14: A Spectacular Court Performance at Florence in 1616. After Callot.

German opera was produced in Dresden, and after that Italian opera companies over-ran Germany. So eager were the Germans for this new art that they could do nothing but import it and imitate it. No real German music was cast in serious operatic form until about 1700, though before that a light type of musical performance called *Singspiel*, with native music, had sprung up. It corresponded to the *opera buffa* in Italy.

Much the same series of events occurred in France. Paris had its first taste of Italian opera in 1645, and it was fifty years before French composers could break from the Italian influence and find themselves operatically. In 1699 an academy of music dedicated to the development of French national opera was founded in Paris, and from that date the public was divided sharply into two camps—those standing by Italian opera, and those supporting its French competitor.

Meanwhile England lagged behind. It listened admiringly to visiting French opera companies, but it did little to develop an opera of its own. English plays had long made use of incidental music, and in 1617 the entire text of one of Ben Jonson's masques was set to music by Nicolo Laniere, a London-born Italian, but it was not until the latter part of the seventeenth century that long plays were converted into operas, and then the work was done almost exclusively by one man, Henry Purcell, who has been called the first and last great English composer of operatic music. A considerable amount of feeling was aroused in England by the success of the Italian companies. Sir William D'Avenant, the leading theatrical manager of the Restoration period, was responsible for the vogue of imported opera, and his innovation was so successful with the public that other managers and their actors rose up in arms against this effective competition with their legitimate dramas. Finally their indignation found felicitous expression in "The Beggar's Opera," by John Gay, which was produced in 1728. This piece, which was designed as a satire against Italian opera, was not a true opera, however, but a ballad-opera. That is, its music was not created as an accompaniment to the text, but was made up entirely of popular ballad music. And it is in this form that the English have ever since excelled. The compositions of Gilbert and Sullivan are in the tradition founded by "The Beggar's Opera."

Eventually (in most cases during the eighteenth century) opera crossed the frontiers of more distant European countries, and wherever it went it carried with it the spirit of Italian music. Each country has in turn achieved something like a characteristic native opera, but nowhere has Italian opera been completely supplanted. The sober academy which started so austerely to resurrect Greek music had no idea what a virile and unruly spirit it was releasing. The Greek ghost suddenly became an Italian demon, and that demon continues to spit fire. Italy, the tomb of ancient theatrical art, became in the Renaissance, the cradle of the modern theatre.

SELECTED REFERENCES

For the most accurate account of the Renaissance theatre in Italy, consult Chapters IV and V in Nicoll's *The Development of the Theatre*. For a detailed history of the comedy of masks see Sand's *History of the Harlequinade* and Smith's *Commedia dell' Arte*. For the opera see Elson's *A History of Opera*. For stage technique see Campbell's *Scenes and Machines on the English Stage During the Renaissance*. For general background see Garnett's *A History of Italian Literature*. The subject is also treated at some length in Volume II of Mantzius' *History of Theatrical Art*. An older work of considerable importance is Riccoboni's *An Historical and Critical Account of the Theatres in Europe*.

CHAPTER X

THE RENAISSANCE IN FRANCE

THE RISE OF THE PROFESSIONAL THEATRE

FRANCE, even during the Middle Ages, was a strong center of dramatic activity. Minstrelsy flourished there as in no other country in Europe, while religious festivals, miracle and mystery plays were extremely popular during the thirteenth, fourteenth, and fifteenth centuries. Farce, too, arose early in the history of French theatricals, incorporated sometimes with the church plays, again existing independently. As early as the fifteenth century brotherhoods were organized in Paris for the purpose of presenting plays, the proceeds being devoted to charity. The best known of these groups was the Confrères de la Passion, which limited its activities to sacred drama, but not to the church itself, for several of its productions were housed by the Hôtel de la Trinité, and later by a specially constructed theatre in the Hôtel de Bourgogne.

Besides these religious brotherhoods, there existed in fifteenth century Paris at least two amateur dramatic societies of a secular nature: Les Enfants sans Souci, and Les Clercs de la Basoche. These were made up of spirited young students, who specialized in the production of farces. One perfect specimen of their repertoire, "Maistre Pierre Pathelin," has survived to the present day, and is still performed with great success throughout Europe and America. The student groups formed the real connecting link between the Mediaeval and Renaissance theatres in France, for they continued their performances throughout the sixteenth century, until they were supplanted by professional companies. The religious brotherhoods, on the other hand, were virtually put out of business in 1548, when Parliament refused to license them any longer.

The sixteenth century marked in France, as in England, the rise of the professional theatre. Several influences contributed to its development. First, the performances of Les Enfants sans Souci at the Hôtel de Bourgogne (taken over from Les Confrères de la Passion in 1548), a purely native dramatic movement; second, the classical movement centering in the universities, and resulting in the study and imitation of Latin drama; third, the appearance in Paris of the *Commedia dell' Arte*, the Italian comedy of masks, brought from Italy by Henry IV (King of France from 1589 to 1610). It was not until the end of the century, under the stimulus of the Italian companies, that French theatricals became well organized on a professional basis, and in 1600 there was still only one professional playhouse in Paris—that in the Hôtel de Bourgogne.

In this theatre the Italians played, and here also were seen the French comedians organized to be their rivals. The room which had been transformed into a theatre was sixty feet long and eighteen wide. The stage was of the simple platform type, the major portion of the audience stood during the performance, though courtiers and ladies were provided with raised seats, the hall was dimly lighted by oil lamps, and performances began at two o'clock in the afternoon.

The French were not slow to profit by the example of the Italians. Not unlike their southern neighbors in temperament and taste, they quickly evolved comic masks (stock characters) in the spirit of the *Commedia dell' Arte,* and thus provided considerable competition for the imported clowns. Three of these French comedians created lasting fame for themselves and the rôles they assumed:

Henri Legrand as Turlupin, Robert Guerin as Gros-Guillaume, and Hugues Gueru as Gaultier-Garguille. The three always performed together, and secured a most devoted following. Their partnership lasted until 1635, when Gros-Guillaume was arrested for having slandered certain magistrates (in the course of his stage caricatures), and was thrown into prison, where he soon died. His two fellow-clowns (old men by now) could not endure the loss of Gros-Guillaume, and within a week they both followed him to the grave.

The death of the three famous comedians cast a temporary pall over the French stage, but new actors soon took their places, for the profession was growing. In the early years of the seventeenth century a second French company, the Théâtre du Marais, had arisen, and now offered itself as a serious rival of the Hôtel de Bourgogne. Its actors were second-rate, but it boasted the services of an extraordinarily good playwright, Alexandre Hardi, the first Frenchman to write a large number of well-constructed dramas. Hardi as a young man had become a strolling player, and had spent some time in Madrid, where he witnessed plays by Lope de Vega and other Spanish dramatists of the romantic school. Returning to France, he wrote in rapid succession at least six hundred plays, and achieved such a success that for a time his work completely eclipsed the older types of French drama. He retired in 1623.

A third Parisian theatre was established in 1632 in a tennis-court on the Rue Michel-le-Compte. It was licensed to put on plays for a period of two years, but before the duration of that period it was restrained by an order of Parliament on complaint of influential householders in that neighborhood, who objected to the blocking of their narrow street by the crowd and its coaches attending the performances.

But although these three companies were the only ones

established in Paris during the late sixteenth and early seventeenth centuries, there were numerous traveling companies which visited all the large French towns, and occasionally performed in Paris at the fairs held there regularly. In fact it is known that in 1599 a company appearing at the Foire Saint Germain (one of the important fairs) caused a sensation sufficient to arouse jealousy among the players at the Hôtel de Bourgogne. It is interesting to note, also, that this same troupe included Marie Vernier, the first professional French actress of whom there is any record.

CORNEILLE AND "LE CID"

Another traveling company worthy of mention was the one headed by Mondori, an actor-manager who later set up his company in Paris. Mondori and his fellows happened to be playing in Rouen in the year 1629, and there they were observed by a young man who was destined to become one of the greatest of French playwrights. Pierre Corneille was the young man's name. He was born in Rouen in 1606, studied law, and in 1627 was admitted to the bar. He was, however, more interested in literature than in the law, and when he saw Mondori's productions of plays by Hardi, he set about at once to write plays himself. Mondori performed Corneille's first work, and later took it to Paris. Corneille followed his play to the metropolis, and began a long career as professional dramatist. In Paris Mondori was affiliated with the Théâtre du Marais, and naturally it was for this theatre that Corneille wrote most of his early plays. Within a short time, however, he was contributing to all the theatres.

By 1635 Corneille had attracted enough attention to be chosen by Cardinal Richelieu as one of the five authors to collaborate on a series of plays to be presented under the

Cardinal's patronage at his palace. Richelieu, in his extreme vanity, wished to have a hand in theatricals, and to that end he conceived the plan of hiring five capable dramatists to write under his guidance, he furnishing the plots and dictating the style. Each author was to do one act. A special salon was decorated and equipped in the Palais Cardinal for the presentation of these plays, and the first to be completed, "Les Tuileries," was given there on April 16th, 1635, but with only fair success. The second work of collaboration, "L'Aveugle de Smyrne," proved Corneille's undoing, for while writing the third act (the one assigned to him) he took the liberty of altering the plot (carefully designed by Richelieu), and thereby brought himself under the acute displeasure of that despot. So great was the breach created between the young poet and his patron that Corneille left Paris for Rouen, where he busied himself at his studies.

During this sojourn in his native city he was advised by an old friend to study Spanish drama as a means of improving his own writing. This he did, and was much impressed by the fiery romanticism of Lope de Vega and his contemporaries. One play in particular, "The Cid," by Guillen de Castro, fascinated him and impelled him to construct a drama on the same theme. His new play finished, he hurried with it to Paris, and had the pleasure of seeing it produced at the Hôtel de Bourgogne late in 1636.

"Le Cid," with its heroic characters, its wealth of exciting situations, and its high flights of poetry, achieved immediately a success never heard of until that time in the French theatre. It set the whole city of Paris in an uproar, and made Corneille the idol of the day. The stir created by the play carried beyond the confines of France, for soon "Le Cid" was performed in London before Charles I, and also in Madrid. Within a few years it had been translated into all the principal European languages

—an event hitherto unprecedented. A deluge of controversy resulted. Jealous Parisian playwrights attacked Corneille in scores of pamphlets, and every possible objection was raised to "Le Cid." Cardinal Richelieu, who had not had time to recover from the slight paid him by Corneille, was furious at the latter's triumph, and plotted to hurt the reputation of "Le Cid" by submitting it to the Academy, whose forty members were supposedly under the Cardinal's thumb. The Academy was given to understand that the play was to be condemned, but much as it feared Richelieu's wrath, it also disliked running counter to strong public opinion, and therefore begged the question. Richelieu, aware of the reason for the hesitancy of the Academy, forced the issue, and finally compelled the Academy to pass rather unfavorably on the play. The report, however, instead of being taken seriously by the public, as Richelieu had intended, was virtually ignored, and "Le Cid" became more popular than ever. The quarrel between Corneille and Richelieu was finally patched up in 1639, when, with a degree of humility, the poet confessed certain private troubles, and the Cardinal, with commendable generosity, helped him out of them.

No sooner had "Le Cid" made its hit than a host of young playwrights set out to imitate Corneille. Most of these have not survived in the annals of the great. But before many years Corneille's young brother, Thomas, achieved a notable success as a dramatist. The younger Corneille was not truly great, but he was decidedly clever, and at one time was the most popular playwright in Paris. In 1656 his play "Timocrate" ran for eighty-four performances at the Théâtre du Marais, and would have run longer had the actors not wearied of it. This long run set a record in the French theatre. The two Corneilles married sisters, and for many years lived in adjoining houses, the best of friends.

OPERA IN PARIS

In 1645 opera was introduced in Paris. Cardinal Mazarin, Richelieu's unpopular successor, was responsible for the innovation. The entire production, opera, singers, and all, was imported from Italy. But it did not prove a success. Two years later Mazarin tried again, with another opera, to win approval for the new art. But his hopes were in vain. French critics of the period were scornful, and the public was indifferent. Finally the irritated Cardinal (bound to win his point) tried a new tack. He commissioned Pierre Corneille to write a French opera. Corneille consented, and composed "Andromède," a musical play, but not in the Italian tradition. This writing was done in 1647, and the production would have ensued promptly, but civil wars prevented, and it was not until 1650 that "Andromède" saw the stage. It was very well liked, although contemporary accounts indicate that its favorable reception was due in no small measure to the manner of its presentation. Instead of being performed on a platform hung with curtains, "Andromède" was mounted with all the elaborate scenery of the Italian theatre. This was provided by one Jacques Torelli, a theatrical craftsman who had been driven out of Venice because of his stage effects. So clever were his inventions that the superstitious Venetians thought him in league with the devil, and actually attempted his life. Fleeing to Paris, he found employment at the court, and in staging Corneille's opera, he gave Parisians a treat in the way of moveable scenes.

THE CAREER OF MOLIÈRE

Now while these things were going on in Paris, other events of tremendous significance were also taking place, though it was not until some years later that their significance was appreciated. In 1622, for instance, was born Jean Baptiste Poquelin. His father was an upholsterer in the service of the court. From infancy Jean exhibited a talent for mimicry, and when he was taken to the theatre he was entranced. His parents often shuddered at the thought that he might become an actor. (The acting profession was not at that time considered an honorable one in France.) When he was fourteen years old, his mother died, and he was sent to a Jesuit school. He was a good student. Later he studied law, and while in college he began participating in amateur dramatics. Presently he assumed the management of a company of young actors, and almost before he knew it he was being sued by costumers and other creditors for unpaid bills. But this did not discourage him in the least. He collected what money his mother had left him, and with his company, which he called the Illustre Théâtre, set forth on the road. At this time, for the sake of his family, who were properly scandalized by his conduct, he changed his name to Molière. The exact date of his departure from Paris is not known, but it was either 1645 or 1646.

For twelve or thirteen years Molière and his fellows played in the villages and provincial cities of France. The company included several women, and one of these, Catherine Debrie, became Molière's mistress. She made him supremely happy, and remained to the end of her life his most faithful friend. Molière not only managed his company and played principal parts, but he wrote farces as well, and these were performed along with the standard repertoire of plays by Corneille and other contemporary dramatists.

The turning point in Molière's fortunes came in 1658, while he was playing at Rouen. There he received a summons to bring his company to Paris and play before the King. Thus it was that on October 24th of that year, on a special stage erected in the guard hall of the Old Louvre, the Illustre Théâtre gave the crucial performance of its career. The whole court was present, led by Louis XIV (at that time only twenty years of age). In the audience were, among other notables, Cardinal Mazarin and Anne of Austria. A play by Corneille was chosen for the occasion, but the performance did not go well. Molière's company did not show to the best advantage in heroic drama. Had matters concluded there, the history of the French theatre might be quite different from what it is. But Molière had waited too long for this opportunity to let it slip away from him. He made a speech, apologizing for the short-comings of his troupe, and asking permission to show one of his own farces. The request was granted, the farce was excellently done, and everyone in the audience was de-lighted.

Following the performance, the King engaged Molière's company to play every Tuesday, Thursday, and Sunday at the Hôtel de Petit Bourbon, where the Italian comedians were playing the other days of the week. A new title was also granted the company by Louis: namely, the Troupe de Monsieur (a title which signified the patronage of the King's brother). The next year Molière produced a play of his own, "Les Précieuses Ridicules," a comedy which sat-irized the affectations of the time so brilliantly that society was fundamentally affected, and the author raised to a pre-eminent position among French playwrights. Other plays of unsurpassed cleverness flowed from his pen regu-larly thereafter, and there were few human weaknesses that escaped his witty invective. His most sensational play was "Tartuffe," acted before the court at Versailles in 1664, and promptly banned, but allowed public presen-tation under the title of "L'Imposteur" in 1667. In nearly all his productions, Molière took the leading part. He re-mains, probably, a unique figure in theatrical history, a

man who excelled in three activities: play-writing, acting
and stage-managing.

The same fortune, however, did not follow him in
private matters. In 1662 he deserted the faithful Mlle
Debrie, and married a young girl in his company, Armande
Béjart. This false step cost him his happiness, for his wife
(nearly twenty-five years younger than himself) proved
flippant, selfish, and undeserving of his affection. In 1664
she gave him a daughter, but on the whole her conduct
was far from that of an ideal wife. Her inconstancy made
life a very hell for Molière, who, while conscious of her
faithlessness, still retained for her an irresistible passion.
During the course of their married life she continued to
act in her husband's productions.

In 1661 the Hôtel de Petit Bourbon was pulled down to
allow an addition to the Louvre, and both companies (the
Italians, and Molière's troupe) were removed to the large
theatrical salon in the Palais Royal, which Richelieu had
prepared in 1639 for his special productions. In 1665
Molière and his colleagues were signally honored by
Louis, who replaced their old title of Troupe de Monsieur
with a new one, Comédiens du Roi—the highest compli-
ment in his power to bestow. At the same time the King
granted a liberal pension to the company, and asked
Molière to become the titular head of the troupe. The
pension was, naturally, welcomed, but the other request
was refused by Molière, who preferred not to set himself
above his fellow-players.

The third of the immortal trio of French dramatists,
Jean Racine, made his début in 1664. Born in 1639, he had
received a classical education and had been prepared for
the church, but his interest turned to literature, and after
gaining some recognition as a poet, he wrote a play and
submitted it to Molière. The latter recognized Racine's
ability, and though he rejected the young man's first offer-

From Mantzius' *History of Theatrical Art.*

Plate 15: Stage of the Hotel de Bourgogne, showing the three farceurs: Turlupin, Gaultier-Garguille, and Gros-Guillaume.

ing, he encouraged him to write on another theme. Racine
took the suggestion, composed "La Thébaïde," and saw it
produced by Molière at the Palais Royal, where it created
a favorable impression. During the next sixteen years
Racine was a steady contributor to the literature of the
theatre. In 1680, strangely enough, he returned to the
folds of the church, married a remarkably devout woman,
and renounced the theatre. He died in 1699. Together with
Molière and the older Corneille, he forms one of the most
illustrious groups of playwrights in the annals of the
theatre.

On February 17th, 1673, Molière died of consumption.
He had been ill for some time, but he refused to stop work.
The afternoon of his death he insisted on playing his part
—that of the hypochondriac in his own play "Le Malade
Imaginaire." In the course of the performance, in the
midst of his humorous portrayal of imaginary illness, he
was seized with a convulsion. The performance was stopped
and Molière was hurried to nearby lodgings. He asked that
a priest be brought, but none would come, for the Church
had suffered too sharply from Molière's wit. He died
within a few hours. The Church then refused him Christian burial, and on the night of February 21st his body was
laid in a small, disreputable cemetery, his friends following
it to the grave with torches. The incident was considered
disgraceful by the host of Molière's admirers, and the
Church made many enemies by its stubborn action.

Hard upon the death of Molière came a shake-up and
readjustment of theatrical matters in Paris. Michel Baron,
one of Molière's best actors, deserted the ranks of the
Comédiens du Roi, and headed a new company of his own
at the old Hôtel de Bourgogne. This company was called
the Troupe Royale. The Théâtre du Marais was closed up
for good; the Palais Royal theatre was dedicated to
French opera, and Mme. Molière, who had meantime as-

sumed the management of her husband's affairs, was forced into new quarters. She found a theatre which had been built in the Rue Mazarine (it was often called the Théâtre de Guenegaud, after an adjacent street) and with the money left by Molière, succeeded in purchasing it. This theatre was large and well-equipped, having an unusually deep stage. Keeping the old company nearly intact, Mme. Molière resumed production at once, and met with success.

FOUNDING OF THE THÉÂTRE FRANÇAIS

Louis, however, had developed a mania for unification, and on the theory that in this way perfection was to be attained, ordered the existing theatres combined into one. In 1680, therefore, the Théâtre Français was established, and was given a complete monopoly of the legitimate drama. The Italian comedians were still allowed to occupy the Hôtel de Bourgogne, but their productions were limited to pantomime and music. The King himself superintended the organization of the Théâtre Français, choosing twenty-seven actors, and listing them in order of importance. He then drew up a salary schedule, which provided that all profits from the theatre, together with the subsidy which he had recently granted, be divided into twenty-three equal parts, the first eighteen players (in the order of their listing) to receive one part each, the next six, a half part each, the last three, a quarter of a part each. The very small remainder after this apportionment was likely devoted to some special (though unspecified) purpose.

On this basis the theatre opened in August, 1680, playing every day of the week, and continuing to operate successfully for many years. The first significant break in its routine occurred in 1689, when, because of congestion in the Rue Mazarine, the company moved to new quarters. After considerable reconnoitering, the representatives of the King had agreed upon the new location, which was an old tennis-court in the Rue des Fossés St. Germain des Pres, constructed originally for Henry IV at the beginning of the century. This tennis-court, it seems, was not a mere enclosure, but a substantial pavilion, which, in the hands of the royal architect, was speedily transformed into a commodious playhouse. It was opened April 18th, 1689, and was given the name of Le Théâtre de la Comédie Française (a name which has ever since been applied to the national theatre of France).

During this period of the late 17th century, the French theatres were still lighted (auditorium and stage) by candles and lamps; there was still a pit without seats (the part of the house nearest the stage, and of course the cheapest) ; there were three tiers of raised seats in the auditorium, including boxes, loges, *et cetera;* there was a special row of seats near the stage for press critics; the stage settings were ornate in the classic spirit, imitated from the Italians; there was a large and splendid foyer, where the elegantly dressed audience promenaded and chatted between acts; the wings of the stage were filled with fops, who fastidiously took snuff and criticised the actors; the front curtain rose at the signal of three knocks on the stage-floor.

SUMMARY

The Renaissance may be said to have accomplished its purpose in France shortly before the close of the seventeenth century. The rise of the French theatre, was, obviously, a peculiar movement because of the restrictions placed upon it. In no other European center of civilization was there quite the same spirit of centralized activity as in Paris. That is one reason why it is relatively easy to focus on a few personalities, a few theatres, a few productions, and still survey rather justly the French theatrical renaissance. But limited as it was in scope, the French theatre found itself by the year 1700 with firm foundations: a wonderful repertoire of native drama, a well-defined tradition of acting, and finally, a liberally subsidized state theatre, wherein the art of its golden age might be preserved for future generations.

SELECTED REFERENCES

The standard work in this field is Hawkins' *Annals of the French Stage*. It gives a detailed, year-by-year account of French theatricals up to the death of Racine in 1699. The whole of Volume III in Mantzius' *History of Theatrical Art* is devoted to Molière and the French stage. For the story of the Italian comedians in Paris see Sand's *History of the Harlequinade*. For specialized biography see Trollope's *Life of Molière*. Considerable information on the subject is contained in the various histories of French literature.

CHAPTER XI

THE RENAISSANCE IN SPAIN

EARLY PROFESSIONAL THEATRICALS

SPAIN during the Middle Ages had expressed its theatrical instinct in much the same manner as the other European countries. The Roman Catholic Church supplied liturgical drama and festival, with miracle plays performed on fixed stages and on floats; the minstrel, in the rôles of singer, acrobat, juggler, dancer, and monologist, contributed the secular entertainment. The Corpus Christi festival (which gave rise to the great religious cycles of miracle plays in England) was established in Spain during the thirteenth century, and reached its highest development (as it did in England) during the fifteenth century. It was not until the sixteenth century, however, that the Spanish theatre was organized and the national drama founded.

But even before a secular drama had developed, professional actors had organized into small groups, and had toured the cities and villages of Spain, performing miracle plays interspersed with songs and dances. It was inevitable that these companies should drift gradually from the religious play to the secular, and that new playwrights should be found who could supply farces, comedies, and historical interludes. The first company of which there is authentic record was one headed by Lope de Rueda, an actor-manager, who toured the principal cities of Spain at least as early as 1554. This manager wrote many of his own

plays, in an excellent prose style, and is said to have invented the domestic farce (at least so far as Spain was
concerned). He and his company traveled in the simplest
possible manner, with no more equipment than could be
carried in a sack. They played, customarily, on a rude platform erected in the village square, and depended for their
success upon witty dialogue and clever acting. No less a
person than Cervantes was a spectator at some of these
performances, and it was from them that the great writer
derived his love of the theatre, an affection which did not
bear sweet fruit, for Cervantes' own plays were failures.
But we have it first-hand from the author of "Don Quix-
ote" that Lope de Rueda's company was entertaining in
spite of its complete lack of theatrical trappings.

But while we are giving Lope de Rueda credit for
founding Spanish drama, we must note the fact that there
were outside influences at work also. The Italians, who
had the start of everyone else, penetrated Spain with their
elaborately mounted classical plays and also with their
modest but overwhelmingly popular *Commedia dell' Arte*.
The latter was seen at a festival in Seville as early as 1538;
ten years later a comedy by Ariosto, accompanied by all
the scenic complexity of the Italian Renaissance theatre,
was performed at the Spanish Court (then established at
Valladolid). During the remainder of the century, Italian
companies were regularly in and out of Spain, influencing
the entire course of Spanish stage and drama.

There was, of course, a certain amount of theatrical research carried on in Spanish universities, and to a much
lesser extent than the Italians, the Spaniards derived their
knowledge of Roman and Greek theatricals from a direct
study of classical literature and art. In 1570, for example,
the students of the college of San Hermenegildo produced
a tragedy in the classical manner, the play itself an imitation of ancient drama. A special stage was erected for the

production, and canvas walls and towers were provided for the setting. But occasional outbursts of formal classicism did not affect materially the growth of the public theatre. Besides, of what use was a study of the Roman theatre, when the Italians had already exhausted the subject and applied its principles to their own stage? Spanish scholarship could not hope to do more than had already been accomplished by the academies in Italy.

THE FIRST THEATRES

It was only a question of time until permanent places of dramatic performance should be designated. As the number of vagabond players increased and the visits of the Italian comedians grew more frequent, the need of theatres in the larges centers of population became more and more apparent. Finally a decisive impetus was given theatrical matters by the establishment in 1560 of Madrid as the capital city. As soon as the court was settled in its new quarters, Madrid became the center of many activities, not the least of which was the drama. But strangely enough the first legitimate theatrical enterprises in the city were not prompted by a professional spirit, but were primarily charitable in motive. In other words, the first theatres were not promoted by actors or actor-managers, but by groups of pious citizens, *cofradias,* who applied for and received licenses permitting them to set aside certain *corrales,* or yards, as permanent places for the presentation of plays, the proceeds of which were to be devoted to the support of hospitals. In 1565 the first *corral* was set aside for this purpose, and within a few years several others were similarly designated.

The word *corral* means nothing more than yard, or enclosure, but during the Renaissance it was the only Spanish word employed in reference to the theatre. Sometime during the seventeenth century the term *teatro* came into use. The *corrales* set aside by the *cofradias* were, then, merely square or rectangular spaces enclosed by the walls of houses—almost identical with the inn-yards which were the prototypes of the early theatres in London. A rude stage was built at one end of the enclosure and spectators were expected to stand in the space around the stage, or else to take up positions in the windows and balconies of adjoining houses. No protection from the weather was provided.

It was no great while, however, before one of these *corrales* was improved. The innovator was an Italian, Alberto Nazeri de Ganassa by name, who headed his own company of *Commedia dell' Arte* players, and had previously performed in France. Taking over the *Corral de la Pacheca* in 1574, he built a roofed stage, installed covered seats along the sides of the *patio* (yard), and stretched awnings over the pit, or standing space in the middle of the enclosure. He and his company performed here many times during the following years.

From the covered *corral* to the permanent theatre structure was but a step, and in 1579 the first theatre building in Madrid was erected by one of the charitable societies. A second structure appeared in 1582. Needless to say, these buildings followed closely the plan of the early *corrales*—the chief difference between them being that the new theatres were complete in themselves, whereas the old ones had made use of houses for their outer walls.

While this development was taking place in Madrid a similar movement was occurring in Seville, a city which not only had its local dramatic companies, but which also was favored with visits of the Italian comedians. Five theatres were built in Seville prior to 1600, and several others at the beginning of the seventeenth century. One of the latter, the *Coliseo,* was the first solidly roofed theatre in Spain, and boasted of an elaborate interior supported by

Doric columns whose bases and capitals were of marble. It burned, unfortunately, in 1620, and was not rebuilt until 1631, when it was made grander than ever, and is said to have seated four or five thousand persons. In 1659 it burned again, and was not rebuilt until 1676.

Another fine theatre, *La Monteria,* was built in Seville in 1626, from plans drawn up by the city officials. It too had a wooden roof, and even contained living-rooms for some of the actors. Its cost was equivalent to about a hundred thousand dollars today. It was financed by the city and turned over to a lessee, who was strictly under municipal supervision. All fees were determined by civic authority, and certain percentages of the receipts were paid to charities. In the rules governing this theatre it was also stated that performances could be given on approximately one hundred ninety-eight days in the year. The closed periods included forty-six days of Lent, every Saturday, and more than two months of summer, when no traveling companies were available.

LOPE DE VEGA

Another city in which drama flourished during the Renaissance was Valencia. Curiously, though, it was an accident that caused her dramatic efflorescence. She had had, naturally, some taste of theatricals, for Spain was over-run by vagabond players, who exhibited in every city and village, but until the year 1588 Valencian theatricals had been ordinary to say the least. The circumstance which altered matters was the banishment of Lope de Vega, the foremost dramatist of the period, from the capital. This prolific and highly successful author was convicted in Madrid of criminal libel, and therefore was banished for eight years from the city of Madrid, and for two years from the kingdom of Castile. The first two years of his banishment he spent in Valencia, and the result was that this city found itself suddenly a theatrical center, for Lope de Vega took with him into banishment all his enthusiasm and ability as a writer and producer of plays.

Regarding Lope de Vega something more should be said. Born in 1562 (two years earlier than Shakespeare) he soon fell under the influence of the swiftly growing theatre, and especially under the spell of the Italian comedy. Trained for the priesthood, he nevertheless devoted himself almost exclusively to dramatic writing, making his début as a professional playwright around the year 1585. Until the day of his death in 1635 (at the age of seventy-three) he labored prodigiously in the theatre, writing literally hundreds of plays on an infinity of themes. Generous and careless, he spent money as fast as he earned it, and died poor. He, like Shakespeare, over-topped all his contemporaries, and created in his country the first great body of national dramatic literature. Like Shakespeare, too, he wrote his plays for money rather than fame, caring no more than the man from Stratford what happened to the manuscripts, once they had been paid for and included in the repertory of the stage.

THE NATURE OF THE PUBLIC THEATRES

The public theatres in Spain during the period of Lope de Vega were all very much alike in their arrangement, use of scenery, and general regulations. Except in one or two cases the pit was open to the sky, the stage was a simple projecting platform surmounted by a balcony which could be used in the action of the play, there was a curtained inner stage and sometimes curtained recesses at the sides of the main stage, the scenery was unpretentious, and did not imitate the elaborate Italian settings, painted in perspective, there were private boxes along the sides of the auditorium, and a balcony which included a special section for women. No men were admitted to the women's balcony, and women were not allowed in most parts of the house. The women's balcony was reached by a special entrance and staircase, but even this isolation did not encourage the attendance of respectable women, for we are told by contemporary witnesses that the atmosphere of the whole theatre was noisy and vulgar, and women were there to be seen rather than to see the play. Those who cared for their reputation came masked, and sat generally in the private boxes with male escorts. In these particulars the Spanish theatre resembled closely the English theatre of the same period.

As regards the appearance of women on the stage, however, Spain followed the Italian rather than the English custom, for we find women licensed to act in Madrid as early as 1587 (permission having been granted first to an Italian company playing there, and the same privilege having been extended to native companies immediately after) whereas the first London production to include actresses was licensed in 1656. There were, it is true, many subsequent discussions of the propriety of women's acting, but the privilege was never withdrawn. There was also a controversy over the matter of boys' taking feminine rôles, for this was an old custom that still held in certain theatres. The King's Council issued decrees from time to time regulating theatre practices, and in 1615 it ruled that women should not represent men on the stage, and boys should not represent women. The same decree prohibited immoral dances on the stage, and insisted that none but actors be admitted to dressing-rooms. Finally, it limited the number of licensed companies to twelve, and arranged for careful supervision of these. That the decree was put into force so far as was possible is proved by the slump in theatrical business which followed. The theatres in Madrid, however, were the ones which suffered most, for they were under the eye of the court. Small touring companies pursued their usual way, carefully avoiding Madrid and its severe restrictions.

The admission fees, too, were controlled in metropolitan theatres by royal or municipal councils. At the door two fees were collected, one by the theatre management, another by a representative of local charities. As has been stated above, all theatrical performances were licensed on condition that they contribute to hospital funds, and this principle was rigidly adhered to. Once in the theatre the spectator was faced with the problem of a seat. He could stand in the yard or pit without additional expense, but if he wished a chair or a place on a bench he had to pay extra for it. Box-seats were the most costly, and could be rented for the entire season, as at the modern opera. A large number of the audience beat their way in. In fact it appears that the average citizen made it a business to enter the theatre without paying. He managed this in various ways, now by assuming an importance that would entitle him to favor, again by slipping past a careless doorman, and not infrequently by organizing a mob of ruffians and crashing the gate.

The audience was as hard to control inside the theatre as at the door. The pit-crowd was especially unruly, and brought with them whistles to blow, ripe fruit and vegetables to hurl at the actors, and swords with which to fight in any brawl that might start. Playwrights were forced to write cringing prologues (called *loas*) to their plays, the chief purpose of which was to obtain the indulgence of the temperamental crowd, whereas the actors were constantly in fear of their lives. Eating and drinking went on constantly during the performance, and expressions of approval or disapproval of the play were given in the noisiest manner imaginable.

THE COURT AND THE THEATRE

Relations between the court and the public theatres altered with changing reigns. Philip II (who died in 1598) was a sombre man, unaddicted to gaiety, and therefore inimical to the theatre. Philip III was more lenient, and, especially as the Queen was fond of plays, frequently held performances at court. But it was Philip IV who showed the greatest enthusiasm for the theatre. He had, indeed, a passion for it. At the age of nine (in 1614) he is said to have played the part of Venus in a court spectacle, and although the movement of the car on which he was mounted made him violently ill, he acted to the satisfaction of everyone. Later in life he built a special theatre in his palace and had plays performed there regularly by professional companies. But it must be admitted that his love of the theatre was closely bound up with his love of actresses. He and his courtiers made the stage their playground, and although they encouraged the drama they cannot be said to have done so from very high motives. Philip's famous son, Don John of Austria, had for his mother Maria Calderón, a popular actress, who, like Nell Gwyn of England, rose from obscurity to the favor of a king.

Partly because of the demoralizing influence of the court, but chiefly because the great creative dramatists were dying off, the Spanish theatre declined rapidly toward the middle of the seventeenth century. In 1650 Calderón was the only important dramatist left. The movement had spent itself, as it had in England a few years earlier. In 1665 Philip IV died, and by order of the Queen every theatre was closed indefinitely. It is true that the next year some of them reopened, but they did not recapture the spirit and vitality of the old days. The Renaissance was over.

It is safe to assume that the early Spanish theatre had

relatively little influence on the theatres of other European countries. Spanish companies did venture abroad, especially into France and the Netherlands (as early as 1618), and a troupe is reported to have played at the English court in 1635, but they did not meet with very enthusiastic receptions, and certainly did not establish any new theatrical art in the places they visited. Certain Spanish dramas were imitated by foreign playwrights, particularly by the French, but it is unlikely that in the arts of acting and staging the Spaniards had much to teach their northern neighbors.

THE BULL-FIGHT

This chapter must not be concluded, however, without mention of a semi-theatrical institution which has long been associated with Spanish life, and which from the standpoint of popularity, completely eclipses the legitimate theatre. This institution is the bull-fight. When it was introduced into Spain and by whom, no one appears to know, some saying it came in with the Romans, others, that it originated with the Moors. At all events, it was planted on Spanish soil long before the Renaissance, and by the sixteenth century had become a national pastime. In 1567 Pope Pius V issued a proclamation against bull-fighting, but the order was revoked in 1576 by Pope Clement VIII, and from that day to this the sport has increased constantly in favor.

While English and French knights met in tournament and jousted for the king's or a lady's favor, unhorsing each other with their pikes, Spanish courtiers tried their strength and skill against ferocious bulls. Even the kings of Spain entered the arena in the rôle of *torero*. With the passing of the age of chivalry, however, passed also the aristocratic amateur of the bull-ring, and in modern times the sport has become highly professionalized.

It is common knowledge that all European countries during the late Middle Ages and the Renaissance had their animal fights. Bulls and bears being baited by dogs and men made entertainment for the mob in all large cities. It will be remembered, for instance, that the first public theatres in London were erected in the midst of arenas given over to animal shows. The first Hamlet soliloquized within stone's throw of such spectacles. In no country but Spain, however, did this rather savage show secure a permanent hold, and flower into a dramatic ritual of beauty and complexity. If the legitimate theatre has suffered in Spain from lack of patronage it is mainly because the people have always had an insatiable love for this drama of colored action enacted by bulls and men.

That the bull-fight matured early into practically what it is today is proved by the fact that an English traveller to Madrid in the year 1623 described an exhibition which he saw, and his description tallies in every important point with the modern bull-fight. The chief difference to be noted is that three hundred years ago there were no large permanent *plazas de toros* (arenas), as there are today; the fights then being held in improvised rings. The first arena of the modern type was built by Philip V in Madrid in 1747.

Let us describe briefly the spectacle of the bull-fight. It begins with the arrival of the President (or referee, as he would be called in America), who has been chosen to preside over the occasion. When this official enters his box, the music strikes up, and the *entrada,* or entrance procession, is started. Into the arena ride a pair of mounted police, in gay uniform, followed by the *espadas* (two or three) on foot, then the *picadores* (about the same number) mounted on the horses which are to withstand the attacks of the bull, then the *banderilleros,* and finally the *muleteros,* with their brightly bedecked mules to be used in dragging off the carcasses of bulls and unlucky horses

This procession circles the arena, salutes the President and prepares for action. The bull is let into the arena and is engaged by the *picadores,* who are armed with pikes This encounter forms the first of the three movements o the bull-fight, and is called the *suerte de varas.* The horse on which the *picadores* are mounted are invariably old and worthless, and are often gored fatally by the bull. If a horse falls and his rider is in danger of the attacking beast's horns, one of the *espadas* (the chief bull-fighters who work on foot, and carry bright red cloths called *muletas*) comes to the rescue and draws off the bull by waving the red cloth before his eyes. In a moment the animal sights another horse and charges at him, when he is piked by the *picador,* with or without doing damage to the second horse. The purpose of this first movement is to get up the blood of the bull, to enrage him sufficiently to ensure a ferocious conflict in the following movements.

When in the estimation of the President, enough horses have been sacrificed, the *picadores* retire, and a bugle announces the *suerte de banderillas.* In this movement the human actors are the *banderilleros,* foot-fighters equipped with short, hooked darts adorned with colored papers. These darts must be handled with great skill, and must be placed in pairs in the shoulders of the bull as he comes charging at the *banderillero.* Once planted in the flesh of the shoulder, they prove a persistent annoyance to the bull. Occasionally, if the animal be lethargic, special *banderillas de fuego* are employed. These are flaming darts, guaranteed to rouse fury in even the tamest *toro.*

When enough darts have been hung on the harassed hero of the performance, the President again gives the word, and the bugle announces the third and final movement, the *suerte de matar,* the killing. Here the *espada,* (or *matador,* as he is also called) tempts the bull to his death. Single-handed this extraordinarily brave and skillful man engages in mortal combat with the frenzied and blood-thirsty creature. Before doing so, however, he advances to a position in front of the President's box, and in a formal speech dedicates the life of the bull. In one hand he carries the *muleta,* the red cloth, in the other, a sword. He waves the cloth, the bull charges, and his horns encounter only the cloth. The animal, bewildered, whirls and charges again, with the same result. The *espada,* who knows all that can be known of the behavior of bulls, knows that his body is not in danger so long as the red cloth is held in the right position. He never runs from the bull, and as a rule does not even move in his tracks as the animal rushes past him. His every move is carefully observed by the crowd, and his reputation is always at stake. At length, when he feels that he has played the bull just long enough, he exe-cutes the final stroke. By the unvarying and long-established rules of the drama he must kill the bull with one thrust of his sword, the weapon passing through the neck and reach-ing to the heart. Such a stroke must be timed perfectly, and must be delivered with a marvellous combination of dex-terity and strength. After the *espada* has finished, an at-tendant comes forward and runs a sharp dagger into the bull's spine near the head, ending its death struggle.

After this climax, the bull is dragged off and another driven in, whereupon the whole performance is repeated. There is no limit to the length of a bull-fight, everything depending on the importance of the occasion. As many as six or eight bulls are sometimes killed at a single exhibi-tion in modern times, while in the eighteenth century two or three times that number were killed at the special fights held on feast days.

Madrid and Seville are the homes of bull-fighting, but there is scarcely a town in Spain without its *plaza de toros.* More than a thousand bulls are needed each year to supply the nation's entertainment, and these are all specially bred for the purpose, the breeders taking pride in the excellent fighting qualities of their animals.

The costumes worn by the bull-fighters are picturesque and gorgeous. Made of satin and velvet, embroidered with gold, they cost enormous sums, and are not at all the flimsy, tinseled outfits that are seen so frequently in our theatre when plays or operas of Spanish atmosphere are performed. Nor is the bull-fighter ever completely free from the mark of his profession, for he wears a short braid of hair at the back of his head, and by this he is distinguished until he retires for good from service, when the braid is cut off.

The *espada* is the idol of Spain. Men do him honor; boys envy him; ladies seek his favor. The more daring his conduct in the arena, the greater his popularity. Yet his position is precarious in more ways than one. Not only is his life constantly in danger; his reputation hangs by a thread. The populace is well versed in the art which he practices, and is eager to find fault. Hundreds of books have been written on the art of the bull-fighter, and every detail of technique is the subject of general controversy. There are technical names for each move made during the course of the fight, and in each audience are connoisseurs in matters taurine. Woe to the *espada* who commits a *faux pas!*

Much has been written and said against the bull-fight. It has been called barbarous by some Spaniards and countless foreigners. The typical Spaniard, however, stoutly defends his native sport, and insists that the cruel elements are exaggerated by its opponents. He admits, generally, that the injuries to the horses are unpleasant, but he points out that the only horses used in the arena are those that have had their day, and are ready for extermination. He insists, furthermore, that whereas the eyes of the foreigner are drawn to the pitiful condition of the injured horse, the eyes of the Spaniard are fixed on the conduct of the *picador* and the *espada*. He admits, perhaps, that *banderillas de fuego* are unnecessarily cruel, but he points out that they are seldom used nowadays. He believes, also, that the foreigner is inclined to attribute human sensitiveness to animals, thereby falsifying the emotional values of the drama. He goes on to say that English and American sports such as horse-racing, automobile racing, prize-fighting, and football, have aspects of cruelty, and that in most instances the injuries attendant on them are sustained by human beings, whose feelings are much finer than those of bulls or horses. Finally he declares that the bull-fight is justified by its beauty, and by its display of heroism and skill. It is stated, too, by competent authorities, that the bull-fight is singularly free from the evils of drinking, gambling, and crooked management. The crowd is orderly, there is no systematized betting, and there is not a case on record of a bull-fight having been "fixed" by its managers.

Whatever may be one's opinion on the foregoing points, it remains clear that the bull-fight is a unique specimen of theatrical spectacle, and one that the Spaniard has made his own.

SELECTED REFERENCES

A complete study of this subject is Rennert's *The Spanish Stage in the Time of Lope de Vega*. Information may also be gleaned from Ticknor's *History of Spanish Literature*. Many references could be given on the bull-fight. Two of the best are: Villiers-Wardell's *Spain of the Spanish,* and Calvert's *Madrid*.

CHAPTER XII

THE RENAISSANCE IN ENGLAND

PROFESSIONAL acting companies were common in England during the early part of the sixteenth century. As has been shown in a previous chapter, these companies composed of four or five men and a boy toured the villages and presented miracle plays, moralities, and interludes. They played in churches, banquet halls, and in the market-place. For purposes of protection they attached themselves to various members of the nobility, and were legally classified as servants.

At this time England was emerging, rather tardily, from mediaevalism. A spirit of expansion was in the air; foreign commerce was increasing; the humanism of ancient art and literature was creeping in from Italy and France. London was the center of English life, and was growing rapidly; at the accession of Elizabeth to the throne in 1558 it was still a walled town with approximately one hundred thousand inhabitants, whereas, at her death in 1603 it had overflowed its boundaries and doubled its population. The court was a center of great activity, and its functions were most elaborate. There were enough Puritans in London to cause a considerable opposition to theatrical and other profane amusements, but the majority of citizens were lively and sport-loving. Holidays were celebrated with enthusiasm, and the fun afforded by athletic contests, animal-fights, *et cetera,* was indulged in by great numbers. It was almost inevitable that in such a center of movement and prosperity, the theatre would find its place.

THE CONSTRUCTION OF PUBLIC PLAYHOUSES

The first public theatre made its appearance in the north suburbs of London in 1576. It was called simply "The Theatre," and was erected by James Burbage, a carpenter who had turned actor and joined the Earl of Leicester's Men. It was a circular structure of wood, costing about six hundred pounds. It housed plays steadily for more than twenty years, and was undoubtedly the theatre to which Shakespeare was first attached in the capacity of actor and playwright. In the years 1598–99 (because of a quarrel over the renewal of the lease of the ground on which it stood) it was pulled down and its timbers used in the construction of "The Globe" on the south bank of the Thames. No account survives of the dimensions or arrangement of "The Theatre," but it cannot have differed greatly from its successors, of which more is known.

In the same year, 1576, the second theatre was built and named "The Curtain," not, as one would suspect, because of the obvious symbolism of the word "curtain," but because the land on which the playhouse stood had long been called by that name. It was smaller than "The Theatre," but was also circular in form. In 1587 "The Rose" was constructed for Philip Henslowe and John Cholmley. We know from Henslowe's Diary (the chief source of information regarding Elizabethan theatres) that it was circular, that it had a tiring-room at the rear of the stage, and that its gallery had a thatched roof. It housed plays quite regularly until 1620, when it was given over to prize-fights and similar spectacles.

The fourth theatre, "The Swan," built about 1594 by Francis Langley, was a twelve-sided structure, with a seating capacity variously estimated at from fifteen hundred to twenty-five hundred persons. It was used for plays until 1597, but infrequently thereafter. It seems to have been poorly adapted to dramatic production, and is thought to have had a portable stage. A crude drawing of "The Swan," made in 1596 by John de Witt, a visitor to London in that year, was discovered in the university library of Utrecht, and published in 1888. "The Globe," next in order of construction (1599), became at once the most important of the public theatres. It burned down in 1613 during a performance, but was rebuilt at once in octagonal form, with a tiled roof. It was the center of Burbage's theatrical activity, and was the home of Shakespeare. Its leading actor was Richard Burbage (son of James, the manager) for whom Shakespeare created his great male rôles. When the decline in drama set in, "The Globe" still kept its banner flying, and was the last playhouse to support Elizabethan drama. It was pulled down in 1644.

"The Fortune" was built in 1600 for Alleyn and Henslowe, and it is the only theatre of the period of which we have the exact dimensions. It, like the pioneer playhouse, was located to the North of London. It was square, and measured eighty feet each way on the outside. Its inside measurements were fifty-five feet each way. The framework was of wood, but the foundations were brick. It had three stories, twelve, eleven, and nine feet high respectively. The two upper stories (the galleries) overhung the ground floor by ten inches. The galleries were twelve and a half feet deep. Stage and galleries were roofed with tile. The stage, which projected to the middle of yard, was forty-three feet wide. The yard (central part of the auditorium) was open to the sky, as were the yards of all the public theatres of the period. A room over the rear of the stage took the place of the gallery along that side. This room could be used in the action of the play, or could house the orchestra. The theatre was occupied by the Lord Admiral's Men, one of the most important theatrical companies. It burned down in 1621, but was rebuilt two years later, entirely of brick, in circular form. This structure stood until the beginning of the nineteenth century.

"The Red Bull" and "The Hope" were the two other public theatres of the period. The construction date of the former is not known, but the theatre was leased in 1605, and must have been built shortly before that date. It was occupied at first by the Queen's Men, but strangely enough it was noted for the sensational nature of its productions, and for the particularly vulgar audience which it attracted. It survived into the period of the Restoration. "The Hope" was built in 1614 for Philip Henslowe, and was probably octagonal in shape. It had brick foundations, a tiled roof, and outside staircases leading to the galleries. It had a portable stage which rested on trestles, and the stage-roof (or "heavens," as it was called) was supported by the main structure, and not by pillars set near the front corners of the stage, as in the case of most of the theatres. Plays were performed in "The Hope" until 1616, when it was given over to bull-baiting and bear-baiting. It served this latter purpose as late as 1682.

THE NATURE OF THE PUBLIC PLAYHOUSES

Whatever the differences in these eight public theatres of London, their similarities were marked. For one thing, they had a common origin. It had long been a custom with traveling companies of players to use inn-yards for their performances. The inn and the church were the two dominant structures in any sixteenth century English town, and they were also the chief places of public assembly. As the plays became secular in character, the inn naturally proved more hospitable than the church, and so it came about naturally that when the first theatre architects drew up their plans, they reproduced more or less faithfully the traditional inn-yard, with its balconies along the sides of the court, and the raised stage at the end opposite the entrance. But they had before them at the same time the circular arenas or bull-pens on the Bankside, with raised seats for the spectators, and a pit or ring in the center. As a result of contemplating these two architectural models, the Elizabethan theatre builders vacillated between square and circular forms, and occasionally compromised with an octagonal or a twelve-sided structure.

Tremendous controversies have raged among scholars as to the details of the Elizabethan theatre, but most controversial points may be omitted as unnecessary to a brief general account such as this. It is indisputable that the stage was an elevated platform extending well into the yard, and that it usually was of a permanent nature. It was wide in proportion to the width of the theatre, but it allowed some standing room between its sides and the inner walls of the building. The actors, then, were viewed from three sides rather than from one. At the rear of the main stage was a smaller inner stage, probably concealed from the audience by a curtain which could be withdrawn during the course of the play. Above this inner stage was a balcony (which may also have been curtained), and above it a "hut" or small building on the roof containing stage-machinery (such as cranes or pulleys) surmounted by a flag-pole from which fluttered the banner of the theatre. The flag was flown only on days when plays were to be performed, and therefore served as an official announcement.

Relatively little scenery was used in these theatres. The Italian revival of elaborately painted backgrounds did not influence the English theatre until later. It came in via court and university productions toward the close of the Elizabethan period, and did not reach the public theatre until the Restoration. We may say, then, that so far as scenery was concerned, Shakespeare's theatre was mediaeval rather than Renaissance. This does not mean, though, that attempts were not made to portray specific localities. The inner stage was often converted into a bedroom, a cave, or a forest glade. The main stage, on the contrary, seems to have been free from decoration, its sole adornments being necessary properties such as tables, chairs, and benches, which were carried on and off in full sight of the audience (for of course there was no front curtain). In the plays of the period, characters frequently announce the locality of the action, and it is possible that signs were sometimes used to indicate setting, but there is no very strong proof that the latter practice was common. The mediaeval principle of the multiple setting (that is, an arrangement whereby several localities are represented simultaneously on the stage) does not appear to have had much hold on the Elizabethan theatre. The main stage was used as a rule for general, unlocalized scenes, such as streets, fields, seashore, *et cetera;* the inner stage for specific, localized scenes requiring special properties. Interior scenes were not always represented on the inner stage, nor were outdoor scenes confined to the main stage; these matters depended on the requirements of each play. The main thing was to obtain a smooth alternation of scenes to assist in the illusion of changing time and place, and at the same time to allow the play to go forward without delays. When the balcony was used in the action, the alternation became more complicated, involving what amounted to three distinct stages. It was this swiftness of production that was lost during the nineteenth century with the development of ponderous realistic settings which took so long to move on and off stage that Shakespeare's plays were distorted, cut to pieces, and rearranged to avoid the rapid alternation of scene which the author had intended. Only in the twentieth century has the true Shakespearian method been recovered, not, to be sure, by a restoration of the actual Elizabethan stage, but by the simplification of scenery: the substitution of drop scenes and draperies for elaborate box-sets, the introduction of the skeleton set, and in some productions, the addition of a forestage.

It is unlikely that any very complicated machinery was employed in early London theatres. The trap-door was certainly a much-used device, for the plays often demanded the sudden appearance of devils, witches, and other supernatural characters. The texts make clear that some of these apparitions rose from beneath the stage; others no doubt were lowered from the "heavens" by means of wires, ropes, cranes, and pulleys. The representation of distant landscapes, clouds, planets, animals and other difficult subjects, with which the Italian producers were already familiar, was almost certainly untried in the public theatres of London during the life of Shakespeare. Nor was there any display of ingenious stage lighting. All performances took place in the afternoon, in broad daylight, and when darkness was to be represented, torches or lighted candles were carried by actors to symbolize the fact.

Although these theatres prospered for the most part, they did not find their way a smooth one. They had many enemies, and their existence was constantly made difficult by attacks from Puritan-minded authorities. They were not allowed at all in the city proper, but were forced either into the suburbs to the north of London, or else into the disreputable district on the south bank of the Thames. The greater number were found in the latter locality, surrounded by brothels, bear-pits, and filth. Licenses were issued to them only on condition that they bring certain revenues to city charities, and whenever a plague was rumored, the theatres were closed up tight. The plague scare was undoubtedly overworked by zealous officials who seized the slightest pretext for striking at the theatres. The weather was another enemy. If heavy rain fell during

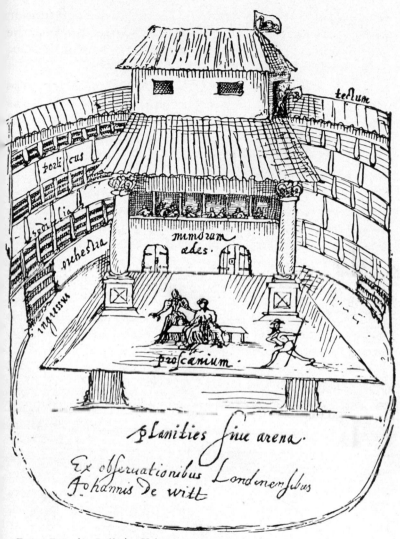

teſtum

porticus

ſedilia

orcheſtra

ingreſſus

mimorum
ædes.

proſcænium.

planities ſiue arena.

Ex obſeruationibus Londinenſibus
Johannis de witt

Plate 16: Swan Theatre, from a contemporary drawing of
John de Witt.

the day, the flags were drawn in and the afternoon performances cancelled, for the theatres offered scant protection from the elements.

A typical audience at a public theatre of the time was
neither cultivated nor attentive. It was made up largely of
men, and was noisy and quarrelsome. Eating and drinking
went on constantly during the performance, and actors
were frequently the targets of missiles and verbal insults.
The yard (standing room in front of and at the sides of
the stage) was filled with rowdies, while the galleries held
the more affluent though not necessarily better-mannered.
Sporty aristocrats occupied boxes in the gallery, and occasionally (though not commonly) sat upon the stage itself.
Very few respectable women entered the theatres, and those
who did so wore masks to conceal their indentity. Vulgar
women of the streets, however, were regular patrons.
When one considers these facts, one realizes clearly why
it was that so much sensational brutality and low comedy
was injected into Elizabethan plays. In fact the marvel
is that so much glorious poetry, profound philosophy, and
delicate fancy could have been created for the entertainment of such an audience.

That the standard of acting in the best public theatres
was high cannot be doubted. Never in the history of the
theatre have great plays been written for poor players.
Had not Richard Burbage been worthy of Hamlet and
Lear, Shakespeare could never have conceived them. Had
not Tarleton and his fellow-clowns been superb comedians,
there could be no Touchstone, no Dogberry. We must even
assume that the boys who took feminine rôles were capable
of exquisite impersonation, else how can we account for
the existence of Juliet, of Rosalind, of Cleopatra? It has
not been mentioned previously in this chapter, but it must
be emphasized that no women played on the Elizabethan
stage. The tradition of the Middle Ages in this regard

held good in England until the re-opening of the theatres at the time of the Restoration. And when we take this fact into account, we understand, for one thing, why such a play as "As You Like It" was plausible at the time it was written, and is rather preposterous today. A boy-Rosalind was a convincing boy in the Forest of Arden. A girl-Rosalind never is. There are plenty of evidences in the history of the theatre that boys can take feminine parts acceptably—the English stage offers but one of many proofs.

THE PRIVATE THEATRES

Let us now consider the private theatres of the period. These grew out of the amateur dramatic movement of the sixteenth century, which centered in the activity of choir-boys. The boys of St. Paul's were perhaps the best known group, but there were several other companies that gave frequent performances of plays. They established their own theatres, not new buildings erected for the purpose, but old ones remodeled. Their ventures wore such an air of respectability that they were allowed to operate within the city proper, and this presented an opportunity to professional theatrical managers which they were not slow in seizing. The Burbages and other theatre magnates soon managed to arrange for special performances by their companies in the private theatres, and shortly were in control of these houses. They coöperated with the boys' companies, and often recruited actors from their ranks.

The most famous private theatre was "Blackfriars," which had been made out of the large rooms in an old priory. It was used for plays before 1600, and in 1608 was taken over officially by the Burbages, who ran it in connection with "The Globe." The company which occupied the open-air theatre on Bankside in summer and good weather, moved into the roofed theatre in the city during winter and bad weather. "Blackfriars" (taking its name from the district in which it was located) was the most fashionable theatre in London, and on its stage were acted the plays of Shakespeare, Ben Jonson, and other great dramatists of the time.

A second private theatre was "Whitefriars" (its name, too, derived from its location), which was used for plays as early as 1590. The name persisted until 1670, though during that time it was applied to more than one building. "Whitefriars" apparently retained more of its amateur quality than did "Blackfriars," and housed boy companies more frequently than professionals.

The third theatre of this type of which we have record is "The Phoenix" or "The Cockpit." Both names seem to have been used commonly. It was located on Drury Lane (famous ever since as a theatrical site), and was opened in 1616. It became one of the most popular playhouses in London, and held performances even during the Restoration. It was in this theatre that Sir William D'Avenant produced his "musical plays" or operas in 1658, introducing scenic effects never before put before the English public.

It must not be imagined that these three theatres were "private" in any strict sense of the word. They were founded for the purpose of housing occasional productions by amateurs for select audiences, but they soon outgrew this "privacy." Still, they continued to be called "private" in order that they might escape the supervision of the censor. There was always about them a certain atmosphere of exclusiveness, even though it was possible for any person to gain admittance at the regular price. The thing which contributed chiefly to this atmosphere was the attendance of ladies and gentlemen of social standing. To patronize the Bankside theatres was extremely unconventional; to patronize "Blackfriars" was fashionable. And yet there were plenty of citizens, and even more citizens' wives, who would have been scandalized at the thought of being seen in even the most reputable of the private theatres. Most of the women wore masks in the theatre, and many of the men were present primarily with a view to flirtation. The prices were slightly higher than at the public playhouses, but of course the accommodations were superior. There was protection from the weather, there were benches in the pit (corresponding to the yard of the public theatre) and there was good illumination. Best of all, the private theatres were located in the heart of the city, and were therefore easily accessible to everyone.

It was very likely in these theatres that the projecting platform stage of the sixteenth century received its first modification. Indoor performances required considerable artificial illumination, and any augmentation of lighting equipment made the inner stage more effective to the audience. We may assume, therefore, that in the private theatre the forestage began to lose its prominence, and that it declined steadily from the early part of the seventeenth century until the latter part of the nineteenth, when it disappeared altogether.

The principal factor in the decline of the forestage, however, was the development of scenery, and to trace that we must turn from both the public and private theatres of Elizabethan and Jacobean times, to the university and the court, where the mechanical achievements of the Italian stage were studied, copied, and perhaps in certain ways, improved upon.

It has been noted in a previous chapter that during the sixteenth century the universities were developing a strong interest in classical drama. Students wrote imitations of Latin comedy, and performed them on their own stages. They also exhibited no little curiosity as to ancient methods of play-production, and like their fellow research scholars of Italy and France and Spain, they were eager to experiment with revivals of old plays. At the same time dramatic presentations at court were becoming more frequent and more elaborate. During the entire sixteenth century court masques and pageants were popular, and toward the end of the century, professional companies were often called upon to perform at royal functions. The children's companies, too, were regular entertainers at the court of Elizabeth. Masques and pageants were often mounted on floats, and exhibited in large castle halls or outdoors; plays and the simpler sort of masques were performed on temporary stages erected at the end of a rectangular room. All court productions were supervised by the Master of the Revels, an official of the court, who was directly responsible to the king or queen. Enormous sums of money were available for such events, and the most elaborte effects were desired. It is small wonder, then, that the art of theatrical scenery should have been cultivated at the court rather than at the public theatres.

INIGO JONES AND SCENIC ART

Henry VII, Henry VIII, and Elizabeth had each encouraged these sumptuous spectacles. It remained, however, for James I, who came to the throne in 1603, to sponsor the first real scenic movement on the English stage —a movement which advanced remarkably during the reign of Charles I (1625–1649), and reached almost a modern plane during the period of the Restoration (1660–1700). And the stimulus for the movement came, as might be expected, from Italy. It rose principally from the work of one man—Inigo Jones, an English architect attached to the court of James I, who, hearing of Italian theatricals, set out to study them at first hand. In 1604 he visited various Italian centers, making careful observation of every thing pertaining to the theatre. He did not overlook the Olympic Theatre at Vicenza. On his return to England, his notebook filled with sketches and plans of stages, moveable scenery, *et cetera,* he set to work enthusiastically to put into practice his newly acquired principles. His first production was at Christ Church, Oxford. There he mounted a tragedy in neo-Greek manner, arranging the three required settings in the form of a revolving triangle, an imitation of the *periaktoi* of the Greek stage, learned from Vitruvius. This experiment, which took place during August, 1605, was not very successful, and it caused Jones to alter his methods. He soon transferred his services to the court, where he became the principal producer of masques, and in this position he developed the mechanics of the modern theatre, making a second trip to Italy in 1613 and another to Italy and France in 1614.

The fundamental motive in Jones's work was, naturally, perspective. He designed and painted every conceivable sort of background for dramatic action, and to accompany these, he invented many effects imitative of natural movement, such as artificial waves, clouds, and monsters. He specialized in the elaborate pastoral masque, for this gave scope to his ingenious fancy. He worked generally on an elevated stage at the end of a large rectangular hall. One of his earliest discoveries was the value of a front curtain, and in 1616 he introduced the proscenium arch in the production of a Ben Jonson masque. This arch (formed by two statues holding a globe) was devised only as a novelty for the particular production, and was not in any sense a permanent architectural feature, but its effectiveness was so marked that for almost every subsequent masque a temporary arch was erected in front of the curtain, and the tradition of the picture-frame stage was established.

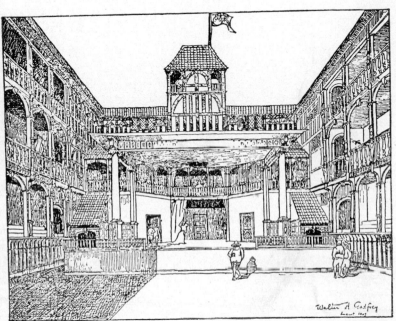

From Cheney's *Stage Decoration*.

Plate 17 : Godfrey's Reconstruction of the Fortune Theatre.

It should be noted, however, that the front curtain employed by Jones was not intended to conceal changes of scene or to mark divisions in the play. It was drawn open at the beginning of the performance, and not moved again until the end. It is a curious thing, but this limited function of the curtain was a characteristic of the English stage for nearly two centuries. Not until the nineteenth century did the curtain really come to play the important part which we assign to it today.

Not the least of the problems which confronted this pioneer of stage-craft was that of scene-shifting. After a long series of experiments, Jones arrived at a system which was relatively satisfactory. He cut in his stage a series of grooves, running crosswise, and in these he operated flats (i. e., flat pieces of scenery made by stretching canvas on wooden frames). Four or five of these grooves cut the stage at regular intervals from front to back, and in the ceiling were corresponding grooves in which were set borders of clouds, foliage, or whatever was required to match the flats resting on the floor. In this way the entire stage could be cut off by a series of sliding screens at any one of the stage levels, and could be opened to view again by withdrawing the screens from the center into both wings. When the full depth of the stage was needed for the action, a drop was hung at the rear, and the flats were shoved out just far enough to form wings and provide side-entrances, as in the semi-modern woodland set, where a landscape back-drop is flanked at right and left by a series of three or more woodwings. We may safely say that the pastoral scene of Inigo Jones did not differ materially from the same scene of the modern realistic theatre, except that grooves have given way to stage-braces and overhead pulleys.

We find, then, that Jones and his associates were responsible for at least four distinct mechanical improvements in English theatricals: perspective in scene-painting, moveable scenery, the rising curtain, and the proscenium arch. But these improvements did not affect the public theatres of London until later. Not until the latter part of the century do we find them employed outside the court. This is partly explained, of course, by the fact that at the time Jones was doing his most significant work, the public theatres were declining. After 1620 legitimate drama fell out of public favor, and in 1642 the theatres were closed by government order. Had the mechanical renaissance occurred twenty years before it did, it would have coincided with the literary renaissance, and the story would be a different one. As things transpired it was inevitable that the splendid technical achievements of Inigo Jones should have to wait for a later flowering of the drama before they could be incorporated in popular theatrical tradition.

In 1643 Jones was dismissed from his court office because of his loyalty to the King, and his place was filled by his pupil and assistant, John Webb, who carried on the work where Jones left it, and played a considerable part in the establishment of the Restoration theatre. Jones died in 1652.

D'AVENANT AND THE DARK PERIOD

It is common to speak of the period between 1642 and 1660 as a complete blank in the history of the English theatre, and it is quite true that there was a minimum of activity while the Puritans were in power, but though the theatres were closed, men's minds were working, and plans were being laid for a new dramatic era. The person most vitally interested in things theatrical during those dark years was Sir William D'Avenant, a poet, playwright, and theatre manager. D'Avenant, who was alive to all that was going on in the world of the theatre, saw early in his career that the stage of the future would be devoted to elaborate scenic displays. He knew what a strong appeal such displays would make to the public, which had grown weary of the barren Elizabethan theatre, and had never tasted the joys of court spectacles. He saw, too, the popular possibilities of Italian opera, and of native plays filled with song and dance. In 1639 he had obtained a license to build an opera-house and produce his dramatic novelties, but before he could realize his ambition the Civil War put an end to his plans. Then, of course, came the closing of the theatres, and D'Avenant was left chafing under the restraining law.

But before the theatres were officially re-opened, this enterprising manager succeeded in getting several productions before the public. In 1656 he presented his opera "The Siege of Rhodes" on a temporary stage at Rutland House, and two years later he obtained special permission to stage two more operas in the old "Cockpit." Cleverly enough he convinced the authorities that there was nothing harmful in reviving the sacred art of the ancient Greeks and Romans (for opera was so considered), and in doing so he established a precedent that has been followed many times since, as any modern New Yorker who has attended "sacred concerts" on Sunday evenings in the theatres of Broadway will testify.

"The Siege of Rhodes" was a notable performance in more ways than one. It marked the appearance of opera in England, it introduced to the London public the new stagecraft, it broke the tradition which excluded actresses from public theatricals. Mrs. Coleman, who appeared in this production, was, so far as is known, the first English-woman to appear on the public stage. French actresses had been seen in London theatres as early as 1629, acting with touring French companies, but they had been hissed and hooted by the English audiences. Obviously, too, women had taken part in court masques and pageants, but these were in the nature of private theatricals, and it is also unlikely that they took important acting parts. It remains to the credit of D'Avenant to have established woman in the English theatre. One reason, perhaps, why the innovation met with relatively little opposition was that opera was considered less profane than legitimate drama; another was that women's voices were needed for Italian music; still another, that during the closed period of the theatres, boy actors had grown mature, and a new generation had not been trained to take their places as feminine impersonators.

THE RESTORATION THEATRE

D'Avenant did not have long to wait for official sanction of his activities, for in 1660 Charles II returned from exile in France, and was restored to the throne. In a grant of August 21st of that year, Charles authorized Thomas Killigrew and William D'Avenant to organize two companies of players, and to install them in suitable playhouses. While in France the King had developed a decided taste for the theatre, and during the years of his reign he indulged this taste to the full. He maintained a private theatre at Whitehall, and personally supervised the operation of the public theatres. He set the fashion for rhymed plays, acted as judge in all theatrical disputes, lent the actors his robes of state for costumes, and pressed his favors upon the actresses. He made Nell Gwyn (first an orange-girl in the theatre, later an actress) his mistress, and had children by her, bestowing upon them the titles of Lord and Duke. He was the first English sovereign to attend regularly the public theatres. He and his courtiers had absorbed from French life only those characteristics which inclined toward vicious gaiety, and they made the theatre a hotbed of aristocratic immorality.

The company headed by Killigrew was under the personal patronage of King Charles, and whatever playhouse it occupied was known as the Theatre Royal. D'Avenant's company was patronized by the King's brother, the Duke of York, and its house was called the Duke's Theatre. These two were the only licensed companies of players during the Restoration period. A few small troupes toured the provincial towns, but seldom if ever performed in London. Construction of two new theatres was begun at once: a Theatre Royal in Drury Lane (also called the Theatre Royal in Bridges Street, Covent Garden) for Killigrew, which was opened in April, 1663; another in Lincoln's Inn Fields for D'Avenant, opened in May, 1662. These new theatres were probably designed by John Webb, pupil of Inigo Jones, though they may have been based upon designs left by Jones himself. They were comparatively modern structures, roofed and well equipped. While they were building, the two licensed companies occupied make-shift theatres, among these being the old "Red Bull," the "Cockpit" in Drury Lane, and the Salisbury Court Playhouse.

In 1668 it was agreed that D'Avenant should have a new theatre, and plans for it were drawn by the architectural genius of the age, Sir Christopher Wren. In that same year D'Avenant died, but the new theatre was erected in Dorset Garden, and was occupied by the Duke's company in 1671. In 1672 the Theatre Royal in Drury Lane was destroyed by fire, and Killigrew's company withdrew to the Lincoln's Inn Fields house, where they remained while a new Theatre Royal, designed by Wren, was going up in Drury Lane. The latter house, costing four thousand pounds, was opened in 1674.

Competition between the two theatres was keen. Catering to virtually the same audience, they were obvious rivals, and neither spared time or expense in its attempt to outdo the other.

They took full advantage of the recent advances in stage mechanics, and built productions which were sensationally novel. Their repertoire included Shakespearian plays, heroic dramas by Dryden and other Restoration poets, and prose comedies of a realistic and highly sophisticated nature. In spite of the fact that only two theatres were in the market for their products, the playwrights of the period were extremely fertile, and an enormous number of new plays found their way onto the stage. The reason for this becomes clear when one realizes that the audiences of the time were drawn from a very limited circle—about four-fifths of every audience being composed of court ladies and gentlemen, and courtesans. The general public shunned the theatres as places of corruption, and only occasionally slipped into the gallery to get a view of the aristocrats and their light o' loves disporting themselves shamelessly in the pit and boxes. In other words, the same persons filled the theatre day after day, and they demanded a constant change of bill. It was unusual for a play to run for more than two or three performances, and not infrequently it was withdrawn after the first performance. This rapid change of program was excessively hard on the actors, and it was not very fortunate for the playwrights, inasmuch as it was customary to give the author of a play a percentage of the third day's receipts as his sole remuneration, and if the play did not reach a third performance, the author was left unpaid. The actors were abused in still another way: they were constantly harassed by unruly and intolerant auditors. Drunken noblemen not only hissed the play from the pit when they felt like it, but often made their way to the dressing-rooms (to which they had access on payment of a small fee), where they flirted with the actresses, and sometimes stumbled through the wings onto the stage proper, where they interrupted a scene, started a fight, or at least abused the actors until they were led or thrown from the stage. Fights among members of the audience (over women) were common, and more than once men were killed while a play was in progress.

Yet the actors, or at any rate some of them, maintained a high standard of acting. Thomas Betterton, leading man with the Duke's company, and the outstanding actor of his time, evidently upheld the dignity of the profession, and his rival, Michael Mohun, at the Theatre Royal, is said to have been a very capable performer. Among the actresses, Mrs. Bracegirdle is the most noted, with the exception of Nell Gwyn, whose reputation as a royal mistress has perhaps given her name a lustre that it would never otherwise have possessed.

The managers certainly were not free from trouble. They were responsible to the King for the financial success of their enterprises, yet they were hard put to it to collect the regular admission fees from a large number of the audience. It was the custom in Restoration theatres to collect a small fee from everyone who entered, then to pass among the audience after part of the performance had been given, and collect larger amounts (varying according to the seats occupied). This second fee was often dodged by auditors who moved artfully from place to place as the collector made his rounds. And even the door fee was avoided by the nerviest of the courtiers, who, with insolent bravado, forced an entrance or else insisted that the charge be "put upon the books." Such debts were seldom if ever paid, but if the manager complained to the King, he was apt to be reprimanded for daring to question the credit of a gentleman of the court.

SUMMARY

From the above survey it is apparent that during the closing years of the seventeenth century the theatre in England attained its maturity. For the first time in its history it possessed all the fundamentals of the modern theatre. It had an extensive repertoire of drama, romantic, classical, and realistic; it had well organized companies of actors, comprising both men and women; it had beautifully designed playhouses, and well equipped stages with moveable scenes and elaborate machinery for spectacular effects. The Renaissance had finally transformed every branch of English theatrical art, and had laid permanent foundations for its future development.

SELECTED REFERENCES

Hundreds of books contain matter relevant to this subject. The most complete and authoritative account of the English theatre to the death of Shakespeare is Chambers' *The Elizabethan Stage.* Other standard references of a similiar nature are Thorndike's *Shakespeare's Theater,* Adams' *Shakespearean Playhouses,* and Lawrence's *The Elizabethan Playhouse.* There are several biographies of Shakespeare. A standard one is Lee's *A Life of William Shakespeare.* A valuable study of staging is Poel's *Shakespeare in the Theatre.* A book which contains, besides a good summary of the Elizabethan theatre, a valuable chronological table and a useful bibliography, is Schelling's *Elizabethan Playwrights.* The clearest and most authoritative discussion of the Restoration stage is contained in Nicoll's *Restoration Drama.* For a splendid survey of the work of Inigo Jones see Campbell's *Scenes and Machines on the English Stage.* For a biography of the leading actor of the Restoration see Lowe's *Thomas Betterton.*

CHAPTER XIII

THE RENAISSANCE IN OTHER EUROPEAN COUNTRIES

THE Renaissance theatre belongs almost entirely to Italy, France, Spain and England. No other European country gave birth to a significant theatrical art until the eighteenth century. There were, however, during the sixteenth and seventeenth centuries various manifestations of the dramatic impulse at work in Germany, Russia, and Scandinavia, and these manifestations, largely inspired by foreign example, laid the foundations for later theatrical developments.

GERMANY

Germany was not wanting in mediaeval theatricals. She had her miracle plays, her farces, her folk-song-and-dance plays, her religious processions, and her minstrels. Around the city of Nuremberg, in particular, the amateur drama flowered during the fourteenth and fifteenth centuries. Here were composed and performed by townspeople the pieces known as Shrovetide plays, made up of song and dance and dialogue, oftentimes excessively vulgar, and generally satirical of peasant life. The authors of these crudities are nearly all unrecorded, the two exceptions being Hans Rosenplüt and Hans Folz, both of the fifteenth century. Their names, however, are insignificant today. The first important name in the history of the German theatre is Hans Sachs.

Sachs, called the father of German drama, was born in

1494, the son of a tailor. As a boy he was apprenticed to a shoemaker, and learned from him the trade that he followed all his life. Possessed of a roving disposition, he traveled much during his youth, and visited Vienna, Cologne, Munich, and other large cities, cobbling as he went, and indulging at the same time in musical and dramatic activities. At the age of twenty-two he returned to his native city, Nuremberg, and devoted himself to a reformation of German drama. It is interesting to contemplate the fact that at the very time this young shoemaker was pressing his ardent idealism into the service of the drama, another idealist, even more ardent, was heading a religious movement which was destined to make his name immortal. The Reformation (which resulted in the establishment of the Protestant church) was the fruit of Martin Luther's labors. The efforts of Sachs bore no such mighty results, but they are not to be ignored in a history of the theatre.

Sachs had no professional companies of actors to inspire him. The only dramatic organizations were those sponsored by the trade-guilds or by the church. Nevertheless, he composed approximately two hundred plays, in addition to a large number of fables, epic poems, songs, et cetera. He was not a man of classical training, yet he felt vaguely the influence of the classical movement, and frequently made use of Greek themes. He reflected somewhat, too, the form of the classic drama, for he divided many of his plays into acts—a habit hitherto unknown in Germany. His plays never achieved a high degree of unity or compactness, but they were definitely advanced in technique over the compositions of his predecessors. Everything, old and new, was grist for his mill. He used Biblical material, folk legend, classical motifs, and contemporary realistic themes with impartiality, and all too frequently, from the aesthetic point of view, mixed them into plays. He was, therefore, in essence a mediaeval writer, for he did not hesitate at incongruity. On the other hand he is best considered a transition figure from the Middle Ages to the Renaissance, for he took the first steps in the direction of classical revival.

The companies directed by Sachs and his contemporaries had no actual theatre in which to work. They performed in convents, in inn-yards, and in churches. They had little or no scenery, but they laid great stress on good acting. Under the thumb of the church, they were allowed to give performances only between Epiphany and the beginning of Lent (from January 6th to the fortieth day preceding Easter). The price of admission to their shows was regulated also by the church. This state of affairs existed throughout the sixteenth century in Germany. Sachs died in 1576, the very year in which the first theatre building was erected in London, and long after professional companies had been formed in Italy. It was many years after Sachs' death before the German theatre was organized and placed upon a firm foundation.

It would have been natural for the theatre to rise in Germany at the beginning of the seventeenth century, but events ran counter to such a logical development. Internal strife was the chief obstacle. The Thirty Years' War (1618–1648) consumed the energies of the people, and left the country in a completely exhausted condition. It also left it divided into a large number of autocratic principalities, each with its miniature court and its provincial prejudices. While London and Paris were centralizing the activities of the English and French, no city was doing a like service for Germany. Without an intellectual and artistic metropolis, the German theatre could scarcely come into existence. The various courts were, it is true, eager to emulate the brilliant court of France, but no one of them possessed the money or the necessary number of gifted persons to do so.

Into this country divided against itself came from time to time during the seventeenth century the theatrical troupes of Italy, France and England. Elizabethan tragedy vied with the *Commedia dell' Arte* for German favor, and both won their place. Many of the foreign companies were so well received that they stayed on for long engagements at certain of the courts. Gradually Germans worked their way into these visiting troupes, learned to act, and eventually formed companies of their own. They contributed to the repertoire some of their own farces, too. There had developed during the sixteenth century in Germany a type of play known as the Hanswurst play, or Pickelherring play, a crude slapstick variety of drama taking its name from the low-comedy character around which the action centered. Hanswurst or Pickelherring fitted in not so badly with the clowns of the Italian comedy, and for many decades held first place in the hearts of German audiences. In Vienna he was transformed into Kasperl and Jackerl, characters who still appear in farce and puppet-shows.

In the latter part of the seventeenth century, then, the Germans began to organize their theatre. At first, however, it was a motley affair. From the English it took a bombastic style of delivery, from the French its deportment (formal and rigid), and from the Italians its notions of scenery and stage mechanics. The three classical scenes: palace, cottage, and wood, made their inevitable appearance, and though they were executed poorly, they served the purpose, and gave the Germans something better than they had ever had before.

By the end of the century German companies were not only touring their own country, but were venturing into Russia and Scandinavia. They had no definite native tradition, but they had plenty of imported examples from which to draw, and they were at least making the effort which was necessary as a first step toward something truly representative of their ideals. They had as yet no playwrights of great ability, but they had translations of English and French masters, and between these they could always insert a Pickelherring play. The actors were poorly paid, were despised by the respectable, were forced to endure unbelievable hardships, and were not united by the bonds of any common principles, but they were intrepid, and they paved the way. In the eighteenth century the German theatre emerged from this dramatic chaos.

RUSSIA

In Russia during the sixteenth and early seventeenth centuries there existed the usual precursors of the professional theatre: individual performers, such as minstrels and jesters, religious groups performing crude miracle plays, and educational groups performing Latin comedies. These activities, however, did not give rise to any native drama or to any native tradition of acting. About the middle of the seventeenth century the Russian court first began to reflect the taste of southern capitals, and to feel the need of a national theatre. Consequently in 1660 the Tsar Alexis, who had hitherto looked askance at such frivolity, decided to emulate his neighbors and acquire a company of court players. He commissioned an Englishman to organize the company, but for various reasons the commission was not executed. In the first place, there were no Russian actors available for such a company, and in the second place, it was difficult to entice foreigners to far-off Moscow. The plan was temporarily abandoned.

In 1672 another attempt was made to establish a court theatre. Actors from Copenhagen were engaged, but they did not fulfill the engagement. Conditions in semi-barbarous Russia did not appeal to them. Before the year was over, however, a German named Grigori, a resident of Moscow,

came to the rescue and organized a company of his country
men under the Tsar's patronage. A special wooden hal
was erected for the performances, and was opened in Octo
ber, 1672. These comedians, whose repertoire consistec
mostly of typical German farces, continued to act there fo:
four years, until the death of the Tsar.

Toward the end of the century Peter the Great, whc
became Tsar in 1682 at the age of ten, revived interes
in theatricals, and cultivated this art as he did all the
civilized institutions of the more advanced European coun
tries. He built a new theatre in Moscow, and encouragec
native acting. His encouragement, however, was slow ir
gaining results, and for a long time German actors anc
German plays were the only fare at the Russian court.
The plays were performed in the German language, anc
consequently were only slightly understood by the audience
It was found advisable, ere long, to close up the theatre
In one sense the movement had failed, but in another i
had succeeded, for, although it did not lead immediately
to the establishment of a native professional theatre, it a
least instilled in the upper classes a taste for the drama
and in the half-century which followed, amateur dramatics
flourished among the aristocrats, and private theatrical:
became the vogue. When, in the course of the eighteentl
century, the Russian theatre came into being, it had, as a
result of these early strivings, a somewhat fertile soil ir
which to send down its roots.

SCANDINAVIA

In Sweden, during the middle ages, folk-plays had flour
ished, and these, during the sixteenth century, had giver
way gradually to religious and school plays, the latter, o:
course, being chiefly Latin classics. Early in the seventeentl
century the religious drama waned, and was supplanted by

the secular drama with classical theme. About 1650 the French influence became apparent, with the result that in court circles, poetic allegory and ballet-performances held sway, while at the universities classical tragedies were produced. In 1660 a theatre was built at Upsala Castle, and a company of amateurs installed therein. The life of this company was brief, but it was replaced in 1686 by another troupe of similar standing, which after a time moved to Stockholm and played publicly for several years. Until the close of the century dramatic interest was reasonably strong in Sweden, though it appears to have given rise to no very well-organized profession. Thereafter, although poetry was cultivated, drama declined rather than advanced.

In Denmark and Norway a rather similar state of affairs existed, except for the fact that at the Danish court during the seventeenth century it was customary to engage French and Italian companies to give regular performances. The common people, without access to the court, contented themselves meanwhile with exhibitions by touring German companies. It is probable, too, that an occasional English troupe ventured into the Scandinavian countries during this period. Norway had not as yet obtained her independence from Denmark, and therefore had no artistic life of her own. It was not until the eighteenth century that a Danish-Norwegian drama was established.

SELECTED REFERENCES

The beginnings of native theatrical art in Germany are traced in Mantzius' *History of Theatrical Art*. Notes on the rise of the theatre in Russia may be found in Bakshy's *The Path of the Modern Russian Stage*. Occasional bits of information concerning the theatre in Scandinavian countries are to be found in literary histories.

CHAPTER XIV

THE EIGHTEENTH CENTURY

AN AGE OF ACTORS

I T has been remarked by nearly every historian of the theatre that the eighteenth century was a period of great actors. The statement is certainly true. The Renaissance had given most of the European theatres a well-equipped physical theatre, a repertoire of worthy plays, and a wide-spread interest in theatricals. The stage was set, and it was time for the actor to appear.

We must not forget, however, that the eighteenth century was also a period of great scenic art and mechanical ingenuity. The elaborate settings and machines devised by Italian artists and technicians during the seventeenth century had established a tradition, and that tradition persisted for more than a hundred years. Torelli had taken it to Paris; Bibiena passed it on to his sons and his grandsons, who in turn carried it all over Europe. The Bibiena family, most famous of all scenic artists, created settings so enormous in size and so rich in ornate detail that mere drawings of them shock the eye and bewilder the imagination. Judged by modern standards they are architectural monstrosities; judged by post-Renaissance standards they were superb. Baroque art may some day return to favor. If it does, the Bibienas will again be gods.

ITALY

Although we have subscribed to the common assertion that the eighteenth century was primarily an age of great actors, we must admit that when we think of the Italian theatre of that period we do not think of actors, but rather of scenic artists and a playwright. The Bibienas and Goldoni. That there were excellent actors on the Italian stage must not be doubted, but none of them stands out as a world-figure, and in this narrative we must concern ourselves with major theatrical forces. Goldoni was the first great Italian playwright—he is still the greatest Italian playwright.

That Italy should not have produced a dramatist of the first rank until so late a period may seem strange, but the fact becomes less unaccountable when we consider that during the Renaissance Italian theatrical genius had been poured into three molds, neither of which was designed to bring into being the highest type of drama. First, there was the classical literary movement, sponsored by the academies, which bore dead imitations of antique drama; second, there was the *Commedia dell' Arte,* which achieved superb success at home and abroad, but which depended largely on improvisation and upon clever dumb-show, and therefore could not, so long as it retained its true nature, evolve into complete and well-made drama; third, there was the opera, constantly attaining greater and greater vogue, and dividing into several types. In opera the emphasis is inevitably upon the music; librettos may be good or bad, but they are seldom worth much without the score. And still another reason why Italian drama was slow in forming was that during the Renaissance Italy was a strongly divided country. It was composed of many independent provinces and city-states, and lacked, therefore, a national consciousness. It even lacked a pure national language, for although the dialects of various localities had a common foundation, they diverged considerably, and in that way seriously affected the progress of Italian literature.

So much for the background. Carlo Goldoni was born at Venice in 1707, the son of a rather eccentric physician. He was educated at various schools, and finally was prepared for the law. But from boyhood his chief interest was the theatre, and he began composing plays while he was still at school. At the age of fourteen he ran off from Rimini with a troupe of players, but was soon reclaimed by his parents. He took part in amateur theatricals whenever opportunity allowed, and although he did not aspire to the profession of actor, he found it impossible to stay far away from the theatre. He wrote every conceivable kind of work for the stage. Under the influence of Renaissance drama- tists, he tried his hand at poetic tragedy, but met with cold failure when he showed the results to producers. He then essayed the opera, a most tempting field from a remunera- tive standpoint, but he was soon convinced that he knew too little of operatic traditions to succeed in that line. Finally he caught his real inspiration. He realized, after a thorough study of the situation, that what Italy needed was a realistic drama. With Molière as a guardian spirit, he began to compose comedies of the life about him, draw- ing deeply from his own experience, and depicting character with sharp, clear strokes. His plays caught on, and he at- tached himself by contract to various managers, for whom he turned out plays with the regularity of an artisan. Oftentimes he travelled from town to town with the com- panies that were using his plays, and in that way broadened his experience. By the middle of the century he was well established as the leading playwright of Italy.

Goldoni attempted deliberately to reform the theatre of his native land. He attacked the conventions of the *Commedia dell' Arte,* and in the end succeeded in destroying their power. For this he has more than once been criticized, for the Comedy of Masks was a rare and delightful institu- tion, and far preferable to most types of theatre. But to

Goldoni it appeared too crude, too limited, and too weak in the portrayal of character. Goldoni loved the theatre, but he loved literature, and particularly that literature which mirrors life clearly. He did employ, to be sure, many of the stock figures of the Comedy of Masks, but he did so chiefly because they were essential in the minds of the actors and audiences for whom he was writing. He did not allow the masks to limit him; he altered their significance when he pleased, and greatly increased their range of expressiveness, thereby vitiating their fundamental power, and weakening the traditions which had secured them. Modern romanticists, therefore, are inclined to blame Goldoni for his reforms, even while admitting that he gave us, by way of recompense, some of the finest comedies ever written. Among these, the best known in English translation are "The Mistress of the Inn" (*La Locandiera*), and "The Liar." The great majority of his plays are not translated into English at all, partly because they contain so much dialect. He used the Venetian dialect most frequently, and permitted certain characters to speak nothing else. He even began the compilation of a dictionary of this provincial language, but became too bored with the task ever to complete it.

In 1761 Goldoni was invited to Paris, where he was to furnish plays for the Italian company located there. It is somewhat doubtful whether he would have accepted the invitation had things continued to go well with his affairs in Venice, but it so happened that at this time a rival of Goldoni's, Carlo Gozzi by name, had created a furore in the Venetian theatre with his dramatic fantasies, and Goldoni smarted so severely under Gozzi's success that he was in a proper mood to leave his native city and try his fortunes elsewhere. Gozzi hated Goldoni's realism, and Goldoni hated Gozzi's ridiculous romanticism. The fairy tale won the day temporarily, and Goldoni went to Paris, where he remained until his death more than thirty years later. In Paris things came none too easily to Goldoni. He was disappointed in the Italian company for which he was to write, and furthermore this company was gradually losing its hold on French favor. The dramatist found it difficult to earn enough money to support himself and his wife comfortably, and had to engage himself as tutor to some of the children of the royal family. In spite of his advanced age he mastered the French language, and had the temerity to compose two plays in it, both of which were performed by the Théâtre Français. Toward the end of his life he wrote his Memoirs, and retained up to the year of his death the liveliest interest in life and literature. When he died in 1793, he left behind him approximately two hundred and fifty compositions for the stage, most of them comedies. He was, therefore, the third most prolific playwright of whom there is record (Lope de Vega and Alexandre Hardi ranking first and second in that respect).

It might be imagined that Goldoni's Memoirs would supply us with ample information regarding the Italian theatre of the eighteenth century, but the fact is that in the whole work there are not a half-dozen specific details of the theatre. Goldoni knew the theatre, but he was not primarily interested in its mechanics or its history. He loved it for its gaiety, and for its humanity, but in his attitude toward it he was always the literary rather than the theatrical man.

He does tell us, however, that during his youth Venice had seven theatres, two of which were generally devoted to grand opera, two to light opera, and three to plays. He implies that this apportionment was a typical one. Again he informs us that in certain sections of Italy which were under control of the Pope, women were not allowed to perform in plays, and remarks on the fact that when he returned to Venice from school at Perugia (which was in the Pope's dominions) he saw women on the stage for the first time in his life. Being an ardent realist, besides a most enthusiastic admirer of pretty women, he could hardly fail to approve of this enlightened custom.

In spite of Goldoni, in spite of everything, opera carried all before it during the eighteenth century in Italy. Raised to a plane of dignity and brilliance early in the century by such men as Zeno and Metastasio, it captured the Italian theatre once and for all. The Italian is born a singer and a lover of music. His most natural dramatic expression is in opera, and for that reason opera has become for Italy what the bull-fight is for Spain—a truly national form of entertainment.

FRANCE

In the French theatre, meanwhile, things were following a normal course. Provincial touring companies were active, but the real center of theatrical interest was still the Comédie Française in Paris. This institution since 1680 had held a monopoly of the legitimate drama, and during the greater part of the eighteenth century it continued to hold it. Subsisting mainly on seventeenth century drama, it cultivated stilted manners, refined declamation, and costly dress at the expense of naturalness and originality. The scenery was not improved, spectators were still allowed to sit on the stage, and the theatre continued to be the fashionable resort of the aristocrats. Without competition and without fresh ideas, the Comédie Française passed through a period of decided decadence. Its routine was illuminated only now and then by a brilliant performer such as Adrienne Lecouvreur, a young woman who, after learning her art in the provinces, made her Paris début in 1717, and acted steadily at the Comédie Française until her mysterious death in 1730. This actress stands out in all accounts of the French stage because of the individuality of her style. Possessed of a sincere nature and abundant natural charm, she made a sharp contrast to the over-mannered and affected company that surrounded her. Unlike most of her colleagues she preferred tragedy to comedy, and was at her best in the plays of Racine.

In 1729 a new force was felt in the Paris theatre, for in that year Voltaire returned from three years' exile in England where he had been much impressed by the drama and theatrical customs. He had come under the spell of Shakespeare, for one thing, and also he had been forced to the conclusion that the French theatre harbored a host of absurd conventions. He immediately wrote a number of plays, conducted their rehearsals himself, and succeeded in instilling a reasonable degree of warmth in the cut-and-dried actors of the Comédie Française.

One of the things that Voltaire fought for was the recognition of the actor's profession as a dignified and honorable one. In this he succeeded slowly but surely. Largely as the result of Voltaire's constant propaganda, the French actor attained during the eighteenth century a social position which placed him for all time above the stigma of public scorn. The theatrical vice that Voltaire hated most was the habit of seating spectators on the stage. Attacking this long-established prerogative, he waged savage war upon it for thirty years, and in the end (1759) had the satisfaction of seeing his proposal enforced at the Comédie Française. This step, which meant remodeling the theatre, to say nothing of offending its snobbish patrons, was probably the most significant event in the French theatre during the century, for it left the stage free for the actor.

Another innovation ascribed to Voltaire is the claque, or group of invited guests at a first-night performance, whose duty is to applaud the play vigorously. The ethics of such

an institution may well be questioned, but the modern
theatre has made effective use of it, and tradition has sanc-
tioned it. It is hardly probable that Voltaire was the first
playwright to safeguard the reception of his play in this
manner, but it may well be that he was the first to handle
the claque efficiently and establish it as a recognized theatrical custom.

The Comédie Française in 1750 had seventeen actors
and nine actresses in its regular employ. The outstanding
actor was Lekain, a protégé of Voltaire's, and a tragedian
of the first order. It was he who brought back to the French
stage the dignity that it had lost, and that Voltaire considered so desirable. About this time, too, comedy became
more refined, and a number of high-class comedians came
into public favor. Among these were Mlles. Gaussin and
Dangeville, and Messrs. Préville and Molé. The latter
acquired such a devoted following that in the year 1766,
when he was taken ill, and it was learned that his doctor
had ordered him to drink plenty of good old claret with
his meals, he received as gifts in one day as many as two
thousand bottles of wine.

In 1778 Voltaire, who had been living outside France
for a number of years, paid his final visit to Paris. He was
nearly eighty-four years of age, and was in very poor
health. He attended a special performance in his honor at
the Comédie Française, and was accorded an ovation
which has rarely been equalled in the theatre. He was
crowned with a wreath of laurel and hailed as the greatest
living Frenchman. Two months later he died, and his death
marked the close of a theatrical epoch.

Excellent as the theatre of Voltaire's time had been, it
was, after all, judged by modern standards, extremely affected and hide-bound by classical traditions. It had technique, but its technique was ill-adapted to the expression
of individuality. It was founded on the worship of form,

even as was the social life of the same period. Aloof and
aristocratic in point of view, it was doomed to change with
the social order. When the political revolution broke in
1789 with the storming of the Bastille, the theatre registered the shock, and never recovered its former composure.
Influences from without and within worked the transformation.

In 1791, for example, the National Assembly abolished
the long-standing state monopoly of the stage and drama,
and decreed that anyone could erect a theatre and perform
what plays he liked. For the first time in France since the
establishment of the professional theatre, therefore, the
theatre became a democratic institution. The result was
that whereas at the time of the revolution there were only
five theatres in Paris, by 1799 there were forty-five.

The Comédie Française was preponderantly conservative, and continued to act reactionary dramas in the old
manner. This tenacity of point of view led the company
into difficulties, for in 1793 a number of the players were
arrested on political grounds, and the theatre itself was
forced to suspend performances. In 1799 the company was
combined with that of the Théâtre Français de la Rue
de Richelieu, its chief rival (founded 1791 and established
in the Palais Royal), and allowed to resume production.
During the entire revolutionary period the theatre was a
hot-bed of political controversy. Plays were construed as
propaganda whether they were or not, and performances
frequently deteriorated into heated debates and actual riots.
No new plays of value appeared, however, for the simple
reason that there were no good playwrights.

The man who stands out above all the excitement and
change in the theatre of the revolution is François Joseph
Talma, born 1763, the son of a valet. As a boy he was
trained for the profession of dentistry, and actually practiced this profession in France and England during his years

From Nicoll's *Development of the Theatre.*

Plate 18 : Theatrical design by Giuseppe Bibiena.

of early manhood. But he was drawn to the stage, and after attending a French school of elocution, he made his début in 1787, and worked his way into small parts at the Comédie Française, specializing in tragedy.

Talma found himself out of sympathy with the classical actors of the Comédie Française because he was inclined toward naturalism, and insisted on developing his parts from that point of view. In a Roman play, for example, he startled his colleagues by performing with bare arms and legs (correct from an historical standpoint), whereas they followed the French custom of wearing contemporary court dress no matter what period or nationality the play. Eventually this annoying naturalism of Talma's got him ejected from the company, but meanwhile he had won favor with the public, and after considerable pressure on the part of his admirers, he was re-admitted to the Comédie Française.

By 1800 Talma was the leading French actor, and when Napoleon came into power (1804) he and Talma directed their energies to the elevation of their national theatrical art, Napoleon, with characteristic assurance, advising the actor how to play his parts. His advice, as a matter of fact, may have been helpful, for he seems to have cautioned Talma against the over-use of gesture and loud vocal exhibitions. He took particular pleasure in coaching the star in the rôle of Caesar, for reasons that are all too apparent. The Emperor's pride in the Comédie Française was so great that he frequently ordered Talma and the rest of the company to join him at his military headquarters, during foreign campaigns, there to display before the eyes of generals and princes the artistic glory of the Empire.

Talma's tragedy was that he lived at a time when France was barren of playwrights. He longed for a new drama that possessed reality and that was free from the restraints of seventeenth century classicism. Napoleon realized the lack, and ordered a national poet to arise. But the imperial summons was unheeded. The Muses demurred. In 1826, when Talma was sixty-three years old, and ill in the bargain, he was introduced to a fiery young man of twenty-four, who told him of a play he was writing. It had to do with Cromwell, and was to break with the stylistic traditions of the past, aiming at a realistic portrayal of human character. The young man was Victor Hugo. Talma was excited. The day for which he had waited was now at hand. Hugo went home to complete the play, but a few months later, before it was done, Talma died of a cancer. He had spent his life and the richness of his art on a drama that could not inspire him. The wave of romantic revolt, on which he could have risen so happily, then swept the French theatre.

SPAIN

In Spain the eighteenth century was a period of theatrical activity and experimentation, marked by conflicts between native and foreign types of drama, sharp clashes between church and theatre, and physical improvement of the theatre buildings. A large number of playwrights and critics favored the French type of drama (that is, the unified imitation of classic models) whereas others defended the romantic and loosely knit forms characteristic of Lope de Vega and Calderón. The former encouraged the acting of plays by Racine and Corneille, the latter supported the traditional Spanish melodrama and farce. The latter won the day. The most popular dramatist of the century was Ramon de la Cruz, (born 1731), who wrote several hundred pieces for the stage, most of them short sketches, in careless but witty verse. The outstanding actors were Moratin the elder, and his son Moratin the younger, who inclined toward the French manner, and who, with their studiously perfected style, made a strong impression on the public. Not a strong enough impression, however, to win popular favor away from the native tradition. It was, after all, the critics who cried up the French theatre as an example; the common people never accepted it.

Throughout the century theatres were closed by order of the church, only to be reopened when righteous indignation had subsided. Old plays were constantly being banned on the grounds of blasphemy, and many of them were dropped completely from the national repertoire. Good taste no longer permitted the curious mixtures of sacred and profane elements that had characterized many a sixteenth century masterpiece.

At the beginning of the century the open *corral* was still commonly used for plays, but gradually this type gave way to modern playhouses, entirely enclosed, and comfortably appointed. Impetus was given to physical improvement by Queen Isabel, who, in 1737, caused one of the *corrales* to be remodeled into an opera house after the Italian manner. Soon other *corrales* were subjected to similar alterations, and for a time opera was the vogue. But its ornateness had little appeal outside court circles, and it failed to take root in Spanish soil.

In summary it may be said that the eighteenth century in Spain represented the challenge of foreign theatrical styles, ending in their virtual defeat, and the triumph of the native tradition.

ENGLAND

In England the eighteenth century brought more than one significant change to the theatre. First of all, it changed it from an aristocratic to a middle-class institution. The court no longer ruled the stage. This meant that more theatres were built, more playwrights were developed, and the plays themselves became sentimental rather than cynical.

During the first half of the century eight important theatres were operated in London (not all at once, to be sure). These were: Drury Lane, Lincoln's Inn Fields (old house), Dorset Garden, Haymarket (also called Queen's Theatre, Opera House, and King's Theatre), Lincoln's Inn Fields (new house), Little Haymarket (also called French Theatre), Goodman's Fields, and Covent Garden. In addition to these principal playhouses there were a dozen or more of lesser importance devoted to operas, puppet-shows, and minor theatricals.

It was during this period, too, that playhouses made their appearance in smaller cities. Fashionable resorts, such as Bath, Richmond, and Tunbridge Wells, had their show-halls and booths during the summer months, and traveling companies made the rounds of them, playing the latest London successes. Dublin became a theatrical center, and contributed both actors and plays to the English stage. Even Scotland, inhibited heretofore by Puritanism, allowed the theatre to cross its border and profane its sanctimonious atmosphere.

Changes in the physical structure of the theatre and in the methods of mounting plays were not extraordinary, however. It was a time of expansion rather than of alteration. The closing years of the seventeenth century had seen the English stage pretty well equipped with settings and machinery. The stage-apron was cut down slightly, but it remained an important place for action; the proscenium doors (opening onto the apron) continued in use; the front curtain was still used to open the play, but not to mark scenes or acts, and was not always used even at the end of the play; flats or curtains were drawn laterally across the stage (in the Inigo Jones manner) to conceal or reveal tableaux; the Italian trinity of palace, cottage, and wood-land sets still reigned, and most of the stage designers were Italians or Frenchmen. Old manners obtained, too, in costuming. Period dress was sketchily, if at all, suggested. Women invariably wore eighteenth century hoop-skirts regardless of the nature of the play, whereas men compromised and achieved a ludicrous mixture of antique and contemporary style. They were consistent in one thing (at least in enacting tragedy) and that was that they always wore plumed head-dresses.

The audience of the time, though numerically greater, was not so much better behaved than its seventeenth century predecessor. The gallery was still filled with rowdies, the pit with flirts, and the wings of the stage with privileged spectators. Fashionable young men made a practice of attending first-nights and hooting the play off the boards, with the result that the claque was resorted to by authors in self-protection. Riots over prices were common, and fights between members of the audience not uncommon.

Plays, as has been indicated, were written with more sentiment than had been employed in Restoration days, and the dialogue was far less sophisticated. On the other hand, playwrights and producers found more than one way of catering to the vulgar, and what the dialogue lacked in spice was made up for by entr'acte dancers imported from the Continent, or by pretty young actresses dressed in boys' attire. The modern leg-show (though it has evolved considerably since) is of eighteenth century origin.

Of the lighter forms of theatrical entertainment, especially of the Continental variety, Christopher Rich was the chief sponsor. Following the lead of Sir William D'Avenant, he imported Italian and French novelties, operatic, acrobatic, *et cetera,* and succeeded in developing among London playgoers a real demand for that sort of thing. His son John, who succeeded his father as manager when the latter died, was the first English Harlequin, and instigated a type of pantomime (not all dumb-show, but a medley of song, dance, dialogue, and trick scenic effects) which endured in the English theatre until the beginning of the present century, when it gave way to modern vaudeville, burlesque and musical revues. Young Rich acted under the name of "Mr. Lun" (the name of a famous French clown).

In 1714 the elder Rich built a new theatre in Lincoln's Inn Fields (to supplant the older one there), and took considerable pride in its decorations and appointments. But in November of that year, when the house was virtually completed, he died, and it was left for his son John to superintend the opening, which took place in December. For a number of years thereafter Lincoln's Inn Fields Theatre was highly successful commercially, and proved a serious rival, with its pantomimes, to the legitimate attractions at Drury Lane. Its productions were often considered cheap, but occasionally we may be sure they were far from that. For example, in 1728 it housed the production of the first true English opera, "The Beggar's Opera," written by John Gay. This piece, which has served as model to so many composers and librettists, and which has been revived in our own time with such tremendous success, ran continuously for sixty-two performances, establishing a new record in the English theatre, and making, as the quip has it, "Gay rich, and Rich gay." The piece satirized not only the Italian opera, which had been encroaching on English drama, but English politics as well, and therefore gave rise to much controversy. More than one of its witty barbs was aimed at Sir Robert Walpole, Prime Minister (identified with the character of Lockit), and although Walpole did not take steps to close the production he nevertheless paid off the score by refusing permission for a performance of the sequel to "The Beggar's Opera," namely, "Polly," which Gay wrote immediately after his success with the first piece.

The Little Theatre in the Haymarket went in for novelties, also, and was a kind of catch-all for the theatrical odds and ends of the time. Opened in 1720, it was devoted chiefly to opera and pantomime until 1766, when it came under the management of Samuel Foote, the comedian trained by Garrick at Drury Lane, and was legitimatized. It was this theatre which in the seventies fell into the hands of George Colman the elder, who kept it on a high plane and increased its popularity.

But it is of the great actors of the eighteenth century that the most has been written, and it is the actors who have given their names to the periods which compose it. The first of these is Colley Cibber.

Cibber made his début in 1690 (at the age of 19), under the greatest of Restoration actors, Thomas Betterton. The young man is reported to have failed miserably in executing the small part assigned to him, but because of his amusing personality was allowed to stay on in the company. Presently it was perceived that his eccentricities were adapted to comic rôles, and that by exaggerating his own defects he could move an audience to hysterical laughter. He had a piping, ridiculous voice, an impossible memory, and an unheroic figure, but he was a remarkable mimic, and an excellent manager. He also had the gift of writing successful comedies. The result was that he became the most popular person in the English theatre, and the first three decades of the eighteenth century are commonly called the Cibber Period.

In 1714 Cibber, with two other actors, Robert Wilks and Barton Booth, acquired control of Drury Lane Theatre, and operated it for a number of years under a license granted by King George to Sir Richard Steele, who acted as supervisor and was responsible for the moral character of the plays presented. Cibber was chief comedian in his own company, Wilks was romantic leading man, and Booth the tragedian (supreme in that field after the death of Betterton in 1710). In the same company were two excellent actresses, Mrs. Oldfield and Mrs. Porter. This group flourished and prospered, and for more than a decade preserved a unity that won for them the loyal admiration of London playgoers. But in 1728, with the retirement from the stage of Booth, their fortunes began to decline. In 1730 Mrs. Oldfield died, and in the following year Mrs. Porter became an invalid. In 1733 Cibber himself retired and sold his interest in Drury Lane, though he did not die until 1757, when he was eighty-six years of age.

For a few years following the disintegration of Cibber's company the London stage was not dominated by any single personality, and is therefore referred to as a period of transition. The outstanding actors were James Quin, an all-round actor of the old school, and an incomparable Falstaff; Charles Macklin, his rival, who is said to have been the founder of naturalistic acting; and Kitty Clive, one of the most celebrated comediennes in the history of the English theatre, and of whom the great Dr. Johnson said: "She was a better romp than any I ever saw in nature." Drury Lane Theatre itself suffered from bad management at this time. When Cibber gave over control, it fell into the hands of a Mr. Highmore, who was a dabbler, and whom the actors hated. A short time later it passed to a Mr. Fleetwood, wealthy and only twenty-one years of age, who did not improve matters much. But during the Fleetwood régime occurred an event so significant that it must be reported in some detail.

On October 19, 1741, handbills were circulated in London announcing a performance of Shakespeare's "Richard III" at Goodman's Fields Theatre, the title part to be filled by "A Gentleman who never appeared on any Stage."

The performance was duly given, and the incognito "Gentleman" created a sensation which has rarely been paralleled. He was none other than David Garrick, twenty-four years of age, the son of a wine merchant, French and Irish in blood, a little under middle size, and very handsome.

It was not really true, incidentally, that he had "never appeared on any stage." For several years he had acted in amateur performances, and under assumed names in professional theatres (notably in the provincial house at Ipswich), but without attracting any particular attention. It testifies to his innate business sense that he served his apprenticeship incognito in order that he might burst suddenly forth in his own name, a full-blown actor.

Sensing his power, and consumed with ambition, Garrick now launched a series of Shakespearian and contemporary plays, instilling new life into familiar rôles, and astonishing all London with his versatility. From the beginning he ignored the traditions of acting, broke all the rules, eliminated the "grand manner" of his predecessors, and humanized Shakespeare's characters as they had never before been humanized. He reached Lear when he was only twenty-five!

Goodman's Fields could not hold such a star. He was hired by Fleetwood for Drury Lane, and moved there in 1742, at a salary of six hundred guineas yearly (a large sum for that time). There he ran counter to Macklin, who resented Garrick's sudden rise to prominence. When the smoke of battle lifted, Macklin was out of Drury Lane, and Garrick was firmly established. At this time he formed the acquaintance of Peg Woffington, a clever Irish actress, and that acquaintance became a love affair, which did not, however, culminate in marriage, as Peg seems to have hoped it would.

Fleetwood was a spendthrift and soon was in arrears

with his actors' salaries. Garrick, a natural leader, and always hasty of action, went out on strike for three weeks in the spring of 1743, and persuaded most of the company to follow him. Fleetwood promptly hired other actors to fill their places. Garrick tried in vain to find financial backing for an opposition theatre and ended by compromising with the manager over the salary dispute. But he was still dissatisfied, and two years later left for Dublin where he was enthusiastically received by Irish audiences. On his return to London, a short time later, he accepted an engagement at Covent Garden (since its opening in 1732 chief rival to Drury Lane) under the management of John Rich. Here he met opposition in the person of Quin, who, like Macklin, resented Garrick's popularity and insistence on leadership. But Garrick had his way, as always, and ruled the Covent Garden company with a strong hand. Even this situation did not satisfy his craving for power. He wanted a theatre of his own. He did not have long to wait, for in 1747 he discovered that the Drury Lane patent was on the market. Together with James Lacy he bought it, his half interest costing eight thousand pounds. He had saved some money; the remainder he borrowed. So at the age of thirty he was the leading actor and the chief theatrical manager in England.

He organized what was very likely the most brilliant company of players ever assembled. Some of them he had inherited with the theatre, the others he trained. His ideal was that of a perfect ensemble (an ideal realized in our own time by the Moscow Art Theatre) and he achieved his aims by working himself and his company to the limit of their endurance. By nature he was a tyrant, but the sort of tyrant who inspires love, and whose ends seem to justify the means. In spite of the exacting duties of managership and leading rôles, he found time to compose forty-odd plays of his own and many of them proved great successes

From Cheney's *Stage Decoration*.

Plate 19: Drury Lane in 1778. Production of *The School for Scandal.*

in the theatre, though none of them is marked by real literary genius. He continued his Shakespearian repertoire, and kept that rich body of drama alive to the people of the eighteenth century.

At the age of thirty-two he married an Austro-Italian dancer named Eva Maria Violetti, with whom he lived happily all his life.

In September, 1763, tiring somewhat of the grind of Drury Lane, and anxious to add new lustre to his name, he embarked on a grand tour of the Continent. He and his company played in all the principal cities of Europe, and were accorded royal receptions everywhere. When he returned to London in April, 1765, he brought with him certain ideas for the improvement of the theatre, and chief among these was a new notion of stage lighting, namely, the use of footlights, suggested to him by French and Italian theatres. It was his opinion that the introduction of footlights would allow the removal of the large chandeliers previously hung above the heads of the actors, and would therefore improve the visibility of the stage from the auditorium. His plans were put into effect at Drury Lane and met with general approval, though there may have been some who felt what modern producers have come to realize, that the footlight has serious disadvantages unless used very moderately. Garrick also had installed groups of lights in the wings (invisible to the audience) using altogether three hundred lamps on the stage. The auditorium was lighted by two hundred and seventy wax candles.

Although he remained active manager of the theatre, Garrick gave up acting on his return from the Continent. He was well-off and no doubt felt that his tour constituted a climax to his career. But the public clamored for his return to the boards, and six months after his return to London he was served with a royal request (from King George III) to resume acting. To this request he acceded, and from then until 1776 he filled his old rôles, but did not create any new ones. In the latter year he gave a series of farewell performances, and at their close retired definitely. He died January 20, 1779, leaving a considerable fortune to his wife, who survived him many years.

It is thought by most authorities that David Garrick did more than any man before or since his time to elevate the art of the theatre. He not only carried his personal art to a pinnacle of excellence, but he ennobled the entire business of the theatre with his ideals of management and production. His influence extended far beyond the confines of his own country, and may be traced throughout the theatres of all Europe. His death, said his friend, Dr. Johnson, "eclipsed the gaiety of nations."

But before the light of Garrick's genius faded from the scene another, almost as brilliant, showed on the horizon. Richard Brinsley Sheridan, a young Irishman from Bath, whose father was Thomas Sheridan, a veteran provincial show-man, and whose mother was a writer of plays, set about to get control of Drury Lane. Young Sheridan (born 1751) had already written a remarkably successful play, "The Rivals," which was produced in January, 1775, at Covent Garden under Colman's management, and had unbounded faith in his own ability. He persuaded his father-in-law, Dr. Linley (for Sheridan had recently married Elizabeth Linley, a singer) and two other friends to help him raise the necessary money, and by borrowing a large sum in addition to what these men contributed, he succeeded in achieving his purpose. The transaction involved an extraordinary amount of money, and probably more than a man of good business sense would have risked, but Sheridan was young and reckless.

In September, 1776, Drury Lane opened under the management of this young plunger, who immediately installed his father as stage-manager, his wife as keeper of accounts,

his father-in-law (who was a composer) as musical director, his mother-in-law as mistress of the wardrobe, and
himself as general supervisor and chief contributing playwright. Forthwith he produced his new play, "The School
for Scandal," and won with that production not only a
great deal of money, but also a literary reputation which
reached throughout the world.

It must be remembered, when considering Sheridan's
overwhelming success in the theatre, that he had inherited
from Garrick's régime a matchless company of actors, and
in addition, the priceless good-will of the London public toward Drury Lane. The only contribution required of him
was sound management and new comedies. The first of
these he failed utterly to provide, and the second he provided for a very limited time, for he never wrote a play
after he was twenty-eight years of age. Spoiled with his
immediate success, and avid of social position and flattery,
he paid less and less attention to his theatrical obligations
and as time went on, became a virtual stranger to his own
company. In 1780 he stood for Parliament and was sent
there, distinguishing himself for many years as a political
debater and orator. He dressed magnificently, dined with
the élite, drank much, gambled extensively and lived always
beyond his income. The box-office of Drury Lane was the
bank on which he drew, and more than once the actors
were left unpaid because he drained the till. Nor was this
his company's only grievance; they could not stand the
tyranny of the elder Sheridan, and eventually the young
manager was forced to discharge his own father. As a matter of fact the new stage-manager, one Thomas King,
proved little better, so for some time there was disquiet
behind the scenes.

Drury Lane Theatre, meanwhile, was decaying physically. The old building, designed by Sir Christopher Wren,
had stood for more than a hundred years, and was in a

serious condition. In 1791, therefore, Sheridan had the house pulled down, and a new, larger and better equipped building erected in its place. Old Drury Lane had seated approximately two thousand persons; New Drury Lane seated thirty-six hundred. The auditorium of the new building was fifty-six feet high from floor to ceiling, the proscenium arch was forty-three feet wide and thirty-eight feet high. The stage-lighting system was largely concealed from view, the exceptions being two handsome chandeliers hung in the proscenium. Elaborate precautions were taken against fire: an iron curtain (forerunner of the modern asbestos) was hung in the proscenium, water-taps were numerous, and the stage was so devised that it could be turned into a veritable lake. In fact at the opening of the theatre, March 12, 1794, the stage *was* turned into a lake, and a man rowed a boat around it to impress the audience with their safety from fire.

The ironical sequel to this opening night display occurred on February 24, 1809, when the theatre caught fire. Sheridan was at the time on the floor of the House of Commons, debating on the subject of the war with Spain. Word of the fire was brought to him, but he refused to give over his debate. When his oratory subsided, at two o'clock in the morning, he walked to Drury Lane and discovered the smoking ruins of his only financial asset. He was completely ruined. He attempted to raise money enough among his wealthy friends to restore the theatre, but his reputation as a gambler and spendthrift worked against him, and he was forced out of the theatre business for good. A fund to rebuild Drury Lane was soon thereafter raised by Samuel Whitbread, a brewer, and the new house opened in 1812, its cost totalling, it is said, the huge sum of four hundred thousand pounds.

Sheridan was a bankrupt until the day of his death in 1816. Up to the very end he played the beau, moved in high social circles, borrowed from his sporty friends whenever possible, and so kept up appearances. But he was in many ways a pitiable figure, particularly to those who realized what genius he had brought to the theatre, and how much of it he had thrown away.

We must now turn to a consideration of two other great personalities of the late eighteenth century English stage, two who, like Sheridan, lived on into the early years of the nineteenth century, but who belong chiefly to the eighteenth.

In the summer of 1775 David Garrick had heard from some friends that down in Cheltenham there was a touring company of players whose ranks included a young woman of great ability and charm. Garrick dispatched an assistant to the scene, who on his return reported that indeed the young woman was worth watching. Her name was Sarah Kemble Siddons, and she was twenty years of age. She was the daughter of Roger and Sarah Kemble (in whose company she had played since a child) and the wife of young William Siddons, an unprepossessing actor also in her parents' employ.

Garrick, after some further investigation of her merits, engaged her at five pounds a week to play at Drury Lane, and by way of a tryout, allowed her to appear as Portia in "The Merchant of Venice," in December of that year. But although fortune seemed to have turned upon her, Mrs. Siddons was doomed to bitter disappointment. Her début was a flat failure. She was a tall, slender young woman, rather gawky really, her voice was weak and unsuited to the large auditorium of Drury Lane, and her manner was coldly aloof. Garrick saw that she had possibilities, and that her restrained, classical manner could be brought to an effective point, but he was near to his retirement, and did not, we may assume, feel enough interest in her to undertake her development. He allowed her to stay on with the company for the season, but when Sheridan took over the theatre, Mrs. Siddons was not retained.

It was not a very pleasant experience for the gifted young actress, but she showed well the strength of character which came later to be recognized in her by everyone, and went back to her acting in the provincial theatres, determined to improve herself until she should be ready to try again before a London audience. For seven years she followed her old life, and in October, 1782, made her second début at Drury Lane. The Mrs. Siddons of this time was a far more mature person than the one who had failed under Garrick. She now had perfected her style, and was capable of creating an emotional effect such as the English theatre had seldom if ever experienced. She was still restrained, but hers was the restraint that suggests terrific reserve power, and that through its dignity and poise achieves sublime effectiveness.

Meanwhile Mrs. Siddons' older brother, John Philip Kemble (born 1757), had completed his education in France, and had gone to Dublin to enter upon his acting career. Sarah, soon after her London triumph, joined him in Dublin, and after a joint engagement there, they returned to London and became the principal actors at Drury Lane, John Philip's first appearance being in the rôle of Hamlet.

These two Kembles (there were a host of others, for they were part of a family of twelve children, most of whom went on the stage) were alike in most respects. John Philip was tall, handsome, and as coldly dignified as his sister. He lacked versatility, and no doubt would appear to a modern audience insufferably stiff and affected. But as is ever the way with the public, taste shifts from romantic to classic, and back again to romantic, *ad infinitum*. Garrick's flexibility and complete humanism had had its day— the Kemble style was a change, and it had its vogue. In

1788 Kemble succeeded King as stage-manager for Sheridan, and held that commanding position until the close of the century. He and his sister were, during the late eighties and nineties, undisputed sovereigns of the London theatre, and in the domain of tragedy their achievements were undoubtedly of the first order. They specialized in Shakespearian repertoire, and maintained toward the classical drama the grandest of grand manners.

In 1803 the Kembles could stand Sheridan's financial irregularities no longer, and with their brother Charles took control of Covent Garden, where they inaugurated a conservative and consistently successful régime. Among the actors in their employ was the famous George Frederick Cooke, a drunkard who was the real precursor of the wildly romantic school of acting, of which Edmund Kean became the most celebrated example. Cooke was opposite to Kemble in every way, and his "acting by inspiration" often disturbed the latter's poise and temper, but Kemble always made allowances for Cooke's vagrant ways, and treated him like a gentleman.

In September, 1808, Covent Garden Theatre burned down, bringing a great loss to the Kembles. Through the support of wealthy patrons, however, it was rebuilt at once and opened in September, 1809. Three years later Mrs. Siddons retired. Her farewell performance was as Lady Macbeth, and the effect of her sleep-walking scene was so great that at the conclusion of it the audience demanded that the play be stopped at that point in order that there might be no anti-climax to the magnificence of her triumph. After her retirement, the tragedienne lived the life of a stately dowager, honored and admired wherever she went. She died in 1831 at the age of seventy-six, and found a high place in theatrical annals not only because of the excellence of her acting, but also because she was the first English actress of prominence to lead a sane and virtuous life. No scandal was ever successfully linked with her name. She was also the first actress to have a public monument erected to her memory.

With the opening of the new Covent Garden in 1809 John Philip Kemble faced the ordeal of his life. Made necessary by the cost of the structure, a new scale of prices of admission had been put into effect. This rise the public vigorously denounced. On the opening night of the theatre the audience booed the actors and chanted in unison, "Old Prices! Old Prices!" so that the actors could not make themselves heard beyond the footlights. This racket was kept up the whole evening, with the result that "Macbeth" was played virtually in dumb-show, the actors stubbornly sticking to their guns. The Riot Act was read from the stage, but without result. On succeeding nights the disturbers reappeared, better organized than ever. The management had many arrested but others took their places. Bullies and prize-fighters were hired and stationed in the theatre to intimidate the objectors, but they could not be intimidated. Cow-bells, horns, and other noise-makers were used to augment the din. This terrible state of affairs continued for two months. On the sixty-first night Kemble came before the curtain and granted the demand for "old prices." It hurt his pride, but he was at his wit's end. So the stubbornness of the British public scored another victory.

Kemble retired in 1817, his farewell performance being in the rôle of Coriolanus. The ovation given him is said to have eclipsed even that accorded his sister five years before. He died in 1823.

THE ENGLISH PROVINCES

So much for London. Let us now take a moment to survey the spread of theatres throughout the provinces. The

most famous playhouse outside the metropolis was the
Theatre Royal at Bath. There had been some sort of theatre at this fashionable resort ever since 1700, though it
was not until the middle of the century that a house became
really profitable. In 1767 the existing building was reconstructed, and shortly after was granted Letters Patent by
George III, becoming thereupon a real Theatre Royal, and
the third in England to receive the title (Drury Lane and
Covent Garden having been first and second). Here the
most admired of London actors performed on occasion
before the highest society.

In Bristol the first theatre was opened in 1729 by John
Hippesly, a London comedian, but because of official opposition, the house was located a short distance outside the
city. In 1766 a theatre was built within the city, and two
years later received a Royal License. It offered performances only once a month in winter, and three times a week
in summer. Mrs. Siddons acted at Bristol (and at Bath)
frequently around 1780.

In Exeter a theatre opened in 1749, but proved a very
incommodious place, and did not attract much attention.
Plymouth had its first playhouse in 1758, Newcastle in
1789, Norwich in 1759, Sheffield in 1762, and Tunbridge
Wells in 1770. Liverpool had an unlicensed house toward
the middle of the century, but not a duly patented one until 1772. Brighton, a popular resort, had makeshift theatres throughout the century, but did not acquire a permanent house until 1744. In York a theatre was patented
in 1759, in Leeds, one in 1771, and in Leicester, one in
1750.

Three temporary theatres opened in Birmingham about
1740, but a good house was first constructed in 1752. No
Royal Patent was obtained in that city until 1807, about
the time that Edmund Kean and his wife were playing
there. In Manchester the Theatre Royal opened in 1775,

and the next year Mrs. Siddons played in it. This house burned down in 1789, but was rebuilt at once.

Other centers acquired theatres of their own during the latter half of the century, but the most important ones are listed above. Some of the provincial houses maintained, for at least a portion of the year, independent stock companies, which alternated between three or four adjoining towns, and were supplemented from time to time by visiting stars. In these circuits many of the greatest English actors of the eighteenth century got their early training, and many of them, too, after they had risen to stardom on the London stage, returned to the circuits to augment their incomes during lean months, and to renew acquaintance with audiences that had applauded them when they were "green."

SCOTLAND

In Scotland theatrical art had a hard row to hoe. Although Edinburgh was a large city, and might be thought to have proved profitable to showmen, there was in existence there too staunch a brand of Puritanism. It was not until 1736 that any effort was made to establish a legitimate Scottish theatre, and that effort met with fatal results. Taking over a booth erected a short time previously by Madame Violante, a French dancer, whose vogue was great throughout the British Isles, Allan Ramsay reconstructed it and began the presentation of plays. He was abused roundly by officials, and inside of six months was put out of business by a prohibitive licensing act. That was the end of plays in Edinburgh for a while. About ten years afterwards, however, a Concert Hall was opened in the city, and the astute manager began giving plays between the various musical numbers. In this way he dodged the licensing act, and gradually acquired a public following. In 1752 John Lee, an actor from Drury Lane, took over the management of the Hall, and brought the entire Haymarket company north for a theatrical season. When business was dull in Edinburgh he and his company paid visits to Glasgow, Newcastle, and Scarborough. But in the end he found the venture unprofitable, and cleared out, having lost all his money in an effort to entertain the Scotsmen. His place was taken by an intrepid Irishman named West Digges, who came from the famous Smock Alley Theatre in Dublin. His fate was not much better than that of Lee.

Eventually, in 1767, a Patent was obtained for the house, and it promptly became the Theatre Royal. The Patent was issued to David Ross, an actor who had had experience with Garrick. Possessed of legal authority, Ross was emboldened to build a new theatre, which he opened in December, 1769. To this house came at a later date Henry Siddons as manager, and Sarah Siddons as star. By the close of the century Edinburgh was in close theatrical communication with London, and although the four hundred intervening miles proved a considerable barrier to travel, many of the leading English actors went to the northern city during the summer months for special engagements. Slowly, very slowly, in fact, a few other Scottish cities established theatres, but in many large centers of population the actor never gained a foothold.

IRELAND

In Dublin conditions were much more favorable. There was a theatre (the first recorded) there in 1634, although it was closed by the authorities in 1641. In 1662 (coincident with the opening of the Drury Lane Playhouse in London) the most famous of all Irish theatres opened its door. This was the Smock Alley Theatre, a leading center of theatrical activity for more than half a century, on whose stage Robert Wilks and James Quin both made their début.

The first serious rival to the shows in Smock Alley was the renowned Madame Violante, with her dancing and acrobatic performances. Coming to Dublin in 1727 she remained for several years, and was excessively popular. One of her most famous performances was a children's production of "The Beggar's Opera," and it is interesting to note that the child who played Polly was Margaret ("Peg") Woffington, ten years of age, who later was to have all London in her train.

In 1734 the first rival legitimate playhouse was opened. This was the Theatre Royal, and to its boards came (later) guest actors from London, among whom was David Garrick. The two theatres were amalgamated in 1743, and Thomas Sheridan was installed as stage-manager, but later a split occurred and rivalry was resumed. The third Dublin theatre of importance was erected in 1758 in Crow Street by Spranger Barry, an Irish actor who later in his career moved to London, and became Garrick's most formidable rival. It was at this time, too, that Henry Mossop gained his fame in Dublin, and then went to London, where he entered Garrick's company, and earned for himself the title of one of the great actors of the eighteenth century.

From this time on there was an exceedingly close connection between the Dublin and London stages. Dublin invariably gave rousing welcomes to London performers of merit, and London was forced time and again to acknowledge its indebtedness to the city that sent it such brilliant actors and actresses.

GERMANY

As has been indicated in an earlier chapter, Germany, for several reasons, had been slow in acquiring a native theatrical system. The chief of these reasons was, it will be recalled, that the country possessed no large center of intellectual and artistic life. The eighteenth century remedied that situation, for in the early 1700's Leipzig became such a center. The movement began with the formation of poetry societies, whose ambition was to organize and promote German art and literature along lines already laid down by the French. The leading spirit in this movement was a young man named Gottsched, who was, it is to be feared, rather a prig, but who at least was intensely sincere about the whole business.

Into Leipzig came, at this opportune moment, a traveling company of German actors headed by Frederika Caroline Neuber and her husband, Johann. It was the year 1727. Mrs. Neuber was an actress of real ability, and possessed a considerable amount of business sense. She was ambitious to accomplish something great in a theatrical way, whereas Gottsched was only too eager to acquire a disciple. Between the two of them a plan was evolved for elevating the German drama and stage. The first conclusion they reached was that Mrs. Neuber's company should throw overboard the old folk-plays of which the common people were so fond, and perform instead, literary masterpieces. The chief obstacle in the way of such an idealistic program seemed to be that no German dramatic masterpieces existed. Gottsched solved that problem temporarily by proposing that French classics should be translated and offered to the German people until plays of similar worth should be forthcoming from native pens. Mrs. Neuber agreed, and with her company took to the road. But French masterpieces did not take so well as had been hoped, and the crusaders found it necessary generally to add a Harlequinade or a Hanswurst farce to the bill in order to satisfy their auditors. They fared best of all in Hamburg, perhaps because of the cosmopolitan character of the population, but even there they failed in the course of time, and in 1735 returned to Leipzig, in which vicinity they acted whenever interest warranted.

With Gottsched Mrs. Neuber continued to consult, until a quarrel arose between them in 1739, occasioned by the former's insistence that the company use a translation of a Molière play made by his wife. Mrs. Neuber, with the independence which she often asserted, preferred another translation, and used it. This insult Gottsched never forgave, and from that time on he attacked his former friend and colleague at the slightest opportunity. Mrs. Neuber shortly thereafter began another tour, stopping again at Hamburg, and going finally into Russia, where she met with failure because of the vogue for Italian opera which was then sweeping the Far North.

When Mrs. Neuber started on this tour she left behind her the chief comedian of her company, Schönemann. This actor, with his wife, promptly allied himself with Gottsched, and through his assistance, set up a company of his own, so that when Mrs. Neuber returned in 1741 she found herself supplanted. Undaunted, however, she entered the lists, and defied Gottsched's artistic tyranny in Leipzig. He had, as a matter of fact, become increasingly dogmatic and oracular. Seeing himself a German Boileau, an arbiter of taste and fashion, he regularly informed the public what it should and should not enjoy. Annoyed by Mrs. Neuber's independence, he issued a series of scathing critiques on her productions, and among other things objected to her custom of dressing plays of older periods (Roman, Greek, and the like) in contemporary style. It was really strange that Gottsched should have taken this view, for it was common in all European countries at the time to dress these plays in a modern manner, but he was looking for any possible ground on which to quarrel, and this, obviously, was a controversial point.

Mrs. Neuber, displaying a strategy which did honor to her sex and her profession, announced a performance of Gottsched's own play (so-called, though it was actually a steal from Addison) "The Dying Cato," in correct historical costume. The performance was duly given, and when the audience saw Romans dressed as Romans they howled with laughter. They had never seen anything so ridiculous on the stage. So Gottsched's pedantry was turned against him, and his power was partly broken. At least from that time on he was taken less seriously, and his other enemies took heart and joined Mrs. Neuber in her fight against his priggish dominance.

One of the far-reaching effects of Mrs. Neuber's productions in Leipzig was the influence they exerted on certain young men studying at the University. Among the students who got their first knowledge of the theatre from these performances were Weisse and Lessing, the latter becoming one of Germany's most renowned playwrights and dramatic critics. During the years 1746–48 Lessing was in constant touch with the Neuber company, and although he was only seventeen years old in 1746, he was nevertheless allowed to make translations for their use, and even had one of his own farces produced by them.

As Mrs. Neuber grew old she lost her grip on the business and gradually went from bad to worse. In 1753 she tried her fortunes in Vienna, but failed miserably. Six years later her husband died, and she survived him only one year. She died a pauper. But her example remained with the German people, and she deserves to be remembered as the first woman to succeed at all in elevating the art of acting in Germany, and in inspiring intellectual young men to write for the theatre.

Let us now return to trace briefly the fortunes of the company formed by Schönemann in 1740, when Mrs. Neuber set forth on her Russian tour. In this company were

Konrad Ernst Ackermann, a versatile but reckless young man, Sophia Schröder, a charming young lady who had deserted her husband (a drunkard) in Berlin, and fled to Leipzig, and Konrad Ekhof, a clerk who had no experience in acting, but who could not resist the lure of the stage. These, besides Schönemann and his wife, were the principals. The company made its début in the town of Luneburg, where there was no theatre building, a riding academy serving the purpose.

For a year the company held together and fared well. Then Ackermann and Sophia Schröder withdrew and formed their own company. They, too, went on the road. Schönemann, as the years went on, ceased taking an active part in his own company, and became a sportsman, caring more about his horses than about his actors. This indifference finally drove Ekhof out of the company, for the erstwhile clerk had come to take the art of the theatre seriously, and he had made such remarkable progress as an actor that he was actually become famous. So serious was he that in 1753 he founded what he termed an "Academy of Actors" (the membership made up of the actors of the company), before whom he lectured, and whom he instructed in the technique of the stage. His fellow "Academicians" did not, as might be guessed, take him as seriously as he would have liked, but the important thing is that Ekhof really knew what he was doing. He was laying the foundations for modern German naturalistic acting. The fact that he was a pioneer made it rather difficult for him, of course.

When Ekhof deserted Schönemann, the company dissolved. The other members then came to Ekhof to lead them. This he consented to do, but loathing business responsibility, he engaged a manager named Koch, who acted in that capacity for six years. At the end of that time Ekhof could tolerate Koch no longer, so he left the company and immediately accepted an engagement with his old friends Ackermann and Schröder. This was in 1764. Ekhof was now rated the finest character actor in Germany, and as his associates were scarcely less renowned, the three constituted a brilliant trinity of stars.

Now it happened that twenty years previous to this event, Sophia Schröder had been party to a short-lived reconciliation with her husband, the drunken musician of Berlin, and the result of that reconciliation had been a son, Friedrich Ludwig Schröder (born 1744). The husband had then sunk back into oblivion, Sophia had rejoined Ackermann, married him, and toured with him in Russia, Switzerland, and all parts of Germany. When Ekhof came to them in 1764, young Schröder was acting in the company. The older man perceived at once that Schröder had the making of a great actor, and with his customary seriousness set about training him. They were in the same company for five years, and in that time the young man developed marvellously, though he quarreled constantly with his instructor, and insultingly refused to admit being improved by him. Schröder, it would seem, had been badly reared by his mother, and in consequence had grown so arrogant as to be almost unendurable. None but a passionate enthusiast like Ekhof would have spent any time or energy on him. As a matter of fact when Ekhof did leave the company it was largely because he could not stand Schröder's insults any longer.

In 1765, the year after Ekhof joined the troupe, Ackermann had a theatre built in Hamburg especially to house his productions. It was not a very good house, but it was at least a theatre, and that was something unusual in Germany, where most performances still had to be given in halls built for other purposes. Here the company performed regularly for a couple of years, and then an interesting thing happened. A group of leading citizens in Hamburg decided to found the first German National Theatre. Concentrating their energies they managed to squeeze out Ackermann and obtain a lease on the building. It opened in March, 1767. To give the venture intelligent publicity, the managers had hired Lessing to write reviews of all their productions for the public journals. Lessing's articles were extremely competent, but they were not very optimistic. The playwright-critic felt that Germany was still lacking in the unity necessary to insure the success of a National Theatre. And his fears were justified, for in November, 1768, the theatre closed its doors through lack of public support. Meanwhile Lessing had advanced some interesting ideas on drama, one of which was that Voltaire was not a great playwright (a popular German idea at that time) and another was that Shakespeare was *the* great dramatist. The English poet was vaguely known in Germany, through occasional performances by English troupes, but he had not become a familiar figure.

After the break-up of the National Theatre, Ekhof, who had been retained as one of its players, drifted about the country, picking up what employment he could find. Eventually he became manager of the small Court Theatre in Weimar. Here he remained until the theatre burned down in 1774. He was then recommended to the Duke of Coburg-Gotha, who built a small Court Theatre and installed him as manager. In this post the old actor (he was not quite sixty, but he was in poor health) spent the final years of his life happily, and died in 1778. The last part he played was the Ghost in "Hamlet."

In the meantime young Schröder, who was an excellent athlete, dancer and acrobat, had joined a mixed company of German and Italian players who had engaged in a kind of *Commedia dell' Arte*. He made a huge success in this line, excelling in grotesque pantomime, and also in the art of improvisation, which is so essential to the Italian form of popular comedy. After a year or so of this he returned to Hamburg, where he was well known, and found that Ackermann (his step-father) had resumed production there. Shortly afterward Ackermann died, and the management of the company fell to Schröder. Throwing the old French repertoire overboard, the young man took up the new German drama (plays by Lessing and Goethe in particular) and introduced a new and vital realism to the German people—a realism which has characterized the best German theatrical efforts ever since.

In 1776 he took an even more spectacular plunge—into the plays of Shakespeare. His first production was "Hamlet," and it was the first production of that play in the German language, though it had been given in Germany by a traveling English company as early as 1625. So great was the success of "Hamlet" that Schröder produced eleven Shakespearian plays in the next four years. He played the leading rôles himself, and his greatest part is said to have been King Lear. At the time he first produced "Hamlet" he was thirty-two years old.

From this time on Schröder was the great actor of the German stage. In his time he created seven hundred rôles, and many of these were masterly characters in the dramas of Shakespeare, Molière, Lessing and Goethe. In 1782 he accepted an engagement in Vienna at the Burgtheater, which had been founded in 1741 as a Court Theatre by Empress Maria Theresa, and changed in 1776 by Emperor Joseph into a National Theatre (in imitation of the Comédie Française). Schröder remained in Vienna four years, where he was eminently successful. In 1786 he returned to the control of the Hamburg theatre, and stayed twelve years, building up by far the best company of players in Germany, and prospering financially at the same time. He then retired to lead the life of a country gentleman, and with the exception of a brief period of theatrical activity in 1811–12 had nothing more to do with the theatre. He died in 1816. By all accounts he was the embodiment of everything that was excellent in eighteenth century German theatricals. He did for acting in that country what Garrick did for it in England—humanized it and ennobled it. He lifted the yoke of French artificiality, and revealed the possibilities of true German realism. He encouraged native drama by performing the best examples of it then available; he gave the German people their first insight into the power and beauty of Shakespeare—an insight which has grown clearer and deeper ever since, for Shakespeare is still played more frequently on the German stage than on that of any other country. In theatrical annals one finds the name "The Great Schröder." One can scarcely question the appropriateness of that appellation.

The last of the major actors of eighteenth century Germany was Iffland, who like Schröder, owed something of his excellence to the old veteran, Ekhof. Iffland was in the company employed at the Coburg-Gotha Theatre when Ekhof was manager there, and this same company moved in 1778 to Mannheim to occupy the National Theatre. A short time afterwards the young romantic poet Schiller came to Mannheim and for two years served as official playwright to the theatre. In 1782 was produced there his famous and epoch-making drama, "The Robbers." Iffland continued in this engagement until 1796, when he was offered a position with the Court Theatre in Berlin (a position which carried with it not only the highest remuneration, but also the greatest honor of any on the German stage). Here he remained until his death in 1814. He was greatly admired by King Frederick William II, and also by his son, Frederick William III, who came to the throne in 1797. Besides being an actor of outstanding ability, Iffland was the most popular playwright of his time. He is not so famous now, of course, as Schiller, for Schiller was ahead of the people. Iffland's plays were simple and realistic; Schiller's were born of the romanticism which had not yet permeated German life.

The last personality in the eighteenth century German theatre whom we shall consider is Johann Wolfgang von Goethe (born 1749), the greatest literary man Germany has ever produced. It will be recalled that at one time the actor Ekhof was manager of the Court Theatre at Weimar, and that he left that position when the theatre burned down in 1774. Weimar was one of the many tiny principalities composing the Germany of that period, each of which took itself seriously as an independent state, and insisted upon artistic and intellectual as well as political independence. The life of the Duchy centered in the palace, where resided the reigning Duke, Karl August, with his young bride and his mother, the Dowager Duchess. The Duke had met Goethe in Frankfurt, and was much impressed by him. He therefore invited him to take up his residence in Weimar, and Goethe accepted the invitation. This was in 1775.

For the next five years theatrical entertainments were given in the halls and gardens of the palace under Goethe's direction, and many of the plays were written by him especially to suit the occasion. Goethe acted parts himself, and was considered a good comedian, but he did not take either his acting or his other dramatic offices very seriously. He was a man of varied interests, and was at this time more enthusiastic over politics and scientific study than he was over the theatre. He fulfilled his position as theatrical director chiefly because he had been brought there for that purpose, and depended upon it for his living.

In 1780 a combined theatre and ball-room was built by the Duke and four years later a very poor professional company of players (mostly Austro-Italians) was engaged to perform in it at regular intervals. Between their Weimar engagements the company made journeys to nearby towns and repeated their plays. This relieved Goethe somewhat of his duties, and he set off for Italy in pursuit of his studies. In 1790 he was recalled by the Duke, who informed him that the Austro-Italians had taken their departure. Largely because he did not care to offend his patron, Goethe obeyed the summons and resumed his post, which he held thenceforth for a period of twenty-six years. Soon a new company of players was hired, and Goethe put in charge of them. Determined to make the most of a situation which he found it difficult to get out of, the poet (now a little past forty years of age) gave a great deal of thought to the art of acting. He drew up rules for the guidance of his actors, and saw that they were religiously observed. Pedantically he reduced the most personal and plastic art to a set of instructions absolutely military in their precision, and would tolerate not the slightest deviation from them. In costumes and scenery he had less interest. The Weimar productions were all done before the most meagre combinations of back-drop and wings.

Goethe's favorite player was Christine Neumann, who began acting for him when she was only thirteen, married an actor when she was fourteen, was the mother of two children by the time she was seventeen, and died when she was nineteen. In this girl the poetical, philosophical Goethe discovered his own ideal of feminine charm, and her influence on his life was very strong.

In 1798 another dramatic poet, Schiller, was attracted to Weimar by Goethe, and during the seven years which followed (Schiller died in 1805) the two worked together under conditions of mutual inspiration. Schiller was by nature more theatrical than was Goethe, and from Schiller Goethe learned a good deal about the spirit of the theatre. He imbibed from him, too, some of the romanticism that was destined to sweep Europe in the early decades of the nineteenth century. But Goethe never was at home in the theatre. In spite of the fact that his greatest poetical work, "Faust," was cast in dramatic form, its greatest qualities are literary rather than theatrical.

In 1808 Goethe handed the Duke his resignation. The reason for his action was that he could no longer stand the tyranny imposed on him by the Duke's mistress, Caroline Jagemann, who had come to Weimar in 1797 to sing in operatic productions, and who had gradually become the ruling personality in the Duchy. Goethe was a tyrant himself, and could not brook interference with his prerogatives, least of all from a rather silly woman. He was persuaded to stay on temporarily, but eight years later, when Caroline and the Duke insisted on producing a melodrama in which the star was a trained poodle, he revolted and left Weimar never to return. His later years were devoted to scientific study, and he died in 1832.

Goethe's influence on the slowly developing German theatre was considerable. His plays became a part of classic German drama, and his system of acting was copied in other parts of the country. His company made a successful tour of Germany early in the nineteenth century, and succeeded in stamping their style on a large number of young actors. The stiffness and pedantic correctness to be found in German acting even today is said to be traceable to the Goethe régime.

RUSSIA

It is questionable whether further space should be given to the eighteenth century theatre, but perhaps a word may be said regarding the progress of Russian and Scandinavian theatricals, and the founding of the Polish theatre.

In Russia things went slowly. After the death of Peter the Great (in 1725) his daughter Elizabeth founded a theatre to which were attracted two Russians, Fyodor Volkov and Ivan Dmitrevsky, the first an organizer, the second an actor, and it is these two who are called the fathers of the Russian theatre. No doubt they deserve the title, for until their time court theatricals had been almost entirely dependent upon foreign (especially German) actors.

The amateur dramatic movement among the upper classes had gradually developed a taste for drama in a considerable number of people, and by the middle of the century, when these two men put forth their efforts, a Russian theatre was not an impossible ideal. In 1765 Dmitrevsky paid a visit to France and England, where he absorbed theatrical information, and is said to have made the acquaintance of David Garrick. On his return to Russia he carried with him a repertoire of French plays, and a hearty admiration for French acting.

From then on the Russian theatre developed along typical eighteenth century lines, learning from the French, the Italians, the English, and the Germans what there was to be known about plays and their production. The periodical visits of German dramatic companies and Italian opera troupes undoubtedly hastened the process. By the end of the century there were two state-controlled theatres in Russia; one in Moscow and the other in St. Petersburg. These became the standard, and when, during the nineteenth century, theatres spread to many provincial cities, the two pioneer houses were copied in nearly every respect. It is considered doubtful whether there was anything strongly native about them until the fourth decade of the nineteenth century, when the Russian drama arose, and it is extremely doubtful whether they made any important contributions to the technical art of the theatre until the very end of that century. What the modern Russian theatre has given to the world will be discussed in a later chapter.

SCANDINAVIA

In Scandinavia the eighteenth century theatre centers about the work of one man, and (as in the case of Italy during the same period) that man was a dramatist. Ludwig Holberg was born in Bergen, Norway, in 1684. While still a young man he spent several years in England, and studied for a time at Oxford University. From England he went to Denmark, where he lectured at the universities and at the same time wrote poetry. Now in 1722 a Frenchman named Capion obtained permission to build a theatre in Copenhagen. The house was opened in September of that year with a repertoire of French and German plays. Holberg was invited to write for the new national theatre. Although he had not previously written any plays, he was familiar with English, French and Italian drama, and was an admirer of Molière. He accepted the invitation and in the course of a year and a half composed fifteen original comedies. Thenceforth his work belonged in the repertoire of the theatre and he continued to contribute to it until the end of his life (he died in 1754). This so-called national theatre of Denmark was forced to close its doors in 1728 (because of Puritan antagonism), but reopened in 1747. Holberg gave it all that was truly native in its character, and his plays, which are still read and performed widely, remain among the most significant contributions of the Scandinavian countries to the world-theatre.

POLAND

Poland, the prey of avaricious neighboring states, was, for obvious reasons, slow in creating a national theatre. She had her folk-play traditions, and during the Renaissance had felt the classical dramatic urge, but the fight for political independence occupied her best energies at the

time when most European countries were founding theatres for the entertainment of their citizens.

The man who really founded the Polish theatre was
Albert Boguslawski (born 1757), who after his training in
a Catholic school, became a page in the household of Ka-
jetan Soltyk, Bishop of Cracow. Soltyk was a very learned
man, and counted among his interests the classical dramas
of France. He even had some of these plays performed in
his palace, and young Boguslawski took part in them. Thus
was the germ planted.

Later, when the young man had become a soldier, the
idea of creating a native theatre burned strongly within
him, with the result that he quit the military and organized
a troupe of players. In this he was encouraged and aided
by a Frenchman named Montburn. Boguslawski made an
operatic arrangement of a native comedy and produced it.
He then worked up translations of several foreign plays,
and with his small company, started on tour. This was in
1783.

As a result of Boguslawski's rather successful venture,
the King ordered a playhouse built in Cracow. This was
completed in 1799, and Boguslawski was appointed director. In this capacity he continued for fifteen years, and during that time he perfected the organization of the theatre,
even to the extent of founding a dramatic school in connection with it. Polish dramatists soon appeared, and a
native drama was a reality. Furthermore, other Polish
cities followed the lead of Cracow, and within a few years
there were playhouses in Wilna, Grodno, Lemberg and
Posen.

Boguslawski is looked upon as a national hero, for it
was his intense patriotism that led him to launch a difficult
movement toward a national theatre and drama. It is felt
that without his intelligent pioneering Poland would have

taken a great deal longer to throw off the yoke of foreign drama, and Polish life would have been much poorer on the side of artistic expression.

CONCLUSION

In concluding this chapter it seems scarcely necessary to point out the fact that the eighteenth century was an era of personalities—actors, playwrights and directors. So far as the physical nature of the theatre is concerned, the period marked but little advance over the achievements of the Renaissance. But there is no century in the history of the theatre which is so alive with dynamic humanity as the eighteenth. The stage of that time was indeed peopled with giants.

It must be apparent, too, that as we come forward with this outline, our subject broadens with ever-increasing rapidity. Details are multiplied with geometric speed, and by their number preclude all possibility of inclusiveness. Selection, therefore, must be our watchword. Only those personalities, ideas and events which are vital and far-reaching in their influence can be dwelt upon at all.

SELECTED REFERENCES

The story of the rise of great actors in the eighteenth century is told well in Volume V of Mantzius' *History of Theatrical Art*. The French, Italian, and English theatres of the period are described excellently in Chapters VIII and IX of Nicoll's *The Development of the Theatre*. An important record is Hawkins' *The French Stage in the Eighteenth Century,* and another is Thaler's *Shakspere to Sheridan*. There are innumerable biographies, memoirs and critiques relating to the period, some of the more important being: Goldoni's *Memoirs,* Chatfield-Taylor's *Goldoni: A Biography,* Cibber's *Apology,* Knight's *David Garrick,* Rae's *Sheridan: A*

Biography, and Macklin's *Memoirs*. A full account of the English stage is given in Fitzgerald's *A New History of the English Stage*. A brief story of the development of the theatre in Russia is to be found in Bakshy's *The Path of the Modern Russian Stage*.

CHAPTER XV

THE NINETEENTH CENTURY

GENERAL CONDITIONS

THE beginning of the nineteenth century found every country of Europe with an established theatre. The story of the following hundred years is therefore one of expansion rather than innovation. Progress was made in the matter of physical equipment, and particularly in the matter of lighting, but fundamentally the theatre remained what it was.

The theatre is essentially a metropolitan institution. With the development of great cities during the nineteenth century, therefore, the number of theatres increased extraordinarily. In London, for example, there were in 1807 only ten theatres operating during the winter season, whereas in 1870 there were thirty. In Paris a similar increase occurred, especially after 1864, when the freedom of the theatres was restored. Natural expansion had been curtailed in 1807 when Napoleon had revoked the measure passed by the National Assembly in 1791 allowing anyone to produce legitimate plays. In England the monopoly of the legitimate drama by Drury Lane and Covent Garden was broken in 1843 by act of Parliament, and freedom of the theatres established.

England and France succeeded in centralizing their civilizations in their capital cities, with the result that the London stage was the English stage, the Paris stage, the French. Something the same was true of Spain and Madrid, but the Spanish theatre was left far behind during the progress of the nineteenth century, and can therefore be neglected. In Italy, a country composed of many small states, each with its principal city, no great center could be formed, even though, midway in the century, these states were welded into a kingdom. There have been many attempts to make Rome the heart of Italian life, but sectional differences and sectional pride interfere. The theatres of Italy are still divided between Rome, Milan, Bologna, Venice, Genoa, Florence, Turin, Naples, and other seats of traditional culture, a half-dozen or more to each city. In the German-speaking countries a somewhat similar condition obtains. In recent years Berlin has become the metropolis and nowadays ranks with London, Paris, and New York as one of the four great theatrical cities of the world, but during the large part of the nineteenth century it was no more important theatrically than Munich, Dresden, or Vienna. In Russia, Moscow and Leningrad (St. Petersburg, Petrograd) have consistently divided honors in the race for theatrical supremacy.

There are obvious advantages in a centralized system, but there are distinct disadvantages, also. A large and sophisticated group of regular theatregoers provides incentive for high-grade productions, and at the same time creates a salutary competition among the many theatres which naturally come into existence. But this same large public makes possible and well-nigh inevitable the long run, which is so decidedly detrimental to the artistic health of a theatrical company. While Italy is lamenting its lack of a theatrical metropolis, and is suffering from an over-supply of third- and fourth-rate touring companies, each of which is too impoverished and too itinerant to afford decent scenic equipment or a respectable ensemble, London protests against the deadly routine of a production which plays for a year or more in one theatre. The remedy for both situations is the same, as anyone can see: the repertory theatre, with a fairly permanent location. And indeed so far as improvements are being made in the organization of theatrical affairs, they are being made on the basis of the repertory idea. But the repertory plan does not always succeed. In the first place, it is expensive; in the second place, it demands an extraordinary *esprit de corps*. We shall have more to say on this subject presently. It must be borne in mind, however, that from the middle of the nineteenth century on to the present day the theatre has been considered primarily as a business (that is, a money-making institution), and although since the fifth century B. C. certain individuals have managed to make a living from the practice of theatrical art, it is only in recent times that financiers have been in control of the theatre and have determined its policies.

CHANGES IN THE PHYSICAL THEATRE

The nineteenth century signifies the multiplication of theatres, to meet the enormous growth in population, especially the urban population. It also signifies certain modifications in the theatre building itself. First of all should be mentioned the disappearance of the forestage, or apron, as it is sometimes called. The extension of the stage into the auditorium, which in Shakespeare's day was the stage proper, but which in the time of Garrick had shrunk to half its previous size and importance, receded steadily from 1800 on, until by the close of the century it had vanished utterly from the newer theatres, and survived after the fashion of an appendix in the older ones. And with the decline of the apron occurred as a matter of course, the disappearance of the proscenium doors, those permanent entrances in front of and at either corner of the proscenium arch. By 1900 the up-to-date playhouse was possessed of a purely picture-frame stage, with the audience assembled in front of it, and the traditional boxes either conspicuous by their absence or else rendered ridiculously impractical from the standpoint of vision. As a matter of fact the stage boxes have persisted in many theatres as pure ornament, in others as a traditional concession to high society, whose interest in the theatre is not always well grounded in aesthetics.

The evolution toward the picture-frame stage was accompanied, logically enough, by a readjustment of the entire auditorium. As the scene moved farther and farther back behind the proscenium, the extreme sides of the audience had to be pulled in toward the center, and the side extensions of the balconies had to be abandoned altogether. These alterations were made, let us remember, in those theatres which were intelligently designed. Far too many, alas! continued to follow the floor plan of older houses, even though the picture-frame stage had been adopted. It is still possible to find plenty of theatres in any country in which many seats give practically no glimpse of the stage.

It was during the nineteenth century, also, that efforts were first made to provide theatres with really comfortable seats. In the eighteenth century the audience had sat on hard, backless benches. About 1850 they began to enjoy upholstered chairs. It is odd, in this connection, that at the very time when comfort was being provided the audience, the length of performances was being greatly reduced. In the early years of the nineteenth century, for example, it was customary for London theatres to start the evening's entertainment at half-past six, and to continue it until after midnight. A farce, a complete Shakespearian drama, and a light opera were often found on a single bill. Occasionally an audience would be let out as late as half-past one in the morning. The theory was that something light and unimportant had to be presented first, to amuse the *bourgeosie,* who are always eager to get places. The *pièce de résistance* was saved until the arrival of the fashionable, who dined rather late. Then, having seriously taxed the minds and emotions of the audience with classic drama for three hours or more, it was up to the management to relieve them with perhaps two hours of frivolity, and send them home wide-awake and jolly. After nine o'clock, incidentally, admissions were reduced to half-price. Grand opera, the ultra-fashionable, was an exception to this time schedule, however, and began at eight o'clock.

About 1840 certain theatres began to curtail their performances, and at the Olympic Theatre, London, Mme. Vestris, an innovator of great distinction, closed her shows at eleven o'clock, much to the astonishment of the public. Her lead was followed by one manager after another, until finally it became the accepted rule.

The matinee performance, strangely enough, had passed out of existence during the eighteenth century (with the improvement in artificial lighting) and during the period of 1800 to 1850 was scarcely thought of. But in the second half of the nineteenth century, after a series of experiments, it came back into vogue as a supplementary performance. "A morning performance" it was called by the Victorians.

The tendency in stage settings during the nineteenth century was definitely toward realism. Indeed the realistic impulse was the guiding motive in all branches of theatrical art. Playwrights, notably from 1850 onward, strove with undisguised efforts, to capture the atmosphere and character of the people and events which surrounded them. Actors, comic and tragic, endeavored to cast off the artificial mannner of their predecessors: the grand manner of the tragedian, the stock tricks of the comedian, and to portray in human and convincing terms the characters for which they were cast. The scene painter, with considerable skill, and certainly with untold patience and ingenuity, contrived landscapes guaranteed to deceive the most cunning eye, whereas the stage mechanic busied himself with problems of scene shifting, and with spectacular effects which were for the most part simulative of natural phenomena.

Three stage devices of considerable importance were evolved: the diorama, the sinking stage, and the revolving stage. The diorama was a continuously moving landscape drop, which, when operated, gave the audience the sensation of motion. Such an apparatus was in use at Drury Lane Theatre, London, as early as 1820. It may very easily have originated on the Continent. The sinking stage is said to have been employed first by the Germans. As may be surmised, it is an arrangement whereby the entire section of the stage floor occupied by the setting is lowered to the basement, where the setting is removed and another slid into its place, the section then being raised into position again. Such a device allows complete settings to be prepared during the progress of the play without interference with the action, and therefore minimizes the waits between acts. The revolving stage serves the same purpose in a slightly different manner. In this case the stage must be unusually large. A huge disc is cut in the floor and mounted so that it revolves easily. It is then marked off into segments, the outer circumference of each segment corresponding to the width of the proscenium opening. Three or four complete settings may then be constructed in advance on the disc, and the whole play run through without any appreciable delay or labor in shifting during the performance. Although the revolving stage made its first European appearance in Germany during the late nineteenth century, it cannot be said to have originated there, for it was employed on the *Kabuki* stage of Japan more than a hundred years before.

Contemporary with these mechanical developments was the gradual heightening of the stage-roof. As settings became more and more elaborate, and as more and more mechanical effects were tried out, it became increasingly obvious that overhead space was needed. The easiest way to handle scenery is to lift and lower it by lines and pulleys. When lifted, it is out of everyone's way, and when needed it can be dropped in a moment. To take a tall scene up out of sight requires an extraordinarily high stage-roof. To handle a number of scenes in this manner requires a carefully planned and fairly complicated overhead equipment. The modern stage-building, projecting oftentimes high above the roof of the auditorium, with its elaborate gridiron (the metal framework in which the pulleys are fitted) and its maze of depending lines, is the result of these considerations.

THE EVOLUTION OF STAGE-LIGHTING

But more interesting, and of vastly greater importance, than any of these physical improvements in the theatre, is the evolution of theatrical lighting, and it is to the nineteenth century that that evolution chiefly belongs.

Before the end of the eighteenth century an English engineer had succeeded in manufacturing gas in sufficient quantities for illuminating purposes, but it was not until 1803 that an attempt was made to apply this kind of lighting to the stage. In that year the Lyceum theatre, London, was equipped with gas lights, and the new illuminant was a revelation to the public. For the first time in the history of the theatre, a stage was lighted brightly enough to make visible every detail of scene and action, every subtlety of facial expression. Futhermore, it was now possible to control stage-lighting; that is, to darken or brighten the stage at will, for the feed pipes were brought to a central point, where a mechanic could decrease or increase the flow of gas.

In Paris gas was first used at the Opéra in 1821. There, and in fact at every theatre which installed a gas-lighting system, a special plant for gas-manufacture was also installed. It was a number of years before commercial companies supplied it for such purposes.

The chief objections to the new system were that considerable gas escaped, creating a bad odor in the auditorium, and that the open flames were flickered by currents of air. The latter fault was practically eliminated, however, by the introduction of glass chimneys to protect the flames. The odor was never entirely corrected, though it was diminished.

The next illuminating device employed in theatres came into use about 1860. This was the lime-light: made by playing a burning mixture of oxygen and hydrogen on a block of lime. The lime, when heated to a certain temperature, became incandescent, and produced a strong white light. This was found to be admirably adapted to localized lighting, such as is needed in creating the effects of sun rays, streams of moonlight, *et cetera*. It was also well adapted to "spotting" a portion of the scene, or a character, and this use gave rise to the familiar expression, "in the lime-light." From this invention it was a fairly easy step to the incandescent gas mantle, which quickly supplanted the open flame jet.

Color-lighting, which had been tried earlier, but with weak effect, now made rapid progress. Silk and other transparent materials were placed in front of "limes," and a rich color thrown upon the stage. Henry Irving, the famous English actor-manager of the late nineteenth century, was one of the first to make effective use of color-lighting.

Experiments with electricity were being conducted in laboratories early in the century, but the first record of an electrical effect on the stage is that of the representation of a sunrise at the Paris Opéra in 1846, when an arc and a reflector were combined to throw a beam of light on a silk screen. For several years thereafter mechanics were employed at the Opéra to experiment with electrical effects. Lightning, a rainbow, and an electric spotlight were three of the results of these experiments. In 1879 it was discovered that the paintings which hung in the foyer of the Opéra were being destroyed by vapors from the gas-lights, and this emergency led to the installation in 1880 and 1881 of a complete system of incandescent electric lights—the first installation of such a system in any theatre.

In 1882 there was held in Munich an Electro-Technical Exposition, and one of the features of the Exposition was a model theatre completely lighted by electricity. Color-screens were used in connection with the lamps on the stage, and diffused or indirect lighting was employed in the auditorium. So remarkable was the effect of this demonstration that in September of the same year, at a Congress of Theatrical Managers, a report was issued favoring the installation of electricity in all theatres and public halls. Before the end of the year the Savoy Theatre, London, had made such an installation, and so had the Bijou Theatre in Boston, U. S. A.

A few years later this illuminant, which was to revolutionize the theatre, was brought sharply under control by the invention of rheostats, or "dimmers," which permit the operator to control easily and smoothly the flow of electricity through the various circuits, and make possible infinite gradations of light at any point on the stage or in the auditorium. Needless to say, also, myriad types of electrical stage-lighting units have lately been devised: spotlights, bunch-lights, borders, floods, *et cetera,* operated from every conceivable angle, and giving unlimited scope to the stage electrician.

Let us now speak of some of the great actors of the nineteenth century. Our list cannot include many, but it must include those whose careers dominated theatrical styles of the period, and whose names are still heard wherever the art of the theatre is discussed.

PERSONALITIES OF THE ITALIAN STAGE

In Italy the two pioneer actors of the century were Louis Belloti Bon (1810–1883) and Gustavo Modena (1803–1863). They were pioneers in the sense that they both strove to cast off the older manners of Italian acting, and to create a theatre of realism. Belloti Bon was influenced directly by the French company of Meynardier, which toured Italy about the middle of the century, and presented a most striking example of perfect ensemble acting. Italian productions had heretofore suffered extremely from the star system, under which a leading actor gave an effective but exaggerated performance, while the rest of the company acted in a very ragged fashion. The visiting French troupe, on the contrary, performed as a unit, and that unit was strictly subordinated to the drama itself. In consequence, the new realistic plays in which they appeared (the work of Dumas *fils* and Augier) became highly convincing representations of life. There was in existence in Italy at this time neither a body of realistic modern plays nor a school of realistic actors. Belloti Bon founded such a company, and was soon the inspiration of new playwrights.

At the same time, or perhaps a little earlier, Modena was striving mightily, more from instinct than from foreign influence, to achieve something very similar in the way of acting and production. He introduced realistic period costumes on the Italian stage, and sought a natural effect in his own acting and in the acting of his associates. He discarded both the violently active style of comic acting, which had had its origin in the *Commedia dell' Arte*, and the heavy, stilted manner of classical tragedy. Not only did he realize a modern ideal in his own art: he communicated it to many others, among whom were two great actors, Tommaso Salvini and Ernesto Rossi. Salvini, whose life embraced the bulk of the century and extended into our own period (he was born in 1829 and died in 1913) was the dominant figure of the Italian stage for fifty years, and was one of the supreme interpreters of the tragic rôles of Shakespeare.

Parallel with Salvini, and of equal greatness, was Adelaide Ristori (1822–1906), who possessed as completely as any actress of the century a combination of natural charm, nobility, and exceptional intelligence. Born of actor parents, she was literally raised on the stage, and at the age of fifteen was a famous leading woman. During her career she performed in all the principal European countries, and established herself as the chief actress of the time.

All this pioneering came to flower in the person of Eleonora Duse (1859–1924), also a child of the theatre. Duse reached the zenith of her power at the very time when the modern realistic drama was at its height—the final decade of the century. This was a most happy coincidence, for whatever rôle Duse touched she made utterly true and utterly beautiful. Not that she limited herself to the Ibsen drawing-room drama; she was equally at home in poetic tragedy; but it was fortunate that the realists should have an interpreter who could lift their prose to spiritual heights and at the same time retain most marvellously its fidelity to fact. Duse's acting drove even the harshest critics to speechlessness or else to ecstatic praise. She was possessed of the subtlest arts, the finest shadings, an infinite variety of expressive powers. She surpassed every other living actress, and her sublime idealism combined with her supreme technique to make her the embodiment of a world ideal.

Three men stand out as leaders of the Italian stage at the close of the century: Ermete Zacconi, Ermete Novelli, and Giovanni Grasso. Zacconi attained fame as a master of realistic detail, and was for many years principal actor with Duse. Novelli, born early enough to receive six years of schooling with Belloti Bon, became the foremost character actor of his native theatre, and appeared in all the countries of the Occident. In 1900 he made a courageous effort to give Italy a national theatre by founding at Rome a permanent repertory company, patterned after the Comédie Française. The fact that the venture failed does not lessen the significance of his attempt. Italy was not ready for such a theatre. Grasso, a Sicilian, performed only in his native environment until 1903, when he went to Rome and immediately created a furor. Later he traveled abroad, and with his own company has established an international reputation. He excels in peasant drama, where his dynamic, brutally fiery style is displayed to best advantage. His technique is said to be instinctive rather than acquired, and is peculiarly effective.

Italians, according to those well-informed, are born actors. Possessed of passionate natures, strong, musical voices and expressive bodies, they meet naturally the fundamental requirements of the theatre. Their weakness lies in their tendency to over-act, to be carried away by emotion, and to indulge themselves in an excess of sheer theatricalism. This proclivity is not so detrimental to opera (their forte), but it often ruins a modern play in which the intellect is uppermost or at least emphasized equally

GRIMALDI, Bold Dragoon in Pantomine of the Red Dwarf

Plate 20: Grimaldi as the Bold Dragoon.

with emotion. When the Italian fire is tempered, as it was in Duse, for example, it is an ideal spirit for the theatre.

PERSONALITIES OF THE FRENCH STAGE

From the French theatre of the period we must mention but a few actors. The list should be headed by Frederick Lemaître (1800–1876), for his reputation is the greatest. Lemaître served his apprenticeship in minor Parisian theatres, and for a time appeared with pantomime companies, who represented the survival of the Italian comedy. But he did not entirely succeed in this line for the reported reason that he could not make his entrance on a tight-rope, and the pantomime actors insisted on such a spectacular entrance for every character. Lemaître finally got small parts to play at the Odéon, and later went to the Ambigu-Comique, a theatre specializing in melodramas and horror plays. Here he registered his first great success, and within a few years had become the most excellent romantic actor in Paris. Back at the Odéon again, he starred in the dramas of Victor Hugo, and in them reached the pinnacle of fame. Like Edmund Kean, his English contemporary, he was of a wild disposition, and drank heavily. Like Kean, too, he symbolized the romantic movement of the early nineteenth century.

While Lemaître was winning glory in the field of romantic melodrama, another actor, Jean Gaspard Deburau (1796–1846) was working in quite a different *genre* to attain a place of no less honor. Deburau had come to Paris in his father's acrobatic troupe, and in the French pantomimes had made his way to the top of the clowning profession. Although he was a versatile performer, he made a specialty of the Pierrot character, and stamped that traditional rôle with a temperament and set of mannerisms which clung to it long after he himself was dead. Pierrot, in the hands of Deburau, ceased to be merely a clown, and was transformed into a poetical, tragic figure—a creature of melancholy seriousness, with depth and subtlety. Traces of this Pierrot are still to be found in our versions of the Harlequinade. The tradition was carried on, but not so successfully, by Charles Deburau, son of the great actor.

In classical tragedy and in high comedy the second half of the century provides two great names, Mounet-Sully (1841–1916), and Constant Coquelin (1841–1909). The former was the most powerful and the noblest tragedian of the French stage since Talma; the latter was supreme both in realistic and romantic comedy. Coquelin's greatest rôle was Cyrano de Bergerac in the play of that name written especially for him by Edmond Rostand, and produced for the first time at the Théâtre Porte Saint-Martin in Paris, 1897.

Among French actresses of the century, three tower above their sisters. These are Mlle. Rachel (1821–1858), Mme. Réjane (1856–1920), and Sarah Bernhardt (1844–1923). Rachel was noted for her superb diction (always prized by the French) and for her perfectly poised interpretations of the dramas of Racine. For fifteen years she was the reigning queen of the Comédie Française, and in 1855 embarked on a tour of America, under the business management of her brother, who saw the possibilities of a fortune in the venture. Her company, which included three of her sisters, was the first to perform in America in a foreign language, and although it did not reap a huge financial reward, it attracted a great deal of attention. After a number of performances in New York, Boston, and one or two other cities, Mlle. Rachel contracted a cold, which developed into consumption, and led to her premature death not long after her return to Paris.

Mme. Réjane was a woman of intellect. Her acting was characterized by remarkable brilliance and by a superior realism. During the last two decades of the century she took a keen interest in the new drama of Becque and other French realists, and performed a service for them not unlike that performed by Duse.

Bernhardt is, of course, a more familiar name to the average reader. "The Divine Sarah," as she was known to publicity agents, led a hectic and scandalous life, but commanded the infatuation of the whole world by her histrionic skill. Her versatility was amazing, her courage unlimited, and her vital energy unmatched. Throughout her long life she was an indefatigable worker in the theatre, not only as actress but as manager. She played every sort of part, from Camille to Hamlet, and nearly always succeeded in creating a sensation. She had an absolute mastery over the tricks of acting, and was particularly skillful in the use of her voice, which had an unusual range. What she lacked was sincerity and spiritual depth. She was in many ways the antithesis of Duse. Duse's art was lighted with a white flame; Bernhardt's with red fire.

PERSONALITIES OF THE GERMAN STAGE

Few names from the German theatre of the nineteenth century hold an international significance. Among actor-managers who influenced the course of German acting and stage-craft may be mentioned Iffland (already dealt with in a previous chapter), who in the first few years of the century combated the Weimar school, and laid the foundations, at the National Theatre in Berlin, for modern directors; Josef Schreyvogel (1768–1832), a follower of Iffland, and director of the Burgtheater in Vienna; Karl Immermann, (1796–1840) founder of the theatre at Düsseldorf; Heinrich Laube (1806–1884), of Vienna and Leip-

zig, who was one of the first to use modern realistic set
tings, and to insist on an adequate number of rehearsal
with scenery and properties; Ludwig Tieck (1773–1853)
director of the Court Theatre at Dresden, and a strong
proponent of originality and freedom in acting; and Lud
wig Devrient (1784–1832), the romantic actor *par excel
lence* of the German stage.

Devrient made his début in 1804, and was an immediate
success. He played chiefly in Breslau, Berlin, and Vienna
and was a great favorite everywhere, for he epitomized the
spirit of romanticism with which the air was charged. Akir
to Kean of England and Lemaître of France, he lived at
a frantic pace, and drank himself into a breakdown and
early death. English and French romanticism were feverish
enough varieties, but the German sort was maniacal. De
vrient, who gloried in representation of the diabolical and
the grotesque, was fond of the rôles of Falstaff, Shylock
and King Lear. The impersonation of Lear, however,
was such a strain on his energies that he could not essay
it frequently. Such wholesouled acting was a violent de
parture from classic principles, and was almost as far
removed from the newer realistic principles, but it was
a comprehensible phenomenon when considered in the light
of the time and environment from which it sprang. It was
a desperate attempt to set utterly free the most ecstatic im
pulses of man; and behind it was a powerful, if hazy, mys
tical conception of the sublime. The spirit which animated
Devrient a hundred years ago is not altogether unfelt in
modern Germany, although the end of the century brought
in a sweeping tide of realism, which not only affected the
style of acting, but turned the mechanical genius of the
German people to excellent account. The personalities of
this realistic movement: Brahm, Reinhardt, and others,
will be discussed later.

PERSONALITIES OF THE ENGLISH STAGE

When we turn to the celebrated personalities of the English theatre of the nineteenth century we are embarrassed by their number, but inasmuch as this book is written primarily for the American reader, and considering that the American theatre is an offshoot of the English, it seems justifiable to devote a rather large amount of space to the London actors and managers whose careers are such an important part of our theatrical tradition.

The recital begins with an illustrious name: Edmund Kean. Born in 1787, the illegitimate son of Anne Carey, a minor actress, who left him half-frozen on a doorstep when he was three months old, the greatest of all romantic actors made a sensational début on the stage of the world. He was taken care of by a charitable but otherwise obscure actress named Miss Tidswell, and by other players attached to Drury Lane Theatre. He was later adopted by Moses Kean, a ventriloquist and traveling showman, who may possibly have been the boy's father, and by him was taught the tricks of the stage, including fencing, tight-rope walking, and the acting of Shakespeare's plays.

Edmund was a daring child. He ran away so frequently that he was made to wear a dog-collar bearing the inscription, "Drury Lane Theatre." At the age of eight he disappeared from London, and was found at a French port, where he had landed as a stowaway.

When he grew up he became a strolling player, a Harlequin and a Hamlet. He could do anything required of an actor, and yet in everything he did there was originality. At the age of twenty he married a Miss Chambers, and together they played the provincial theatres, earning a bare living. Eventually he caught the eye of London managers, and was given a début at Drury Lane on the 26th of

January, 1814. His rôle was Shylock. Except for his confidence in himself, the circumstances were inauspicious. The Drury Lane players were hostile, the audience was small and indifferent. Even his wife could not be present; she had to stay at home and look after their child.

But Kean was electric, and the cold audience warmed. In fact they thrilled. It was the greatest London début since Garrick's. And it is interesting to note that one member of that astonished audience was the eminent critic, William Hazlitt. Kean had been promised, in case his tryout was successful, a salary of six pounds a week. The next day he was offered twenty. At Drury Lane he then played in quick succession the great parts: Richard III, Hamlet, Othello, Macbeth. His characterizations were vivid, exciting and new. He acted "by inspiration," evoking the memory of George Frederick Cooke, but surpassing in brilliance and passion even that fiery romanticist. The poet Coleridge testified that, "To see Kean play is like reading Shakespeare by flashes of lightning." He triumphed not only in the stormy classics, but in the new melodramas, filled with Gothic gloom and secret crime.

His success, artistically and financially, was stupendous. He earned during his first thirteen years in London more than two hundred thousand pounds (and a million dollars was a great deal of money a hundred years ago). It was too much, in fact, for Kean. He lived recklessly, drank heavily, and finally involved himself in a domestic scandal which alienated him temporarily from the London public, and resulted in a tour to America (1825). He reappeared at Drury Lane in 1827, and was forgiven and idolized.

Meanwhile his son Charles had, against his father's wishes, become an actor. By doing so he found it possible to support his mother, whom his father had deserted. The elder Kean, now estranged from wife and son, and declining rapidly in health, performed intermittently at various theatres, but was too irregular in his habits and too weak physically to maintain his former glory. His final appearance on the stage was on March 25, 1833, at Covent Garden, where Charles was then engaged. At the suggestion of the management a special production of "Othello" was arranged, in which Kean played the title part, and his son Iago. Toward the end of the play the older man collapsed, and fell, clinging to Charles, saying, "I am dying—speak to them for me." The curtain was dropped, and the broken tragedian was taken home. He died two months later, at the age of forty-six, being actually an old and exhausted man.

Charles Kean was not the actor his father was, but he was a good producer. From 1850 to 1859 he managed the Princess's Theatre, and staged in notable fashion the list of Shakespeare's plays. His method was to mount these plays as lavishly as possible, and at the same time to emphasize historical accuracy. In this he contrasted strongly with Samuel Phelps, his contemporary, whose Shakespeare productions at Sadler's Wells were triumphs of acting, but simple in staging. Charles Kean is given credit, too, for having brought the upper classes back into the legitimate theatre and in that way renewing theatrical prosperity. Queen Victoria, unlike her immediate predecessors on the British throne, supported the drama, and beginning in 1849 had a series of plays given at Windsor Castle under Charles Kean's direction. Ending his Princess's Theatre management in 1859, Kean embarked on a long tour of America and Australia. He died in England in 1868.

The most interesting actress of the first half of the century was Mme. Vestris (born Eliza Lucy Bartolozzi, and married in 1813, at the age of sixteen, to M. Armand Vestris, a famous ballet-master). This young woman was an accomplished dancer, an excellent opera-singer, and a winning actress. She made her début in 1815 in Italian opera, and was an instantaneous success. In 1819 she separated from M. Vestris, and joined the Drury Lane company, where she enjoyed tremendous popularity, particularly in so-called "breeches parts." At the same time she acquired a scandalous reputation, and was, it is feared, the sweetheart of entirely too many London beaus.

In 1831 Mme. Vestris assumed control of the small Olympic Theatre, where she produced operas, burlesques, and musical farces. In these she imitated the French revue, or follies. She could not do legitimate drama, for Drury Lane and Covent Garden still held the monopoly. In her company was John Liston, the foremost low comedian of the time, and in 1835 she was joined by Charles Mathews the younger, whom she married in 1838. This young man, whose father was renowned for his monologues and character sketches, felt that Mme. Vestris had the only company in London which offered attractive possibilities to a true light comedian. Without doubt her productions were new in spirit. They were clever, satirical, and dominated by excellent taste. Mathews wished to avoid the old lines of comic acting, and to substitute a style based on observation of contemporary life. His desire was gratified, and he really introduced to London audiences a type of comedian whose elegance and wit contrasted markedly with the old and coarse buffoon.

Vestris and Mathews toured America immediately after their marriage, and on their return to London in 1839, took control of Covent Garden Theatre, where, of course, they were free to present legitimate drama. At the Olympic they had depended chiefly on the novel dramatic compositions of J. R. Planché, an extremely versatile writer, who not only turned out dozens of burlesques, fantasies, and operettas, but who also was a distinguished antiquarian, and exerted a great influence on the London producers of the time in regard to correct costumes and settings. At

Covent Garden, Vestris and Mathews brought into the public eye the young playwright, Dion Boucicault (1820–1890), one of the major pioneers in realistic drama, whose first success was "London Assurance," 1841.

The Covent Garden venture was not a great success, however, and was given up in 1842. After various engagements, Vestris and Mathews took over the Lyceum, where from 1847 to 1854 they specialized again in burlesque and extravaganza. Mme. Vestris retired in 1854, because of illness, and died two years later. Mathews gave up the Lyceum in 1855, and two years afterward made an American tour, in the course of which he found another wife. Returning to London, he continued to act at various theatres for twenty years longer. Toward the end of his life his style of acting, which had been revolutionary in the thirties, was considered rather old-fashioned. The realist had been out-moded by time, and by a newer realism.

In tragedy the field was led by William Charles Macready (1793–1873), who began his London career at Covent Garden in 1816, the year before John Philip Kemble retired from that theatre's management, leaving it in the hands of Charles and Fanny Kemble, his brother and his niece. Macready was the upholder of the Betterton-Kemble tradition, although he combined with the dignity of that manner, some of the passion of Kean, and the easy, matter-of-factness of the French actor, Talma, whom he had seen in Paris. He was a peculiar combination, therefore, of many styles, and while he lacked the creative imagination necessary to originality, he nevertheless was possessed of a good intellect, and turned the experience of others to good account. In 1823 he left Covent Garden for Drury Lane, and remained there until 1837, when he returned to Covent Garden as manager. In Shakespeare, and in the new dramas of Bulwer-Lytton, he achieved artistic success, but financial failure, and in two years moved to

the Haymarket, and later to Drury Lane, where he repeated his failure. Discouraged, he made another American
tour, and also acted in Paris. It was on this, his third, trip
to America, that he quarreled with the American tragedian,
Edwin Forrest, who accused Macready of having incited
a London audience to hiss Forrest's performance of Macbeth. So strong was the feeling aroused that Macready
had to leave America hurriedly and in secret. Back in
London the veteran performed at various houses until
1851, when he made his farewell as Macbeth. He was, we
may conclude, primarily the champion of classics. He had
a stubborn nature, and would never consider the commercial aspect of a production. He played what he liked in
the way he liked, and damned the public if they did not
support him. He had the true temperament of the tradi-
tionalist.

Another actor of the classics, contemporary with Macready, was Samuel Phelps. As a matter of fact, Phelps had
been partially trained by Macready at Covent Garden. In
1844 he acquired a controlling interest in Sadler's Wells
Theatre, a suburban house famous since the previous century, and for eighteen years made it the home of Shakespeare and other poetic dramatists. Altogether he mounted
thirty-two of Shakespeare's plays, and performed them
on an average of four nights out of every six. He minimized the use of scenery, and stressed good acting. This
emphasis was in contrast to Charles Kean's method at the
Princess's, where historical costumes and settings, combined
with pageantry, well-nigh buried the plays themselves.
Phelps's best acting parts were those requiring extraordinary comic technique, such as Falstaff and Malvolio. He
drew to his playhouse all those who loved sound acting;
he left to Charles Kean those who preferred superficial
and extravagant effect. He gave old Sadler's Wells its best
years of a long and mottled career, and made it a glorious

reality for his own day, a noble legend for posterity.

There remains one more great name among the early nineteenth century actors: Joseph Grimaldi (1778–1837), father of modern clowns, and the greatest comic idol in the whole history of the English stage. Grimaldi, of Italian descent, was born in London, the son of Giuseppe Grimaldi, a Harlequin player and ballet-master who had been at various times attached to all the principal theatres of London. Joseph was trained to a very limited extent by his father, for the latter died when the boy was ten years old.

Joseph inherited all the tricks of the *Commedia dell' Arte* tradition. They seem to have been born in him. He could play straight dramatic rôles as well as any actor in London, yet he was the supreme buffoon. He performed at Sadler's Wells, at Covent Garden, at Drury Lane, and other houses. In the English pantomimes, which were largely Harlequinades, he played not Harlequin, but Clown, for he was short and plump, with a full-moon face. Not only was his dumb-show superb; his creative ingenuity was remarkable. He invented the most astonishing transformations (mechanical illusions which allowed one object or scene to change suddenly into another of a quite different character) and built up all sorts of apparatus of a comical and spectacular nature.

Grimaldi hoped that his name would be borne honorably in the theatre by his son, J. S. Grimaldi, but although the young man showed great promise, and made an early success, he led such a wild life that he lost his mind and died wretchedly five years before his father. The old clown's style was not completely lost, however, for it survived in several of his pupils, chief among them being Tom Matthews. Later the style reappeared, with more or less modifications, in such pantomime and music-hall comedians as Dan Leno, the various Paulos, "Whimsical" Walker, Grock, and finally Harry Tate and Charlie Chaplin. But although no clown since Joseph Grimaldi has quite lived up to that famous name, even the humblest of the profession answers to the name of "Joey" and is ennobled by the implication.

Other actors who attained fame in the first half of the century were: R. W. Elliston, a first-class comedian, and at various times manager of the Olympic, the Surrey, and Drury Lane theatres; James Wallack, an associate of Edmund Kean's, and one of the best melodrama actors of the early decades; Henry Compton, said to have been the finest Shakespearian clown of his day; J. B. Buckstone, a favorite low-comedian and author of popular melodramas; T. P. Cooke and Tyrone Power, melodrama actors who were featured members of the famous Adelphi company during the twenties, under the management of Daniel Terry and Frederick Henry Yates. It was this company which is said to have done for melodrama what Vestris and Mathews did for comedy—civilize it and rid it of its traditional crudities.

Let us now consider the leading personalities of the English theatre between 1850 and 1900.

We may begin with a foreigner. Charles Fechter, a well-known French actor of the time, began a series of performances in London in 1860. He played at first in French, later in English, and exhibited such a novel style of acting and staging that for a few years his influence on the London stage was very great. He ignored the English conventions in regard to Shakespeare, and played even "Hamlet," the most sacred of tragedies, in a realistic manner, treating it as a refined melodrama, and introducing novel bits of stage-business throughout. He also used (for the first time on the English stage) solid sets of scenery, with realistic ceilings instead of borders. Even more startling was his use of a sinking stage (later perfected by the Germans), which allowed changes of scene to be handled in the basement. He is reported, furthermore, to have lowered the footlight trough to a point where the lamps and reflectors were entirely invisible to the audience.

Fechter's mechanical innovations, combined with his unusual interpretations of classic drama, made him a sensation. His vogue passed, but his influence was added to that of others, before and after him, to hasten the freedom of the theatre from a heavy load of conventionalities.

In 1856 Miss Marie Wilton made her début at the Lyceum in musical burlesque. Her vivacity and charm made her an immediate favorite. Two years later she moved to the Strand, where she starred in a series of extremely successful burlesques written by H. J. Byron. Charles Dickens, who saw her during this period, called her, "the cleverest girl I have seen on the stage in my time, and the most singularly original." She was a refreshing actress of the soubrette type, whose impudence and pertness were delightful and in good taste.

In 1865 Miss Wilton, in partnership with H. J. Byron, took control of the old theatre which had been known at various times as The Queen's, The West London, The Regency, and The Fitzroy. It was a poorly furnished house, and catered to a cheap audience. By special permission it was now christened the Prince of Wales's Theatre, was thoroughly renovated and fitted with upholstered seats (then a novelty), and in every way made attractive to discriminating playgoers. It was opened with burlesque, but very shortly afterward was given to a new line of comedies, the first of which was "Society," by a rising young playwright, Tom Robertson. Robertson had already achieved one success with "David Garrick," which had been produced at the Haymarket with E. A. Sothern in the title rôle. "Society" included in its cast, Miss Wilton, Squire Bancroft, and John Hare—three excellent performers. It was a tremendous hit. Four more of Robertson's comedies followed: "Caste," "Ours," "Play," and "School."

Nearly all of them enjoyed long runs, and together they established the Prince of Wales's as a leading playhouse. It was a new kind of comedy that Robertson had given to the English stage. It was not great, but it was highly significant in the general movement toward realism. A pleasant picture of the forward-looking young dramatist is given by Pinero in his famous comedy, "Trelawney of the 'Wells,' " in which the character called Tom Wrench represents Robertson.

The spirit of the new realism dominated the Bancroft régime. (Miss Wilton had married Bancroft in 1867.) Modern interior settings of a very realistic sort were constantly used, and the acting was keyed to the settings. Although Fechter had employed many realistic devices in London as early as 1860, the Bancrofts were the first to standardize them and make them a tradition.

In 1879 the Bancrofts moved from the Prince of Wales's to the Haymarket, where they continued until 1885. That year marked the end of their management, though they appeared individually in certain productions during the late eighties and the nineties. Their long and successful efforts in elevating the art of comedy were rewarded by extraordinary expressions of affection from the public, and by a knighthood conferred on Mr. Bancroft by the Crown.

John Hare, who was one of the mainstays of the Bancroft company, left them in 1874, and launched a company of his own at the Court Theatre, where he established the same high standards of acting as obtained at the Prince of Wales's. Among those whom he engaged were Mr. W. H. Kendal and Mrs. Kendal (formerly Madge Robertson, sister of Tom Robertson, playwright), who had been acting at the Haymarket, where they had made a notable success in the early plays of W. S. Gilbert. In 1879 the Kendals joined with John Hare to take control of the St. James's Theatre, which they held until 1888. After that the Ken-

dals toured America, and Hare moved to the newly built
Garrick Theatre, where he remained until 1895. From
then on he was in and out of various theatres. His productions were always smart, always permeated with the spirit
of high comedy, and were always extremely fashionable.

The Haymarket Theatre, during the sixties and seventies, was a very successful house, managed by J. B. Buckstone, the popular comedian and playwright. Its typical bill
was long and varied, including comedies, tragedies and
farces. But probably its most successful production during
those years was that of Tom Taylor's play, "Our American Cousin," with E. A. Sothern in the rôle of Lord Dundreary, which took London by storm in 1861. Sothern had
played the part first in America, where it had proved a
triumph. Although the play itself was of small merit, the
eccentric character created by Sothern was irresistible, and
Lord Dundreary mannerisms became the talk of the Eng-
lish-speaking world. They have since been imitated countless times on the stage. Sothern's next step was into the
part of David Garrick, in the play of that name by Robertson. His performances in these parts stamped him as probably the foremost character actor of the English theatre
during the years 1860–1870.

But of all late nineteenth century actors the most renowned is Henry Irving (John Henry Brodribb), born in
1838. After years of apprenticeship in the theatres of Edinburgh, Glasgow, Dublin, Liverpool, Manchester, and other
cities, he made his first London appearance at St. James's
Theatre in 1866, having by that time mastered the technique of acting. After a year's engagement there he assumed the management of the Queen's Theatre, and in the
first season played opposite Miss Ellen Terry in "Taming of
the Shrew," a significant event in the light of the future.

In 1871 an American, Hezekiah L. Bateman, known as
"The Colonel," settled in London and bought control of

the Lyceum Theatre, an old house which was dilapidated and unpopular. His idea was to exploit the talent of his daughter Isabel, who had already acted on the stage of the Adelphi. Bateman engaged Irving as leading man, and promised to make him the foremost actor in England. The first two productions were failures, and "The Colonel" grew discouraged. Then Irving suggested playing "The Bells," a horror play with a tragic ending. Bateman demurred, but Irving insisted, and won his point. When "The Bells" appeared it took the town by storm, and started Irving and the Lyceum on the road to prosperity and fame.

His second triumph was in Bulwer-Lytton's "Richelieu," which electrified the public; his third was in "Hamlet" (1874), which proved the most climactic of all. With his first performance as Shakespeare's tragic hero, Irving became the most commanding figure on the English stage. Without rhetorical stunts, without elaborate scenic devices, but by sheer magnetism and mastery of natural acting, Irving held his audiences spellbound. By one leap he had reached the side of Garrick and Kean.

In 1875 Bateman died, and the Lyceum passed to the hands of his widow, who retained control until 1878, when she sold out to Irving. One of the latter's first acts as manager of the theatre was to engage Ellen Terry as leading woman. Miss Terry, now thirty years of age, had been playing meanwhile with the Bancrofts at the Prince of Wales's, and with John Hare at the Court. She had not been associated with Irving for eleven years.

The first production in which Irving and Terry appeared together at the Lyceum was "Hamlet," with Miss Terry as Ophelia. Later they did "The Merchant of Venice," with great success, Miss Terry's Portia being considered one of her finest rôles, and Irving's Shylock as great as any of his major characterizations. Their best efforts in comedy were made in "Much Ado About Nothing," where, in the rôles of Beatrice and Benedick, they are said to have been truly superb. Irving's less successful attempts were in the characters of Macbeth, Othello, and Romeo. He was primarily an intellectual actor, and did not shine in parts which demanded an exhibition of blind passions.

Irving took his company to America during the season of 1883–84, where he was received in an absolutely royal manner. Shortly after his return to London he was knighted (1895). From that time on he met with considerable ill luck: he had difficulty in finding new plays which suited his genius; he was the victim of a fire which destroyed the scenery and properties for forty-four of the plays in his repertoire. In 1899 the Lyceum was taken over by a joint-stock company, in which Irving held certain shares, but the new management was unable to revive the prosperity of the theatre. Irving and Terry played together for the last time in 1902, when the Lyceum was closed, prior to being remodeled and opened under other auspices as a low-priced, popular house.

Irving performed steadily in various theatres for the next three years, making a farewell tour of America shortly before his death. In the autumn of 1905 he began a final tour of England, but the tour lasted only eleven days. In the town of Bradford he died after a performance of "Becket," given on Friday, the 13th of October.

Briefly now let us mention other celebrated actor-managers of the time. Charles Wyndham appeared first in the sixties. In 1869 he took his own company to America, where he played for three years. In 1875 he became part owner of the Criterion Theatre, London, and made it his headquarters for twenty-three years. He visited America again in 1883 and in 1889. His most pronounced success was in Sothern's rôle, David Garrick. He translated the play into German, and performed it in Berlin, Moscow, and St. Petersburg, always to enthusiastic audiences. In

1899 he opened the new Wyndham Theatre, London, and in 1902 was knighted.

George Alexander made his début at Henry Irving's Lyceum in 1882. In 1891 he became manager of the St. James's Theatre, and inaugurated a series of high-class modern plays, the best of which were written by Henry Arthur Jones, Arthur Wing Pinero, and Oscar Wilde. His company was a distinguished one, and included such actors as Mrs. Patrick Campbell, Irene Vanbrugh, H. B. Irving (son of Henry Irving), Marie Tempest, and Henry Ainley.

Wilson Barrett was a melodramatic actor of great distinction. He became manager of the Court Theatre in 1879, and of the Princess's in 1881. He toured America several times, and twice visited Australia. In 1884 he played "Hamlet," but without much success. His most popular vehicle was the religious melodrama, "The Sign of the Cross," which he presented at the Lyric Theatre in 1896. His acting was pretentious and vigorous, but was lacking in subtlety.

Herbert Beerbohm Tree made his London début at the Prince of Wales's Theatre in 1881. In 1887 he became manager of the Haymarket, where he presented a mixture of modern drawing-room comedies and Shakespearian dramas. His revival of the classics followed the style of Charles Kean, with its emphasis on pageantry and historical detail. In 1897 he opened the elaborate Her Majesty's Theatre, which then became the home of lavish Shakespearian productions.

John Martin Harvey had his early training under Irving at the Lyceum. A romantic actor of unusual charm, he is known best for his portrayal of Sidney Carton in "The Only Way," a dramatization of Dickens' "A Tale of Two Cities," which was first seen at the Lyceum in 1899.

Johnston Forbes Robertson is another actor who was associated with Irving, and who has won an enviable reputation in romantic drama. Of the same generation are Cyril Maude, Charles Hawtrey, and Arthur Bourchier, all actor-managers of high standing.

In melodrama William Terriss outshone all his contemporaries. Trained by the Bancrofts and by Irving, he was one of the idols of London until his death in 1897. Of equal popularity was J. L. Toole, the comedian, who retired in 1895.

Others whose names loomed large during the last decade of the century were: Mrs. Patrick Campbell, Mrs. Langtry, Irene Vanbrugh, Gerald du Maurier, Henry Ainley, Olga Nethersole, Seymour Hicks, Edward Terry, Marie Tempest, and H. B. Irving. This is a very incomplete list, but for lack of space it must suffice.

THE SPIRIT OF REVOLT

It must be made clear that throughout the century the theatre was monopolized by the actor-manager, who in most cases combined the ability of a star performer with the responsibilities of stage-director and owner or lessee of one or more theatres. In some countries, Germany, France and Russia, particularly, the principal theatres were under the direct supervision of the state, and in many instances were heavily subsidized. In England the large theatres were the property of private capital. But everywhere the actor-manager was the keystone of the structure, the nucleus of a star system.

At the same time the arts were evolving in the direction of realism. Dramatic literature, acting, and painting were coming nearer and nearer to actual life; stage machinery was making possible the illusion of reality. And this evolution did not harmonize well with the organization of the theatre, for state-controlled houses were inevitably conservative in policy, and were loath to experiment with new (radically realistic) plays, while the star system, so dear to the despotic actor-managers, was positively inimical to the chief corollary of the new realism: i. e., a producing method which would subordinate every player to the play itself, and which would create and sustain its illusions by means of a perfect ensemble. The results of this conflict between facts and ideals was a strong dissatisfaction on the part of many intellectuals, among whom were young playwrights, critics, actors, and a certain number of the playgoing public. Action of some kind was unavoidable. A new theatre had to be established, and its guiding principle had to be freedom from the characteristic features of the established theatre. Freedom from the old drama, freedom from the actor-manager and the star, freedom from state or capitalistic control. It was therefore not at all strange that when the first of the new theatres was founded it should be called The Free Theatre. Nor was it strange that it should be founded in France, where so many revolutionary movements have had their birth.

THE FREE THEATRE IN FRANCE

Balzac, Zola, Becque—these were some of the leaders in the so-called "naturalistic" literary movement in France. They were the arch-enemies of romanticism; and it was one of their young admirers who carried their ideals into the theatre. André Antoine was a self-educated boy who loved everything pertaining to the theatre. In 1875 (he was then about eighteen years of age) he secured a membership in the official claque at the Comédie Française. Soon he became the leader of the claque. Having learned all he could from sitting in the audience, he became a "super" on the stage, and in that capacity studied the technique of all the Comédie Française actors. In addition to this, he attended elocution school. But soon he was claimed by the government for compulsory military service, and served in the army for five years.

In 1883, back in Paris, Antoine earned his living by working as clerk for a gas company. His theatrical ambitions still active, he joined one of the Montmartre dramatic clubs, the Cercle Gaulois. This group of amateurs produced a play a month. Antoine wished them to produce a group of one-acts by new playwrights. A few members supported him; the majority did not. He seceded. The owner of the hall where the club produced its plays (a cheap little hall seating 343 persons) turned against him and said he could not use the hall unless he paid a hundred francs rental. The Cercle Gaulois said he could not use the name of the club. Antoine waited until he could afford the hundred francs out of his salary at the gas-works, then gave his first performance. The date was March 30, 1887. He called his company of amateurs the Théâtre-Libre (the Free Theatre). News of the venture had spread, and in the audience were several distinguished *littérateurs,* notably Zola and Becque. Antoine made a hit as an actor, and was immediately taken seriously as a director.

In May another bill was presented under the same auspices, and plans were laid for a full season beginning in October. A few subscriptions were received, and the company was moved to a theatre which seated 800. Seven productions were offered between October and June of the next year. There was a financial deficit, but the artistic accomplishment was felt to be considerable. At last there was a theatre in Paris which opened its doors to the interesting work of new writers—writers who had little or no chance of being heard in the sacred precincts of the Comédie Française or the Odéon.

Antoine's first idea was to serve the rising playwrights of France; his second was to introduce the work of foreign dramatists. In February, 1888, he produced Tolstoy's "The Power of Darkness," and from that moment his little theatre possessed an international significance. Early in 1890 he produced a play by Turgenev, and in May of the same year he gave the first French performance of Ibsen's "Ghosts." The following year he did another Ibsen tragedy, "The Wild Duck." At later dates he gave first performances of plays by Strindberg, Björnson, and Hauptmann, three other giants of the realistic movement.

Among French playwrights whose work he encouraged and presented were: Georges Ancey, Georges de Porto-Riche, Henri Lavedan, Léon Hennique, Jean Jullien, François de Curel, and Eugène Brieux. Those are the brilliant names; there were many more who owed much to Antoine.

At the close of his 1889–1890 season Antoine drew up a rather elaborate plan for a model theatre. By doing so he hoped to interest subscribers, for he was badly off financially. His plan included actual designs for a theatre, and outlined the ideals which would govern it. The house was to seat 900, and every seat was to offer a good view of the stage. It was to avoid the old circular form of auditorium, and was also to eliminate boxes. It was to be fireproof, well ventilated, and equipped with smoking-rooms. The company was to include thirty-five actors, who were to share in the profits of the theatre. Plays were to be changed every two weeks, regardless of success or failure. There were to be no stars, and no favoritism.

Where did Antoine get these ideas? Not altogether from his own mind. Becque, the dramatist, had previously listed several of the points in a critical attack on the conventional theatres. Zola had expressed himself on the subject from time to time. In 1876 Richard Wagner had opened his Festival Playhouse at Bayreuth, and news of its physical characteristics had reached Antoine. In 1888 Antoine had visited Brussels, and while there had seen performances by

From *Theatre Lighting: Past and Present.*

Plate 21: Lighting and Control System Employed at the Paris Opera during the Eighties.

the famous German troupe sponsored by the Duke of Meiningen. From them he had learned much regarding ensemble acting. August Strindberg, the Swedish dramatist, had been in Paris at the time of Antoine's first venture, and had voiced many revolutionary ideas. Strindberg advocated: elimination of boxes, elimination of footlights, concealing the orchestra, discarding the old style of scenery, reduction of the amount of make-up on actors' faces, and similar reforms in the direction of realism.

Antoine had gathered ideas from many quarters. He synthesized them in his plan for an ideal theatre. But subscriptions did not pour in, and he was forced to struggle along in a poorly equipped theatre. In the summer of 1894 he gave up and went on tour. He stranded in Rome. A friend of his, Larochelle, kept the Théâtre-Libre alive for two more seasons, then he succumbed. Antoine, still in debt, made a tour of South America. In 1897 he was back in Paris opening a theatre under his own name. The Théâtre-Antoine pursued the same policy as the old Théâtre-Libre. It favored realism; it favored new playwrights; it stressed realistic effects in acting and setting. It continued until 1906, when Antoine was made director of the Odéon, a state theatre. At the Odéon he was forced to exercise care, and to produce chiefly classics, though he managed to intrude Tolstoy, Hauptmann, Becque, Ibsen, and Zola. In 1914 he resigned, leaving behind him a tremendous debt.

The artistic success of the Théâtre-Libre could not but inspire imitators, both in France and abroad. The most notable French offshoot was the Théâtre de l'Oeuvre, founded in 1893 by Lugné-Poe, an actor who was for a time in Antoine's company. Lugné-Poe combined, better than did Antoine, the artistic with the practical, and his theatre has therefore prospered as the Théâtre-Libre never did. Like its prototype it has laid the emphasis on new French plays of merit, and on significant foreign plays, but it has not

been quite so insistent on realism. Its first production was
Maeterlinck's poetic tragedy, "Pelléas and Mélisande."
Another theatre which may be considered a successor of
the Théâtre-Libre is the Vieux Colombier, founded in 1914
by Jacques Copeau. But an account of its life would be
chronologically inappropriate to this chapter.

THE FREE THEATRE IN GERMANY

In the eighties Berlin made a strong bid for the theatrical leadership of the German-speaking countries. During the middle decades the leadership had rested with
Vienna, where the Burgtheater maintained an extraordinary
standard of excellence, but the challenge came in 1882,
when the Deutsches Theater was founded in Berlin by
Adolf L'Arronge, a dramatist, and again in 1888, when
the Lessing Theater was founded by Oscar Blumenthal,
also a dramatist. But although these theatres specialized in
good acting and good staging, they did not encourage new
playwrights, and for that reason there was still need for a
theatre such as Antoine had established in Paris.

In the summer of 1889 a committee of nine, headed by
Otto Brahm, was formed for the purpose of creating a
society for the presentation of new plays, native and foreign, and on September 29th of the same year they gave a
special performance at the Lessing Theater of Ibsen's
"Ghosts." This play had been shown once before in Berlin,
but had been withdrawn by the censor. The new society
called itself the Freie Bühne (the Free Theatre), in frank
imitation of its Parisian prototype.

On October 20 the Freie Bühne gave a first performance
of Hauptmann's "Before Sunrise," a strong and sordid
piece of naturalistic writing, and the opening gun in the
German dramatic revolution. Later they did plays by Tolstoy, Sudermann, Zola, Becque, and Strindberg. Their high-

est achievement was the production, in 1893, of Hauptmann's "The Weavers," which later proved a climactic
piece in the repertoire of Antoine's Théâtre-Libre.

The Freie Bühne ceased functioning in 1894, for two
reasons. First, Otto Brahm was in that year installed as
director of the Deutsches Theater; second, the commercial
theatres of Berlin had capitulated to the new movement,
and had opened their doors to the young dramatists. The
fight was won much more easily in Germany than in France.
Indeed the state theatres in Paris are still the strongholds
of conservatism.

German imitations of the Freie Bühne sprang up in Berlin and elsewhere. Two in Berlin were the Deutsche Bühne
and the Freie Volksbühne; others appeared in Munich, in
Leipzig, in Breslau, in Hamburg, and in Vienna.

But before we leave Germany we should take some account of the establishment of a unique theatre; a theatre
which, while not dedicated to the major principles of the
Free Theatres, had, nevertheless, much in common with
them, and served, in a sense, to inspire them. This was
Wagner's opera house at Bayreuth.

Richard Wagner (1813–1883) devoted a lifetime to
the cultivation of native German opera. As a young man
he became a musical conductor, and was attached to various
theatres and traveling companies. In 1839 he went to Paris,
where he did hack work for a living. In 1842 his opera
"Rienzi" was produced at Dresden. In 1848 he launched
a movement for the foundation of a German national opera
house, but the public could not be interested in the project,
and there was little faith in Wagner. He then allowed himself to be involved in political matters, with the result that
he was forced to leave the country. For fifteen years he
made his headquarters at Zurich, Switzerland, and there
he began the composition of his great opera cycles. In 1864
he was invited to Munich by Ludwig II, of Bavaria, and

he accepted the invitation. Ludwig was so enthusiastic over Wagner's music and his dreams of an opera house that he planned to build a theatre for him. But public opinion was too strongly against the enterprise, and it was temporarily dropped. Plans for the theatre had even been drawn.

In 1871 Wagner happened to be in the village of Bayreuth. So struck was he by the beauty of the place that he decided his theatre should be built there. He succeeded in interesting a number of persons who helped solicit subscriptions, and the money secured in this manner was augmented by a considerable amount raised by Wagner through a series of public concerts. Finally Ludwig was persuaded to advance enough money to start operations, and the theatre was constructed. Rehearsals under Wagner's direction began in the summer of 1875, many musicians sacrificing their vacations in order to participate, and the theatre was opened in 1876. The artistic success of the event was unquestioned, but the financial loss was very great, and it was not until the season of 1882 that the second festival was held. Wagner died in 1883, after the third series of productions in the theatre which represented all his theatrical and musical ideals, and which still stands as a shrine to his greatness.

The Bayreuth playhouse is a red brick building, simple in architecture, with seating for approximately 1500. All but a few of the seats are on the main floor. Nine boxes are situated at the back of the auditorium, and over these is a small gallery. The orchestra pit is unusual in that it is composed of a series of steps which begin at the front of the auditorium and run under the stage. Each step or level is occupied by a specified group of instruments. Nearest the audience are the violins; farthest away are the heavy brasses. The entire orchestra is concealed from the audience by screens.

The stage, scenery-rooms, and dressing-rooms are large

—as large, together, as the auditorium. Such an apportionment of space was rather revolutionary when the theatre was built, but it was necessary for the elaborate scenic
effects so essential to Wagnerian drama, and it was one of
the ideals of Wagner, who felt that no existing German
theatre suited his needs. The practical nature of the Bayreuth structure had a good deal of influence on later Continental theatres.

THE FREE THEATRE IN RUSSIA

Let us turn Eastward now, and note the birth of another
theatre, in some ways the most illustrious of all. Another
"free theatre," but not called by that name. The Moscow
Art Theatre.

In the sixties and seventies the state theatres of Russia were in a flourishing condition, both in Moscow and
St. Petersburg. Permitted to draw liberally on the treasury
of the Tsar, they presented in the most fashionable and
elaborate manner the standard native dramas, the foreign
classics, Italian opera, and the most gorgeous ballets. The
great actors of all Europe appeared in them. Dramatic
schools were attached to the theatres, and a distinctly Russian style of acting was emerging. At this time, too, it was
the rage for cultured landowners to maintain private companies of actors on their estates. Theatricals, professional
or amateur, were everywhere popular.

In 1863 there was born in Moscow one Constantin Ser-
geievitch Alexeiev. Throughout his boyhood he evinced the
liveliest interest in the theatre, and was consumed with ambition to be an actor. As a very young man he organized what
was known as the Alexeiev Dramatic Circle, which included, besides himself and certain members of his family,
several professionals. This group gave plays and operettas
in one wing of the large Alexeiev house. Constantin also

went to acting and singing school, and finally began to appear in amateur vaudeville performances elsewhere than in his own home. It was at this time that he adopted the name Constantin Stanislavsky, for his family name was entirely too respectable to be used in the atmosphere of vaudeville.

In 1888 Stanislavsky (as we shall call him henceforth) assisted in forming the Society of Art and Literature, which was in reality a play-producing group, and this society presented plays by Molière, Pushkin, and other literary dramatists. Money was lost, but artistic prestige was gained, and more important still, Stanislavsky acquired valuable experience in acting and managing. About this time, too, he learned something from the German company of the Duke of Meiningen, who played in Moscow. He learned from their performance the beauty of perfect ensemble (something which Stanislavsky later perfected), and also the despotic system of stage management, exemplified in Kronek, director of the Meininger. The lesson in despotism Stanislavsky later regretted.

Other influences upon him during his apprentice years in the theatre were: the Comédie Française, which he observed at first hand in Paris; Ernesto Rossi, the Italian actor, in Shakespearian performances at Moscow; Tommaso Salvini the elder, also of the Italian stage, in Shakespeare, and particularly as Othello, at Moscow; and the principles of acting as expounded by Mikhail Shtchepkin, said to have been the greatest dramatic teacher of the century in Russia.

During these same years he enjoyed the friendship of one of the most brilliant young men in Moscow, Vladimir Ivanovich Nemirovich-Danchenko, who was a dramatist, a teacher of dramatic art, a stage-director, a critic, and a thoroughly good business man. More or less accidentally, Stanislavsky and Nemirovich-Danchenko, in the course of a casual conversation at a Moscow restaurant during the early summer of 1897, laid the foundations for the Moscow Art Theatre.

They were expressing their mutual dissatisfaction with existing conditions in Russian theatres, and were advancing their own theatrical ideals. They ended (after an uninterrupted conversation of at least fifteen hours) with an agreement to launch a theatre which would embody these ideals, and which would use as a nucleus, Stanislavsky's semi-professional society of actors, and Nemirovich-Danchenko's advanced dramatic students. A few professionals were to be added to the two groups. The theatre was to be controlled by two executive bodies, the Council and the Direction. The Council was to have absolute control of the artistic policies, and was to be headed by Stanislavsky; the Direction was to be headed by Nemirovich-Danchenko, and was to have absolute control of the business policies. The theatre was to be organized on a profit-sharing basis, and actors in the company were privileged to be stockholders.

A year went by. Then, in the summer of 1898 rehearsals began in a barn that was lent for the purpose by a friend. This barn was situated in the village of Pushkino, a short distance from Moscow. It was remodeled and given a stage. Here, in seclusion, and in the oppressive heat of midsummer, the assembled company of enthusiasts rehearsed two plays a day: the first from eleven in the morning until five in the afternoon; the second from seven in the evening until eleven.

Meanwhile they rented one of the poorer Moscow theatres, and on October 14 the Art Theatre made its début in "Tsar Fyodor," a play by Alexei Tolstoy. A week later was given "The Merchant of Venice," then, on December 2, Goldoni's "The Mistress of the Inn"; finally, on December 17, the play which made them famous, and which gave them the symbol by which their theatre has ever since been known, "The Seagull," by Anton Chekhov. This play, the essence of realistic subtlety, had been tried two years earlier by a theatre in St. Petersburg, but had failed lamentably, and by its failure had frightened Chekhov away from theatrical writing. From the time of the first performance of "The Seagull" by the Moscow Art Theatre it became apparent that a perfect affinity had been discovered. Three other plays by Chekhov became a part of the theatre's repertoire, two of them written especially for this company, and more would have followed but for the untimely death of the playwright in 1904. Subordination of every actor to the play itself, infinite attention to detail, meticulous characterization, deep sincerity of acting, and absolute avoidance of conventional theatricalism—these were the governing principles of Stanislavsky's company, and they were the only principles under which Chekhov's plays could succeed.

The Moscow Art Theatre became the foremost repertory theatre in the world. In its first twenty years of life it made sixty-one productions, each of them as nearly perfect as a production can be. Approximately half of the plays were by Russian authors; the rest were chiefly by Sophocles, Shakespeare, Molière, Goldoni, Maeterlinck, Ibsen, and Hauptmann. Most of these productions were dominated by what Stanislavsky himself has called a "realism of the spirit." That is, a realism which does not depend primarily upon externals, but which is based on a sincere desire to realize and to communicate to the audience the inner (emotional, intellectual) realities of a play as conceived by the playwright. Nevertheless it is true that a great many of the Moscow Art Theatre productions are staged and acted with considerable emphasis on external realistic effects, and it is also true that several members of the company, Meyerhold for one, and Tairoff for another, have seceded and carried out their own opposing ideas in other theatres, largely because they objected to this emphasis. One of the few exceptions to Stanislavsky's realistic principle was the production of Maeterlinck's "The Blue Bird," in 1908, the first performance on any stage. In this, pure fantasy was the guiding spirit.

Stanislavsky also admits that in the early years of the theatre he and his colleagues leaned slightly backward in their eagerness to create something new, something different from the conventional. This tendency toward the revolutionary, the unorthodox, can easily be understood, of course, by anyone who considers how rigid the state theatres were in the late nineteenth century, and how annoying this rigidity must have been to a temperament such as Stanislavsky's. Two of the rules adopted by the Moscow Art Theatre, and retained by them, are that there shall be no applause at their performances, either between acts or at the end of the play, and that there shall be no music between acts or as an overture.

Stanislavsky was, from the beginning, one of the finest actors in the company. Of almost equal greatness and fame are Katchaloff, Luzhsky, Gribunin, and Moskvin. Among the women, those who stand out are Mme. Knipper (widow of the dramatist Chekhov), Marie Lilina (wife of Stanislavsky), Nadiezhda Butova, Maria Germanova, and Maria Zhdanova. It is generally felt, however, that the actresses are not quite as brilliant as the actors.

The Moscow Art Theatre overcame very nearly all of the objections raised against the commercial and state theatres. They avoided the star system; achieved a perfect ensemble, in which the smallest rôle was played as skillfully and conscientiously as the largest; produced only plays of distinction; struck a nice balance between native and foreign plays; introduced new playwrights; kept each production in rehearsal until it was absolutely ready for presentation; rotated their productions rapidly, thus avoiding long runs and the consequent deadening of the performers; substituted an artistic atmosphere for a social one within the theatre; discarded traditional stage-settings, and conceived new ones in the spirit of each play; operated the theatre on principles of sound finance, and shared the profits with the workers in that theatre. There have been few such achievements in theatrical history.

THE FREE THEATRE IN ENGLAND

In England during the eighties there was considerable dissatisfaction with the theatre, at least among critics. The most outspoken detractors of the actor-manager system, so strong in London, were William Archer and George Moore. These writers not only criticized the producing system; they deplored the lack of a new English drama. They realized, also, that the two points were related, and that a worthy modern drama could not arise until a theatre was founded to welcome it. They followed with keen interest and approbation Antoine's experiment in Paris, and cried out for an English counterpart. Their cry was heard, and answered, by Jacob T. Grein, a native of Holland, but an established resident in England. In the spring of 1891 he organized a producing group called the Independent Theatre (a conservative synonym for Free Theatre), and on March 9th this group presented for the first time in England that battle-cry of freedom, Ibsen's "Ghosts." The British Isles rocked with moral indignation. A Zola play followed, then plays by various Continental and English authors. In 1893 came George Bernard Shaw's first play, "Widowers' Houses," an event which obviously was of the greatest importance. Had the Independent Theatre done nothing more than to sponsor the début of the foremost dramatist of the modern era, its existence would long be memorable.

The productions of this group were housed in the Royalty Theatre and in the Opéra Comique. They were supported by a rather small number of subscribers (never more than 175), but on the list were many distinguished persons, including Thomas Hardy, George Meredith, Arthur Wing Pinero, and Henry Arthur Jones.

The Independent Theatre ceased activity in 1897, having presented in its short life twenty-six new plays, and having completed the ground-work for the intellectual English theatre and drama of the twentieth century. It was succeeded by the Stage Society, founded 1899, which produced a series of brilliant plays, by the world's greatest modern dramatists: Ibsen, Gorky, Maeterlinck, Hauptmann, Brieux, Shaw, Barker, Yeats, and others. This series, given chiefly at the Court Theatre, led soon after to the famous Barker-Vedrenne management of the Court (1904–1907), one of the bright spots in modern English theatre annals.

THE FREE THEATRE IN IRELAND

Last in our account of the "free theatres" is the Abbey Theatre of Dublin. In its early years, however, it was not known by that name. It would have been strange indeed if the so-called Irish Renaissance had produced no theatre to serve as the home of its literary aspirations. Irishmen are too theatrical by nature to neglect the drama and the stage when there is something they wish to say.

The first step was taken in 1899, when W. B. Yeats, Edward Martyn, and Lady Gregory founded the Irish Literary Theatre. (This was, of course, only a society, not a playhouse.) Their motives were: to encourage Irish drama of beauty and truth to take the place of the false and sentimental plays which then represented the Irish people to the world; to make Ireland independent of English drama; to bring the poetry of ancient Irish legend back to the people as a living thing.

The first production of the Irish Literary Theatre was shown in the Ancient Concert Rooms, Dublin, on May 8, 1899. There were two plays on the bill: Yeats's "Countess Kathleen," and Martyn's "Heather Field." Because there were no Irish actors of the right sort available, an English cast was brought over and employed in the performance. In 1901 the name of the group was changed to the Irish National Dramatic Company; in 1903, it became the Irish National Theatre Society, and in 1905 this was modified to the National Theatre Society, which it has been ever since.

Three things in particular stood in the way of this organization's success: poverty, the lack of Irish actors sympathetic with poetic drama, and the theatre-licensing law, which forbade the performance of plays except in the three licensed houses of Dublin, the Gaiety, the Queen's, and the Royal. The obstacle of poverty was removed in 1904 by the generous assistance of Miss A. E. F. Horniman, who paid for the remodeling of an old building into a theatre (the Abbey Theatre), and paid the rent for six years in advance. The lack of sympathetic native actors was remedied in 1902 and shortly thereafter by the discovery of the brothers William and Frank Fay, amateurs possessed of real genius, and by the gradual development of an excellent company around the nucleus of the Fays. The licensing difficulty was overcome in the early days of the Society by a special act of Parliament giving it the right to perform plays, and later by a regular license issued to the Abbey Theatre.

New playwrights, notably J. M. Synge and Padraic Colum, were brought to light in the first few years of the new century, and Synge became to the Abbey Theatre what Chekhov was to the Moscow Art Theatre, its greatest and most inspiring contributor.

As early as 1903 the Irish players gave performances in London. Later they toured all the principal cities of England and Ireland, and in 1911 made their first trip to America. They performed in Boston, Philadelphia, New York, Washington, and Chicago, to the delight of many, and to the annoyance of certain Irish-Americans who objected to some of Synge's phrases as being sacrilegious.

The history of the Abbey Theatre lies, as can be seen, largely in the twentieth century. The writer feels, however, that the foregoing résumé belongs in the present chapter because the Abbey Theatre was a direct product of late-nineteenth century forces and opinions, and must be considered a true specimen of the "free theatre" type, inspired partially by the Théâtre-Libre and the Independent Theatre. Its courageous beginning in the last year of the century makes a noble gesture with which to close our account of a period which multiplied its evils enormously, but which redeemed itself in the eyes of the critical by discovering certain antidotes, and in a few cases, administering them.

SELECTED REFERENCES

The first part of the century is interestingly chronicled in Volume VI of Mantzius' *History of Theatrical Art*. Two very good records of the English theatre are Watson's *Sheridan to Robertson*, and Sharp's *A Short History of the English Stage*. An outstanding biography of a great actor is Hawkins' *The Life of Edmund Kean*. A valuable autobiography is *Mr. and Mrs. Bancroft On and Off the Stage*. A brief description of the English theatre may be found in Chapter XI of Nicoll's *The Development of the Theatre*. A fascinating book dealing with the lighter forms of theatricals in this period is Disher's *Clowns and Pantomimes*. A summary of Italian theatre art may be found in MacClintock's *The Contemporary Drama of Italy*. For the theatre in Russia see Wiener's *The Contemporary Drama of Russia*, and Bakshy's *The Path of the Modern Russian Stage*. For France see Chandler's *The Con-*

temporary Drama of France, and for Germany see Witkowski's *The German Drama of the Nineteenth Century.* The fullest account of the free theatre movement is Waxman's *Antoine and the Théâtre-Libre.* The memoirs and biographies having to do with the nineteenth century theatre are too numerous to mention.

CHAPTER XVI

THE EARLY TWENTIETH CENTURY

GENERAL CONDITIONS

A LTHOUGH at the time this is written only a little
more than a quarter of the twentieth century has
passed, the theatre has undergone so many changes,
has endured so many and such varied "movements," has
become such a colossal organization, that any attempt
to record it in a comprehensive manner must fail lamentably. Yet it is possible to indicate the main lines of its development, to interpret the significance of certain of
its most interesting phases, and to mention a few of the
major human figures who have been, or are now, dominat-
ing it.

The reader must first be reminded that when we use the
word theatre today we may mean any one of many kinds
of theatrical institutions. Since the Renaissance there has
been a steady tendency toward differentiation of types of
theatres, and in this century (an age of specialization and
social complexity) that tendency is most marked. To mention some of the general types only, we have: the repertory
theatre (usually subsidized by the state or municipality);
the metropolitan commercial theatre (devoted chiefly to
long runs of legitimate drama, light opera, or musical
comedy); the grand opera (usually subsidized by public or
private capital); the revue (glorified variety show); standardized vaudeville (a chain of theatres with central booking of acts); dramatic stock (a resident company playing
each show one or two weeks); burlesque (low comedy, with

musical features) ; the road show (touring companies without a home of their own) ; the circus; the motion picture, the cabaret. And in addition to these professional types there are many amateur and semi-professional organizations, such as the school and university theatre, the community theatre, the church theatre and the workingmen's theatre.

This diversity of types is due more than anything else to the increase in population, and to the modern city, where, by means of swift transportation facilities, several million people are enabled to concentrate their activities. The greater the population from which a theatrical center can draw patronage, the greater the necessity for specialized appeal. The sophistication of metropolitan life soon develops in the individual a decided taste, and a demand for its satisfaction. A countryman goes to a "show"; a city-man goes to a revue, an intellectual comedy, a light opera—to the specific form of theatricals which his taste or his immediate mood dictates.

In London today, with its potential theatregoing population of seven or eight million persons, there are in the heart of the city between forty and fifty theatres devoted exclusively to legitimate drama, opera and musical comedy. In the suburbs there are at least a dozen more devoted to the same purposes. Of variety houses and music-halls there are about thirty-five of importance, though the total number is much greater. Besides these, there is a profusion of motion-picture theatres.

In Paris, with its population of more than three million persons, there are fifty theatres devoted to opera, legitimate drama, and musical comedy; ten important vaudeville and revue theatres, four permanent circuses, a great many cabarets, cafe-concerts and motion-picture houses. Berlin, with approximately four million inhabitants, has almost exactly the same number of theatres as Paris. Important, but somewhat smaller cities, such as Moscow, Leningrad

(Petrograd), Vienna, and Madrid, have from ten to fifteen theatres each, exclusive of vaudeville houses, cabarets, circuses, and motion-picture houses.

TECHNICAL DEVELOPMENT

Let us now ask ourselves what are the artistic and technical changes that have come to these theatres in the last twenty-five years. The first portion of the reply will be that to many of them there has come no change at all. To others, a great deal.

It will be remembered that during the final years of the nineteenth century two ideas were fighting their way into the theatre: the idea of a free theatre (free from commercialism, free from the star system, free from conventional drama, acting, and staging), and the idea of realistic representation. And the two ideas were closely united. They were found by most persons strikingly harmonious. While playwright and actor strove for naturalness of dialogue, of action, of diction, the mechanic of the theatre strove for stage-lighting devices and scene-shifting apparatus which would further the cause of illusion—the illusion of reality. The search for a realistic technique of writing and acting was successful in more than one country; the triumph of the stage-mechanic belongs chiefly to Germany.

More than one critic has accused the Germans of having turned the theatre into a machine-shop, and the accusation is probably a just one if at the same time we recognize the definite artistic value of some of the machines. The revolving stage, introduced in Europe in 1896, by Karl Lautenschlager of Munich (though its real place of origin was Japan), was one of the most important innovations of the German mechanics, and its value in the production of certain plays is still agreed on. It permits of several complete settings being arranged in advance on a turn-table, thereby decreasing the labor and the time between acts. The sliding stage, serving a similar purpose, allows a complete setting to be slid into the wings at right or left, and another brought into the frame of the proscenium arch from the opposite direction. The setting in the wings can then be changed during the act, and the process repeated. The sinking stage, said to have been invented by Fritz Brandt of the State Opera, Berlin, and perfected by Adolph Linnebach and Max Hasait of Dresden, is the third and most complicated of these scene-shifting machines. The stage is divided into several sections, each section running the width of the playing stage. The front section (bearing a complete setting) is lowered to the basement, where it is slid off to right or left. A new setting can then be rolled into place from the opposite side of the basement and raised to the stage level, or else (according to Mr. Hasait's scheme) when the front section is lowered, a rear section of the main stage, bearing a new setting, is rolled forward to the proscenium, and when it has served its purpose, is rolled back again, and the front section raised from the basement, bearing still another setting. During the ensuing scene the rear section can be re-set, and the process repeated *ad infinitum*. A fourth device, simpler and less costly, which the Germans devised, is the wagon stage. This is nothing more than a strongly built carriage or wagon, about six feet wide by twelve long, to the sides of which may be lashed large sections of scenery —a whole wall, or a staircase, for example. Several of these wagons are used at once, and by means of them a heavy and cumbersome setting can be moved easily and quickly into place.

Each of these inventions has been hailed in its time as a god-send, but each has its disadvantages. And certain disadvantages they have in common. For one thing, they were intended to save labor, but often they have required the services of a large corps of expert mechanics. Again, they were intended to cut short the intervals between acts. This they can do, except for the fact that frequently the *entr'acte* delay is caused not by scene-shifting, but by costume changes. It is obvious that although a setting may be changed in thirty seconds, a costume or a make-up may require five minutes. Another difficulty which appears with the use of most of these devices is that the settings must all be shallow. In other words, with a sliding or a sinking stage, if several settings are to be employed, no one setting can monopolize anywhere near the entire playing depth of the stage. For outdoor scenes this limitation is serious. Then, in the case of the sliding stage, another technical difficulty occurs. When the setting is slid into the wings it runs against the plaster dome, or permanent cyclorama, which is a part of the standard equipment in so many continental (particularly German) theatres. In other words, if a sliding stage is used, the dome cannot run forward as far as it should, or else it must be constructed especially so that it can be moved back out of the way when the sliding stage is in operation. Both alternatives have been resorted to in German theatres. The revolving stage, on the contrary, works very well in conjunction with the dome.

A word regarding the nature and value of this sky-dome may be intruded here. In the early years of this century M. Fortuny, an Italian, devoted a great deal of energy to experimentation in stage-lighting. His chief contribution was a system of indirect illumination in which light from an arc was thrown against colored bands of silk, which diffused the light and reflected it onto the stage. Further, he devised a silk sky to enclose the stage, and by throwing his diffused light upon it, he obtained even greater diffusion. The silk dome, which curved clear around the stage, and at the same time curved forward at the top (making it concave) was held in place by a rigid framework, and was kept free from wrinkles by being sewed double and then inflated like a balloon. This system, although extremely important in the evolution of the modern stage, did not survive long. It overcame wonderfully the harshness of previous stage-lighting, and it introduced the principle of the sky-dome, but it failed because it was very costly, not only in equipment, but in waste of electricity, and because the invention of powerful incandescent bulbs made such indirect lighting unnecessary.

The Germans supplanted the silk sky of M. Fortuny with a plaster one. They called it a *kuppelhorizont*. Such a dome, when lighted skillfully with incandescent bulbs and glass or gelatin color-screens, gives an absolute illusion of airy space. The light diffuses in such a way on its concave surface that the eye cannot detect the presence of the material dome itself, but loses itself in distance. Another type of dome is the *rundhorizont,* simply a semicircular wall enclosing the stage but not curving forward at the top—in other words, a cyclorama. It was soon discovered, too, that canvas could be substituted for plaster, with the advantage of being mobile, though it is rather difficult to keep a canvas cyclorama from wrinkling.

These sky-domes were, even in the days before the Great War, a part of the standard equipment at the best German theatres, and have gradually found their way onto foreign stages. They were the product of the realistic spirit, of the theatre of illusion. Recently, of course, they have served other than strictly realistic purposes. That is their remarkable value. They lend themselves as easily to the hands of the imaginative decorator as to those of the nature-imitator. They are plastic, practical and beautiful. It is hard to fancy them ever being discarded from the theatre.

There is in use in certain European theatres nowadays a very successful improved cyclorama. Said to have been invented in Germany by either Hasait or Linnebach, it has been incorporated into what is called the Ars System (controlled by a Swedish company). This cyclorama travels on a track which runs in a semicircle round the stage. It is made of canvas, and winds on a roller. It can be completely rolled up or unrolled in half a minute. Besides a traveling cyclorama the Ars System includes an elaborate stage-lighting equipment, with portable floor lights to illuminate the lower portion of the cyclorama, and a battery of lighting units which work from above the proscenium arch, and are capable of throwing on the cyclorama all manner of colors, as well as special effects, such as clouds in motion.

Finally we may mention in connection with the sky-dome the projection machine attributed to Linnebach and called the Linnebach Lantern. This device consists chiefly in a special reflector, which, with a single powerful bulb, is able, from a distance of only a few feet, to throw a design over the whole surface of a transparent dome or back-drop. The lantern is placed behind the scene, facing the audience, and the design is painted on a glass plate. This invention, which has already found considerable use in the modern theatre, has led some to predict that the painting of stage settings with paint will soon be a thing of the past, for it is so much easier and so much more economical to paint them with light.

ENTER THE ARTIST

Having thus indicated briefly some of the major technical accomplishments of the realists, it will now be necessary for us to retrace our steps to the beginning of the century and follow a different course forward. We may suggest what this course is by stating that no sooner had realism approached its zenith than it was subjected to a devastating attack. The three giants who led the charge were Adolphe Appia, E. Gordon Craig, and Max Reinhardt. Their followers were legion.

Adolphe Appia, an Italian Swiss, was at work during the

eighteen-nineties, formulating new theories of stage art, and paying particular attention to the artistic use of electricity. His views were first published in 1895, and have ever since been held in great esteem by students of the theatre. Taking Wagner's music-dramas as his experimental material, Appia designed settings for them, and planned the lighting and action along lines which were then revolutionary. His dominant motive was to create a plastic scene—that is, a scene which, by the elimination of traditional painted backgrounds lighted in a perfectly flat manner, would depend upon solid structural forms and strong shadows. In other words he wished to create a three-dimensional setting which would harmonize with the three-dimensional actor, and which would be as vibrantly alive. This sense of the discrepancy between a dead setting and a live actor, between a human body of three dimensions and a back-drop of two (patently false in its attempt to achieve the third by means of perspective) was not original with Appia. It had been felt by acute observers before him, but Appia was the first modern to resolve the problem into something like an acceptable solution. He was probably the first to realize fully the potentialities of electricity as an art medium on the stage. His weakness as a pioneer was that he did not apply his theories to a great enough variety of productions. Satisfied with a few applications, and resting his case on their merits, he became the subject of adverse criticism, and therefore had less influence than certain others who pushed ahead, ever eager to meet new problems and enlarge or alter their theories to fit them.

Gordon Craig, an Englishman, son of Ellen Terry, the great actress, is also fundamentally a theorist. But as is always being pointed out to his detractors, he is a practical man of the theatre as well. In the first place he was an actor—in the company of Henry Irving—from 1889 to 1896. When he left the acting profession he became a designer of scenes, and later a producer. He became also, in a sense, a philosopher. Suffering from an immense dissatisfaction with the whole theatre system as it existed in the nineties, he began laboriously to acquaint himself with its history, its principles, and its future. Like a good philosopher he started with questions. Like Descartes he began by accepting nothing, and ended—but he has not yet ended.

He could scarcely have been nurtured in a better school than that of Henry Irving, for there he learned at first hand the practices of the realistic producer, *par excellence.* If one is destined to become, let us say, a foe of Christianity, it will stand him in good stead to have been reared in the house of a bishop. Irving's love of lavish realism was, and still is, notorious. Craig's reaction to that realism, much as he respected its proponent, was as violent as it was effective. By 1900 he had developed a point of view toward the theatre, and had prepared some extremely interesting designs for settings. These designs he began to exhibit publicly in 1902. They were shown in London, Berlin, Vienna, Munich, Dresden and other European cities. Everywhere they caused discussion, but only in Germany were they greatly appreciated. Craig wanted to found a school of the theatre in England, but the necessary endowment was not forthcoming. He made a few productions in London theatres, but this activity left his countrymen cold. In 1904 he was invited to Berlin to stage a production of "Venice Preserved." He returned to his theories and designs. His first book on theatre art appeared in 1905. The next year he staged "Rosmersholm" in Florence, Italy, for Eleonora Duse. Later he founded his dramatic school in Florence. He continued to publish his ideas and his pictorial suggestions for stage settings. In 1911 he was invited to Moscow, where he designed for Stanislavsky's Art Theatre a production of "Hamlet." The settings were composed of screens arranged to give effects of architectural solidity and dignity. The screen setting, used many times since then, was Craig's invention.

Wherever this man went, his ideas took root. Wherever his essays and drawings went, something new and beautiful occurred in the theatre. His influence has been strongest in Germany, weakest in England. Perhaps because he is English. He is still writing, still drawing, still inspiring all who come within range of his powerful personality. Only a year ago he was in Copenhagen, by invitation of the Royal Theatre, staging Ibsen's "The Pretenders." He lives most of the time in Italy, but he is a world figure—the father of modern theatre art.

It is assumed, of course, that whoever reads this book will read or will have read Gordon Craig's books. They are essential to an understanding of what is new in the theatre. But that fact need not prevent our summarizing the main points contained in them.

Craig insists that the theatre should be noble, not tawdry. It should be the home of the artist. It should be ruled by the artist. And the artist in the theatre should learn from the past, but should not strive to reproduce the past. He should be creative, not imitative.

Further, a production should be the vision of one man. Only thus can unity of effect be achieved. A production must be harmonious in all its parts. It may be realistic, or it may be conventionalized, but it must not be both. Harmony is the essential in any work of art. Realistic acting, a poetic, non-realistic play, scenery which is half realistic and half stylized, lighting which strives for but scarcely achieves the natural, facial make-up which half-disguises the personality of the actor—some such conglomeration as this is common in the theatre, and is definitely opposed to artistic principles.

The arts of the theatre should be reorganized and made consistent. Those who wish a realistic theatre should produce plays in natural settings (in the open air, in buildings suited to the play, or before scenes which are constructed of actual building materials, such as wood, brick, *et cetera*). Actors in this theatre should be chosen for their resemblance to the characters of the play, and should employ no disguise. The play itself should be a faithful representation of life, its action plausible, its dialogue colloquial. The theatre should be lighted by the sun, the moon, or the stars. On the other hand, those who wish an art theater (i. e., a theatre of creative imagination) should eschew all naturalistic effects, should devise settings of decorative appropriateness but innocent of visual deception, should choose plays of poetic or stylized qualities, should use artificial lighting for atmosphere, mood, and design, without regard to the laws which govern the light of nature, should disguise the actors beyond recognition (by the use of masks) or else discard the flesh-and-blood actor altogether and replace him with the marionette, and, finally, should insist upon a technique of acting (posture, gesture, delivery of dialogue) conventionalized and suited to the play in hand.

A theatre of the first sort will strike almost any person as stupidly restricted; one of the second sort will appeal to some as ideal, but to others unnecessarily artificial. There is no doubt but that Gordon Craig himself realizes fully that some compromise is unavoidable in the theatre, but he was quite right in thus analyzing and re-grouping the several theatrical elements. Such an examination and evaluation is extremely important in any theoretical study of the stage.

Like all pioneers, Craig has been forced to exaggerate in order to waken a drowsy public consciousness and stimulate thought. He has annoyed many persons greatly by his emphasis and insistence on certain principles, but less emphasis and less insistence would have accomplished nothing. He has perhaps exaggerated the importance of the mask and the marionette, the two oldest properties of the theatre.

But these had fallen into such neglect and disrepute that only the most violent propaganda could reinstate them in public favor and win for them again the admiration and reverence which for so many centuries was theirs. Craig objects strenuously to the dominance of the modern theatre by the human personality of the actor. Such dominance seems to him vulgar, vain, and inartistic. He blames women for creating such a state of affairs, and suggests that the stage would be improved were it to become (as in old days) purely masculine. But he objects to men and women alike as actors on the ground that no creature of flesh-and-blood can serve the artist-director faithfully. He cannot be brought under perfect control, for his own emotions, his moods, his personality, will intrude themselves into the pattern of the play. The marionette is a true art material, for it is subject only to the will of the director. It has no temperament; it is tireless; it is unchanging. If man persists, then, as an actor, he must become less a man and more a marionette—an über-marionette.

Craig's designs for stage settings have often been criticized as impractical. Many of them are impractical if taken literally. They are consciously ideal, and their purpose is not to provide working plans for the stage-craftsmen of the world, but to instruct them in the principles of design: the value of simplicity, the art of selection, the dramatic use of light and shadow, the strength and dignity of architectural forms. As a matter of fact, although they are intended chiefly to inspire, most of the designs can be realized literally in a certain kind of theatre—one whose stage is sufficiently large and adaptable. It will be remembered that Craig's fundamental point is that the scene-designer be creative—not imitative. Those who attempt to use his designs in their own productions are therefore violating the whole spirit of his work.

The third of the giants, Max Reinhardt, is in every sense

of the word a "practical" man. It is doubtful if he has
ever formulated a theory without putting it immediately
into practice. While Craig dreams and writes, and only
occasionally ventures into the field of public activity, Reinhardt rushes from theatre to theatre, controls armies of
workmen and actors, experiments with plays of all periods
and styles, with small stages and large stages, and hesitates at nothing. He is very likely the most dynamic man in
the history of the theatre.

Reinhardt was born and raised at Baden, near Vienna.
He started acting, as an amateur, in the latter city, with
the great tradition of the Burgtheater for inspiration. His
first real engagement was as a character actor at the Municipal Theatre of Salzburg, during its opening season, 1894.
There he was observed by Otto Brahm, then director of
the Deutsches Theater, Berlin. Brahm took him to Berlin
and introduced him to the naturalistic stage art which was
then in the ascendant. Reinhardt, though successful as an
actor, soon became a director, and began to produce plays
independently. At first he followed the naturalistic course,
but gradually he emerged as a romanticist. A milestone in
his career was his production in 1905 of "A Midsummer
Night's Dream," at the Neues Theater. This production,
which broke so many of the accepted traditions in the German theatre, won the day for the young *régisseur,* and
ushered in a new era.

Meanwhile, in 1902, Reinhardt had opened the Kleines
Theater, a tiny house in which he experimented with the
drama of intimacy. In 1905 he opened another small theatre, the Kammerspiele. His larger productions were housed
in the Deutsches Theater. But he soon gave his ambitions
even greater scope. He was dreaming of the spectacle—
the theatre colossal. In 1910 he produced at the Circus
Schumann (a very large building remodeled somewhat for
the occasion), the Greek tragedy, "Oedipus Rex." A few

years later he took over this huge circus and had it completely rearranged and redecorated by his architect, Hans Poelzig. It thereupon became the Grosses Schauspielhaus (Great Playhouse). The plans called for it to seat five thousand spectators, but it did not quite live up to that expectation. Here during 1919, 1920 and 1921, Reinhardt presented a series of magnificent spectacles, including "Danton," "Julius Caesar," and the Greek trilogy, "Oresteia." In these productions an attempt was made to revive certain ancient theatrical modes. Much of the action was carried out into the audience, and mass effects were emphasized.

Although the Grosses Schauspielhaus venture was hailed the world over as a magnificent achievement, the *régisseur* was disappointed in it. The public approved it, but Reinhardt's own restless spirit did not. Weary of his Berlin theatres, the master showman retreated to the village of Salzburg, for which he had nourished a sentimental affection ever since his début there as an actor, and set to work at an enormous project—the construction of a Festspielhaus (Festival Playhouse), a group of theatre buildings devoted to drama and opera. Associated with Reinhardt in this scheme were Hugo von Hofmannsthal, the Austrian poet-dramatist, Richard Strauss, the renowned composer, and several architects. One of the purposes of the Festspielhaus was to enshrine the spirit of Mozart (who was born in Salzburg), as the spirit of Wagner was enshrined at Bayreuth.

While these plans were going forward Reinhardt sojourned in Vienna, where he was given possession of the Redoutensaal, a richly decorated eighteenth century ballroom in the palace once presided over by Maria Theresa. Here he has presented a number of plays (chiefly classics), utilizing the spirit of the hall, and employing a formal stage, without a curtain, and with only a few conventional

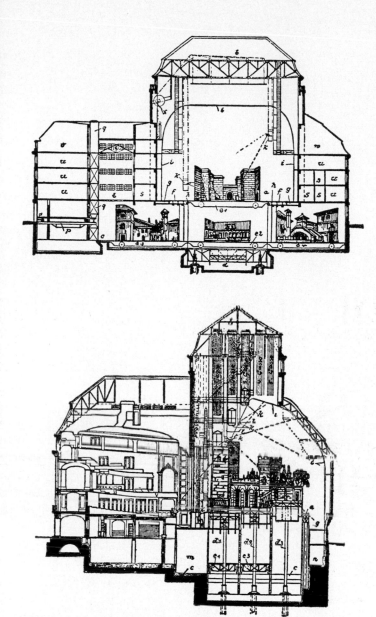

Plate 22–23 : Sliding and Sinking Stage in a Dresden
Theatre.

decorative screens and pieces of furniture by way of stage scenery.

One of the strongest influences on Reinhardt has been the ritual of the church, especially the Roman Catholic Church. More than once he has staged plays in a ritualistic style, but the most ambitious and the most celebrated of his efforts in this direction was the spectacular pageant-drama, "The Miracle," which he produced in London as early as 1911, in various European cities thereafter (Berlin, 1914), and in the United States (New York City), 1924. In this production the essential theatricality of Christian ritual was carried to its ultimate point, and the powerful appeal of mediaevalism was fully realized.

Many of the members of Reinhardt's old companies are world-famous now. During his active years in the theatres of Berlin he trained and directed skillfully more good actors than one can enumerate. But the financial depression which followed the Great War played havoc with these wonderfully organized repertory companies, and many of the leading members were forced to enter the motion pictures or else to take to the road as stars, surrounded by a group of poorer, cheaper actors. Among the most famous Reinhardt players may be listed: Alexander Moissi (rated by many critics the greatest actor in the world today), Albert Bassermann, Max Pallenberg, Leopoldine Constantin, Camilla Eibenschütz, Paul Wegener (seen by Americans in the German film, "The Golem"), Victor Arnold, Gertrud Eysoldt, Rosa Bertens, Wilhelm Diegelmann, Elsa Heims, Emil Jannings (motion-picture star of Europe and America), Rudolf Schildkraut (also a motion-picture star), Ernst Lubitsch (motion-picture director in America), Werner Krauss (known the world over as Dr. Caligari in the film "The Cabinet of Dr. Caligari," and as the brilliant star of other German films), Helen Thimig, Hugo Thimig, Hermann Thimig, and Conrad Veidt (film star now in

America, and known previously to Americans by his marvellous acting in such German pictures as "The Cabinet of
Dr. Caligari," "The Three Waxworks," and "The Affairs
of Lady Hamilton").

To summarize Reinhardt's work (though it is by no
means finished), we may say that he has been the most vital
agent in the modern theatre, that he has made the theatre
a place in which to see as well as to hear (i. e., has brought
pictorial drama back to the legitimate stage), that he has
raised the standard of acting for the entire world, that he
has put into effect many of the major principles of Craig
and Appia, that he has combined art and business with remarkable success, that he has caught up all the threads of
theatrical history and woven them into a wonderful pattern, and finally that he has set an example of industry,
courage, patience and constant growth, which may well inspire workers in the theatre for a long time to come. The
first German *régisseur* to be invited to other countries to
produce plays, he has justified his reputation by making the
theatre international. He is perhaps the first true *régisseur*
in the history of the theatre, for a *régisseur* is a producer
who understands and combines all the arts of the theatre .

WAYS OF ESCAPE FROM REALISM

To study the contemporary theatre is to discover in almost every country an acute dissatisfaction with the realism
of the late nineteenth and early twentieth centuries. The
majority of theatres even today do not reflect very strongly
this dissatisfaction, for they are expressive of the conservatism and aesthetic indifference of the average citizen. But
in practically every theatrical center there are playwrights,
critics, actors, musicians, dancers and designers who are
struggling mightily to escape from the realistic formula—
partly because they are weary of it, and partly because they

feel that it is not true to the best ideals of modern life. And inasmuch as it is these groups who are contributing what is new in the theatre, it is our business to consider them in this chapter. The hosts who remain unmentioned are for the most part concerned with the perpetuation of the nineteenth century tradition, and therefore, whether good or bad, are not much in need of elucidation.

There are several ways of escape from nineteenth century realism, and they have all been taken advantage of. There is, for example, the formal stage; i. e., the stage with a permanent or semi-permanent setting of a three-dimensional, architectural nature. This may follow the Greek style, the Elizabethan, the Chinese, or any other which does not depend upon false perspective to give its illusion, and which relates the actor closely to the audience by bringing the action forward, and by eliminating, or at least minimizing, the importance of the front curtain.

A second way of escape is via the so-called "relief stage"; i. e., a shallow setting with decorative curtains or flats, painted with frank artificiality and forming a background rather than an environment for the actor. This, like the formal or architectural stage, brings the actor nearer the audience, but does not, as the formal stage does, attempt harmony between actor and setting in the matter of dimensions.

A third method is that of the circus. Here the drama is made spectacle, and the action takes place *within* the circle or half-circle of audience. Scenery is of little or no use in such a scheme, but costumes and massed figures take its place.

A fourth method is to replace the living actor with the marionette, or, as a compromise, to put masks on the living actor and turn him into a dancer. Stage and scenery may then be of any style, so long as they are harmonious with the acting.

Fifth, there is expressionism. This is a word which one hesitates to use, for its implications are many, and its abuses legion. It is not an exclusive term; in fact, it might correctly be applied to certain productions mounted in any one of the four previously mentioned non-realistic manners. It does not depend on the nature of the stage, the lack or presence of a curtain, the nature of the actor, the dimensional values of settings, or upon any other physical condition. It is strictly a point of view. Expressionism, in brief, is a name for any method of theatrical production which is opposed to representation for its own sake. In other words, whether the materials of production (actors, scenery, properties, *et cetera*) are real or artificial, recognizable imitations of natural objects, or abstract symbols of mood and feeling, does not matter. They are expressionistic if they are used to convey a significance other than that of mere representation. For example, a common chair and a table will signify, in the typical realistic production, nothing more than their obvious qualities of "chairness" and "tableness." But in the hands of an expressionist they will be so placed or so related to their surroundings that they will carry, in addition to their obvious qualities, a subtle, but appreciable emotional significance. They will, theoretically at least, contribute actively to the drama in the same sense that the actor contributes to it.

Expressionism includes such art-movements as cubism, vorticism, constructionism, and certain varieties of futurism and post-impressionism. As an artistic principle it belongs chiefly to the realm of stage design, though it functions also in the technique of acting. It is not such a mysterious theory as it has sometimes been made out. It has often failed in its purpose, but it has often succeeded. Some of its failures may be laid to the desire for the novel or sensational effect, regardless of aesthetic propriety; others to the use of abstract

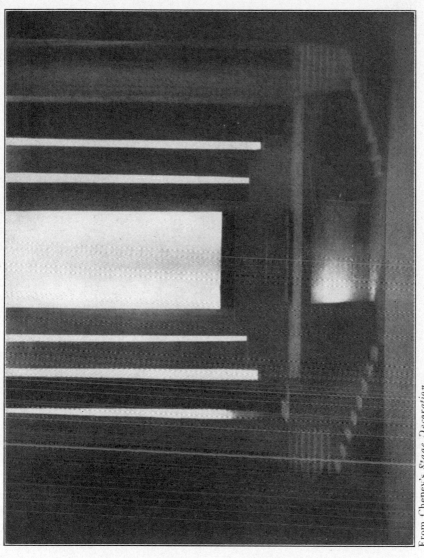

Plate 24: Setting for Claudel's *The Tidings Brought to Mary*, by Adolphe Appia.

or non-representational forms which are too personal to transmit their emotional values to a sufficient number of the spectators. In this connection it must be remembered that a symbol (a concrete representation of an object, an emotion, or an idea) is dependent for its success on a rather general recognition. In long-established, ritualistic theatres, or in ritualistic churches, we find many symbols in use, but these symbols are effective because nearly all who behold them are familiar with their significance. On the other hand, when a modern scene-designer places on the stage a painting or a structural property which he declares represents nothing but his emotional reaction to that portion of the play in which it is to serve, he can scarcely be surprised if ninety-nine percent. of the audience fail to derive from the symbol an emotional experience corresponding to his own. What will have meant "terror" or "vaulting ambition" to the artist, may suggest to the average spectator nothing so much as a gigantic potato or a comb with broken teeth. The mind will inevitably labor toward identification, and will usually arrive at the ludicrous.

Such unfortunate reactions occur, of course, when the artist has gone too far in the abstracting process. He may distort a natural form (of a door, a tree, or a face) and thereby give it expressionistic force; he may simplify a natural form to its last essential characteristic, and thus achieve a beautiful simplicity. But in both these instances he will, presumably, keep the object within the realm of recognizability. Few sensible persons object to this sort of conventionalization. It is the thing to expect in a theatre, where severe limitations are forever interfering with completely realistic representation. But when the object is not identified, trouble begins. The public is angry or amused, and only a few technical enthusiasts appreciate, or pretend to appreciate, the esoteric significance of the symbolic object.

REVOLT IN THE RUSSIAN THEATRE

Having thus indicated briefly the theories of the modern theatre, let us enumerate specifically the places and the persons most conspicuous in their application.

If we consider the contemporary movement one of revolt, we shall not be surprised to find the Russians taking a leading part in it, for it is surely unnecessary to remind the reader that political and social revolutions are certain to be reflected on the stage. Long before the great upheaval precipitated in Russia by the Great War, the spirit of revolt was working, and was finding a degree of expression in the theatre. The Moscow Art Theatre, which at its founding near the close of the nineteenth century had seemed radical, appeared before the end of the first decade of the twentieth century to be the stronghold of conservatism. Its solid realism, even when its spiritual implications were considered, proved too stodgy for many Russians, and the fact that Stanislavsky and his company were so successful and influential, only served to fire their opponents with greater zeal. In order to perpetuate his ideals, and to provide definitely for the future of his theatre, Stanislavsky during the early years of the War opened the First and Second Studio Theatres. Each of these consisted of a small auditorium and a company of advanced students from the dramatic school which had always been operated in conjunction with the Moscow Art Theatre. In these subsidiary playhouses the promising young actors presented plays to the public, and received instruction from the leading members of the mother company. Those who fulfilled their promise obtained small parts at the Art Theatre, and understudied the principals. In 1921 the Third and Fourth Studio Theatres were added, and in the same year a fifth, the Musical Studio Theatre, devoted to opera, under the personal direction of Nemirovich-Danchenko. These well-

conceived and intelligently-guided studios are the pride of
Stanislavsky, but they are only so many thorns in the side
of anyone who dislikes the theatre of realism.

Chief among the dissenters is V. E. Meyerhold, at one
time a member of the Moscow Art Theatre company. He
seceded because he could not continue in agreement with
Stanislavsky's realism. For many years now he has promoted the "theatre theatrical"—i. e., the theatre which is
frankly artificial. Most of his productions have been made
in the theatres of the capital, Leningrad (Petrograd), and
he has experimented with opera as well as with legitimate
drama. He brings the actor close to the audience and frequently keeps the auditorium lights on during the performance, in order that the actor may see his audience and
register its reactions. Meyerhold does not follow the custom of most presentational theatres, however, by insisting
on a bare stage. He often employs rich settings provided
chiefly by the artist A. Y. Golovin, and indulges in colorful costumes and a rich assortment of properties. What
he protests against most bitterly is the "peep-hole" theatre
—with its audience sitting in darkness, peering through a
hole in the wall at a representation of actual life. Such a
theatre seems to him an exhibition of vulgar curiosity. Since
the Revolution Meyerhold has become the ideal of the radicals, and many theatres have adopted his principles as the
true expression of the modern Russian mind.

Still more radical is the Kamerny Theatre, Moscow,
founded in December, 1914, by Alexander Tairoff. Associated with Tairoff was Alice Koonen, an actress who had
left the ranks of the Moscow Art Theatre. Their first production was "Shakuntala" of Kalidasa, and this was followed by an international assortment of plays which
included the work of Shakespeare, Goldoni, and Wilde. All
their plays are mounted expressionistically, and most of
them in a cubistic manner. Stage settings and costumes are

chiefly the work of Alexandra Exter, a woman artist attached to the Kamerny. The theatre operates on a repertory
basis, and has been remarkably successful. Tairoff is an
energetic, clever *régisseur,* and in spite of his fondness for
cubism, does not adhere strictly to any one method. His
ideal is a theatre which is utterly plastic.

Most radical of all, possibly, is the theatre advocated by
N. N. Yevreynoff, and exemplified in certain productions
which he has made in Leningrad and elsewhere. Yevreynoff
is an ardent theorist, and has written a considerable number of essays on theatrical art. The theatre, as he views it,
is a place for the presentation of psychological phenomena,
a place where a group of persons may enter fully into the
secret life of an individual. He has composed "mono-
dramas" which embody this ideal, and in which the action is
sustained by a single character, with whom the audience is
completely *en rapport.* The stage decorations change to
represent the changing world which surrounds the actor, and
also to represent changes within himself. This actor is referred to by Yevreynoff as the "I," for he embodies the
subjective experience of the individual in the audience. It is
interesting to note that Yevreynoff did not formulate his
theory of monodrama first and then write a play to exem-
plify it, but that he composed a monodrama (the form being dictated by the plot) and evolved the theory later. He
is not so narrow in his beliefs as to deny the value of other
forms of drama and other methods of presentation, but he
is convinced of the essential rightness of his theatre, and
feels that its power to express the spiritually significant is
greater than that of the older types. His aim is not the traditional one, "unity in variety," but the exact opposite,
"variety in unity."

On a much more normal plane was the theatre founded
in Moscow in 1914 by Fyodor Kommissarzhevsky in memory of his sister, the gifted Vera Kommissarzhevskaya, who

in her day was one of the great favorites on the Russian
stage, and who died in 1910 shortly after a disappointing
tour to America. This theatre really was an outgrowth of
a dramatic school which Kommissarzhevsky had established
in 1910, and it was an extremely modest venture, its auditorium seating only 150 persons. Its importance lies partly
in the fact that it was one more playhouse devoted to the
anti-Stanislavsky cause. Kommissarzhevsky leaned definitely
toward the "theatre theatrical," but he did not indulge in
any ultra-radicalism. His methods were always sound and
interesting, and expressionistic chiefly in the sense that they
did not aim at realistic illusion. In recent years he has been
in England and the United States, and has produced plays
for the Theatre Guild of New York City.

More frivolous, but certainly not less artistic, than the
foregoing is the theatre founded as a cabaret entertainment
in Moscow in 1908 by N. F. Balieff. The cabaret bore the
name Letutchaya Muish (The Bat). When Balieff later
took his show on a tour of the principal cities of Europe its
name was translated into French, and became The Chauve-
Souris. Like so many founders of unusual Russian theatres,
Balieff was at one time an actor under Stanislavsky. But his
taste did not run to the serious drama; he was essentially a
clown. He therefore originated a super-cabaret—an inti-
mate vaudeville which at first was operated as a semi-private
affair, patronized principally by members of the theatrical
profession, but which soon became a successful public entertainment, and eventually an international triumph. The
Chauve-Souris offers a variety of short acts, just as does a
French revue or an American vaudeville bill, but its acts are
wittier, more original, and more charming. There is a delightful whimsicality which runs through the whole program, and at the same time a spirit of sophistication which
provides balance, and which never touches the plane of
vulgarity. Balieff himself is always present to act as master

of ceremonies, introducing each act with an amusing speech, and creating the proper mood in the audience. Recently the Chauve-Souris has alternated between Paris, Berlin, London, and New York, and besides delighting a large public in each of these centers, has exerted a considerable, though decidedly insufficient, influence on the variety shows of Western Europe and America.

An even more thoroughly internationalized product of the Russian theatre is the ballet. In imperial Russia the ballet was the pride of the Czars. It was the most generously subsidized form of theatrical, and was housed, together with the opera, in two of the finest playhouses in the world: the Marinsky Theatre, Petrograd, and the Great Imperial Theatre (now the Great State), Moscow. Since the Revolution it has been adopted by the radicals, who wish to free it from the conventions which governed it so long, and which savor so strongly of the old régime, but the Soviets have been under too great a financial embarrassment to support it properly, and it has not flourished at home as much as abroad. Of course the Ballet Russe had established itself firmly as an international art long before the Revolution, but in recent years it has been of necessity a wanderer (and a welcome one) over the earth. Introduced to Western Europe by Serge Diaghilev, it has drawn into its service many of the most brilliant dancers, painters, and musicians in the world. It has three great choreographers: Fokine, Nijinsky, and Massine. It has, besides these three, a host of superb dancers, including: Pavlova, Mordkin, Karsavina, Bolm, Krieger, Anderson, and Fokina. Among Russian painters who have contributed ballet settings and costumes are: Bakst, Benois, Roerich, Golovin, and Korovin. Among Spanish and French painters: Picasso, Derain, Matisse, Laurencin, Gris, and Braque. Especially brilliant musical composers for the ballet are: Stravinsky, Rimsky-Korsakov, and Satie.

Although many ballets popular in the theatre today are conservative in every respect, others represent some of the most radical phases of expressionism. An artificial form to begin with, the ballet has a comparatively short distance to go ere it arrives at the pole opposite the realistic theatre. That is obviously why it attracts painters and musicians of the "extreme left wing." On the other hand, whatever contributions are made to it by the artists of other nations, the ballet remains essentially Russian. Like Italian opera, it carries with it ever the fragrance of the soil from which it sprang.

Since the Revolution theatrical experimentation has been rife in Russia. Many workers' theatres have been founded, and in most instances these have followed an expressionistic course. The Theatre of the Revolution and the Proletkult Theatre are two playhouses which are devoted to drama for the laborers, and both these are directed by disciples of Meyerhold. The Proletkult (run by workers), in its attempt to create new and appropriate forms of drama, has gone so far as to move out of the playhouse into the factory (for special productions) and there, surrounded by machinery, with factory hands as actors, to stage plays dealing with the life of the worker. This sort of production, which may be in a sense expressionistic, is also very near to the acme of realism. It represents not so much an escape from the external verities of life as a ritualization of them. It is a new kind of mystery play, with the machine as god.

Climactic events in the Revolution have also been commemorated in drama. Anniversaries of these events have been celebrated by spectacles held in the very public squares which were the original scenes, and thousands of the populace have participated in them. This sort of thing, which has a distinct patriotic value, is, like the factory play, expressionistic because it is formal and ceremonial. The facts relived are real enough, but the motivation is spiritual.

The aim is not illusion, but soul-experience, as in the case of the Dionysiac revels of Athens or the Passion Plays of mediaeval Europe.

Since the Revolution three other distinctive theatres have appeared in Moscow. One, the Semperante (its name derived from a Latin phrase meaning "Art Always Before Life"), is directed by Bykov, and is devoted to the art of improvisation, following the pattern of the *Commedia dell' Arte*. The other two are racial: the Jewish Kamerny Theatre, with plays performed in Yiddish; and the Habima Theatre, also Jewish, but with plays performed in classical Hebrew. The latter is the only one of its kind in existence. It has only recently visited the United States, and appeared in the large cities of the East. Both these theatres indulge in expressionism, and their stage settings are often extremely effective examples of grotesque conventionalization. The chief plays in the repertoire of the Habima group, "The Dybbuk," and "The Golem," are, because of their intense folk-legend quality, beautifully adapted to that manner of expressionism which depends upon decorative distortion.

Finally we may mention briefly the recent Russian motion pictures, two or three of which have been received cordially in Western Europe and America. The film "Potemkin," the first of these to find wide distribution, is declared by thoughtful critics to have ushered in a new period in the art of the motion picture. Commemorating, as it does, an historical event in the annals of the Russian navy, this picture makes use of only natural scenes and properties. Its originality lies in the technique with which these realistic materials were used to create patterns of extraordinary strength and emotional appeal. Men, guns, water, and ship's quarters were all photographed so as to achieve the utmost dynamic effectiveness. Movements of masses were balanced by simultaneous counter-movements, and several planes were employed for these movements. No action in

Plate 25 : Interior of Max Reinhardt's Grosses Schauspielhaus,
Berlin.

the picture was at all lacking in naturalness or plausibility, yet the emotional force created was infinitely greater than that which would have been produced by less complex and less ryhthmical manipulation. It is very likely true that "Potemkin" offers the first clear-cut illustration of a motion-picture technique based on an expressionism which does not distort reality, but merely utilizes its dynamic possibilities.

REVOLT IN THE THEATRES OF CENTRAL EUROPE

Turning westward now to Germany, Austria, and Czecho-Slovakia, we find another scene of modernistic effort. Of the amazing Max Reinhardt we have already spoken. We shall not reiterate his many achievements in the direction of the non-realistic theatre. It should be emphasized, however, that his interest has centered chiefly in the spectacle, in the revival of classic and mediaeval forms, and not in the search for new and abstract patterns. He has worked with many designers, and several of these—notably Alfred Roller and Ernst Stern—have created settings and costumes with markedly modern characteristics, but Reinhardt's taste is obviously founded on a love of the normal, and is seldom freakish.

A *régisseur* of definitely expressionistic tendencies is Georg Fuchs, who, as early as 1907, introduced at the Munich Künstler Theater what has already been referred to as the "relief stage," i. e., a shallow stage which brings the actor forward, and on which the settings are frankly two-dimensional.

More vital, perhaps, than Fuchs, on the modern German stage, is Leopold Jessner, who though inclined toward radicalism, has in recent times held the post of director at the Schauspielhaus (The State Theatre) in Berlin. Jessner, with the aid of his chief designer, Emil Pirchan, has made himself world-famous for his skillful use of steps as an integral part of the stage setting. In some of his productions the greater part of the stage space has been taken up with steps, arranged so as to form an effective design and at the same time to assist rather than hinder the necessary action. Used cleverly, steps can materially increase the effectiveness of entrances and exits, can give a strong, three-dimensional value to the scene, and more important yet, can allow the use of many actors on the stage at the same time without any being hidden from the view of the audience. This fetish of Jessner's has been ridiculed, but it has also been greatly admired and imitated. It is obviously derived from Gordon Craig's theories and suggestions.

Jessner is a consistent expressionist. He uses light without regard to imitation of the natural, but always from the standpoint of theatrical, frequently symbolic, significance. His actors are kept as perfectly under control as living actors can be, and are not allowed spontaneity. Everything which contributes to the production is purposeful, and therefore expressive. There is no room for the accidental, or the casually realistic.

Another German expressionistic director who has been successful in applying theories is Jurgen Fehling, who, at the Volksbühne (Workmen's Theatre) in Berlin has achieved powerful effects in the non-realistic manner. Fehling, who has no use at all for realism, is one of the most radical of all German directors, and in his production of the revolutionary play, "Masse-Mensch," proved himself a master of modern stagecraft. His stage-designer is Hans Strohbach.

At this point we may remark parenthetically that modern ideals of stagecraft have extended into the auditorium, and have materially affected the architecture of the entire playhouse. The Germans have been leaders in these general improvements, just as they have been in the development of stage machinery. It is not hard to realize that the typical theatre of the nineteenth century was a hangover from an aristocratic age; that it was modeled directly after the court theatre of the Renaissance and the eighteenth century. In those older playhouses the architect's guiding principle was a social rather than an artistic one. Showy boxes, horseshoe balconies, and elaborate decorations all served the purpose of the upper classes. The twentieth century, with its democratic and aesthetic ideals, demands that the theatre be physically altered. The outstanding theatre-architect in Europe today is Professor Littmann, who has designed many of the newest German playhouses. He has discarded the circular auditorium (Italian Renaissance), and substituted one which runs almost straight back from the corners of the stage. The auditorium floor he has pitched at a very steep angle, so that no seat has an obstructed view. When he includes balconies he insists that they be short, in order that they shall not interfere with the acoustics. Also for the sake of good acoustics, he employs wood as a wall surface as much as possible.

Since Professor Littmann's pioneer work along these lines, theatre-architects in several countries have been awakened to the problems that confront them, and in many cases have evolved very satisfactory structures. The tendency is still, however, to look upon a theatre as a traditional type of building, and to build upon some antiquated plan, without reference to the requirements of modern staging or the character of modern audiences.

Returning now to our main path, we must mention the widespread interest in marionettes exhibited among the Germans and other peoples of Central Europe, for this interest is surely a part of the revolt against realism. We cannot afford space here to trace in detail the long popularity of the puppet; we must be content merely to point out that although puppet-shows have never died out completely, they were at very low ebb at the end of the nineteenth century. When modern forces set to work, however, one of the results was a revival of the inanimate actor. And nowhere has his resurrection been hailed more enthusiastically than in Germany, Austria, and Czecho-Slovakia. The War, instead of obliterating him, popularized him more than ever, and there are now good puppet theatres in practically all the large cities of those countries, and in countless villages as well. The great puppet centers are Munich, Vienna, Baden-Baden, Pilsen and Prague. The most famous puppet play-house is the Marionette Theatre of Munich Artists, which is operated by a group of writers, painters, and puppeteers, with Paul Brann as director. It is equipped with all the most modern appliances, including a revolving stage and an in-tricate lighting system. Its stage settings are excellently de-signed, and its actors skillfully manipulated.

In Baden-Baden the chief puppeteer is Ivo Pühony, whose dolls are all carved from wood. This theatre spends its sum-mers at home, its winters on tour. Its dramatic repertoire is large and varied, including classic and modern plays. In Vienna the most celebrated marionettes are those created by Richard Teschner. They are the most sophisticated of all theatrical dolls, and are the very antithesis of the old-fashioned, naïve and clumsy creatures descended from mediaeval times. Many of the Teschner puppets are nude, and their bodies are extraordinarily slender and graceful. Some of them are fairly realistic; others are fanciful; all are the essence of subtlety. They are exhibited in private circles only.

Czecho-Slovakia has always been hospitable to the pup-pet, but never so decidedly as during and since the War. It is said that although in war-time a strict censorship was im-posed upon the newspapers, the puppet-shows were over-looked (by the Austrians), and that the Czecho-Slovaks used them to excellent advantage in spreading propaganda and in maintaining the morale of their countrymen. Since the War they have been utilized in the educational system, and are playing somewhat the same rôle that the motion pictures are playing in the United States. It is reported that more than 1500 puppet-theatres have been established by the authorities in Czecho-Slovakia since the War, and that they have been prescribed for military units as well as for schools. Certainly as an economical, artistic, and entertaining method of disseminating national ideals and information, the puppet-show has many distinct qualifications. And it belongs fundamentally to the expressionist movement, whether it be a survival of the crude folk-type or a sophisticated modern derivation. In any form it is sufficiently artificial to be ruled out of the theatre of realism.

A word now regarding that cousin of the puppet-show, the motion picture. Of all European countries Germany is the one that has steadily made progress with the motion picture as an art form. Recently, of course, Russia has made some notable films, but her accomplishments are few compared with those of Germany. Following the end of the War, German designers and actors set to work, with more art than money, and in a short time produced a series of films which were years ahead of anything then known to the rest of the world. "The Cabinet of Dr. Caligari," directed by Robert Wiene, was the first application of purely expressionistic principles to the motion picture, and is still, relatively speaking, an advanced work of art. Made at a total cost of approximately ten thousand dollars, it eclipses practically every million-dollar film that has been put upon the market. As a highly unified specimen of expressionism (the variety which uses distortion as a principle of design) it is matchless. The story, the acting, the settings, are in one key, and that key is an appropriate one for motion pictures.

"The Golem," with expressionistic settings designed by Hans Poelzig, decorator of Reinhardt's Grosses Schauspielhaus, is almost as successful as "Dr. Caligari." It is hampered somewhat in its imaginative flight by the necessity o considering historical architecture and detail, but it is never theless an inspiring and harmonious work.

Even in relatively realistic films the Germans have se standards. In such historical romances as "Deception," "Passion," "Peter the Great," "The Affairs of Lady Hamilton," and "All for a Woman," there has been exhibited a spirit, an understanding of the technique involved in the re-creation of an older period, which has been generally lacking in non-German films of a similar type. And in the definitely modern, realistic drama there can be no question of German superiority. "The Last Laugh," "Variety," "Shattered," and many others of this sort have already become models. The acting of Emil Jannings, Werner Krauss, and Conrad Veidt (all from the Reinhardt family) has easily overshadowed the work of any other group of motion-picture actors in the world. That is, if we consider only legitimate actors. Clowns are considered separately.

In still another category are the romantic-mythological films, such as "Siegfried," and "Faust." Here the Germans have blended the fantastic and the realistic, with eminently satisfactory results. "Siegfried" is probably the most majestic, the most spiritually beautiful film yet produced. It is music and poetry, architecture and painting, grandly combined.

The German studios have not usually had the technical equipment desirable in the making of motion pictures, but what equipment they have had they have used superbly. They were the first to realize that the camera need not be stationary, and that discovery almost revolutionized movie technique. They were the first to make a successful picture without sub-titles—a picture free from the literary quality that linked the spoken and the silent drama. They were the first to make a picture with settings entirely creative, and of one artistic point of view. These accomplishments need no elaboration; they illustrate clearly enough that Germany has led the world in taking the motion picture seriously as an art form. That leadership may, for one reason or another, pass elsewhere, but the pioneering years should not be forgotten.

REVOLT IN THE FRENCH THEATRE

The leading spirit in the modernistic French theatre is M. Jacques Copeau, whose small Paris playhouse, the Théâtre du Vieux Colombier, was opened in 1913. During the war the house closed down (M. Copeau directed productions in New York City for two seasons, 1917–1919), but it was reopened in 1920, and continued to operate until 1924, when financial embarrassment overtook it. M. Copeau is not a radical of radicals, yet he dislikes the illusionary stage, and reacts from it in the direction of formality. At the Vieux Colombier he used no front curtain, and there were no wings; there was a forestage, and on the main stage a semi-permanent setting, with exits into adjoining rooms. His settings were brilliantly designed by Louis Jouvet. Since 1924 M. Copeau and his troupe have worked in semi-retirement (on co-operative terms) at an old château in the Côte d'Or, whence they issue periodically to delight the audiences of various European countries with their original and harmonious performances of modern and classic plays. Molière is their *forte*.

Other French producers who fit into the general category of expressionists are Georges Pitoëff, Firmin Gémier, Jacques Rouché, and M. Lugné-Poe. M. Pitoëff, a Russian by origin, lays emphasis on modern design, and his productions at the Théâtre des Arts have attracted wide attention. M. Gémier, formerly classed as a radical, was in 1921 appointed director of the Odéon, the second State Theatre. He is not remarkably original, for he follows in the footsteps of the Germans, and of Reinhardt in particular, but he has had the courage to adopt modern styles. M. Rouché, a man of private wealth, founded in 1907 the Théâtre des Arts, and later became director of the Opéra. Lugné-Poe, who has been mentioned in a previous chapter as founder of the Théâtre de l'Oeuvre, in 1893, has continued the Free Theatre tradition even to the present day, though his work was suspended during the War, and since then has been of a semi-private nature. Both Gémier and Lugné-Poe were colleagues of Antoine in the early days of the Théâtre-Libre.

There have been many other attempts to inject the modern spirit into the French theatre, but most of them have been short-lived. It is undeniable that although Paris is the center of artistic radicalism, most of the radicals are foreigners, and have very little influence on French institutions. The French theatre as a general thing is extremely old-fashioned, and the public appears quite satisfied with it. Compared with the German or the Russian theatre it is shockingly reactionary. This may be explained partly by the fact that the French have a strong literary interest in the theatre, and are more concerned with the arts of playwriting and acting than with the art of stage design and the mechanics of stage effects. A few modern French painters have contributed to the Ballet Russe, and to certain legitimate productions, but their work has been too slight to stand comparison with that of their northern and eastern neighbors.

REVOLT IN THE ITALIAN THEATRE

In Italy there have been a few isolated and brilliant efforts in the cause of expressionism. As early as 1909 Signor Marinetti was experimenting at Milan with a theatrical style which has been classified as futurism. It may also be called constructionism or machine-expressionism, for it in-

From *Theatre Arts Magazine.*

Plate 26: Russian Realism. A scene from Gorki's *The Lower Depths.* At the Moscow Art Theatre.

volves the use of mechanical objects as vital actors in the play—that is, it emphasizes the dramatic value of the inanimate, and demands plays in which scenery, lighting effects, and properties have values other than those given them by their relations with the living actor, and may therefore "act" independently.

With a more particular emphasis there is also Ricciardi's theatre of color, which endeavors to prove that color is the most fundamental element in the theatre. In Ricciardi's productions (which have not exactly triumphed) the psychological values of color have been entertainingly, if not convincingly, tested, and although it seems unlikely that such productions can do more than amuse for a brief time, it is possible that they have demonstrated something useful to other directors.

Still another extreme theorist is Scardaoni. His approach to the theatre is via the path of visual beauty. He refuses to admit the supremacy of dialogue as a theatrical element, and insists that the theatre should be a temple of light, of gesture, of movement. It can scarcely be doubted that this conception is derived from the theories of Craig and Appia, and it is quite clear that although it has admirable points, it is nevertheless a difficult conception to objectify.

We may mention next the Independent Theatre of Signor Bragaglia, which has the distinction of being located in the recently excavated baths of Septimus Severus at Rome. Here, within walls decorated by Italian futurists, are presented modern plays selected from the literature of several countries. But critics have not been overly warm toward this group of expressionists (or should we call them excavationists?), for they feel that there is too much slavish imitation in their methods, and not enough sincerity.

Finally, and no doubt of greatest importance, is the Teatro Odescalchi, opened in Rome in April, 1925, under the direction of the brilliant dramatist, Luigi Pirandello. The founding of this playhouse represents the latest and most auspicious attempt to establish an Italian Art Theatre— that is, a theatre which will present the finest examples of intellectual drama, native and foreign. The theatre seats only 340 persons, and caters to the sophisticated. If it fails it will only prove what has been proved many times before, that the Italians have no great interest in prose drama. The opera, it must be remembered, is still the theatre in Italy.

REVOLT IN THE ENGLISH THEATRE

The English, in spite of their illustrious countryman, Mr. Gordon Craig, have not taken much stock in expressionism, and then only in its more conservative styles. There were, to be sure, the few productions made by Craig himself in London at the beginning of the century, but these did not have much influence. Then came Mr. Granville-Barker, with a series of Shakespeare presentations in a modified Craig-Elizabethan manner. These really caused a considerable stir, and, although subjected to some sarcastic comment, were successful enough to bring forth imitations. Mr. Granville-Barker's fundamental motive was to rid the stage of the elaborate clap-trap of nineteenth century scenery, and to put in its place a combination of decorative curtains and simple architectural units which could be handled swiftly and easily, thereby restoring to Shakespeare's plays their natural tempo and proper sequence of scenes.

More strictly antiquarian in point of view have been the productions of the London Stage Society and its offshoot, the Phoenix Society. The former limited itself to revivals of classics; the latter limits itself to the revival of English classics, and almost exclusively to Elizabethan plays.

Few English designers have shown an interest in expressionism. The work of the late C. Lovat Fraser may be considered non-realistic, for it was based upon a love of eighteenth century styles. It was a beautifully simplified treatment of an older manner, and while not radical was at least decorative and artificial in spirit. Norman Wilkinson, Paul Nash, and a few others have made modern designs for the English stage, and Paul Shelving, George Sheringham, and George Harris have done work which is not lacking in imagination, but which is nevertheless primarily realistic. It is safe to say that expressionism has failed to interest the English theatre. It has appeared less frequently since the War than before, and has therefore apparently not taken root.

It is extremely unfortunate that space does not permit this chapter to go further in its quest of the strictly modern art of the theatre. Interesting work has been done in many European cities of secondary or minor theatrical importance: in Stockholm, at the Royal Opera; in Prague, at the National Theatre of Czecho-Slovakia; in Amsterdam, Brussels, Hamburg, Madrid, Budapest and elsewhere. But what these cities offer is after all but a reflection of the experiments and accomplishments in the great centers. We have traversed the main thoroughfares; the bypaths must be neglected.

THE THEATRE AND THE WAR

It is more urgent that before we close this subject we indicate briefly the effects of the Great War on the European theatre. The effects varied strikingly in different countries. In England, for example, the War years brought more evil than good. Taking advantage of the chaotic condition into which the theatre was plunged, a combination of commercial managers tightened its hold, and secured practically a monopoly of the playhouses. It then proceeded to exploit as fully as possible the rampant emotionalism of the time. A flood of cheap patriotic plays and sensual revues

and musical comedies was loosed on London, with results
that were patently demoralizing. Little or nothing was done
to use the theatre as an idealizing and ennobling force. The
work of great dramatists (except for some Shakespeare
revivals at the "Old Vic") was scarcely in evidence during
the period of moral and spiritual stress—the time when it
was if ever needed. The Government took no action toward
control of the situation, and the theatre was allowed to run
headlong toward degradation. After the War things improved somewhat, but meanwhile the damage had been
done.

Before the War the repertory theatres had gained headway in the British Isles, and seven of them were operating
successfully. These were situated in Dublin, Birmingham,
Bristol, Glasgow, Liverpool, Huddersfield, and Manchester. Only two of these (the Abbey Theatre, Dublin, and
the Birmingham Repertory Theatre) survived the War.
The rest disbanded. Among the favorable signs of post-war
theatrical development, however, is the amateur movement,
which is gaining headway rapidly. The leader in this field
is the Maddermarket Theatre in Norwich, which was formerly a church, but which has been remodeled into an Elizabethan playhouse, and is used by the Norwich Players.
There are signs, too, that there are to be a number of community theatres for the working classes, sponsored by the
Labour Party. A few efforts in this direction have already
been made.

In France conditions during the War were almost as bad
as in England. The Paris theatres were more thoroughly
commercialized than ever before, and only the presence of
the State Theatres prevented a complete débâcle. Classics
continued to be performed at these houses, but privately-
owned theatres went wild on the subjects of nationalism and
sex.

In Germany the theatre held up its head through the

From Cheney's *Stage Decoration.*

Plate 27: German Expressionism in the Motion Picture. A scene from *The Cabinet of Doctor Caligari.*

storm. The large number of State and Municipal Theatres kept before the public a wonderful repertoire of native and foreign classics. Shakespeare was played regularly, opera was as strong a favorite as ever (whereas in France and England it almost disappeared), and German classics, especially those based on the lives of national heroes, served to keep up the morale of the people in an intelligent and artistic manner. In Vienna, even, when the Austrians were starving to death, the famous Burgtheater, the Volkstheater, and the Opera all held to their normal standard of first-rate productions of masterpieces.

In Prague the Czecho-Slovaks maintained the customary repertoire of international classics at the National Theatre, and in 1916 presented a cycle of Shakespeare's plays in honor of the Tercentenary of his death. The Poles exhibited an equal if not greater courage and faith in the theatre. Warsaw, occupied and sacked first by the Russians, then by the Germans, stripped of food, of shelter, of clothing, exhausted with privation and disease, miraculously kept its theatres running, and offered only the highest theatrical fare.

Russia, in a maelstrom of foreign strife and internal revolution, never forsook the theatre. When the Soviets came into power they quite naturally utilized the drama for political propaganda, but in doing so they paid tribute to its power. They did not ignore or insult it. They encouraged coöperative theatres for the workers, praised and aided men like Meyerhold, whose artistic radicalism harmonized more or less with their ideals of society, and respected, even though not agreeing with, the conservative Moscow Art Theatre of Stanislavsky. It is obvious that the officials of the Soviet Government have enforced some very silly rules regarding the drama. They have, for example, blackballed the plays of Shakespeare and Shaw, because they do not harmonize with Soviet social ideals. They may commit further absurdities. The point is, however, that the theatre as an institution has been strengthened rather than weakened by the turmoil in Russia. It has not been sold out to the money-grubbers.

This summary is not a pleasant one for the reader with English or French sympathies, but the facts should be faced. War is the test of any public institution; if it goes to pieces it is weak. It must be that among the people of northern and eastern Europe the theatre is something vital—not merely a place in which to kill time.

APOLOGY FOR A QUICK CURTAIN

To stop at this point may appear heretical. A cry will go up: What of all the sane, substantial playhouses, filled with competent, even famous actors and painters who have never even heard of expressionism? Do they not belong in this chapter? No doubt they do, but there is not room for them. And they do not need explaining. If we have laid undue emphasis on the abnormal, it is only because it is the new thing in the theatre (or else the very old). We are living in a strange time, and an interesting one.

SELECTED REFERENCES

The three best general references on the contemporary European theatre are: Macgowan's *The Theatre of Tomorrow*, Macgowan and Jones' *Continental Stagecraft*, and Moderwell's *The Theatre of Today*. Also broad in scope, but with a different approach, is Carter's excellent *The New Spirit in the European Theatre*, 1914–1924. More specific treatises, but of unusual value, are: Sayler's *Max Reinhardt and His Theatre*, the same writer's *The Russian Theatre*, Stanislavsky's *My Life in Art*, Howe's *The Repertory Theatre*, Lady Gregory's *Our Irish Theatre*, and five books by Edward Gordon Craig: *On the Art of the Theatre*, *Towards a New Theatre, The Theatre—Advancing, Scene,* and *Books and Theatres.* A complete record of important artistic events in the European theatre since 1918 may be found in the files of *Theatre Arts Monthly* (formerly *Theatre Arts Magazine,* a quarterly).

THE THEATRE IN AMERICA

CHAPTER XVII

BEGINNINGS: THE EIGHTEENTH CENTURY

IT would be obviously untrue to say that no theatricals existed in the American Colonies before 1700, for even the slightest understanding of human practices tells us that the dramatic impulse asserts itself, perhaps timidly and without skilled direction, wherever society exists. It is true that the Puritans of early New England frowned upon frivolity and show, yet even they could not always resist the lure of occasional entertainment. The more cavalier residents of Virginia and the Carolinas, on the other hand, leaned frankly toward the gaieties of life.

But there is no record of any professional companies of players in the Colonies before the year 1700, and the only recorded amateur production of an actual stage play is that of "Gustavus Vasa," a tragedy written by Benjamin Colman and acted by the students of Harvard College in 1690. This is thought to have been the first play written by an American and played in America.

The first license to perform plays professionally was granted in New York some time during the period 1699–1701 to one Richard Hunter, whose origin and career are utterly unknown. The next record has to do with Anthony Aston, an English actor, who toured the Colonies at the very beginning of the century, probably in 1703. Details of his associates and their performances are extremely scanty.

In 1716 was built at Williamsburg, Virginia, the first playhouse in America. It was erected by William Levingston, a dancing master, and probably housed some legitimate productions as well as exhibitions of dancing. There is no record of these, however. In 1735–36 it was used for amateur performances by the students of William and Mary College, and possibly by visiting companies of professionals. In 1745 it was converted into a town hall, and its theatrical life ceased.

New York City got its first playhouse in 1732. It was called the New Theatre, and was merely a large room (seating about 400) with a platform stage, in a building owned by the Hon. Rip Van Dam, acting governor of the city. The players came, it is thought, from England, and they acted as a rule three times a week, their principal piece being the popular English Restoration comedy, "The Recruiting Officer," by George Farquhar. The room was lighted by candles, and the scenery employed was slight. The success of the venture, however, is attested by the fact that these performances continued more or less regularly for about a year and a half.

There were plays given in Charleston, S. C., as early as 1735, though who the players were is a question. Possibly they were the same that performed in Williamsburg and in New York. Philadelphia, then the principal American city, had plays by 1749, in spite of strong opposition from the Quakers. In 1750 a group of amateurs, assisted by two professionals from England, gave in a coffee house in Boston a performance of Otway's "The Orphan." Such a sensation was caused by this ungodly event that laws were immediately passed forbidding all forms of play-acting in that Colony.

The first half of the century offers no more records than the foregoing. Other theatrical events of minor significance may have occurred, but if so, the few newspapers of the time were too disdainful to give them space.

From 1750 on, however, the story is clearer and more complex. In that mid-century year a company of players arrived in New York from Philadelphia, where, it is assumed, they had been performing. They were headed by Walter Murray and Thomas Kean, thought to have been English actors who came to America via the West Indies. They stayed in New York two seasons and there gave a series of popular English plays, including John Gay's "The Beggar's Opera," which was probably the first light opera performed in America.

In 1752 there arrived from England the first complete and well-trained dramatic company. It had been organized in London by two brothers, William and Lewis Hallam, both actor-managers. The former did not join the expedition, but left the management entirely to Lewis. The troupe included twelve adults, Hallam and his wife making two, besides the three Hallam children. They landed in Virginia, and with the Governor's permission, acted in Williamsburg for almost a year. They then (1753) moved up to New York, and after constructing a new playhouse on Nassau Street, enjoyed a successful season. In the spring of 1754 they removed to Philadelphia, where, after much altercation with the authorities, they succeeded in obtaining permission to perform. This engagement lasted only two months. During that time, however, William Hallam arrived from England to collect his share of the profits, and then promptly returned home. Following the Philadelphia season the company sailed for Jamaica, West Indies. There Lewis Hallam died, and upon his death the company disbanded. Mrs. Hallam, however, was later seen in America in the company organized by David Douglass, an Englishman, whom she married in 1758.

David Douglass, besides acting as head of this new company, was America's first great theatre builder. He built, among others, the first permanent (brick) playhouse in Philadelphia, the Southwark Theatre, in 1766; another, of similar construction, in Annapolis in 1771; and the John

Street Theatre, New York City, in 1767. Wherever he and his company went they left theatres behind them, and while these were small and crude compared with modern playhouses, they were not at all bad for their period. They seated anywhere from 300 to 600 persons, were imitative of English theatres of the time so far as arrangement and general architecture were concerned, were heated by a single stove in the foyer (around which the audience gathered between acts), and were commonly painted red (symbolic of just what is not clear).

Douglass at first called his actors "The Company of Comedians from London," but during the sixties, when anti-British feeling was growing in the Colonies, he prudently changed this to "The American Company." His leading man was Lewis Hallam, Jr., one of the children in the Hallam expedition of 1752. Young Hallam became the foremost actor in America, proving himself a Hamlet when he was 21, and a Lear when he was 26.

At the outbreak of the Revolution, Congress recommended the prohibition of play-acting, and several of the States acted in accordance with the request. The Revolutionary period would therefore have been practically devoid of theatricals had it not been for the usurpation of playhouses by British military troops. Wherever British soldiers were quartered, dramatic performances were given, usually with charity as an ostensible motive, but with the natural craving for entertainment the fundamental one. Private gain entered into the matter, also, for many of the soldier-actors received pay for their services.

The John Street Theatre, New York City, was renamed the Theatre Royal, and was the scene of many British productions. The Southwark Theatre, Philadelphia, was another important house adopted by the usurpers, and in Boston, where no theatre existed as yet, plays were nevertheless

Plate 28 : Interior of the Old John Street Theatre, New York.

given. This British occupation of the American stage extended from 1776 to 1783.

Following the Revolution the American theatre was quick to revive. It came back stronger than ever, in fact, for there was now an acute national consciousness, and this inspired native art. Baltimore had opened its first theatre in 1781, and shortly afterward became one of the chief theatrical centers; a small crop of playwrights began writing plays with American atmosphere; Pennsylvania repealed in 1789 its law against play-acting; and in 1792 Boston christened (not very willingly), its first theatre.

Of these native playwrights the most prominent were Royall Tyler, a graduate of Harvard, whose comedy, "The Contrast," was acted at the John Street Theatre in April, 1787; and William Dunlap, the first American to make a profession of playwriting, who in 1798 became one of the lessees and managers of the Park Theatre, New York, at the opening of that famous house. Dunlap wrote many plays, and even though they were superficial, they helped lay the foundation for an American Drama. Tyler is credited with having introduced, in "The Contrast," for the first time on the stage the stock Yankee character who was to appear so frequently in plays thenceforth. Tyler's conception of the comedy of manners, which he applied to American life, was, it is said, derived from the plays of Sheridan.

As has been stated above, Boston acquired its first playhouse in 1792. Although the law forbidding stage presentation was still in effect in Massachusetts, that law was circumvented by a group of theatre-loving Bostonians, who raised by private subscription a sum of money sufficient to erect a building with a seating capacity of about 500, and possessed of all the basic requirements of a theatre. It was opened under the name of the New Exhibition Room, and

322   THE STORY OF THE THEATRE

was ostensibly for the presentation of such harmless entertainment as tumbling, dancing, and wire-walking. It opened
in August and proceeded cautiously, but during September
the managers risked a little drama. The heavens did not
fall, so more drama was risked. Shakespeare was played,
as were later English dramatists. But on December 5th,
during a performance of "The School for Scandal," a sher-
iff entered, stopped the performance, and arrested the manager. The New Exhibition Room was closed.

But, like all unjust prohibitions, this one but served to
augment the desire for that which was prohibited. Another
subscription was taken, and in 1794 an even more pretentious building was erected and opened boldly as "The Boston Theatre." It contained as additional features, a dancing
hall, card-rooms, and tea-rooms. A company of players was
brought from England, and the whole affair was carried off
successfully. It was in this theatre, incidentally, that Miss
Arnold, comedienne and singer, the mother of Edgar Allan
Poe, made her début in 1796. The building burned in 1798
—the first American theatre to be destroyed by fire. But
Boston was not without a playhouse then, for in 1796 the
Haymarket Theatre, a large wooden structure, had been
opened.

The most important theatre established in America during the closing years of the century was the Park Theatre,
New York City. This house, designed by a French engineer,
was constructed of stone, had three tiers of boxes, a gallery, and a pit. The seats in the boxes and pit were cush-
ioned. The stage was well equipped, and the scenery was,
for the time, excellent. It opened in January, 1798, with
William Dunlap and John Hodgkinson as lessees, and became the home of American drama. For thirty years the
John Street Theatre had been the leading playhouse of the
country. It now closed its doors, and the Park Theatre took
its place. Performances were given four days a week: Mon-

day, Wednesday, Friday, and Saturday. The doors were opened at five o'clock and the curtain was at a quarter past six.

Next in importance among the theatres of the nineties was the Chestnut Street Theatre, Philadelphia, established in 1794, and managed by Thomas Wignell, one of the most active theatre magnates of the period. On its stage appeared practically all of the best contemporary actors, including Thomas Abthorpe Cooper, a young English tragedian imported by Wignell; William Warren, father of the well-known American star bearing the same name; and John Bernard, a famous London comedian.

By 1800, although the American-born actor had not yet come into his own, and the American-born playwright had barely made himself heard, the theatre was a firmly grounded institution, and was ready for the great era of expansion and progress which began early in the nineteenth century.

SELECTED REFERENCES

The most recent and the most authoritative account of the beginnings of the theatre in America is to be found in Odell's *Annals of the New York Stage,* Vol. I. Another first-rate study of the subject is contained in Hornblow's *A History of the Theatre in America.* An older work is Seilhamer's *History of the American Theatre.* For the colonial drama, and to a considerable extent, the theatre itself, see Quinn's *A History of the American Drama from the Beginning to the Civil War.*

CHAPTER XVIII

THE FIRST HALF OF THE NINETEENTH CENTURY

THEATRE DEVELOPMENT 1800–1850

W E have seen how the theatre was established in the large Eastern cities before 1800. The first decades of the nineteenth century brought not only a multiplication of playhouses in these centers, but also the extension of theatrical art to interior regions of the country. As there were in existence no railroads, and no highways reaching back any distance from the coast, travel inland was a slow, difficult, and dangerous venture. But actors have never been long deterred by such obstacles. In 1815 the first Western touring company was organized by one Samuel Drake, a stage-manager, and with Kentucky as an objective, the troupe set out via Pittsburgh, performing wherever possible along the way. Much of the trip was made by water, as that was the easiest means of transportation. After many hardships the company reached its goal, and performed in Louisville, Frankfort, Lexington, and other Kentucky towns. The following year it moved on to Nashville, Tennessee, where it remained some time.

During the next few years other troupes penetrated what was then (and still is, to many residents of the East Coast), the West. St. Louis, a small town, received its first visit from a professional company in 1819, and acquired a playhouse in 1837. Cincinnati was favored at about the same time as St. Louis. Mobile, Alabama, could boast of its first theatre (a brick one) in 1824. New Orleans, with the advantage of a seaport, had both French and American theatres early in the century, and in 1835 acquired what is said to have been the finest playhouse in America—the St. Charles Theatre. Chicago saw its first professional performance (given in a hotel) in 1837, but did not possess a theatre until ten years later, when the town's population had grown to 17,000.

Towns which could be reached by river-travel naturally attracted theatricals earlier than their land-bound sisters. And about 1830 a new type of theatre came into being: the show-boat. On the Ohio and the Mississippi rivers particularly, these floating theatres operated. Crude flatboats, with a stage and a small auditorium, they "made" all the river towns, and provided a picturesque life for the pioneer actors who inhabited them. All through the century they flourished, and are not extinct even now.

Meanwhile new playhouses, several of which are famous in the annals of our stage, were appearing in the large cities of the East. In 1820 the Chestnut Street Theatre, Philadelphia, was destroyed by fire, but was rebuilt and opened in 1822. An equally famous Philadelphia house, the Walnut Street Theatre, was opened in 1820. That same year the old Park Theatre, New York City, burned down, and was rebuilt the following year. Until this new house was destroyed in 1848 it remained the most distinguished playhouse in America, and on its stage appeared almost every great actor, native and foreign, who performed in this country. It housed, too (in 1825), the first American productions of Italian opera, with Italian singers.

In 1826 another important house, the New York Theatre, Bowery, was opened in the metropolis. Although it was first known by its full name, it became as early as 1830, merely The Bowery. The tenth playhouse to be erected in New York City, it had the longest and most interesting life of them all, in spite of the fact that it burned down and was rebuilt four times betwen 1826 and 1845. It retained its popular name until 1879, when it was rechristened The Thalia, and given over to unimportant productions.

In 1830 another historic theatre had its beginnings. In that year was built the house known as Niblo's Garden. Seven years before, William Niblo, proprietor of a coffee house, had taken charge of an amusement park theretofore known as Columbia Garden. Giving the park his own name, he erected a small concert pavilion, the success of which was so decided that he soon (1830) put up a much larger building, wherein he offered light forms of entertainment. By 1849 it had become a legitimate theatre as well as the home of spectacular novelties, and was for many years the most fashionable center of entertainment in New York City. Almost every attraction of merit appeared there, and in 1866 it housed the record-breaking melodramatic spectacle, "The Black Crook," with its elaborate scenic display, gorgeous costumes, and ballet of a hundred London chorus girls, dressed as scantily as the traditions of the period allowed. This show ran for more than a hundred nights continuously —a record in the American theatre at that time.

The year 1841 contributed two events of unusual interest. One was the opening of the Boston Museum; the other, the opening of Barnum's Museum. The two had little in common. The Boston Museum, following the precedent of the New Exhibition Hall, sailed under false colors. It did have, to be sure, a display of stuffed animals, but these were camouflage. The main attraction was a hall wherein various theatricals were shown. Legitimate plays were not given until 1843, but after that year were the regular thing. In 1846 it moved to a large new building, a first-rate dramatic company was installed, and for the next half-century the house held a prominent place among American theatres. William Warren, Jr., one of the best-loved American actors

From *Theatre Arts Magazine.*

Plate 29 : Interior of the Park Theatre, New York.

of the nineteenth century, was identified with the Boston
Museum the greater part of his life.

P. T. Barnum, whose name is still an international by-
word, was born in Connecticut in 1810. After a trial of many
routine occupations during his youth, he drifted into the
precarious paths of showmanship. His first venture was the
purchase in 1835 of a terribly old and emaciated negress,
named Joice Heth. This mummified creature he exhibited as
the nurse of George Washington. The ruse was successful
enough to settle Barnum's occupation, and thenceforth he
devoted his energies to the collection and display of rari-
ties. In 1841 he opened his Museum in New York City.
Without any knowledge of plays or the stage, he still could
not resist dabbling in legitimate theatricals, and installed in
his Museum an auditorium which he hypocritically called a
"Moral Lecture Room." But the "moral lectures" delivered
therein were oftentimes current stage successes, and the
"lecturers" included some of the best actors of the time. In
other words he ran a professional theatre. Barnum knew
that once inside the walls, his patrons would enjoy the show;
but he knew also that many of them had scruples against the
word "theatre."

Barnum's career is such a familiar one that it need not be
recounted in detail. Throughout his strenuous life he displayed a sense of showmanship so marvellous as to stagger
the common mortal. His exploitation of such characters as
General Tom Thumb and the Swedish singer, Jenny Lind,
gained for him an international reputation, whereas his
later activities in the traveling circus field were so sensational as to immortalize his name. He died in 1891.

ACTORS ON THE AMERICAN STAGE 1800–1850

Let us glance now at some of the names which drew
crowds to the theatres of America during the first half of

the nineteenth century. It is a very imposing list, indeed, for it includes not only the first native actors to achieve lasting fame, but also practically every bright star of the English stage. Such a procession of celebrated performers crossed the Atlantic that the Park Theatre and The Bowery became virtually another Drury Lane and Covent Garden.

Joseph Jefferson (1774–1832) made his American début in Boston, 1795, and appeared in New York the following year. He was born in England, the son of Thomas Jefferson, an actor in Garrick's company at Drury Lane. His son and grandson, both bearing his name, were brought up as actors on the American stage, the latter renowned and justly loved as the impersonator of Rip Van Winkle.

Thomas Abthorpe Cooper (1776–1849) was brought to the Chestnut Street Theatre, Philadelphia, by Thomas Wignell in 1796. The son of an Irish doctor, he went on the stage when he was sixteen, and played in Edinburgh and London. He became in America one of the foremost tragedians of the time, and excelled as Macbeth. In 1806 he became manager of the Park Theatre, New York.

John Howard Payne (1792–1852) was American-born, and made his début at the Park Theatre in 1809. He was looked upon as a genius and was nicknamed the "American Roscius." Under that title he went abroad and played at Drury Lane. But although he was an able actor, his fame rests today chiefly upon his composition of the song "Home, Sweet Home," which was contained in his play, "Clari, or the Maid of Milan." In 1832 Payne deserted the acting profession and devoted himself to literary work, and to consular service in Europe.

George Frederick Cooke (1756–1812), the romantic English actor, appeared at the Park Theatre in 1810, opening in "Richard III." His American appearance was the sensation of the day, and was accomplished only by the adroitness of Cooper, then manager of the Park, who engaged him while visiting in England. Cooper had offered him a hundred and twenty-five dollars a week for a ten-month tour of America, in addition to traveling expenses and benefit performances. But in spite of the attractiveness of these terms the English public insisted that Cooke had been inveigled on board ship while drunk. However that may have been, Cooke got to drinking heavily soon after his arrival on our shores, and kept it up until it killed him, in 1812. England never saw her hero again, for he was buried in St. Paul's Church, New York City. In 1821 at the request of Edmund Kean his bones were removed to the churchyard, and a monument erected over them. This monument was repaired thrice in after years by great actors: Charles Kean, E. A. Sothern, and Edwin Booth.

James William Wallack (1795–1864) came to America from England in 1818 and appeared first at the Park Theatre. Born of a theatrical family, he had acted with Edmund Kean at Drury Lane, and was considered equally good as a comedian and a tragedian. Although he visited his native country several times, he spent most of his life in America, becoming manager of the National Theatre, New York, in 1837, and opening in 1852 Wallack's Lyceum, which housed a brilliant company and established his name firmly in the annals of the American stage. His son, Lester Wallack, also an actor-manager, will be considered later in this chapter.

Edwin Forrest (1806–1872) was born in Philadelphia, and in that city, at the age of fourteen, he made his first stage appearance. His real début, however, occurred at the Bowery Theatre, New York, six years later, when he essayed the rôle of Othello with extraordinary success. Distinguished in bearing and possessed of noble features, Forrest became America's foremost tragedian. Devoting himself chiefly to Shakespearian drama, he amassed a huge fortune, and exerted in many ways an admirable influence on the theatre. One of his generous acts was to offer prizes for original American plays, but unfortunately, although his inducement brought forth a number of manuscripts, not many were worth consideration.

Edmund Kean (1787–1833), one of the immortal English actors, came to America in 1820 and electrified the country with his brilliant romanticism. He was scheduled to appear at the Park Theatre, but that house burned down just before his arrival, and he was therefore accommodated at the Anthony Street Theatre. Prices of admission went sky-high, and crowds fought to see him. His first performance was in "Richard III." Later he filled an engagement in Boston, but this resulted disastrously, for, the season being summer, the audiences were small, and this so enraged Kean that he refused to perform. The result was a public controversy in which his popularity suffered. Piqued by the rebuff, he returned abruptly to England. In 1825 he again visited America, finding London uncomfortable after he had become involved in a domestic scandal. But the scandal had preceded him across the Atlantic, and this, coupled with the memory of his former quarrel in Boston, served to turn the American public against him. At the Park Theatre he was pelted with rotten apples, and in Boston was treated in the same manner. After public apologies and pleas for consideration had proved futile, he went home once more, and stayed there until the pitiful close of his life.

Charles Mathews, Senior (1775–1835), noted English comedian, made his American début in Baltimore in 1822. Later in the same year he appeared in New York, and was received most enthusiastically. If we are to believe the critics of that period he was the finest comic actor seen on our stage during the first half of the century. Just before his death he made a second visit to this country.

Junius Brutus Booth (1796–1852), the English tragedian, and chief rival of Edmund Kean, came to America in

1821, playing first at Richmond, Virginia, and shortly afterward at Baltimore, Philadelphia, New York, and Boston. In 1822 he appeared in New Orleans, and years later in California. Soon after his arrival in this country he acquired an estate near Baltimore, and, except for one trip back to England, spent the remainder of his life here. He had four sons, three of whom became actors on the American stage: Junius Brutus, Jr., John Wilkes (the assassin of Lincoln), and Edwin. Mention of Edwin Booth will be made later.

James H. Hackett (1800–1871) was the first American-born actor to become a star of the first magnitude. His début was at the Park Theatre in 1826, and although it was not successful, the young actor persevered, and made a great success four years later in the original characterization of Rip Van Winkle. In 1832 he leaped suddenly to stellar fame by his portrayal of Falstaff in Charles Kean's production of "Henry IV" in Philadelphia. Indeed he is thought by certain critics to have been the greatest Falstaff in the history of the theatre. He was also a theatre manager, and controlled, at different times, three playhouses in New York City.

William Charles Macready (1793–1873), the eminent English tragedian, first visited America in 1826, appearing at the Park Theatre. His second and third visits occurred in 1843 and 1848. The 1848 tour was disastrous, however, for it led to a sensational squabble between Macready and Edwin Forrest, in which the former, undoubtedly the victim of unjust persecution, had to leave the country suddenly to save his life. Forrest charged Macready with having incited the audience to hiss him when he played Macbeth in London. This accusation, spread in America by Forrest, caused an outcry against the English actor when he appeared in Philadelphia and New York, and culminated in the riot at the Astor Place Opera House, New York, on May 10,

1849, when twenty-two persons were killed, and thirty-six others injured. The whole affair reflected badly on the American public.

George Holland (1791–1870), an eccentric English comedian, came to this country in 1827, and following his début at the Bowery Theatre became the most popular comedian of the day. He remained on the American stage until his death, and left three sons, all of whom became successful actors. When Holland died, his friends requested burial services at a fashionable church in New York City, but were refused, supposedly because an actor was not quite respectable, even when dead. They were advised to apply at "a little church around the corner," where such scruples were not held. The advice was taken, and since then the Church of the Transfiguration in East 29th Street has been adopted by the acting profession as its own, and has been affectionately called "The Little Church Around the Corner."

Louisa Lane, later Mrs. John Drew, (1820–1897) was brought by her mother, an actress, from England in 1827, and appeared that year at the Walnut Street Theatre, Philadelphia. She had been on the stage since she was a year old. Throughout her long life she was the most brilliant and versatile actress in the American theatre, and from 1861 until shortly before her death was manager of the Arch Street Theatre, Philadelphia. Her third marriage was to John Drew, an Irish comedian, in 1850. She had four children: Georgiana, John, Sidney (adopted), and Louisa. The first three attained success on the stage, and Georgiana, after her marriage to Maurice Barrymore, became the mother of the most noted family on the American stage today: Ethel, Lionel and John Barrymore.

Charles Kean (1811–1868) made his first American tour in 1830, opening at the Park Theatre in "Richard III." A capable manager and a polished actor, he aroused considerable admiration, but did not equal his father's success. He visited this country twice later, in 1839 and 1845.

Charles Kemble (1775–1854), a gifted member of the famous English theatrical family, opened in New York City at the Park Theatre in 1832. His "Hamlet" was a great success. He was supported on this tour by his daughter Fanny.

Tyrone Power (1798–1841) came to America in 1833 and established himself as the chief delineator of Irish character parts. His grandson, bearing the same name, is a well-known actor on our stage today.

Charlotte Cushman (1816–1876) was the first American-born actress to become a great star. Born in Boston, of Puritan parentage, she entered the theatre as a singer in 1835. The next year she went over to legitimate acting, and appeared at the Bowery Theatre, New York, as Lady Macbeth. Thenceforth she was the commanding tragedienne on our stage, and was also a success in London. She was the embodiment of dignity and strength, and was inclined toward masculinity. Her intellectual powers are said to have been exceptional, and she has been compared, as to style, with the celebrated Mrs. Siddons.

Edward Loomis Davenport (1816–1877) was also a native of Boston. Making his début in 1836, he soon became one of the first-rate tragedians on our stage, and next to Edwin Booth was considered the best American Hamlet of the nineteenth century. He left nine children, seven of whom adopted the acting profession. Of these, his daughter Fanny is the most noted.

Charles Mathews, Jr. (1804–1878), and his wife, Mme. Vestris (1797–1856), toured America in 1838, and Mathews himself was an immediate hit. His wife was rather a disappointment. This fashionable and realistic comedian made two later appearances in America.

Anna Cora Mowatt (1819–1870) was primarily a playwright, but was also an eminently successful actress. A gifted child, she began the composition of plays at an early age, and scored a real triumph in 1845, when her comedy of manners, "Fashion," was produced at the Park Theatre. This play was the first by an American to reflect intelligently the social life of the time. Mrs. Mowatt was herself a member of refined New York society, and could therefore write with authority. So elated was she with the success of "Fashion" that she determined to become an actress, and as a matter of fact three months after the opening of the play she made her début as Pauline in "The Lady of Lyons." Later she engaged E. L. Davenport to act opposite her, and the two enjoyed many successes at home and abroad. She retired in 1854 and devoted the rest of her life to literature and society.

It would be possible to continue this list for several pages, but that space is needed for other matters. We may conclude this brief chronicle of players by remarking what is surely obvious: that our large Eastern cities during the period 1820–1850 were not lacking in good theatrical fare.

SUMMARY OF CONDITIONS IN 1850

Until 1825 or thereabouts Philadelphia had been the best theatrical city in America. At least the Chestnut Street Theatre was said to have the finest company of actors and the highest standard of production. But between 1825 and 1830 the New York theatres took the lead, both in numbers and in quality, and by the middle of the century there was no longer any argument as to their supremacy. By 1850 there had been twenty-seven playhouses erected in New York City, though it is true there were never that many in existence at any one time. The Bowery, the National, the Broadway, Niblo's, and Wallack's were the leading houses at that date. The Park had been destroyed in 1848.

But although these mid-century theatres seemed luxurious to many of their patrons, they were, judged by modern standards, rather shoddy. They were generally dirty and ill-smelling, and were frequently infested with rats. The pit and gallery were rowdy in atmosphere, and were therefore seldom occupied by women. In connection with the top gallery there was commonly in operation a bar, which did not improve the moral tone of that section of the house. A portion of the gallery was set aside for negroes. Prices of admission ranged from twenty-five cents for the gallery to seventy-five cents or a dollar for the boxes. The theatres were poorly protected from fire, and were constantly in danger of destruction. In fact it is recorded that between 1820 and 1845 no fewer than twenty-five American theatres were burned down. This number, considering how few playhouses existed at that time, is extraordinary. But in spite of these defects, and also in spite of the war waged against it by the Puritans, the theatre prospered. The country was growing prodigiously in population and wealth, factories were springing up, mills were multiplying, railroads were being constructed (by 1850 approximately 6,000 miles of track was in use) and the majority of people had money to spend on entertainment. Our theatre was still largely dependent on foreign plays and players, but it was evolving surely into a native institution.

SELECTED REFERENCES

The best references here are Odell's *Annals of the New York Stage,* and Hornblow's *A History of the Theatre in America.* Others are Brown's *A History of the New York Stage,* and Crawford's *Romance of the American Theatre,* the latter being a popular rather than a scholarly work. For a chronological record of theatres built, see Dimmick's *Our Theatres Today and Yesterday.* A complete account of the drama, and a great deal of valuable information on the theatre, is contained in Quinn's *A History of the American Drama from the Beginning to the Civil War.*

CHAPTER XIX

THE SECOND HALF OF THE NINETEENTH CENTURY

CALIFORNIA AS A NEW THEATRICAL CENTER

THE year 1849 is almost as famous a date in American history as 1492. And in the history of the American theatre it is a date written in gold. In that year the eyes of the world were turned toward the Far West; the plains of this continent were dotted with covered wagons, and the Horn was rounded by ships from every land.

Inside a few months San Francisco became the liveliest and most picturesque of American towns. Its population was cosmopolitan; the air was charged with excitement; gold flowed in from the hills. It was an atmosphere which could not but give rise to a theatre.

The first professional performances were given in January, 1850, by a hastily recruited company. Shortly afterward an Australian troupe arrived, and following them a French vaudeville company. Eight temporary theatres were built in rapid succession, most of them being destroyed by fire shortly after erection. The first permanently constructed house (brick) appeared in 1853. This was the Metropolitan Theatre, which later housed so many visiting stars. In the next few years many permanent theatres were built.

During the sixties and seventies San Francisco was in every sense of the word a theatrical metropolis. Grand Opera was sung in French, Italian, and English by the finest singers of Europe and America, and beginning in 1869, with the opening of the California Theatre, under the joint direction of John McCullough and Lawrence Barrett, the legitimate drama was presented in a manner unsurpassed by any theatre in the country. Stars of the New York and London stages, attracted by the extraordinary salaries which California offered them, flocked to the Coast and remained for long and successful engagements. Companies when not playing in San Francisco, toured the other towns of Northern California, and ventured even into distant and almost inaccessible mining camps. It was in the midst of this theatrical whirl that David Belasco, a native Californian, laid the foundations for his unusual career. And it was there that Lotta (Charlotte Crabtree), the daughter of a Scotch gold-seeker, sang and played her way into the hearts of thousands—amassing, it is said, a fortune of not less than four million dollars.

San Francisco has never ceased being a theatrical city, even though the gold rush ran its course and became a memory. The palmy days passed, but the tradition survived, and lives now. The City by the Golden Gate is still cosmopolitan, still addicted to gaiety, still hospitable to all fine theatricals.

FAMOUS PRODUCERS AND MANAGERS IN NEW YORK CITY

In 1852 James W. Wallack, the famous manager, assumed control of Brougham's Lyceum Theatre (opened two years before), and gave it his own name. Since that time there has always been a Wallack's Theatre in New York City. In it he installed a very capable stock company, which included his son Lester, John Brougham, Laura Keene, and later, E. A. Sothern. He continued at this house until 1861, when he moved to a new theatre which had been constructed for him. There he achieved a brilliant record, and although he died three years later, his son kept up the Wallack standard and for practically a quarter of a century made his theatre the leading playhouse of America. Some of the actors who contributed to the excellence of the Wallack régime were: E. L. Davenport, Charles and Rose Coghlan, Maurice Barrymore, Dion Boucicault, Steele MacKaye, and John Gilbert. The younger Wallack, besides managing the house, acted successfully in principal parts, and was extremely popular. He moved his company to another new theatre in 1882, but five years later retired from the business, and died in 1888.

In 1872 Albert M. Palmer was offered the managership of the Union Square Theatre. He had had no theatrical experience, but his success was unusual. He remained in that position for eleven years, whereupon he assumed the responsibility of the Madison Square Theatre, which in his hands became one of the leading houses of the city. In 1891 he moved to Wallack's old theatre and renamed it Palmer's. This last venture, however, was not a great success, partly because the house itself was too large for stock productions, and partly because the heyday of the stock company was waning. Palmer retired in 1896, and died in 1905. One of the actors of prominence who rose under his management was Richard Mansfield. He was also responsible for bringing out two of the leading native playwrights of the nineteenth century, Augustus Thomas and Clyde Fitch. His acting corps was not as brilliant as Wallack's or Daly's, but it was competent.

Augustin Daly, of all the American theatrical managers of the last century, assembled and maintained the finest organization. Born in North Carolina in 1838, he early exhibited an interest in the drama, and during the sixties did a considerable amount of playwriting. His compositions, some of which were adaptations of foreign plays, while not distinguished, were still successful. His ambition was to have a theatre of his own. This desire was realized in 1869, when he leased the Fifth Avenue Theatre (a small house), and engaged a company of actors. The venture was remarkably successful, and although the theatre burned down in 1873, it was rebuilt at once, and operated continuously until 1879, when Daly leased and altered Wood's Old Museum and moved into it. This house he christened Daly's Theatre. While the personnel of his company changed considerably in the course of three decades, it was nevertheless an excellent example—the best in the history of the American theatre, in fact—of the permanent stock company. His actors, through years of constant association, developed a wonderful *esprit de corps,* and Daly himself, one of the sternest of disciplinarians, saw to it that every production was perfect in detail.

Among the actors who at various times belonged to the Daly organization may be mentioned: Agnes Ethel, John Drew, Ada Rehan, Fanny Davenport, Mrs. Gilbert, George Holland, Clara Morris, and Otis Skinner. Daly was noted for the excellence of his Shakespearian productions, and also for his encouragement of native playwrights. It was he who brought to the stage the work of Bronson Howard, who is called the Dean of American drama, and who was the earliest of our playwrights to deal in a natural way with the homely materials of American life. In still another matter Daly was a pioneer among managers, for he was the first American to take an entire company to Europe. In 1884 his troupe performed in England, and on subsequent tours, invaded France and Germany. In fact Daly opened a theatre of his own in London in 1893. After a long and noteworthy career he died in 1899.

Steele MacKaye holds a unique place in the annals of our theatre. He cannot be properly catalogued, for he was actor, manager, playwright, teacher, and inventor. No man in any age achieved success in so many branches of the theatrical profession as MacKaye, and few received less in return for their services. It will be impossible in the space available here to review properly the incidents of his career, but their variety and significance can be suggested.

Steele MacKaye was born in Buffalo, New York, in 1842, of Scotch ancestry. At an early age he studied art in Paris, and learned to draw and paint well. Back in America, he served in the Civil War, and during that time developed an interest in acting. Without help from anyone he worked out a system of dramatic expression. After the War he returned to Paris, and met François Delsarte, a Frenchman who had evolved a system of so-called natural acting, which he had taught to a number of actors. MacKaye was thrilled by the Delsarte system, and gave himself up to an intensive study of it. He found that it accorded remarkably with the principles which he had himself originated. Coming back to America, he launched Delsartism, lecturing at universities and giving private instruction to actors. The result of his propaganda was one of the most sweeping fads in the history of our country. Unfortunately hundreds of amateurs began to instruct in the principles of Delsarte, and the whole movement became ridiculous.

In January, 1872, MacKaye made his début as an actor on the New York stage. In the same year he made another trip to Paris, where he studied acting under Regnier, a celebrated director of the Comédie Française. At the close of this period of instruction he appeared as Hamlet at the Conservatoire, playing the part in French. He then went to England, and played Hamlet in English, being the first American actor to attempt that rôle before a London audience.

In America once more, this restless young man engaged in acting, playwriting, inventing, and stage-managing. In 1879 he opened and managed the Madison Square Theatre (formerly the Fifth Avenue). One of the young men whom he engaged to assist him at the business end was Daniel

Frohman, later a leading theatre manager. The next year he remodeled the house and installed several of his patented devices. He reopened it with his own play, "Hazel Kirke," which proved a phenomenal success, and achieved a longer continuous run than any play produced up to that time. It was stopped after 486 performances, not because it was played out, but because a contract demanded that a new play be presented. This record was not broken until 1921, when Frank Bacon's "Lightnin'" set a new endurance mark. "Hazel Kirke" was an epoch-making play in another respect: it was the first to be performed simultaneously in different parts of the country. The idea of sending duplicate companies on the road was MacKaye's. It is interesting to note, in passing, that in the original New York cast was Mrs. Thomas Whiffen, still (1927) a well-loved actress on the American stage. The part of Hazel was originally taken by Effie Ellsler. It has been estimated that "Hazel Kirke" has had more productions than any play ever written. For years and years it vied with "Uncle Tom's Cabin" for popularity, and is still seen occasionally in stock. Yet of the fortune which it reaped, Steele MacKaye received nothing. He lost all his rights in the play because of a disastrous contract which he had previously made with the Mallorys, the financial backers of the Madison Square Theatre.

Finding himself deprived of the income that was his due, MacKaye quit the theatre which he had given such a splendid start, and resorted to barnstorming for his living. In 1885, however, he opened, in association with the Frohmans, the new Lyceum Theatre, to which he contributed extremely valuable technical equipment. In connection with this theatre, under his personal supervision, was established a school of acting, later the American Academy of Dramatic Art, so long presided over by Franklin Sargent, a pupil of MacKaye's. This was the first real school of acting in America.

Among the mechanical innovations attributed to Mac-Kaye are: the double stage (1879); elevator stage for orchestra (1884); folding theatre-chair, with hat- and coat-rack attached (1884); sliding stage (1893); theatre ventilating system (1880); first installation of electric lighting system in a theatre (1885); devices to produce cloud, sun, wave, rainbow effects; a process for fire-proofing scenery; substitution of overhead lighting for footlights; and others too numerous to mention.

The climax of MacKaye's career was tragic. His dream was to embody all his technical and artistic achievements in one grand display at the World's Fair, Chicago, 1893. For this purpose he designed a mammoth theatre, seating ten thousand persons, which he called a Spectatorium. The frame for his stage picture measured 150 by 70 feet, and the sky-dome which encircled the stage (in this he anticipated the Germans) measured 400 by 120 feet. Electricity was to be used for motor power as well as for illumination, and the curtain itself was to be of light. For scene-changes a sliding stage was to be employed. In this theatre, such as the world had never seen, were to be presented musico-spectacle-dramas, combining all the arts of the theatre. For the opening production MacKaye himself wrote a great pageant entitled "The World Finder," with Columbus as a central figure.

Enough money was raised in Chicago to launch the project, but after the frame of the structure was completed, and the dream about to be realized, a financial panic swept the country, and in the storm the Spectatorium was lost. The money to complete it could not be found, and the whole structure was razed. Steele MacKaye collapsed with it. The strain had been too great, and the disappointment too overwhelming. In spite of broken health, he built the following year (1894), a small theatre which he called a Scenitorium, in which he exhibited as well as he could the type of production which he had planned for the Spectatorium. His spirit fighting fiercely against physical weakness, he directed rehearsals from a cot on which he lay, and finally saw the miniature of his dream come true. Three weeks later he was dead, and the newspapers were hailing his achievements.

This man had all the characteristics of genius, including a driving restlessness and an erratic business sense. He was not impractical, but he was hasty. No sooner did he accomplish one thing than he was working at a dozen more. In his impetuous way he sacrificed his own comfort and safety for the sake of his visions. But these visions were never idle, as the records of the Patent Office prove. He was extremely philosophical, but his speculations led to action. The American theatre gave him only a precarious living; he gave it more than any one man had ever given it, or likely ever will.

We must consider now two or three other theatre managers of a less amazing sort. The first is Daniel Frohman. This son of a German-Jewish immigrant got his start with Steele MacKaye at the Madison Square Theatre, and later, after MacKaye's divergence, was manager of the Lyceum. In that house he organized a fairly permanent stock company, which at one time or another included such stellar performers as Mrs. Whiffen, Effie Shannon, Henry Miller, William Faversham, Henrietta Crosman, May Robson, and James K. Hackett. An imposing list. Added to it should be David Belasco as stage-manager, and, with Henry De Mille as collaborator, house playwright. For the past forty years Daniel Frohman has been one of the most successful theatrical managers in America. He was never an actor; he has never contributed particularly to the artistic progress of the theatre; he is purely a business man—one of the first of a now common species; a theatrical magnate with a highly-developed sense of the commercial possibilities of the drama, coupled with a large ability in the field of organization and administration.

Charles Frohman, brother of Daniel, also started at the Madison Square Theatre. After numerous ventures he launched in 1893 the famous Empire Theatre, with its stock company of excellent players. Under his banner marched, among others: Robert Edeson, Ethel Barrymore, May Robson, Arthur Byron, Margaret Anglin, and Henry Miller. But under his régime the old-fashioned stock company remained one largely in name only. It was actually a forcing-bed for stars. And it was he who, during the nineties, exploited more thoroughly than any American manager before him had done, the iniquitous star system. One of the first actors whom he made an independent star was John Drew, weaned away from Daly. Another, who brought a fortune to her manager, as well as one to herself, was Maude Adams. A man without education or artistic interests, Charles Frohman became a theatrical financier— one of the most powerful in the country, and a principal member of the Theatrical Syndicate formed near the close of the century. He died in 1915, a victim of the sinking of the Lusitania.

David Belasco was born in San Francisco in 1859, of English-Portuguese-Jewish stock. He began acting in 1871, and for some time played in his native city and in the mining-camps of Northern California. During these years he also did a great deal of playwriting and adapting— mostly the latter. This craft he learned partly from associating with Dion Boucicault, who was in California at that time. By 1882 Belasco had served his apprenticeship in all branches of the theatre. In that year he accepted an invitation to come to New York City, and on his arrival became stage manager of the Madison Square Theatre. Later he joined Daniel Frohman at the Lyceum in the same capacity, and also wrote and adapted plays for that house.

In 1895 he became an independent producing-manager, and realized a great success with his first star, Mrs. Leslie Carter. In 1900 he "put over" Blanche Bates, an actress who had been with Daly. In 1901 he sponsored David Warfield (theretofore virtually unknown) in "The Auctioneer," and achieved what amounted to a triumph. In 1902 he acquired the Republic Theatre, and after refurnishing it, opened it as the Belasco Theatre. At that house, in 1906, he presented his fourth great "find," Frances Starr. The following year he built his new theatre. But this is running ahead of our limitations; we are supposed to be considering the nineteenth century. In the final chapter something more will be said of Mr. Belasco.

In 1896 occurred the first attempt to set up a theatrical monopoly in America. The business man had got into the theatre, and his eyes were greedy. Six men, Charles Frohman, Marc Klaw, Abraham Erlanger, Al Hayman, Samuel F. Nirdlinger, and J. Frederick Zimmerman were the villains in the case. They formed the famous, or infamous, Theatrical Syndicate, for the avowed purpose of facilitating the booking of tours. The result of this combination was that practically every legitimate theatre in the country was under their direct control, and could not accommodate any attraction not booked by them. Naturally there was a revolt against this situation. Independent producers and actor-managers rose in their wrath and declared their rights. Waving the flag of freedom were David Belasco, Mrs. Fiske, Richard Mansfield, Joseph Jefferson, Francis Wilson, and others. Some capitulated, others did not. Mrs. Fiske proved the most untractable of all. In her defiance she played in tents and roller-skating rinks.

Meanwhile, however, a new enemy of the Trust appeared on the horizon. This was the Shubert family: Sam, Lee, and Jacob. Having started as theatre managers in Syracuse, New York, and later having acquired a chain of houses throughout the state, they invaded New York City in 1900, and started a Trust of their own. The country was then subjected to a war of competition between two great octopuses. It did not matter particularly which won. Both were actuated by the same principles. The theatre was definitely commercialized. An interesting, if not an inspiring, climax to the story of theatre-management in the nineteenth century.

ACTORS ON THE AMERICAN STAGE 1850–1900

John Brougham (1810–1880) was an English actor who made his first appearance on the American stage in 1842. In 1850 he acquired his own theatre in New York City, but failed as a manager, and became a member of Wallack's company. He was also a playwright.

Dion Boucicault (1822–1890) was born in Dublin, of French descent. After a career as actor and playwright in England he came to America (1854) and became one of the dominant personalities in our theatre. Most of his compositions for the stage were adapted from the French, and were extremely melodramatic. His work had considerable influence on the American playwrights of the time.

Lester Wallack (1819–1888) has already been mentioned as an actor-manager of the first rank.

Laura Keene (1826–1873) was born in England, and was a protégée of Mme. Vestris. In 1852 she became a member of Wallack's company in New York City, and later headed a company of her own. She was the first woman theatrical manager in America.

E. A. Sothern (1827–1881) was an English actor who came to this country in 1852. Two years later he joined Wallack's company, and later Laura Keene's. Under the management of Miss Keene he made his first hit, in the rôle of Lord Dundreary in "Our American Cousin" (1858).

He was not a great actor, but he was skillful and ingenious in the portrayal of eccentric characters. As Lord Dundreary he became an international star.

Joseph Jefferson III (1829–1905) was raised on the American stage. As a child he trouped with his parents, and specialized in blackface comedy, which was then coming into vogue. His first New York appearance was in 1849, but he did not attract attention until several years later when he played in "Our American Cousin," with E. A. Sothern. The triumph of his career was his impersonation of Rip Van Winkle, which he revealed first in London in 1865 and the next year in New York City. He played this part for years in all parts of America, and made from it a large fortune.

Edwin Booth (1833–1893) was born on his father's farm in Maryland, and made his début at the Boston Museum in 1849. In the fifties he played with great success in California, and in 1861 appeared in England. In 1864 he played Hamlet for one hundred consecutive nights at the Winter Garden Theatre, New York City, a record run for a Shakespearian production. The next year, following the assassination of President Lincoln by John Wilkes Booth (Edwin's brother), he retired from the stage, but returned by popular request in January, 1866. In 1869 he opened a million-dollar theatre of his own in New York City (Booth's Theatre), where he mounted plays in the most lavish manner. Four years of managerial activity made him a bankrupt, and thereafter he contented himself with starring under the management of others. He was an intelligent and brilliant performer, at his best in the tragedies of Shakespeare. The chief criticism brought against him is that he was content to surround himself with a cheap company. He retired in 1891 and died in 1893, leaving a considerable fortune, besides his home, which he bequeathed to "The Players," a theatrical club in New York City.

Lawrence Barrett (1838–1891) was born in New Jersey, and made his début in Detroit in 1853. He appeared on the New York stage in 1857. During the late sixties he was in California, and afterwards co-starred with Edwin Booth. Because of the general nobility of his manner and appearance he was well adapted to heroic tragedy, and was one of the most deeply admired actors of his time.

John McCullough (1832–1885) was born in Ireland, and made his American début in Philadelphia in 1857. In 1869 he opened, with Lawrence Barrett, the California Theatre in San Francisco, and was responsible for a notable series of productions. He is said to have been an impressive actor in romantic parts, but to have lacked the intelligence of Booth and Barrett, his contemporaries.

Adah Isaacs Menken (1835–1868) was born in Louisiana, the daughter of a Presbyterian minister. At an early age she went on the stage in New Orleans, and later appeared in New York City. She led a varied and sensational life as a dancer, actress, poet, linguist, and sculptor. She first attracted attention on the stage by allowing herself to be strapped to the back of a galloping horse in a performance of "Mazeppa." She is also remembered for her close association with certain European men of letters, whom she seems to have completely charmed. Dickens, Swinburne, and the elder Dumas were among her admirers. Her brief but colorful career ended in Paris, where she died at the age of thirty-three.

Mrs. G. H. Gilbert (1822–1904) was born in England, and became a professional dancer. She came to this country in 1849, and continued her career. In 1857 she made her début as a legitimate actress in the city of Cleveland. Later she became one of the regular members of Daly's company in New York City, and for many years was the chief actress in "dowager" rôles on the American stage.

Fanny Davenport (1850–1898) was the daughter of the

famous American tragedian, Edward Loomis Davenport. She began acting at the age of four, and during the seventies was one of Daly's leading actresses. She is said, however, to have succeeded because of her beauty, rather than because of any extraordinary ability in acting.

Mme. Janauschek (1830–1904) was a German tragedienne who made her American début in 1867. Her first performances were in the German language, but beginning in 1871 she acted in English. She remained on the American stage for a number of years, and was eminently successful in rôles which require majesty and power, such as Lady Macbeth, Mary Stuart, and Catherine II.

Adelaide Neilson (1848–1880) was an English Shakespearian actress who came to this country in 1872, and appeared at Booth's Theatre. Five years later she joined the Daly company, and delighted everyone with her exquisite impersonations of Juliet, Viola, Rosalind, and other classic heroines.

Mary Anderson (1859–   ) was born in California. At the age of sixteen she made her début in Louisville, and two years later was seen in New York. She became one of the favorites of the time, and although she is said not to have been a truly great actress, her popularity has rarely been equalled. Beautiful, refined, and gracious, she did not need more ability than she had. Perdita and Lady Teazle were two of her best rôles. She retired from the stage in 1890.

Rose Coghlan (1850–   ) was born in England, and after achieving considerable success on the London stage, came to America in 1872, where she appeared at Wallack's. The next year she returned to England and played there until 1877, when she rejoined the Wallack company in New York. She was an admired actress on the American stage for almost half a century, and filled a vast number of leading parts in classic and modern plays. From 1909 to 1911 she was a member of the repertory company at the New Theatre, New York, and as recently as 1920 she appeared at the Belasco Theatre in "Deburau."

John Drew (1853–1927) was born in Philadelphia, and made his début in 1873 at the Arch Street Theatre, which was under the management of his parents. He joined Daly's New York company in 1875, and remained under that management until 1892, when he became a star under Charles Frohman. For more than fifty years he was one of the chief figures on the American stage, and was unsurpassed in those parts which require elegance and a sense of high-comedy values. He died in San Francisco while on tour with an all-star cast in Pinero's classic of stage life, "Trelawney of the 'Wells.'"

Helena Modjeska (1845–1909) was a Polish actress who first appeared on the American stage in San Francisco in 1877. Later in the same year she made her New York début, and was soon established as one of our leading actresses. She made two European tours, both successful, and in 1887 was engaged to support Edwin Booth. Her best achievements were in the leading feminine rôles of Shakespeare, and in those of Ibsen, a dramatist whom she introduced to America with her production of "A Doll's House," in 1883.

Charles Fechter (1824–1879) was born in London of German-French-Italian parentage. He was educated in France, and after attaining success on the Paris stage, he went to London, where he created a sensation, both because of his original acting and his mechanical innovations. In 1870 he made his first American appearance at Niblo's. Later he became manager of a theatre in Boston, and after that was connected with the management of the Park Theatre, New York. He was not successful in the capacity of manager, but as a romantic actor he secured a large following. He retired in 1877.

Richard Mansfield (1857–1907) was born in Germany, and began his theatrical career in England. He came to this country in 1882 and did small comedy parts in opera and drama until 1883, when he leaped to success in "A Parisian Romance," produced by A. M. Palmer. Thereafter he was an idol of the American stage, and achieved lasting fame in such plays as "Beau Brummel," "Dr. Jekyll and Mr. Hyde," and "Cyrano de Bergerac." He was a brilliant, personable, eccentric actor, without depth, but with a dazzling technique. Melodrama rather than tragedy was his proper field.

Robert B. Mantell (1854–   ) was born in Scotland and did his first acting in the English provinces. He made his American début in 1878, in support of Mme. Modjeska, with whom he acted for some time. Since the early nineties he has been the most consistent exponent of Shakespeare in this country.

Clara Morris (1846–1925) was born in Canada, but appeared on the stage for the first time in Columbus, Ohio. Her New York début was in 1870, under Augustin Daly. A crude but powerful emotional actress, she created a sensation, and for a number of years was extremely popular. After 1882 she appeared very irregularly on the stage, and from 1894 to 1904 did not act at all. During 1904–1906 she participated in several revivals.

Ada Rehan (1861–1916) was born in Ireland but educated in America. In 1875 she joined Mrs. John Drew's stock company in Philadelphia, and four years later became leading woman at Daly's Theatre, New York. She remained with Daly for twenty years, playing a wide range of parts, and distinguishing herself particularly in romantic comedy. One of her best rôles was that of Katharine in "The Taming of the Shrew," in which she was supported by John Drew as Petruchio. No more spirited comedienne has ever appeared on our stage.

Minnie Maddern, later Mrs. Fiske, (1865–   ) was born in New Orleans of theatrical parents, and was raised on the stage. Her New York début was at Wallack's Theatre in 1870. During her childhood she supported many famous actors, including John McCullough, Barry Sullivan, and E. L. Davenport. In 1890, upon her marriage to Harrison Grey Fiske, she retired from the stage for four years. Since 1894 she has been seen regularly in a great variety of plays, chiefly modern. One of her great successes was "Becky Sharp," another was "Tess of the D'Urbervilles," and she has many times triumphed in the plays of Ibsen. By most critics she is considered the cleverest actress of her generation. Her personal charm is extraordinary, and her technique is equally well adapted to serious drama and high comedy.

E. H. Sothern (1859–   ) was born in New Orleans, the son of E. A. Sothern of Lord Dundreary fame. He was educated in England but made his first theatrical appearance in New York City, at the Park Theatre, in 1879. In 1881–82 he played in London and the English provinces. In 1883 he returned to America, where he filled various engagements for a period of two years. He then became leading man at the Lyceum Theatre, New York, for Henry Frohman, and held that position until 1898. In 1904 he become co-star with Julia Marlowe in Shakespearian and other romantic dramas, and has followed that course ever since.

Julia Marlowe (1870–   ) was born in England, but was educated in America, and began playing small parts in light opera and drama while still a child. She appeared on the New York stage for the first time in 1887. She was recognized at once as a romantic actress of unusual ability, and since that time she has appeared almost exclusively as a star in period plays, chiefly Shakespearian. Her most famous rôles include Juliet, Ophelia, Rosalind, Jeanne D'Arc, and Mary Tudor.

Maude Adams (1872–   ) was born in Salt Lake City, the daughter of Annie Adams, a well-known stock actress. From the time she was an infant she appeared in productions with her mother, and in 1888 made her début in New York City. During the early nineties she acted as leading woman with John Drew under the management of Charles Frohman, and in 1897 became a star in her own right. Her greatest success was in Barrie's "Peter Pan," produced in 1905. Later she starred in other plays by Barrie, and in 1911 scored a tremendous hit in Rostand's "Chantecler." Possessed of a winsome, elusive personality, she occupies a unique place among American actresses. Critics have often remarked that measured by customary standards she has never once proved herself a great actress. The combination of her individual charm and Charles Frohman's managerial ability, however, served to make her the idol of the public and the wealthiest actress in America.

It is a temptation to continue this list of biographical notes, but lack of space forbids. It is impossible, however, to omit entirely the names of many other important players who were identified with the American theatre during the last three decades of the nineteenth century. Without pausing to give detailed information regarding their careers, except to indicate the approximate date of each one's début, we may note the following: Mrs. Thomas Whiffen, 1868; Wm. H. Crane, 1864; Wm. Gillette, 1875; James O'Neill, 1870; Charles Coghlan, 1876; John Mason, 1878; Otis Skinner, 1877; DeWolf Hopper, 1878; Francis Wilson, 1878; Lillian Russell, 1880; Henry Miller, 1880; Henrietta Crosman, 1883; Wilton Lackaye, 1883; May Robson, 1885; Wm. Faversham, 1887; Robert Edeson, 1887; Effie Shannon, 1886; Viola Allen, 1882; Arthur

Byron, 1889; Mrs. Leslie Carter, 1890; James K. Hackett, 1892; David Warfield, 1888; Julia Arthur, 1891; Ethel Barrymore, 1894; Margaret Anglin, 1894; Lionel Barrymore, 1893; Blanche Bates, 1894; Arnold Daly, 1895.

The foregoing are, of course, American actors. Most of them were born and educated in this country. All of them were for years prominent figures on our stage, and many of them are still playing. It may be interesting to mention also a few of the foreign actors of distinction who were seen in America during the period we are discussing. The dates given refer to the first visit of the actor: Mlle. Rachel, 1855; Tommaso Salvini, 1873; Sarah Bernhardt, 1880; Henry Irving, 1883; Ellen Terry, 1883; Coquelin the elder, 1888; Eleonora Duse, 1893; Mounet-Sully, 1894; Mme. Réjane, 1895. Several of these artists made later American tours, Bernhardt and Irving most frequently.

AMERICAN DRAMATISTS 1850–1900

Although there had been plays written in America by Americans before 1850, it was not until after that date that our native drama proved itself a very important factor in the development of our theatre. Mrs. Mowatt had created a stir with "Fashion" in 1845, but one playwright does not suffice for a nation. George Henry Boker contributed his poetic tragedy, "Calaynos," in 1848, his "Anne Boleyn," in 1850, and his masterpiece, "Francesca da Rimini," in 1856, thereby gaining considerable fame and starting the prophecy that the American drama was at last born; but his plays, after all, had nothing to do with American life, and were frankly in the European tradition.

It was not until 1870 that there were visible signs of a drama which reflected native atmosphere and psychology. In that year Bronson Howard (1842–1908) came to the fore with "Saratoga," and won his place as the Dean of

American drama. Later successes of his were "The Banker's Daughter," 1878; "Young Mrs. Winthrop," 1882; "Shenandoah," 1889; and "Aristocracy," 1892.

Contemporary with Howard was James A. Herne (1839–1901), who also achieved fame as a delineator of pioneer life and character. Typical plays of his are: "Hearts of Oak," 1879; "Shore Acres," 1892; and "Griffith Davenport," 1899.

Steele MacKaye, whose career has already been discussed, belongs also in this category of pioneer realists, all of whom were striving to write sincerely on American themes.

The following generation brought forth several well-known playwrights, most of whom are still represented on our stage. Prominent among these is David Belasco, author of "The Heart of Maryland," 1895; "The Girl of the Golden West," 1905; "The Return of Peter Grimm," 1911; and a host of other pieces, many of which were written in collaboration, or were adaptations. Another representative of the group is Augustus Thomas, author of "Alabama," 1891; "In Mizzoura," 1893; "The Witching Hour," 1908; and "As a Man Thinks," 1911. Still another is William Gillette, whose best known plays are: "The Professor," 1881; "The Private Secretary," 1884; "All the Comforts of Home," 1890; "Secret Service," 1896; and "Sherlock Holmes," 1899. Most skillful of all these was Clyde Fitch (1865–1909), who had many extraordinary successes, among which were: "Beau Brummel," 1890; "Barbara Frietchie," 1899; "The Climbers," 1900; "The Stubbornness of Geraldine," 1902; and "The Truth," 1906.

The foregoing dramatists created a large enough body of actable literature to justify the term "American drama." Most of the plays they wrote were not great in a literary sense. They were for the most part sentimental melodrama, and were with few exceptions innocent of subtlety or depth. On the other hand they pictured with a fair degree of faithfulness the fundamental characteristics of the American heart and mind. Composed by pioneers for pioneers, little wonder they were so frequently naïve and homely. They at least pleased the audiences for whom they were intended, and paved the way for native playwrights of a later and more sophisticated era.

SUMMARY

It is now necessary to conclude this survey of a period crammed with important theatrical events. Little attention has been paid to secondary or minor forms of drama, such as opera, vaudeville, circus, and burlesque. An account of these would not only be excessively difficult to formulate, but would be of questionable value, considering the limitations of this book. It has also been deemed inadvisable to attempt an extensive recording of theatre construction during the latter half of the century. The reason for such a decision must be obvious. It would require a separate volume to handle such a subject. Nor, save in the case of Steele MacKaye's contributions, has any time been spent on the matter of theatre architecture, stage machinery, and scenic equipment. The omission of this material is justified, it is to be hoped, by the fact that the American theatre followed technically in the footsteps of Europe, and a fair idea has already been given of the development of stage mechanics in the European theatre.

Two things need to be emphasized. The first is that during the nineties the permanent stock company practically disappeared from large producing centers, and the star system, with its corollary, the indefinite run, took its place. The second is that by the end of the century the American theatre was virtually independent of foreign actors and producers.

Finally it should be mentioned that in 1895 and 1896

Lumière in France and Edison in America made the first moving pictures. What this meant to the theatre of the twentieth century will be indicated later.

SELECTED REFERENCES

For the only thorough account of this period see Hornblow's *A History of the Theatre in America*. Another extremely valuable reference on the whole period is Quinn's *A History of the American Drama from the Civil War to the Present Day*. Similar in character and value is Moses' *The American Dramatist*. For genealogical study consult Moses' *Famous Actor-Families in America*. Specific works of unusual importance are: Tompkins and Kilby's *History of the Boston Theatre, 1854–1901*, Winter's *The Life and Art of Edwin Booth*, the same writer's *The Life of David Belasco*, Towse's *Sixty Years of the Theatre*, Werner's *Barnum*, Daly's *The Life of Augustin Daly*, Belasco's *The Theatre Through Its Stage Door*, Drew's *My Years on the Stage*, Frohman's *Memories of a Manager*, and MacKaye's *Epoch: The Life of Steele MacKaye*.

CHAPTER XX

THE EARLY TWENTIETH CENTURY

THE REVOLT AGAINST THE COMMERCIAL THEATRE

THE first years of the present century were, from the standpoint of the theatre, very definitely a continuation of the closing years of the nineteenth. The Theatrical Syndicate and the Shuberts tightened their hold; the star system prevailed throughout the country; the motion picture was as yet a harmless novelty. In other words the commercialized legitimate theatre had things pretty much its own way. Its chief rival was vaudeville, which, since Tony Pastor gave New York its first well-managed variety house in 1875, had come forward steadily in public favor. Until 1906, however, there was little system in vaudeville. In that year the first central booking agency was established, and thereafter the variety houses gradually came under the same sort of unified control which had been applied to the legitimate. A few stubborn producers and actor-managers insisted on doing as they pleased, when they pleased, but their independent efforts had little effect upon theatrical conditions in general.

"Nativity, once in the main of light,
Crawls to maturity, wherewith being crown'd,
Crooked eclipses 'gainst his glory fight,
And Time that gave doth now his gift confound."

Let us assume that Shakespeare had in mind the Theatrical Syndicate. In which case it will now be our duty to de-

scribe some of the eclipses which fought and are still fighting, " 'gainst his glory." The chief antagonists are: the
repertory theatre, the little theatre, and the motion picture.
The first two are the products of idealism, and are spiritual
enemies of the commercial theatre. The third is the product
of science and business enterprise, and is a rival of the
commercial theatre on its own level.

In 1909, under the auspices of certain wealthy citizens,
an attempt was made in the City of New York to establish
a National Theatre. A very large and handsome playhouse,
called the New Theatre, but later the Century, was built
and dedicated to the repertory ideal. The stage was
equipped with every device then considered valuable by
technicians; a company of actors was employed; Mr. Winthrop Ames, an intelligent young director from Boston,
was engaged as *régisseur;* the advisory committee included
persons of excellent taste in matters theatrical. The opening
production was Shakespeare's "Antony and Cleopatra,"
with Sothern and Marlowe as guest players in the leading
rôles.

The National Theatre enterprise, which had involved the
expenditure of several million dollars, lasted two seasons.
It was, from almost every point of view, a failure. In 1911
the house was taken over by commercial managers, and since
then has been used for musical productions and dramatic
spectacles. The reasons for its failure as a repertory theatre
have been fairly well agreed upon. In the first place, the
auditorium was entirely too large for legitimate drama,
even had the acoustics been good, which they were not. Only
a small portion of the audience could hear satisfactorily.
In the second place, the "permanent" members of the acting company were not great enough artists to command a
following. And by engaging two "stars" as guest players in
the opening production, the management admitted as much
to the public. Two systems, the star and the repertory, can-

not be mixed. They are antithetical in attitude and method. Other reasons besides these have been advanced, and are probably sound. One of the most convincing is that in 1909 America had a relatively poor list of native plays. The National Theatre was therefore dependent upon foreign drama, and could not capitalize the spirit of national pride as it is capitalized in France and Germany at the State theatres. The repertoire may also have been badly chosen, but that is a matter of individual opinion.

About the time that the New Theatre was founded, a number of less pretentious experiments were made with the repertory idea. Several municipal theatres were established, operating on moderate subsidies, and a considerable number of little theatres (private and community) were born. The pioneer municipal theatres were those at Pittsfield and Northampton, both in Massachusetts. The latter was decidedly the more successful, and from 1912 until 1917 maintained a permanent acting and directing staff. The so-called little theatre movement, which has received so much comment, complimentary and otherwise, dates back to the season 1911–1912. To chronicle its development step by step would require more space than can be assigned to it here, but it is possible for us to note the high spots.

The little theatre, that is, the theatre of modest size and equipment, with artistic rather than commercial aims, was a product of the late nineteenth century in Europe, as we have already seen. The Free Theatre of Paris, the Abbey Theatre of Dublin, the Free Theatre of Berlin—these and many others had struck a direct blow at the methods and ideals of the established theatre. It took a few years for that movement to reach America, but when it finally came it had a great effect. It transformed the amateur dramatic world, and in some instances altered the complection of professional theatricals.

If we omit such producing groups as those fostered by colleges and settlement organizations, the first little theatres in America were: the Toy Theatre, Boston, directed by Mrs. Lyman Gale; the Chicago Little Theatre, directed by Maurice Browne and Ellen Van Volkenburg (Mrs. Browne); the Little Theatre, New York City, directed by Winthrop Ames. All three were launched in 1912.

The Toy Theatre operated on a semi-professional basis, and existed for two and a half years. The Chicago Little Theatre (a tiny playhouse seating only 91) had a life of five years. Mr. and Mrs. Browne specialized in poetic drama, and introduced through simplified settings and mood lighting certain of the fundamental theories of Gordon Craig. They also contributed some of the first and most excellent marionette productions to the modern American theatre. It should be mentioned, however, that Chicago had been at least partially prepared for the work of the Brownes by two acting groups: the Hull House Players, who had been producing interesting European plays since 1907, and the Donald Robertson Players, who had performed in the city and adjoining towns, also since 1907, a repertoire of old and modern classics.

But of these pioneer ventures, the only one to be operated on a strictly professional basis was Mr. Ames's Little Theatre, a house seating 299 (thereby coming under more lenient fire regulations than houses seating 300 or upwards). There the artistic standard of production was high, but the result was financial loss. The theatre had to be enlarged. This experiment is thought by many to have proved definitely that a very small theatre must be operated on an amateur or at most a semi-professional basis if it is not to lose money.

In 1915 a somewhat more successful attempt in this direction was launched with the establishment of the Neighborhood Playhouse, New York City. This theatre was an outgrowth of community drama activities in the Henry

Street Settlement, and was generously financed by the Misses Irene and Alice Lewisohn. From the date of its establishment until its change of policy in 1927 it offered a great variety of legitimate drama, dance festivals, music, motion pictures, and revues (the Grand Street Follies). It had loyal workers in all departments, many of whom donated their services. Although it attracted many patrons from all sections of the city, it catered primarily to the residents of its immediate neighborhood on the lower East Side. The house seats 450, and is modern in every way. Its stage was the first in America to be equipped with a permanent sky-dome.

In the same year (1915) a group of artistic radicals (writers, painters, actors, *et cetera*) from Greenwich Village organized the Washington Square Players. This company at first specialized in one-act plays written by its own members, and gave performances only two evenings a week. No salaries were paid, and most of the actors were amateurs. The success of the enterprise, however, soon warranted the presentation of longer plays and more frequent performances. By careful management and wisely directed investments of earnings, the Washington Square Players worked themselves into a secure position. It was from this group that the Theatre Guild sprang in 1918–1919, to become within a short time the most successful repertory theatre in America.

It was in 1915 also that the Provincetown Players started producing their own plays, chiefly for their own amusement, during the summer at Provincetown, Mass. How this company of writers and amateur actors later opened a playhouse in Greenwich Village, and how one of its members, Eugene O'Neill, became America's foremost dramatist, is a story that has frequently been told. The Provincetown Playhouse is still the home of young American playwrights. And that same summer at Christadora

Settlement House, New York City, Stuart Walker presented for the first time in public his Portmanteau Theatre, which later traveled the country over, and delighted thousands of childrens and adults. Mr. Walker (though a young man) was a graduate of Broadway. He had been in the mill long enough to learn how the machinery ran, and long enough to desire something freer and more imaginative. His folding theatre, with its clever simplified settings, its up-to-date lighting equipment, its young, enthusiastic players, and its repertoire of whimsical fantasies, was a change from the commercial theatre of Mr. Belasco, and was also a challenge. Later on it was Mr. Walker who introduced Dunsany to America. That in itself was an achievement.

The year 1916 is remembered by students of the theatre for the productions of the Arts and Crafts Society of Detroit, under the direction of Sam Hume. Mr. Hume was one of the first American producers to make a thorough study of the modern theatre. Starting his study at the University of California, he continued it at Harvard, with Professor Baker, and completed it in Florence, Italy, under Gordon Craig. During his Detroit engagement he put into practice, most effectively, certain new principles of stagecraft (the plastic-unit setting, in particular) and set a standard for little theatre production which proved decidedly inspiring. His work afterward in Berkeley and San Francisco was also extremely interesting.

Between 1911 and the present day hundreds of little theatres have arisen in America. Many have struggled and died. A surprising number have survived and prospered. Among the most successful are: the Pasadena Community Playhouse, the Cleveland Playhouse, the Dallas Little Theatre, the Memphis Little Theatre, the Shreveport Little Theatre, the Berkeley Playhouse, the Lobero Theatre of Santa Barbara, the Indianapolis Little Theatre, the Ram's Head Players of Washington, D. C., the Beechwood Players of Scarborough, N. Y., Le Petit Théâtre du Vieux Carré of New Orleans, the Birmingham Little Theatre, the North Shore Theatre Guild of Evanston, Ill., the Galveston Little Theatre, the Players Club of Chicago, the Santa Fé Community Players, the Ypsilanti (Michigan) Players, the Theatre of the Golden Bough of Carmel-by-the-Sea, California, the Portland (Oregon) Playcrafters, the Cornish Theatre of Seattle, the Arizona Play Actors of Phoenix, the Tacoma Center of the Drama League of America, the Tulsa Little Theatre, the Nashville Little Theatre, the Dayton Theatre Guild, the Civic Players of Grand Rapid, Michigan, the Hartford (Conn.) Players, the Sherman (Texas) Little Theatre, the Civic Theatre of Oklahoma City, the Town Theatre of Savannah, the Little Theatre League of Richmond, Virginia, the Little Theatre of Philadelphia, the Duluth Little Theatre, the Little Country Theatre of Fargo, North Dakota, the Hollywood Community Theatre, and many others. Some of these are mushroom growths, without sufficient support, financial or moral, to insure permanency. Others are well founded and strongly rooted in the life of the community. The Pasadena Playhouse, for example, has in ten years become one of the leading art theatres in America. It now has a beautiful new playhouse, a salaried staff, consisting of director, assistant directors, stage-crew, business manager, publicity director, and box-office assistants. It has a large list of paid subscribers, and operates twelve months in the year. It is and has been from its inception a true community playhouse, drawing on the citizenry for actors, and accepting professional actors only on a volunteer basis. Several thousand persons have taken part in its productions. Mr. Gilmor Brown has served as its director from the time of its foundation.

The Cleveland Playhouse is a little more than ten years old. Its first home was a slightly remodeled church, and its pioneer productions were few and far between. It now occupies a brand-new playhouse with two auditoriums, one very small, the other of moderate size. It offers a dozen new productions a year, with eight revivals of previous successes. Each play runs about two weeks. Unlike the Pasadena Community Theatre, it maintains a fairly permanent company of actors, most of whom have grown up with the theatre, and have taken by way of recompense whatever could be paid. The genius behind this theatre is Mr. Frederic McConnell, who, like Gilmor Brown, has by force of personality and tremendous effort accomplished a most remarkable thing.

The success of such theatres depends, certainly, to a very great extent upon the ability of one or two persons to organize the dramatic forces of a community, to focus them and hold them in focus. The little theatre director must be a combination of business man, artist, and social leader. Failure to be any one of these will kill his chances. That the little theatre has won its place in American life is therefore due to the personal effectiveness of such directors as: Maurice Browne, Ellen Van Volkenburg, Sam Hume, Irving Pichel, Gilmor Brown, Frederic McConnell, Oliver Hinsdell, Alexander Dean, Everett Glass, Arthur Maitland, Clarence Stratton, Walter Sinclair, Lester Raines, Robert Bell, Samuel A. Eliot, Jr., Colin Campbell Clements, Bernard Szold, George Sommes, Mr. and Mrs. Burton W. James, David Owen, Doris Smith, Maurice Gnesin, Ramon Savich, Laura Sherry and others of like standing.

There has been one national organization to support, advise, and correlate the activities of the little theatre; namely, the Drama League of America. This league was founded in 1910 at Evanston, Illinois, and since that time has acted as a clearing house for dramatic information, publishing the Drama, first a quarterly, later a monthly; distributing study outlines, and holding national conventions in the interest of the amateur and professional theatres.

Several hundred centers of the Drama League of America have been established in the United States, some as producing groups, others as writing and study sections. A number of centers have their own little theatres. Under the inspiring leadership of Mrs. A. Starr Best, Mr. Theodore B. Hinckley, Dr. S. M. Tucker, Mr. Harold A. Ehrensperger, Mr. Barrett H. Clark, Mr. J. Vandervoort Sloan, Miss Sue Ann Wilson, and a host of other writers, executives, and organizers, the work of the Drama League has gone forward steadily in spite of financial difficulties. It has been one of the great forces in stimulating and controlling the little theatre movement, and has been of special value to communities whose resources and experience are limited, and whose geographical location prevents their easy access to expert advice and first-rate productions. For several years the New York Drama League existed independently of the larger organization, but its activities have now been merged with the parent group.

THE THEATRE IN THE COLLEGE

About the same time that the professional little theatre made its first appearance in America the universities awakened and began to organize their dramatic activities along artistic and creative lines. In 1911 the Wisconsin Players came into being. This group was not officially sponsored by the University of Wisconsin, but it had its headquarters in Madison, and many of its leading spirits were affiliated with the University. Two acting groups were maintained, one in Madison under the direction of Thomas H. Dickinson, another in Milwaukee under the direction of Laura Sherry. Strong emphasis was placed upon playwriting, and a number of local dramatists were developed.

In 1912 was founded the most famous of all university

theatres, the 47 Workshop of Harvard. This organization was, like the one at Wisconsin, only nominally a university institution. The founder was Professor George Pierce Baker, and the nucleus of the group was his college class, but townspeople shared in the production, and expenses were borne, not by Radcliffe or Harvard, but by private subscriptions. The story of how this group achieved international fame is a familiar one and need not be repeated. It is necessary merely to remind the reader that for many years Professor Baker worked practically without funds and with the humblest equipment, yet managed to provide laboratory experience for many young playwrights, some of whom achieved success on Broadway. Recently, of course, Yale University has stolen Professor Baker from its rival, and has furnished him with a magnificent theatre in which to continue his activities. The far-reaching influence of the pioneer work at Harvard is apparent. Students have gone from the 47 Workshop to all sections of the country, and have carried with them the methods and ideals acquired in Cambridge. The wider opportunities now presented to students by the Department of Drama at Yale should enrich even more greatly the stream of American drama.

Another intensely interesting chapter in the history of university dramatics in this country belongs to Professor Frederich H. Koch, who, following the Harvard example, founded a laboratory for undergraduate playwrights, first in North Dakota, later at the University of North Carolina. In both places he directed the energies of his students to the exploration of their own environment and its traditions, stimulating them to compose folk-plays of true local coloring and remarkable stage effectiveness. The Dakota Playmakers did good work; the Carolina Playmakers, partly because of richer soil, have done even better. They have already created a repertoire of native plays which compares favorably with the repertoire of the Irish theatre, and they are still "play-making." Professor Koch has been highly successful not only in extracting these plays from student writers, but also in producing them skillfully and taking the productions on tour throughout the state, and occasionally farther. He has thus enabled the university to serve its entire community in an artistic and self-revealing manner.

A fourth school of the drama sheltered by an institution of higher learning is that maintained by the Carnegie Institute of Technology at Pittsburgh. Founded in 1914 with Thomas Wood Stevens as director, this school established a four-year course in theatre arts, and was the first institution in America to offer a Bachelor of Arts degree in the dramatic field. It has a thoroughly modern laboratory theatre, and a corps of instructors with professional backgrounds. Connected with the theatre at various times have been Donald Robertson, B. Iden Payne, Sir William Poel, Hubert Osborne, Frank McEntee, Woodman Thompson, Chester M. Wallace, Whitford Kane, Doris Myers, and others of similarly high standing. The emphasis at Carnegie Tech. is different from that at Harvard and other colleges: it is chiefly upon the technical arts of the theatre. Playwriting, while considered, is of secondary importance. This emphasis is natural and proper in a technological institution. In order to give the utmost in practical experience the Carnegie School of the Drama gives a large number of public productions. Several directors working simultaneously make this possible. Students are therefore offered more opportunities for acting, scene-designing, stage-lighting, costuming, and managing than in any similar school in the country.

To enumerate all the American colleges which have recently founded effective dramatic departments would require a long account. We must content ourselves with mentioning the pioneers, and realizing that many followers

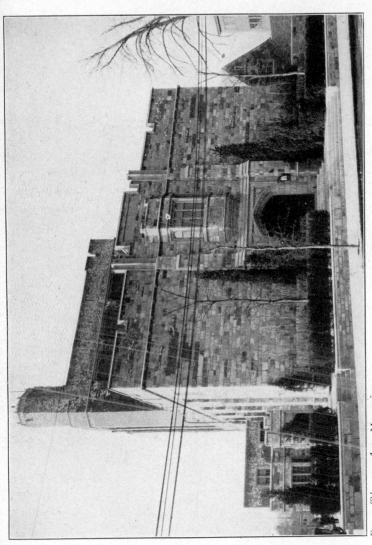

Plate 30: The New Yale University Theatre.

have profited by their example. Professor A. M. Drummond, at Cornell University; Professor E. C. Mabie, at the University of Iowa; Professor B. Roland Lewis, at the University of Utah; Professor C. M. Wise, at State Teachers College, Kirksville, Mo.; Dr. S. M. Tucker, at Brooklyn Polytechnic Institute; Mr. Theodore B. Hinckley, at various institutions in Chicago; Dr. Clarence Stratton, at Cleveland; Mr. Samuel A. Eliot, Jr., at Smith College; Mr. Gordon Davis, at Stanford University; Mr. Sam Hume and Mr. Irving Pichel, at the University of California; Mr. Hubert C. Heffner, at the University of Arizona, and later at the University of North Carolina; Mr. Alexander Dean and Mr. Carl Glick, at the University of Montana; Mr. Allan Crafton, at the University of Kansas; Mrs. Ottilie Seybolt, at the University of Minnesota; Mr. Harold N. Hillebrand and Mr. Wesley Swanson, at the University of Illinois; Miss Gertrude Johnson and Mr. W. C. Troutman, at the University of Wisconsin; Mr. Alfred G. Arvold, at the North Dakota Agricultural College; Mrs. Jeannette Marks, at Mt. Holyoke College; Mr. Randolph Somerville, at Washington Square College of New York University; Mr. Maynard Lee Daggy, at the State College of Washington; Mr. Fergus Reddie, Alice Henson Ernst, and Miss Florence Wilbur, at the University of Oregon; Mr. Albert R. Lovejoy, Mr. Burton W. James and Mr. John Ashby Conway, at the University of Washington; Mr. Lawrence Paquin, at Drake University; Mr. E. D. Schonberger, at the University of North Dakota; Miss Alpha W. Roth, at the State Teachers College, Oshkosh, Wis.; Mr. W. D. Wentz, at Southwestern University; Mr. Arthur C. Cloetingh, at Pennsylvania State College; these are but a few of the men and women who have done dramatic work of exceptional merit in our colleges and advanced schools.

Most of these instructors and producers have had to

meet and surmount the problems of the pioneer. They have usually had to lift dramatics out of a social into an artistic atmosphere; institute fundamental courses in playwriting, acting, and workshop, adapting them to a more or less rigid curriculum; produce plays with meagre equipment on a platform stage before a hypercritical undergraduate audience. Most of them have won the fight. Some of them have already had modern playhouses constructed for them; the rest are working to that end. They have not only enriched the life of the college and its surrounding community; they have taught and inspired countless teachers in the elementary and high schools, who have gone into the cities, the villages, and the wilderness, with a practical and yet idealistic conception of the theatre as an institution of immense social, intellectual and artistic worth. In some instances the graduates of our college dramatic departments have stepped into the professional theatre, where their influence has been considerable, and always admirable. In another fifty years the American drama and the technical arts of the theatre may be chiefly the product of the American college.

THE LARGE REPERTORY THEATRE

If the strictly professional little theatre cannot compete with the commercial theatre, at least it has been proved that the strictly professional repertory theatre can do so. That is, if the house is large enough, the productions good enough, and the business management astute enough. In recent years several repertory groups have made a fair success: the Henry Jewett Repertory Theatre of Boston; Eva Le Gallienne's Civic Repertory Theatre of New York City; the Theatre Guild of New York City. The last mentioned is by all odds the most successful, and therefore deserves particular mention.

The Theatre Guild, built upon the foundation laid by

the Washington Square Players, offered its first production in the spring of 1919, at the Garrick Theatre. Adopting the subscription plan, it secured during its first season, 175 subscribers (that is, holders of season tickets). With the opening of the second season this number leaped to 1,200; the third season to 1,700; the fourth season to 2,600; the fifth, to 5,700; the sixth, to 7,000; the seventh (in which season the gorgeous new Guild Theatre was opened), to 14,000; the eighth, to 17,000; the ninth, to 21,000; the tenth (the present season, 1927–28), to approximately 24,000. These figures are positively alarming, but they are also very cheering, especially to the directors of the Theatre Guild.

This eminently successful organization, although in some respects a repertory theatre, does not change its bill as often as a true repertory theatre should. It allows certain productions to run a very long time, and moves them to other theatres when the home plant is needed for new plays. It does, however, revive its plays occasionally, and by doing so earns a right to the word "repertory." Up to the present it has produced about sixty plays, the great majority of which have been of European origin. It cannot, therefore, be looked upon as a national theatre, but rather as an international one. From a business point of view its policy has probably been the correct one, for an up-to-date international repertoire is interesting to a very large number of playgoers, whereas a native repertoire would appeal to a much smaller number. Nevertheless the Theatre Guild has been severely criticized for its snobbishness toward the rising American playwright.

Recently this theatre has burst the confines of the theatrical metropolis, and has sent a company on tour of the large Eastern cities, with a repertoire of several Guild successes. It also has at the present time a resident company in Chicago. If this policy is carried further, the Guild may easily become a nation-wide force, and (who knows?) perhaps another Trust! In any event it is a rather spectacular example of an art theatre which has proved a commercial success.

CIVIC MASQUES AND PAGEANTS

Another phase of the new spirit in the American theatre is the interest in civic (community) masques and pageants. Several individuals have devoted their energies to this form of theatrical expression: Thomas Wood Stevens, Professor George Pierce Baker, and Percy MacKaye, among others. But of all these, Mr. MacKaye is the outstanding figure. Inspired largely by the dreams and thwarted ambitions of his father, Steele MacKaye, he began as long ago as 1905 to preach the gospel of community drama, and since then, from time to time, has written and directed numerous dramatic festivals, masques, and pageants in different parts of the country. In 1909 he produced his "Canterbury Pilgrims" at Gloucester, Mass., with 1,500 citizens participating. In 1914 he produced, in collaboration with Thomas Wood Stevens, his "Masque of Saint Louis," in the city of that name, over a period of five days, with 7,500 participants. In 1916 he produced, first in New York City and later in Boston, his even more pretentious "Caliban by the Yellow Sands," in celebration of the Tercentenary of Shakespeare's death. In the latter production he had as assistants some half-dozen directors, and a stupendous cast.

There have been in recent years a number of ventures of this kind, some historical, some religious, some of mixed motives. Most of them have been staged outdoors, in amphitheatres, with elaborate scenery, costumery, and lighting effects. A few of them have had artistic merit; the majority have failed to rise above the plane of mediocrity. That even the poorest of them serve a social need cannot be disputed. Neither can it be disputed that this need is better served when the performance is guided by a trained pageant-master, with a sense of art. Thus far the demand for such directors has been too slight to tempt many into the field. How important this form of drama will become in the future is a matter of pure speculation.

PRESENT-DAY PRODUCERS AND STAGE-DIRECTORS

The tradition of the late nineteenth century has been kept alive in the American theatre by a number of producers and directors who had their training in the days before the so-called "art-theatre movement" had crossed the Atlantic. Among these may be mentioned such familiar names as: David Belasco, Wm. A. Brady, Al H. Woods, Sam H. Harris, Edgar Selwyn, Wagenhals and Kemper, George M. Cohan, George C. Tyler, Oliver Morosco, Henry W. Savage, the Shuberts, the late Henry Miller, and John Golden. Not that these men are all old in years; some of them are old only in spirit. For our purpose the most interesting is David Belasco, the Dean of American producers.

Much idolatry has been laid at Mr. Belasco's feet, and as much abuse has been hurled at his head. Friends and enemies alike, however, join in praising him for his industry, his thoroughness, his valuable contributions to the technique of play-production. His laboratory has been engaged for years in the advancement of stage-lighting, and his scenic effects have frequently proved startling in their realism. His actors have generally shown careful training in diction and pantomime, and have therefore helped to maintain a standard in such matters. Mr. Belasco has no patience with hasty effects, with good intentions minus good execution. For this reason, if for no other, he dislikes the amateur dramatic movement. He fights for the maintenance of strictly professional standards in all departments of the theatre. Such an attitude has its merits, obviously. From a certain point of view, however, it is not so admirable. Unless it is joined to a sense of artistic values it is almost devoid of significance. In the whole of Mr. Belasco's career in the American theatre he has produced only a handful of plays that can be called great. His typical productions are of definitely second- or third-rate material. His own plays, for example.

Belasco and Stanislavsky have been compared on the basis of their realism. The Russian, however, easily wins by the comparison, for the simple reason that his productions are fully as meticulous and as finished, are as convincing in their illusion, and at the same time are under-laid and over-laid with spiritual subtleties which a Belasco production never has. One is a seeker after verisimilitude; the other is a poet, a creator.

There is, however, a younger generation of American producers, some of whom at least have reflected the new spirit in the theatre. Of these may be mentioned in connection with legitimate drama: Arthur Hopkins, Brock Pemberton, John D. Williams, Wm. Harris, Jr., Winthrop Ames, Guthrie McClintic, Gilbert Miller, Richard Herndon, Horace Liveright, and Walter Hampden; in connection with musical comedy, revues, and spectacles: Earl Carroll, John M. Anderson, Morris Gest, George White, Florenz Ziegfeld, Jr., Irving Berlin, and Charles B. Dillingham.

In a slightly different category, for the reason that they are stage-directors rather than independent producers, and are therefore in the employ of various producers, should be mentioned men like: Augustin Duncan, B. Iden Payne, Dudley Digges, Frank Reicher, Emanuel Reicher, Robert Milton, Philip Moeller, Sam Forrest, Winchell Smith, and Hassard Short.

ACTORS OF THE TWENTIETH CENTURY

It is exceptionally difficult to set up standards of acting. For that reason there is always a justifiable question in the minds of the public as to whether the actors of one generation are superior or inferior to the actors of another. An old critic will invariably lament that the golden days are over; that the actors of the present cannot compare with those of his youth. A young critic, on the other hand, will either make no comparisons with the past or else will declare loudly that his heroes are as great as heroes ever have been. The old critic's judgment will be called warped, the young one's, callow. There is no one to settle the dispute. A wise layman will therefore worry little about tradition, and will content himself with comparisons of living actors. Instead of trying to settle in his mind whether Hampden is greater than Irving, or Barrymore greater than Booth, let him, if he insists on standards, satisfy himself as to which is the better Hamlet—Hampden or Barrymore. Even then his conclusions will be personal, and subject to debate. It is reasonable to suppose that we have on the American stage today a considerable number of good actors. They give pleasure to people of intelligence and taste. That is all that can be asked of them.

In the previous chapter we listed a number of distinguished players who appeared on our stage before the close of the nineteenth century. Many of these are still with us. But without mentioning them again, we shall put down here the names of certain others who have come into prominence during the past quarter-century. It is an incomplete list, of course, but it is long enough to remind the reader of how rich our stage is in capable performers: George Arliss, Holbrook Blinn, Walter Hampden, Fritz Leiber, John Barrymore, Alla Nazimova, Elsie Ferguson, Grace George, Richard Bennett, Leo Ditrichstein, Emmet Corrigan, Norman Trevor, E. Wynne Matthison, H. B. Warner, Marjorie Rambeau, Lyn Harding, O. P. Heggie, Guy Bates Post, Bertha Kalich, Helen Westley, Nance O'Neill, Ina Claire, Frank Craven, Eva Le Gallienne, Joseph Schildkraut, Jacob Ben-Ami, Alfred Lunt, Lenore Ulric, Peggy Wood, Rollo Peters, Jane Cowl, Basil Sidney, Katharine Cornell, Margalo Gilmore, Ruth Chatterton, Jeanne Eagels, Helen Menken, Emily Stevens, Pauline Lord, Margaret Wycherley, Helen Gahagan, Billie Burke, Geoffrey Kerr, Louis Wolheim, Olga Petrova, Otto Kruger, Florence and Mary Nash, Glenn Hunter, Gregory Kelly, Walter Huston, Helen Hayes, Fay Bainter, J. C. and Elliott Nugent, Wallace Eddinger, Mary Boland, Walker Whiteside, Lester Lonergan, Laura Hope Crews, Frances Starr, Clare Eames, Lynn Fontanne, Judith Anderson, Pauline Frederick, Ernest Glendinning, Louise Closser Hale, Violet Heming, Chrystal Herne, Leslie Howard, Henry Hull, Whitford Kane, Madge Kennedy, Doris Kenyon, Francine Larrimore, Winifred Lenihan, Helen MacKellar, Bruce McRae, Florence Reed, James Rennie, Charles Gilpin, Paul Robeson, Laurette Taylor, Blanche Yurka. Add to this list of legitimate players the names of such brilliant dancers as Isadora Duncan, Ruth St. Denis and Ted Shawn, Margaret Severn, and Ruth Page; such clowns as Frank Tinney, James Barton, Fred Stone, Ed Wynn, Al Jolson, Eddie Cantor, Leon Errol, Chic Sale, Will Rogers, the Marx Brothers, Eugene and Willie Howard; such musical comedy and revue stars as Fannie Brice, the Duncan Sisters, Elsie Janis, Fred and Adele Astaire, Ray and Johnny Dooley, Marilyn Miller, George Jessel, Florence Moore, Mary Eaton, and Helen Ford—and the American theatre of to-day is seen to be overflowing with effective personalities.

MODERN STAGE-DESIGNERS

It has frequently been said that the chief difference be-

Plate 31 : American Realism. *The Return of Peter Grimm,* as produced by David Belasco.

tween the old theatre and the new is that the latter has succumbed to the influence of the modern designer. This statement comes very nearly being true. The European art-movement in the theatre owed more to Appia and Craig than to anyone else. On the American stage the artist now has a foothold, but he did not interest himself in the theatre until 1915 or thereabouts. Until that time scene-painters were essentially craftsmen—very much like sign-painters. They seldom created; they worked from stencils. The settings for most productions in the commercial American theatre are still done from stencils, or might as well be. But the more modern producers employ creative artists, and the non-commercial theatre is very particular about doing so.

We have today a fairly large group of interesting scene and costume designers. Robert Edmond Jones, for example, is a Harvard graduate who studied for a time in Europe, and then returned to revolutionize the American stage. Intelligent, fertile, sincere, daring, he has designed many notable productions, practically all of them for Arthur Hopkins. On one or two occasions he has gone the limit and attempted pure abstraction. Generally, however, he has been content with a reasonable degree of simplification. All his designs exhibit a strongly imaginative quality, and often suggest the influence of Craig.

Lee Simonson, another Harvard man, did his early stage work with the Washington Square Players. Later he became chief designer for the Theatre Guild, and is one of the Directors of that organization. His work covers a wide range, but is always characterized by a fine sense of balance and a certain severity which is extremely effective.

Norman-Bel Geddes, perhaps the most original of the group, was born in the Middle West, studied at art schools in Cleveland and Chicago, did commercial art in Detroit, and while in the latter city became interested in the theatre.

He began making stage designs. Then he discovered Gordon Craig, and was greatly stimulated. He did some work in the Detroit theatres, but soon accepted an invitation to Los Angeles to design productions for Miss Aline Barnsdall's art theatre. In Los Angeles his work created a sensation. After a brief employment in the motion-picture industry he went to New York City, where he was commissioned to do a setting for the Metropolitan Opera. This was in 1918. Since that time he has conceived a vast number of designs: for costumes, settings, and theatre buildings. His conceptions are invariably dynamic and impressive, rich in color, bold in line, spiritual in their implications. No task staggers him; the grander the scale, the happier he is. He gravitated naturally to the Divine Comedy of Dante as a theatre project, and almost succeeded in having that stupendous poem staged according to his plans. When Professor Reinhardt brought "The Miracle" to America, it was to Norman-Bel Geddes that he assigned the problem of designing the whole huge production. This artist is cramped in the ordinary theatre; that is one reason why he has projected new theatre buildings. No one of them has yet been constructed, but it is not impossible that one will be. His ideal theatre eliminates the proscenium arch, allows the stage to flow upward until it merges into the dome of the auditorium, employs light for a curtain, and sinking stages for the changing of scenes. Another of his notions is that space can be saved and sight-lines improved by placing the stage in a corner of the auditorium, rather than in the center of one side. Geddes has the strongest, most powerful vision, of any of our American theatre artists. He is in some respects another Steele MacKaye. It is difficult to predict what he will do next, for he has the fertility of genius, and he is still young.

Joseph Urban must be given credit for having introduced modern stage art to America. Coming here from Vienna shortly before the War, he created interesting settings for opera, and later for revues. His colorful, imaginative designs aroused much discussion, and stimulated native artists. Herman Rosse, a native of Holland, was also an innovator on our stage. In California, Chicago, and New York, he has from time to time done brilliant work, particularly for opera. Other ex-Europeans who have contributed to the beauty of American productions are Willy Pogany, Boris Anisfeld, and Nicholas Roerich.

Mention should be made of many other artists in our theatre. At least eight come to mind as having established themselves definitely as vital and important figures. These are: C. Raymond Johnson, Rollo Peters, James Reynolds, Woodman Thompson, Cleon Throckmorton, Claude Bragdon, Livingston Platt, and Ernest de Weerth. Not one of the foregoing is a stencil-designer. Each is creative, sensitive to the peculiar requirements of theatrical art, and refreshing in manner. They differ greatly from each other in style and point of view, but they all take the theatre seriously, and have brought beauty to it. They have scarcely anything in common with the scene-painters of twenty years ago.

More specialized in their interests, but not unimportant in the advancement of stage art in America, are several men, such as W. T. Benda, Tony Sarg, and Thomas Wilfred. Everyone acquainted with the theatre has seen or at least heard of the Benda Masks. Created first as a diversion for the artist, they later were put to use most effectively on the stage by Miss Margaret Severn and other dancers. Their success, along with the propaganda of Gordon Craig, brought the mask into considerable use, even in legitimate drama. Tony Sarg, whose allegiance is not entirely to the theatre, has nevertheless done it a very great service by reviving the marionette. For several seasons he has brought out delightful puppet-shows, and besides showing them in New York, has sent them touring the country. His example has been widely followed, and all those of the public who admire this ancient (almost sacred) form of theatrical art are distinctly in his debt. Thomas Wilfred has had wide publicity as the inventor of the Clavilux, or light-organ. This instrument, which Mr. Wilfred has exhibited throughout America, is unique and fascinating. It projects light on a screen in continuously changing patterns and color combinations. It achieves the fluidity of music, and is capable of extraordinarily subtle effects. Its creator feels that the Clavilux is the beginning of an utterly new art, and predicts that in the near future light-recitals will be as common and as popular as music-recitals. He also suggests that the Clavilux is a valuable adjunct to the theatre, for it is capable of creating swiftly and easily an infinite variety of moods and backgrounds for the action of a play. Thus far, however, it must be admitted that Mr. Wilfred's prophecies have not shown signs of fulfillment. There seems to be less interest in the light-organ today than there was five years ago. The reasons for this cannot be entered into here, but they will no doubt be apparent to the reader.

CONTEMPORARY AMERICAN PLAYWRIGHTS

This is not a history of the drama, and in most chapters we have given little or no space to dramatic literature, but it is impossible to resist inserting at this point a few remarks concerning the new playwrights in our theatre. It will be pleasant to complete the picture of an American theatre arrived at maturity, at the age of independence.

We have already pointed out that from 1700 to 1850 our stage was almost wholly given over to English drama, and that during the fifty years following, only a handful of native dramatists arose. Of the American playwrights who have secured a hearing in the last quarter-century, few can stand comparison with the master-dramatists of Europe,

From Cheney's *Stage Decoration.*

Plate 32–33: The designs by Norman-Bel Geddes for a proposed production of Dante's *Divine Comedy.*

but many can be put forward without embarrassment as worthy representatives of our literature.

These twentieth century writers can be divided roughly into two classes: pre-war and post-war. In the first group we find William Vaughn Moody, Percy MacKaye, Eugene Walter, Edward Sheldon, George Ade, George Broadhurst, Alice Brown, Owen Davis, Charles Kenyon, Charles Klein, Edward Knoblock, George Middleton, Winchell Smith, Booth Tarkington, Josephine Preston Peabody, Willard Mack, A. E. Thomas, Bayard Veiller, Langdon Mitchell and Channing Pollock, together with a few hold-overs from the nineties: David Belasco, William Gillette, Clyde Fitch, and Augustus Thomas. Many of these men and women are still actively writing for the theatre. They are, for the most part, study craftsmen. Many of them excel in melodrama, one or two in poetic drama, several in light comedy. Their plays are conventional in structure, and with one or two exceptions, undistinguished in style. They give evidence of a real knowledge of the theatre: they abound in action, strong situations, interesting characterization. What they lack, taken en masse, is depth, literary beauty, and psychological subtlety.

In the second group we find: Eugene O'Neill, Zoë Akins, Rachel Crothers, Zona Gale, Susan Glaspell, Elmer Rice, Gilbert Emery, Jesse Lynch Williams, Clare Kummer, Arthur Richman, John Colton, Maurine Watkins, George S. Kaufman, Marc Connelly, Hatcher Hughes, Lulu Vollmer, Maxwell Anderson, Laurence Stallings, George Abbott, George Kelly, Philip Barry, John V. A. Weaver, Brian Hooker, Sidney Howard, John Howard Lawson, Paul Green, John Dos Passos, Kenyon Nicholson, Alfred Kreymborg, Edna St. Vincent Millay, and Alice Gerstenberg. Anyone who is familiar with the work of this group will realize without difficulty that although a certain percentage of it is ordinary and imitative, content to follow well-beaten paths, a larger percentage is restless, original, and even revolutionary. Cynicism takes the place of sentiment, tragedy crowds out melodrama, typical American traits are searchingly appraised rather than blatantly eulogized, sex is handled with unrestrained sincerity rather than with prudish hypocrisy, and expressionism shatters traditional notions of dialogue pattern and act structure.

These changes were the result of many things, but chiefly of the War, which engendered internationalism, destroyed sentimental illusions, and created an intense spirit of longing for new and different things. Another factor was the entrance of college-bred men into the theatre. Still another was the discovery of Freudian psychology. A fourth was the new school of criticism, which cursed and laughed at our older drama until the young men were ashamed to take it as their guide. These are the main factors; the rest we shall not take time to enumerate.

Of our post-war playwrights, Eugene O'Neill is easily the strongest. He is the only American playwright who has become a world figure. From his one-act plays of the sea, written between 1914 and 1919, and acted by the Provincetown Players, through his first successes in the commercial theatre: "Beyond the Horizon," 1920, and "The Emperor Jones," 1920, on to his monumental tragedy, "Strange Interlude," 1927, he has revealed the instincts, the powers, of a true genius of the theatre. "Anna Christie," "The Hairy Ape," "Desire Under the Elms," "The Great God Brown," "Marco Millions," "Lazarus Laughed,"—all these are plays of unmistakable distinction. They are American, but they transcend the boundaries of this nation. Were we to erase all the names listed above, save that of O'Neill, we could still say that the American drama had come of age.

Yet O'Neill's greatness must not eclipse for us the merit of his contemporaries. In the field of satirical comedy we may surely boast of such brilliant writers as George Kelly, Marc Connelly, George S. Kaufman, Philip Barry, Jesse Lynch Williams, Maxwell Anderson, and Laurence Stallings. For psychological subtlety we may turn to Sidney Howard and Susan Glaspell; for powerful treatment of folk-themes, to Hatcher Hughes, Lulu Vollmer and Paul Green; for dexterity and intellectual novelty, to John Dos Passos, John Howard Lawson, and Alfred Kreymborg. Our drama has achieved variety as well as sophistication.

CONTEMPORARY AMERICAN CRITICS

If we have said little about the drama in this book, we have said even less about another important branch of the theatre—criticism. It is too late now to begin with Aristotle and trace the development of his art down through all the centuries. But it seems too great a pity to reach the final page without having paid a little respect to the men who spend their lives under the arching domes of playhouses in order that the world may hear of what is happening on the stage.

It is essential that we take a paragraph or two to suggest that the American theatre of today owes a great deal to these men. Some of them have done the theatre no good; at least they have not contributed to its improvement. They may have increased slightly the box-office receipts. But there are others who have helped tremendously to pull it out of its provincialism, to encourage its best playwrights, its best actors, directors, and designers. These have also acted as interpreters to the public. They have traveled in Europe and renewed their vision. They have even assumed the rôle of prophet.

The rise of the new American critic is almost as startling as the rise of the new American playwright or the new American stage-designer. Whereas two decades ago we had a few theatrical observers who wrote in a genial, leisurely manner of the personalities and occurrences in the theatre, we now have a small army of intense, belligerent, scholarly, exasperatingly keen young men who write not only columns in our dailies, weeklies, and monthlies, but large and bewilderingly intelligent books on the subject of theatrical art! History is their plaything; the world their orange. Nothing daunts them—not even German expressionism in its maddest manifestations.

To be specific: Kenneth Macgowan, Stark Young, George Jean Nathan, Heywood Broun, Sheldon Cheney, Alexander Woollcott, Gilbert Seldes, John Corbin, Robert C. Benchley, Joseph Wood Krutch, Oliver M. Sayler, Brander Matthews, Clayton Hamilton, Walter Prichard Eaton, Barrett H. Clark, Arthur Hobson Quinn, Robert G. Welsh, J. Ranken Towse, J. Brooks Atkinson, Stephen Rathbun, James Craig, Charles Darnton, Burns Mantle, Percy Hammond, Alan Dale, James Metcalf, Robert E. Sherwood, Ernest Boyd, Ludwig Lewisohn, Montrose J. Moses, Thomas H. Dickinson, Lewis Mumford, John Mason Brown—and a great many more.

The discerning eye will catch certain names in this list that suggest anything but modernity, and certainly not youth. The point is well taken, but it is too difficult to draw a line. Think what some of these men have done for our theatre. Kenneth Macgowan, advance man for all that is new, interpreter of all that is obscure. Stark Young, esthete *par excellence,* weaver of subtle theories, caterer to the inner circle. George Jean Nathan, indefatigable iconoclast, incorrigible scoffer at provincialism, barker for O'Neill. Sheldon Cheney, friend of the art theatre, spokesman for the artist in the theatre. Oliver M. Sayler, globe-trotting enthusiast, chronicler of the Russians. Gilbert Seldes, intellectual flash. Ludwig Lewisohn, John Corbin and Joseph Wood Krutch, scholars at the play. Robert C. Benchley,

Heywood Broun, Robert E. Sherwood, wits of rare good sense. J. Ranken Towse, chastener of youth, standard-bearer of the past. Brander Matthews, Clayton Hamilton, Walter Prichard Eaton, Thomas H. Dickinson, Arthur Hobson Quinn, Montrose J. Moses, mellowed and wise historians, essayists, and anthologists. Ernest Boyd, and Barrett H. Clark, virile defenders of the theatre's rights, pleaders for its intellectual and spiritual salvation.

THE AMERICAN THEATRE AS HOST

It would be a serious breach of etiquette were we to ignore in this account certain performances given recently in America by foreign companies. To some of them we are greatly indebted; to others we can at least bow politely. We are not yet so independent that we can afford to turn our backs on the theatrical art of Europe and Asia. If we ever become that independent, we shall be well on the way toward stupidity and decay. We have had as guests, during the past two decades, about a dozen remarkable companies.

The Ben Greet Players, from England, taught us how to play Shakespeare's comedies without more equipment than good actors. The Comédie Française, from Paris, showed us how the classic French drama has been played since the time of Molière. It also demonstrated how French should be spoken. Giovanni Grasso and his Sicilian players illustrated what extraordinary passion may be engendered in the human breast, and how it may be transmitted to an audience. The Russian Ballet opened a new world of rhythmic beauty and extravagant color to Western eyes. The Irish Players gave us the art of Synge and Lady Gregory, and planted in American soil the seed of folk-drama, which has since flowered. The Chauve-Souris, from Moscow, gave us an amazing lesson in the art of vaudeville—a lesson which we have not yet taken sufficiently to heart. The Mos-

cow Art Theatre renewed our faith in the repertory thea-
atre, and revealed to us the finest character acting in the
world. The Théâtre du Vieux Colombier provided a first-
rate example of modern French stage art—modern without
being maudlin. The Habima Company, Hebrew, from Moscow, thrilled those who were susceptible to the grotesquely
beautiful, the profoundly imaginative. The Reinhardt
Repertory Company made the Reinhardt legend a reality,
and excited even those whom it did not satisfy. Eleonora
Duse spread her white hands and touched hidden chords
for the last time on earth. Fyodor Chaliapin shattered the
general belief that a great opera-singer cannot also be a
great actor.

THE MOTION PICTURE

At the beginning of this chapter we made reference to the
eclipses which in recent years have threatened the commercial theatre. Certainly the most ominous of these has been
the motion picture. Invented during the closing years of the
nineteenth century, it became within a decade an extremely
popular novelty. About 1908 its possibilities attracted the
American business man, and from that year to the present
its development has been nothing short of bewildering.
Only thirty years old, the motion picture is today not only
one of the great commercial enterprises of the world; it is
also the most popular form of theatrical entertainment. It
has not totally eclipsed the legitimate theatre, but it has
proved a serious competitor, and has practically killed the
road show. Yet in some ways its influence on the theatre
has been beneficial. By its nature adapted to the representation of violent action, comic or thrilling, and to the purposes
of superficial realism, it has attracted the millions who demand these qualities in drama, and has thus lifted from the
legitimate theatre the burden of providing them. There is

little excuse for a play being done legitimately today unless it depends chiefly on dialogue—the one element missing or at least minimized on the screen. It is almost the test of a good play (good in the traditional sense) to think of it in relation to the motion picture. Shakespeare, Molière, Congreve, Shaw, Ibsen—the work of such men does not depend upon external action. So long, therefore, as the finest dramas in the world demand legitimate production, the theatre will survive, and be purer for having a silent rival.

It is possible, of course, that dialogue will eventually become an important element of the motion picture. Signs point in that direction. On one hand we have the constant efforts to reproduce the human voice in synchronization with movement. Vitaphone, Movietone, and other new processes are certainly impressive. The fact is, however, that many persons prefer a musical accompaniment to a picture rather than an accompaniment of dialogue. Most members of an average audience are mentally lazy, and find it easier to absorb the emphatic emotional values of music than to follow the intricacies of language. On another hand we have the modern tendency to play up the sub-title. This is noticeable particularly in light comedy, where the plot is thin and the action commonplace. Having exhausted the possibilities of exciting action, and being faced with the necessity of turning out quantities of feature pictures, various producers have desperately turned to the wits of the country, the "wise-crackers," in current slang, for help, and have altered the technique of picture-making in such a way that the situations and actions, instead of justifying their own existence, have become merely preparatory material for the climactic sub-titles. In line with this tendency is the remark made several years ago by George Bernard Shaw, to the effect that the movie of the future would consist entirely of sub-titles, and that the idol of the screen would be a modern Oscar Wilde. Mr. Shaw, in this observation, was, as usual, ahead of the time. His prophecy is being gradually realized. In this connection, however, we must bear in mind that so long as motion pictures are made for the million, the sub-titles cannot be very subtle or very profound. As for pictures intended for the few—well, it seems unlikely that the highly intelligent will ever prefer to do their reading in public.

From the business point of view the motion-picture industry has proved a most stupendous success. Like the legitimate theatre, it has been organized until at present it is controlled by a very few men. The free-for-all competition of 1908 has been supplanted by a combination of financiers, who act as producers and distributors; a combination of exhibitors, to protect themselves against the producers; a combination of stars (United Artists) to protect themselves against both producers and exhibitors. There is even an organization (founded in 1922, with Will Hays at its head) to protect the entire industry against the public: by the prevention of scandalous publicity and offensive films.

Some idea of the proportions of this still-young industry can be gained by noting that the yearly production in America of full-length feature films is very close to one thousand. In addition to these are manufactured hundreds of short subjects; comic, scientific, historical, news-reels, and what-not. This output supplies more than twenty thousand motion-picture houses in the United States, as well as hundreds in foreign countries. It is interesting to learn that there are more movie theatres in this country than in all the other countries of the world combined. Germany, for example, has about three thousand; England, the same; France, two thousand; Japan, one thousand; Spain, twelve hundred; India (with a population of more than three hundred million), three hundred; Australia, eleven hundred; Austria, six hundred; Denmark, three hundred and fifty; Holland, two hundred and fifty. In foreign countries the percentage of American-made films exhibited varies between fifty and ninety per cent. of the total.

In the early days of the motion picture, Italy and France vied with America for leadership. Lately England, Germany and Russia have had ambitions in that direction. Seldom, however, has any one of these challenges proved serious. American organization, mechanical expertness, and fabulous wealth have together overwhelmed all competition. At present the two countries that come the nearest to being independent of American films are Russia and Germany. England is busy passing laws regulating the percentage of foreign films that can be shown within her borders, and is putting forth every effort to encourage home production. Thus far, however, British films have been decidedly second-rate. Russia is engrossed in problems of political education. The Soviets have authorized the making of many films, but they are chiefly propagandist, and therefore not adapted to the world-market. An exception is, of course, "Potemkin," which has been discussed in an earlier chapter. The German situation is more complex. In the years immediately following the Armistice a number of excellent films were made in Germany. In some respects they were superior to anything done before or since, there or elsewhere. We have mentioned these films in another chapter. The point to be brought out here is that as soon as American producers began to realize the merit of German movies, they set to work to get control of them. This they did partly by investing money in German playhouses, partly by subsidizing future German films, and partly by hiring, at irresistible salaries, German directors and actors for work in America. Full advantage was taken of the embarrassing financial situation in which Germany found herself after the War.

It is not apparent yet just what will be the final result of this attempt to turn the stream of German movie art into American channels. It is obvious, however, that the immediate results have been both good and bad. We have profited by the acquisition of such brilliant actors and directors as Emil Jannings, Pola Negri, Conrad Veidt, Camilla Horn, Ernst Lubitsch, F. W. Murnau, and E. A. Dupont. We have suffered, however, through the mixture of German and American points of view and motives. A German director is apt not to be at home in Hollywood. He is apt to feel constrained, and therefore work only for his salary. Even when a film is made in Germany with American money, it can scarcely ring true. Occasionally the shadow of the box-office will fall upon the scene, and the picture will falter, lose its unity, its faith in itself as a work of art.

The motion picture has been looked upon as an art since about 1915. Until then it was either a mechanical toy or a poor reflection of the legitimate stage. Upon the appearance of D. W. Griffith's epoch-making film, "The Birth of a Nation," the more thoughtful of the public began to talk and write on "the art of the motion picture." It was realized then that the movies had a technique which was quite distinct from that of the spoken drama; that for the first time in history, the world was being set in controlled motion before the human eye. Since then the specatcle drama, with its emphasis on massed movement, has developed wonderfully: progressing through "Intolerance," "The Covered Wagon," and "The Thief of Bagdad," and culminating in "Ben Hur" and "The Big Parade."

Another discovery of about the same time was that comic pantomime could be recorded most effectively on the screen. Charlie Chaplin, child of London's music-halls, began to delight the world. His first pictures, almost pure slapstick, are still revived and enjoyed. His later pictures, revealing a mature art, has sent millions of spectators into ecstasy, and hundreds of critics into rapture. "The Kid," "The Pilgrim," "The Gold Rush," "The Circus," are pictures that combine popular appeal and subtle artistry in an amazing manner. They establish Chaplin as the chief clown of our time, and one of the greatest comedians of all time. His rivals: Harold Lloyd, Buster Keaton, Harry Langdon, and the rest, have all learned from him, but cannot equal him. The only one who has come near doing so is Harry Langdon, who in his latest pictures has shown flashes of greatness, and in "Three's a Crowd," succeeded in sustaining a character and a mood too subtle, too near to the best tradition of the *Commedia dell' Arte,* for favorable box-office appeal.

It can easily be argued, if not proved, that the chief American contribution to the art of the motion picture (if we except Chaplin) is the animated cartoon. In these short films we have satirical wit, masterly drawing, ingenious imagination. They are truly created. They are free from literal representation, from the evils of photographic realism, and are entirely appropriate to the medium employed. In no way do they encroach upon or imitate the art of the legitimate theatre.

Another type of film which has been brought to a point of excellence by American producers is the picture of actual life. In such a picture we have no pretense at actuality—we have, instead, an artistic arrangement of actuality itself. Notable examples are: "Nanook of the North," "Moana of the South Seas," "Grass," and "Chang."

Of feature films which display unusual artistic imagination we have few. Mme. Nazimova's version of "Salomé" is one; Douglas Fairbanks' "Thief of Bagdad" is another. A possible third is James Cruze's "Beggar on Horseback." We have many films in which there is good acting, and many which are skillfully directed. Most of them, however, are shallow, obvious, sentimental, and innocent of artistic value. Our native ability lies largely in the realm of broad comedy and spectacular melodrama. This, fortunately, coincides extremely well with the demands at the box-office.

When an American producer sets to work on a feature film today he cannot afford to ignore the market value of the forthcoming product. His total expense will be anywhere between two hundred thousand and two million dollars. In 1912 a feature picture cost at the most fifteen or twenty thousand dollars. In those days a star actor received from a hundred to four hundred dollars a week for his work. Today he receives from a thousand to ten thousand dollars a week. In 1912 a director was lucky who was paid five thousand dollars for making a picture. Today it is not uncommon for a director to be paid a hundred thousand dollars for a picture. Under the circumstances, there is little hope for experimentation along artistic lines. The business man has created a vicious circle, from which at present there is no escape. It cost ten thousand dollars to make "The Cabinet of Dr. Caligari," but over two million to make "The King of Kings."

SUMMARY OF THEATRICAL CONDITIONS

Today there are not more than five hundred playhouses in America devoted to the legitimate drama. About a third of these are located in five cities: New York, Boston, Chicago, Philadelphia, and Los Angeles. Very few first-rate companies go on tour; the smaller cities and towns depend upon motion pictures and vaudeville. Some cities have resident stock companies, most of which are decidedly second-rate. Outside the large theatrical centers the legitimate drama is mainly in the hands of tent-show operators, who move, bag and baggage, every week or so. It is estimated that there are approximately four hundred of these tent-shows in the country, playing an average of forty weeks in the year. They have a repertoire of popular comedies and melodramas (not often of recent vintage) and because of low overhead expenses, are fairly prosperous. Their best business is done during the summer months, at least in most sections of the country, for snow and ice preclude the possibility of playing "under canvas."

The trouper, somehow, does not die. He has always been a part of the theatre—sometimes he has been all of the theatre. He is seldom remembered; he does not even care to be. It is he who knows the theatre best, for he creates it wherever he goes. When our great playhouses crumble, and our theories fade, the trouper will still be with us—a living theatre.

SELECTED REFERENCES

The best general survey of the contemporary American theatre is Sayler's *Our American Theatre*. More technical, but extremely useful, is Krows' *Play Production in America*. The amateur movement is throughly chronicled in several volumes: Mackay's *The Little Theatre in the United States,* Dickinson's *The Insurgent Theatre,* Burleigh's *The Community Theatre,* Dean's *Little Theatre Organization and Management,* Stratton's *Producing in Little Theatres,* and Arvold's *The Little Country Theatre.* Pre-eminent in their field are MacKaye's *Civic Theatre,* and *The Playhouse and the Play.* Two references on theatre architecture and equipment are Pichel's *Modern Theatres,* and Kinsila's *Modern Theatre Construction.* Regarding the artists in the theatre see Cheney's *The Art Theatre,* and the same writer's *Stage Decoration.* For the art of the dance in America see Duncan's *My Life,* and Shawn's *The American Ballet.* For the motion picture see Lindsay's *The Art of the Moving Picture,* and Ramsaye's *A Million and One Nights.* For a record of all recent events in the American theatre see the periodicals listed in the general bibliography which follows.

A SELECTED BIBLIOGRAPHY

(*This list is limited to books printed in English. It is made up chiefly of general histories and works which deal with periods and movements rather than individuals or particular events. A few biographies and memoirs of special importance have, however, been included. So far as possible titles have been chosen with a view to illustrating and amplifying the text of this book. It has been deemed advisable to exclude books of plays and critical works dealing solely with dramatic literature. Many of the references contain excellent bibliographies of a more specialized nature.*)

JOSEPH QUINCY ADAMS, JR.
  Shakespearean Playhouses. 1917.
VICTOR E. ALBRIGHT
  The Shakesperian Stage. 1909.
J. T. ALLEN
  The Greek Theatre of the Fifth Century Before Christ. 1919.
MADGE ANDERSON
  The Heroes of the Puppet Stage. 1923.
WILLIAM ARCHER
  About the Theatre. 1886.
  Study and the Stage. 1899.
  Schemes and Estimates for a National Theatre. (With H. Granville Barker) 1908.
ALFRED G. ARVOLD
  The Little Country Theatre. 1923.
GEORGE P. BAKER
  The Development of Shakespeare as a Dramatist. 1907.
H. B. BAKER
  History of the London Stage, 1576 to 1888. 2 vols. 1904.
ALEXANDER BAKSHY
  The Path of the Modern Russian Stage. 1916.

Mr. and Mrs. Bancroft, On and Off the Stage. 2 vols. 2nd. ed. 1888.

HARLEY GRANVILLE-BARKER
  The Exemplary Theatre. 1922.

P. T. Barnum. Written by Himself. 2 vols. 1927.

KATHARINE LEE BATES
  The English Religious Drama. 1910.

MARY P. BEEGLE AND JACK R. CRAWFORD
  Community Drama and Pageantry. 1916.

DAVID BELASCO
  The Theatre Through its Stage Door. 1919.

MARTHA F. BELLINGER
  A Short History of the Drama. 1927.

SARAH BERNHARDT
  The Art of the Theatre. 1925.

MARIO BORSA
  The English Stage of Today. 1908.

WILLIAM B. BOULTON
  The Amusements of Old London. 1901.

FRANK BRINKLEY
  Japan: Its History, Art, and Literature. 1915.

R. J. BROADBENT
  A History of Pantomime. 1901.

✓T. ALLSTON BROWN
  A History of the New York Stage, 1732 to 1901. 3 vols. 1903.

VAN DYKE BROWNE
  Secrets of Scene Painting and Stage Effects. n. d.

LOUISE BURLEIGH
  The Community Theatre in Theory and Practice. 1917.

KATE BUSS
  Studies in the Chinese Drama. 1922.

LOUIS CALVERT
  Problems of the Actor. 1918.

Cambridge History of American Literature. 4 vols. 1917–21.

Cambridge History of English Literature. 14 vols. 1907-16.

LILY B. CAMPBELL
  Scenes and Machines on the English Stage During the Renaissance. 1923.

HUNTLY CARTER
The New Spirit in Drama and Art. 1913.
The Theatre of Max Reinhardt. 1914.
The New Theatre and Cinema of Soviet Russia. 1925.
The New Spirit in the European Theatre, 1914–1924. 1925.

BASIL HALL CHAMBERLAIN
Things Japanese. 1905.

E. K. CHAMBERS
The Mediaeval Stage. 2 vols. 1903.
The Elizabethan Stage. 4 vols. 1923.

H. C. CHATFIELD-TAYLOR
Goldoni: A Biography. 1913.

SHELDON CHENEY
The New Movement in the Theatre. 1914.
The Art Theatre. 1917. rev. ed. 1925.
The Open-Air Theatre. 1918.
Modern Art and the Theatre. 1921.
Stage Decoration. 1928.

CHU CHIA-CHIEN AND A. JACOVLEFF
The Chinese Theatre. 1922.

PERCIVAL CHUBB AND OTHERS
Festivals and Plays. 1912.

COLLEY CIBBER
An Apology for His Life. Everyman's Library ed. 1908.

W. W. CLAPP, JR.
A Record of the Boston Stage. 1853.

REGINALD CLARENCE (COMPILER)
"The Stage" Cyclopædia of Plays. 1909.

BARRETT H. CLARK
How to Produce Amateur Plays. 1917. rev. ed. 1926.
A Study of the Modern Drama. 1925. rev. ed. 1928.

J. P. COLLIER
The History of English Dramatic Poetry. 1879.

DUTTON COOK
A Book of the Play. 2 vols. 1876.
On the Stage. 2 vols. 1883.

CONSTANT COQUELIN, HENRY IRVING, AND DION BOUCICAULT
The Art of Acting. 1926.

EDWARD GORDON CRAIG
  On the Art of the Theatre. 1911.
  Towards a New Theatre. 1913.
  The Theatre—Advancing. 1921.
  Scene. 1923.
  Books and Theatres. 1925.
√MARY CAROLINE CRAWFORD
  The Romance of the American Theatre. 1913.
W. M. A. CREIZENACH
  The English Drama in the Age of Shakespeare. 1916.
PETER CUNNINGHAM AND J. R. PLANCHÉ
  Sketches from Inigo Jones, With Life, etc. 1848.
J. F. DALY
  The Life of Augustin Daly. 1917.
ALEXANDER DEAN
  Little Theatre Organization and Management. 1926.
BASIL DEAN
  The Repertory Theatre. 1911.
THOMAS DEKKER
  The Gull's Horn Book. (Ed. by R. B. McKerrow) 1904.
√THOMAS H. DICKINSON
  —*The Case of American Drama.* 1915.
  The Insurgent Theatre. 1917.
√R. C. DIMMICK
  Our Theatres Today and Yesterday. 1913.
M. WILLSON DISHER
  Clowns and Pantomimes. 1925.
NATHAN HASKELL DOLE
  A Teacher of Dante, and Other Studies in Italian Literature.
    1908.
J. W. DONALDSON
  The Theatre of the Greeks, 8th ed. rev. 1891.
DR. JOHN DORAN
  A History of Court Fools. 1858.
  In and About Drury Lane. 2 vols. 1881.
  Annals of the English Stage. 3 vols. rev. ed. 1888.
FRANCIS DOUCE
  Illustrations of Shakespeare. 2 vols. 1807.

JOHN DREW
  My Years on the Stage. 1922.
ASHLEY DUKES
  Drama. 1927.
ISADORA DUNCAN
  My Life. 1927.
WILLIAM DUNLAP
  History of the American Theatre. 1832.
WALTER PRICHARD EATON
  The American Stage of Today. 1908.
  The Theory of the Theatre. 1910.
  Plays and Players. 1916.
  The Actor's Heritage. 1924.
OSMAN EDWARDS
  Japanese Plays and Playfellows. 1901.
A. ELSON
  A History of Opera. rev. ed. 1926.
ST. JOHN ERVINE
  The Organized Theatre. 1924.
NICOLAS EVREINOFF
  The Theatre in Life. 1927.
ERNEST FENOLLOSA AND EZRA POUND
  'Noh' or Accomplishment. 1916.
PERCY H. FITZGERALD
  A New History of the English Stage. 2 vols. 1882.
F. G. FLEAY
  A Chronicle History of the London Stage. 1890.
  A Biographical Chronicle of the English Drama. 1891.
ROY C. FLICKINGER
  Plutarch as a Source of Information on the Greek Theatre. 1904.
  The Greek Theatre and Its Drama. 1918.
J. G. FRAZER
  The Golden Bough. abridged ed. 1922.
DANIEL FROHMAN
  Memories of a Manager. 1911.
WILLIAM BURT GAMBLE (COMPILER)
  The Development of Scenic Art and Stage Machinery. A List of References in the New York Public Library. 1920.

RICHARD GARNETT
  A History of Italian Literature. 1900.
NORMAN-BEL GEDDES
  Project for a Theatrical Presentation of the Divine Comedy. 1924.
HERBERT A. GILES
  A History of Chinese Literature. 1901.
CARLO GOLDONI
  Memoirs. latest ed. 1926.
HERBERT H. GOWEN
  Asia: A Short History. 1926.
ROBERT GRAU
  The Stage in the Twentieth Century. 1912.
WALTER W. GREG (EDITOR)
  Henslowe's Diary. 2 vols. 1904–08.
  Henslowe Papers. 1907.
LADY AUGUSTA GREGORY
  Our Irish Theatre. 1913.
J. T. GREIN
  The Theatre and the World. 1921.
JOSEPH GRIMALDI
  Memoirs. (Ed. by Charles Dickens) 1838.
A. E. HAIGH
  The Tragic Drama of the Greeks. 1896.
  The Attic Theatre. (3rd. ed. rev. by A. W. Pickard-Cambridge)
    1907.
J. O. HALLIWELL-PHILLIPPS
  Outlines of the Life of Shakespeare. 2 vols. 1890.
CLAYTON HAMILTON
  The Theory of the Theatre. 1910.
  Seen on the Stage. 1920.
NORMAN HAPGOOD
  The Stage in America, 1897–1900. 1901.
CHARLES HASTINGS
  The Theatre: Its Development in France and England. 1901.
LOOMIS HAVEMEYER
  The Drama of Savage Peoples. 1916.
FREDERICK W. HAWKINS
  The Life of Edmund Kean. 2 vols. 1869.

Annals of the French Stage. 2 vols. 1884.
The French Stage in the Eighteenth Century. 2 vols. 1888.

W. C. HAZLITT (EDITOR)
The English Drama and Stage Under the Tudor and Stuart Princes, 1543–1664. 1869.

THOMAS HEYWOOD
An Apology for Actors. 1612.

OLIVER HINSDELL
Making the Little Theatre Pay. 1925.

WILLIAM HONE
Ancient Mysteries Described. 1823.

✓ARTHUR HORNBLOW
A History of the Theatre in America. 2 vols. 1919.

E. P. HORRWITZ
The Indian Theatre. 1912.

P. P. HOWE
The Repertory Theatre: A Record and a Criticism. 1911.

✓JOSEPH N. IRELAND
Records of the New York Stage from 1750 to 1860. 2 vols. 1866–67.

EDITH J. R. ISAACS (EDITOR)
Theatre: 31 Essays on the Arts of the Theatre. 1927.

JOHN J. JENNINGS
Theatrical and Circus Life. 1893.

H. W. JOHNSTON
Private Life of the Romans. 1903.

ROBERT EDMOND JONES
Drawings for the Theatre. 1925.

HELEN HAIMAN JOSEPH
A Book of Marionettes. 1920.

J. A. A. J. JUSSERAND
A Literary History of the English People. 2 vols. 1907–09.
English Wayfaring Life in the Middle Ages. rev. ed. 1920.

JOSEPH SPENCER KENNARD
Goldoni and the Venice of His Time. 1920.

ZOË KINCAID
Kabuki: The Popular Stage of Japan. 1925.

EDWARD BERNARD KINSILA
  Modern Theatre Construction. 1917.
JOSEPH KNIGHT
  Theatrical Notes. 1893.
  David Garrick. 1894.
✓ARTHUR EDWIN KROWS
  Play Production in America. 1916.
W. J. LAWRENCE
  The Elizabethan Playhouse. 2 vols. 1912–13.
  The Elizabethan Public Playhouse. 1927.
R. LAWSON
  The Story of the Scots Stage. 1918.
SIR SIDNEY LEE
  A Life of William Shakespeare. new ed. 1916.
PHILIPPE E. LE GRAND
  The New Greek Comedy. (Trans. by J. Loeb) 1917.
KATHERINE MORRIS LESTER
  Historic Costume. 1925.
LUDWIG LEWISOHN
  Drama and the Stage. 1922.
VACHEL LINDSAY
  The Art of the Moving Picture. rev. ed. 1922.
ROBERT WILLIAM LOWE
  Thomas Betterton. 1891.
M. LUCKIESH
  The Lighting Art: Its Practice and Possibilities. 1917.
HELEN MCAFEE
  Pepys on the Restoration Stage. 1916.
LANDER MACCLINTOCK
  The Contemporary Drama of Italy. 1920.
HALDANE MACFALL
  Sir Henry Irving. 1906.
KENNETH MACGOWAN
  The Theatre of Tomorrow. 1921.
  Continental Stagecraft. (With Robert Edmond Jones) 1922.
  Masks and Demons. (With Herman Rosse) 1923.
CONSTANCE D'ARCY MACKAY
  The Little Theatre in the United States. 1917.

PERCY MACKAYE
  The Playhouse and the Play. 1909.
  The Civic Theatre. 1912.
  Community Drama. 1917.
  Epoch: The Life of Steele MacKaye. 2 vols. 1927.
CHARLES MACKLIN
  Memoirs. 1804.
BURNS MANTLE
  The Best Plays of 1919–1920. 1920. (Similar volumes for each
  succeeding season).
KARL MANTZIUS
  A History of Theatrical Art in Ancient and Modern Times.
  6 vols. 1903–1921.
The Marionette (Ed. by E. Gordon Craig) Vol. I. 1918.
[JAMES] BRANDER MATTHEWS
  Studies of the Stage. 1894.
  The Development of the Drama. 1908.
  The Study of the Drama. 1910.
  A Book About the Theatre. 1916.
F. J. MCISAAC
  The Tony Sarg Marionette Book. 1921.
ADDISON MCLEOD
  Plays and Players in Modern Italy. 1912.
ROY MITCHELL
  Shakespeare for Community Players. 1919.
ASATARO MIYAMORI
  Tales from Old Japanese Dramas. 1915.
HIRAM KELLY MODERWELL
  The Theatre of Today. 1914. new. ed. 1927.
J. FITZGERALD MOLLOY
  Peg Woffington and the Period She Lived In. 2 vols.
  1892.
  The Romance of the Irish Stage. 2 vols. 1897.
✓MONTROSE J. MOSES
  Famous Actor-Families in America. 1906.
  — *The American Dramatist.* rev. ed. 1925.
GILBERT MURRAY
  Euripides and His Age. 1913.

J. T. MURRAY
  English Dramatic Companies. 2 vols. 1910.
GEORGE JEAN NATHAN
  The Popular Theatre. 1918.
  Comedians All. 1919.
  The Theatre, the Drama, and the Girls. 1921.
  The World in Falseface. 1923.
  The House of Satan. 1926.
ALLARDYCE NICOLL
  A History of Restoration Drama. 1923.
  British Drama. 1925.
  A History of Early Eighteenth-Century Drama. 1925.
  A History of Late Eighteenth-Century Drama. 1927.
  The Development of the Theatre. 1927.
✓GEORGE C. D. ODELL
  Shakespeare from Betterton to Irving. 2 vols. 1920.
— *Annals of the New York Stage.* 2 vols. 1927.
T. F. ORDISH
  Early London Theatres. 1894.
JOHN PALMER
  The Censor and the Theatre. 1912.
  The Future of the Theatre. 1913.
JOHN PARKER (COMPILER AND EDITOR)
  Who's Who in the Theatre. 5th ed. 1926.
MARK E. PERUGINI
  The Art of Ballet. 1915.
WILLIAM LYON PHELPS
  The Twentieth Century Theatre. 1918.
IRVING PICHEL
  Modern Theatres. 1925.
J. R. PLANCHÉ
  History of British Costume. 3rd ed. 1900.
WILLIAM POEL
  Shakespeare in the Theatre. 1913.
A. W. POLLARD
  English Miracle Plays, Moralities, and Interludes. 1904.
FREDERICK POLLOCK (EDITOR)
  Macready's Reminiscences and Diaries. 1875.

W. A. PROPERT
  The Russian Ballet in Western Europe. 1921.
ARTHUR HOBSON QUINN
  —*A History of the American Drama from the Beginning to the
  Civil War.* 1923.
  *A History of the American Drama from the Civil War to the
  Present Day.* 2 vols. 1927.
W. FRASER RAE
  Sheridan: A Biography. 2 vols. 1896.
TERRY RAMSAYE
  A Million and One Nights: The History of the Motion Picture.
  2 vols. 1926.
HUGO A. RENNERT
  The Spanish Stage in the Time of Lope de Vega. 1909.
LUIGI RICCOBONI
  An Historical and Critical Account of the Theatres in Europe.
  1741.
WILLIAM RIDGEWAY
  The Dramas and Dramatic Dances of the Non-European Races.
  1915.
ROMAIN ROLLAND
  The People's Theatre. (Trans. by Barrett H. Clark) 1918.
EDWIN O. SACHS AND E. A. WOODWARD
  Modern Opera Houses and Theatres. 3 vols. 1896–98.
MAURICE SAND
  The History of the Harlequinade. 2 vols. 1915.
OLIVER M. SAYLER
  The Russian Theatre Under the Revolution. 1920.
  The Russian Theatre. 1922.
  —*Our American Theatre.* 1923.
  Max Reinhardt and His Theatre. 1924.
  Inside the Moscow Art Theatre. 1925.
FELIX E. SCHELLING
  Elizabethan Playwrights. 1925.
GEORGE O. SEILHAMER
  — *History of the American Theatre, to 1797.* 3 vols. 1888–91.
GILBERT SELDES
  The Seven Lively Arts. 1924.

R. Earquharson Sharp
A Short History of the English Stage. 1909.

Ted Shawn
The American Ballet. 1926.

Frank Shay
The Practical Theatre. 1926.

Errol Sherson
London's Lost Theatres of the Nineteenth Century. 1926.

André Smith
The Scenewright: The Making of Stage Models and Settings. 1926.

Milton Smith
The Book of Play Production for Little Theatres, Schools, and Colleges. 1926.

Winifred Smith
The Commedia dell' Arte. 1912.

Matthew Lyle Spencer
Corpus Christi Pageants in England. 1911.

Constantin Stanislavsky
My Life in Art. 1924.

H. T. Stephenson
Shakespeare's London. 1905.

Marie C. C. Stopes
Plays of Old Japan; The Nō. 1913.

Clarence Stratton
Producing in Little Theatres. 1921.

Donald Clive Stuart
Stage Decoration in France in the Middle Ages. 1910.

John Addington Symonds
Shakespeare's Predecessors in the English Drama. 1900.

Arthur Symons
Plays, Acting, and Music. 1909.

Linwood Taft
The Technique of Pageantry. 1921.

François Joseph Talma
Reflexions on the Actor's Art. 1915.

Alwin Thaler
Shakspere to Sheridan. 1922.

GEORGE TICKNOR
History of Spanish Literature. 3 vols. 6th ed. 1888.

R. J. E. TIDDY
The Mummers' Play. 1923.

ASHLEY H. THORNDIKE
Shakespeare's Theater. 1916.

EUGENE TOMPKINS AND QUINCY KILBY
The History of the Boston Theatre, 1854–1901. 1908.

J. RANKEN TOWSE
Sixty Years of the Theatre. 1916.

HENRY M. TROLLOPE
Life of Molière. 1905.

T. G. TUCKER
Life in Ancient Athens. 1906.

FRANK VERNON
The Twentieth Century Theatre. 1924.

JANIE VILLIERS-WARDELL
Spain of the Spanish. 1909.

VITRUVIUS POLLIO
The Civil Architecture of Vitruvius. (Trans. by William Wilkins) 1812.

ARTHUR WALEY
The Nō Plays of Japan. 1922.

CHARLES WILLIAM WALLACE
Evolution of the English Drama up to Shakespeare. 1912.

A. W. WARD
History of English Dramatic Literature to the Death of Queen Anne. 3 vols. 2nd ed. 1899.

WARD LEONARD ELECTRIC COMPANY
Theatre Lighting; Past and Present. 1923.

ERNEST BRADLEE WATSON
Sheridan to Robertson. 1926.

SAMUEL MONTEFIORE WAXMAN
Antoine and the Théâtre-Libre. 1926.

M. R. WERNER
Barnum. 1925.

H. W. WHANSLAW
The Bankside Stage Book. 1925.

LEO WIENER
   The Contemporary Drama of Russia. 1924.
J. D. WILSON (COMPILER)
   Life in Shakespeare's England. 2nd ed. 1913.
WILLIAM WINTER
   The Life and Art of Edwin Booth. 1893.
   Other Days. 1908.
   The Wallet of Time. 2 vols. 1913.
   Vagrant Memories. 1915.
   The Life of David Belasco. 2 vols. 1918.
CLAUDE M. WISE
   Dramatics for School and Community. 1923.
ROBERT WITHINGTON
   English Pageantry. 2 vols. 1918–20.
ALEXANDER WOOLLCOTT
   Mrs. Fiske: Her Views on Actors and Acting. 1917.
   Shouts and Murmurs. 1922.
   Enchanted Aisles. 1924.
STARK YOUNG
   The Flower in Drama. 1923.
   Glamour: Essays on the Art of the Theatre. 1925.
   Theatre Practice. 1926.
A. E. ZUCKER
   The Chinese Theatre. 1925.

CURRENT   PERIODICALS

The Billboard. (Weekly) Cincinnati.
The Drama. (Monthly from Oct. to May) Chicago.
The Film Year Book. (Annual) New York.
The Mask. (Quarterly) Florence, Italy.
The Stage Year Book. (Annual) London.
Theatre Arts Monthly. New York.
Theatre Magazine. (Monthly) New York.
Variety. (Weekly) New York.

INDEX